Oct 2000

Dearest Gersh & Syp,

Enjoy reading.

Lots of love

Geoff & Esther

X X X X X
X

Flavours of South Africa

PETER VELDSMAN

TAFELBERG

Dedicated to Johan Odendaal,
friend and colleague, as a token of appreciation and as
a retrospective of our culinary heritage on which we can base our
future true South African cuisine

ACKNOWLEDGEMENTS
All the CAIA students
The staff of Emily's Restaurant
Joan Kruger, editor of *Rooi Rose*,
for permission to use some of the photographs which
I originally commissioned for the magazine
David Briers for the photograph on the back page
The Cornelia Ragni bequest for the use
of a transparency of Sannie Smit in the introductory chapter
Miriam Moss
Johan Odendaal
The following writers: Betsie Rood, Lannice Snyman, Rina Pont,
Dine van Zyl, Renata Coetzee, Anna de Villiers, Laurens van der Post,
C Louis Leipoldt, Annette Kesler and S J A de Villiers
Etienne van Duyker
Johan Wilke
and, naturally, Hennie Aucamp,
with whose anthology *Borde borde boordevol* -it all began.

Also available in Afrikaans as *Kos van die eeu*.

Translated by Pat Barton and Elizé Lübbe
Photography by Johan Wilke (except the photograph on page 3)
Design by Etienne van Duyker
Set in 10.5 on 11 pt Baskerville by Tafelberg
Printed and bound by National Book Printers, Drukkery Street, Goodwood, Western Cape
First edition 1998
ISBN 0 624 03715 0

Contents

A spark from the flint-stone

THIS IS HOW IT BEGAN: One afternoon at Emily's, my Cape Town restaurant, over generous helpings of quince bredie, Danie Botha of Tafelberg Publishers came to the point. 'Would you be interested in working with Hennie Aucamp and providing recipes for his anthology and essays on Afrikaans short stories about food?' I was flattered, because I have the greatest admiration for Hennie. He then gave me a list of the stories and the recipes they contained.

I soon realised that these recipes reflect our country's culinary heritage over the past centuries: a cuisine with a present and a past. Those members of our population who are searching for their spiritual roots and cultural traditionswill find out how our culinary traditions originated and developed. But more than this: they will also realise that our country has many faces – much cultural cross-pollination has taken place. The Nguni, Sotho, British, French, Italian, German, Dutch, Portuguese, Greek, Malay and Indian influences have influenced the way we think about food. A nostalgic cuisine, seen with the benefit of hindsight. A cuisine that ends an era, but also heralds a new one on which Africa will continue to put her stamp. Think, for example, of the creative way in which the Tswana used offal, and how quickly, over the past few years, chillies have given our dishes the fifth taste dimension.

This book also attempts to provide a frame of reference for a new generation of cooks. It is concerned with not only traditional dishes, and not only regional food, but especially with dishes which have stood the test of time, even though some were confined to certain geographical areas or used by small groups of people – a small spark.

PETER VELDSMAN
Kenilworth, Cape
1 May, 1998

Introduction

A taste of nostalgia

There's no doubt that South Africa speaks with many voices when it comes to food. The first flavours came from food cooked on the braai fires of the San and the Khoi, followed by the beer which the Sotho and Nguni brewed from sorghum. Jan van Riebeek established vegetable and fruit gardens at the Cape. Malay slaves and exiles added zest to Cape food with spices and herbs. The British conquerors toned down these flavours temporarily, but when the large numbers of Indian people arrived in Natal and Zululand they brought with them new flavours to enhance our dishes. Meanwhile, trek farmers and the Voortrekkers developed a unique style of cooking. A century of wars followed. It is against this background that we first visit the past in an attempt to assess the food of the twentieth century.

The San were the first hunters. They did not domesticate animals or work the soil. Neither were they potters; they used calabashes and ostrich egg shells to store milk. They were nomadic, forever moving on in search of game and plant foods from the veld. They lived in caves and under rock overhangs. While the men hunted, the women gathered wild fruits, berries, leaves, bulbs and the roots of various plants. Dassies (rock rabbits) and small game formed part of their diet, and sometimes they trapped larger, dangerous wild animals like the hippopotamus, elephant and rhinoceros to supplement their diet. Remains of shells, crayfish and seals found in caves along the coast attest to their skill as fishermen.

About 2 000 years ago, in the area known today as Botswana, the lifestyle of the Khoi changed. They came into contact with the sheep of the nomadic Sudanese from the north and the cattle of the Bantu from the east. One of the oldest dishes in South Africa is the Khoi's *kaiings* (crackling), crisply fried sheep-tail fat which they enjoyed with wild leaves – probably broad-leaved sorrel (*Oxalis* spp, *surings*, or wild cabbage (*veldkool*).

The Nguni and the Sotho

Research has shown that people were living in southern Zimbabwe during the Iron Age and that by 450 BC they were already established in the Soutpansberge. The present St Lucia on the east coast was already inhabited by 300 BC. These people lived on plants from the veld and game. Sorghum grew wild in large parts of northern South Africa, and there are indications that it was ground between two stones and used to brew beer. In the north, large shallow dishes were made of clay and used to evaporate water, so that salt was fairly freely available by 250 BC. Salt pans like those in the Soutpansberge, as well as areas where mining took place, became centres for gatherings and trading.

By the time the Portuguese seafarers arrived in the second half of the fifteenth century, there were two main language groups among the black population: the Nguni and the Sotho. The seafarers noted that the Nguni had fat cows and worked the soil. Calabashes, beans and maize, in particular, were grown. Sweet melons (*spanspek*) were known in the Eastern Cape before Van Riebeek planted them at the Cape. The Nguni had a decided preference for gooseberries, and centuries later persuaded the British settlers to try them. And that is how gooseberry fool made its way to the South African table. The settlers also encountered a vinegar named *tjala* and all kinds of beer made from *boermanna* (a wild grass with seeds resembling those fed to canaries). The Tsonga women caught fish and other seafood in fishing baskets, while Xhosa men used spears. To my knowledge, the Mpondo were the only black people who were fond of crayfish.

The Sotho group consisted of the South Sothos (Basotho), the North Sothos (later split into two groups – the Pedi and Lobedu), and the West Sothos, or Tswanas. Their earliest foods included sorghum, of which there were six varieties. Melons (*Citrullus lanatus*) were plentiful and were favoured by the Sothos. They cooked the young shoots and dried the seeds to serve with porridge. Two kinds of indigenous bean were the main providers of protein. Ground nuts and pumpkin were added later. Children shot pigeons, as well as other birds, with catapults or caught them in cages. Fieldmice were caught and fried. And then there was the marula. The seeds were much more important than the flesh and were roasted and eaten with porridge.

The Sothos followed the honey bird to find honey, which they usually ate on the spot, taking only a portion back to the kraal where it was served as a dessert. Veld plants and the green leaves of certain trees were collected by girls and women for the preparation of *morogo* or *imifino*. There was a choice of more than a hundred kinds of green leaves, which were cooked slowly and served with porridge – particularly to pregnant women.

Bartering

During the sixteenth and seventeenth centuries, the Khoi became accustomed to the ships that called at the Cape. A number of Khoi – including Herrie, who belonged to an immigrant group of Khoi known as Strandlopers – were taken to the East, Holland and Britain by the Dutch and the British and brought back to the Cape to act as interpreters. While in foreign parts, the visitors learned how to trade, which stood them in good stead. Herrie even became a postmaster for the British.

Victims of shipwrecks often stayed at the foot of Table Mountain until a passing ship picked them up. The Dutch East India Company and its controlling board, the Here XVII (Council of 17), had realised that a halfway station between Europe and the spice islands of the East was essential for the wellbeing of seamen. One in six were dying of scurvy for lack of vitamin C. A settlement therefore was established at the Cape to provide fresh foods. Van Riebeeck was sent to the Cape for this task.

Immediately after his arrival, Van Riebeeck appointed Hendrik Boom to cultivate a garden.

Van Riebeeck is, to me, a very important figure in the development of South African cuisine. Coming from a country with no shortage of water to a country with dry and searing winds and devastating rain storms, it is amazing what he accomplished in his ten years at the Cape.

Fish was the main source of protein, but occasionally lamb and even dassies were eaten. Most of the hunting trips were unsuccessful, and penguin eggs had to supplement the protein. Van Riebeeck wrote an ecstatic entry in his diary about the first turnips cooked with lamb. Vegetables and salad greens were grown with relative success: turnips, cauliflower, beetroot, cucumber, pumpkin, *kadjang* (Indian beans), watercress, radishes, cabbage, lettuce, endives and spinach.

The first successful fruits were watermelons and sweet melons (*spanspek*). A year later, red cabbage, chervil, onions, parsley, carrots and asparagus followed and, a year or two later, cherries, plums and peaches, quinces, medlars, apples, pears, oranges and, naturally, grapes. On 2 February 1659, Van Riebeeck wrote in his diary with great enthusiasm: 'Heden is Gode loff van de Caapse druyven voor de eerste mael wyn gepaerst …' ('Today, praise God, wine was pressed for the first time from Cape grapes …')

At that time, salt was the most important preservative. Van Riebeeck found salt just a few kilometres from the fort, on the banks of the Diep River. Before long, salt had become the first export – to India. Salt, sugar and saltpetre were used to preserve fish and meat. (Remember – there were no refrigerators.) For this reason, the offal was eaten first, then biltong was made, leftover pieces of meat and some of the offal were used to make brawn, cuts which we know today as roasting cuts were pickled, and neck was used to cook bredies (stews), which were topped with a thick layer of fat and kept for days.

THE FIRST CHEESE

There was enough fresh milk for the needs of the settlement. Annatjie Boom, wife of the gardener Hendrik, was (compared with Maria van Riebeeck) less refined, more practical and dominated her husband. They were the first settlers to live outside the fort, but still within the company garden. She was industrious, made the first cheese at the Cape and, by the time Van Riebeeck left the Cape, was offering a fairly good cumin cheese for sale. She was later the first innkeeper at the Cape. With one of her sons, Job, she was also the first purveyor of milk, from the Company's cows, which she got at a fixed price – this probably made her the first 'free burgher' at the Cape. *Melkkos* (milk noodles) was a popular dish at Annatjie's inn, and also at the fort. She catered for most receptions, particularly wedding feasts, serving dishes like ham, roast pork, roast chicken with rosemary, yellow rice, pumpkin purée, green beans and a *Waterbul* for dessert. Annatjie and her family thrived until Commissioner Ryklof van Goens put a spoke in the wheel. Annatjie lost everything during the VOC-Khoikhoi War and the family returned to Holland. What a loss to industriousness!

SLAVES AND POLITICAL PRISONERS CHANGE THE CAPE'S DIET

The local population showed no interest in working for the settlers and as a result the first black slaves, from Angola and West Africa, were obtained from a passing ship. Incidentally, by 1748 there were more slaves than free burghers at the Cape! The first imported slaves came from Mauritius and Madagascar, and afterwards from the East Indies and many other countries in the East. Among them were political prisoners (including princes) from various countries, sent here to serve their sentences or to live in exile. Their diets differed greatly from those of the Dutch and German settlers. Because rice was their staple food, large quantities had to be imported. Rice from Batavia became the Cape's first staple food, and remained so until the First World War, after which it was imported sporadically. For almost a decade during and after the Second World War only a little rice was available, until the establishment of the Tastic Rice Company in 1961.

This diet cried out for spices like pepper, cinnamon, cloves, ginger, nutmeg, coriander, turmeric and saffron. Because of the monotonous dishes of the Dutch, these spices were soon adopted, and so the Cape cuisine got its characteristic spicy flavour. Dishes like *bobotie*, *sosaties*, *pienangvleis* and *denningvleis*, *tasal*, curry, *bredies*, *kebabs*, *atchar*, *sambals*, *blatjang* (chutney) and *samoosas* – of which there are a wide variety – have survived up to the present.

THE ARRIVAL OF THE HUGUENOTS

The first horses arrived in the Cape from Batavia in 1660, which meant that expeditions could be undertaken to the interior. The main goal of these expeditions was to expand the barter trade. Outposts were established at Saldanha Bay and Hottentots-Holland. The first French Huguenots arrived at the Cape in 1688. After a sojourn in the Netherlands, where they began to adapt to the Dutch lifestyle, these civilised, godfearing people were settled away from Cape Town, most of them in the vicinity of Drakenstein and Olifantshoek (the present Franschhoek). Many food writers today hold the Huguenots in high esteem; all kinds of confectionery are (incorrectly) attributed to them. What we do know is that they baked good bread. Le Vaillant (a French botanist) attested to this during his visit to the Cape. We also know that one of their greatest contributions to our cuisine is the creation of must buns (*mosbolletjies*), and that they cooked with wine. 'Fransche ragoe', a dish of braised wood pigeon in a meaty wine sauce, is the forerunner of casseroles which became particularly popular in the second half of the twentieth century with the arrival of the slow-cooker.

The Cape got its first governor, Simon van der Stel, in 1679. He was a man of vision who laid out the farm Constantia behind Van Riebeeck's Bosheuwel, where he greatly improved viticulture at the Cape and made the first wine of any note. Years later, this farm would produce some of the most famous wines in the world, which were held in high regard by all the illustrious people of the time. On his deathbed, Napoleon requested a glass of Constantia. Part of Van der Stel's task was to expand the colony. He established the town of Stellenbosch, named after himself and his wife, and farmers settled along the Eerste River.

The eighteenth century

In the period 1710-20, after the Cape farmers had survived the outrageous Willem Adriaan van der Stel, there was a glut of grain and wine, and the local population was faced with impoverishment for the first time. In 1708 the first fat-tailed sheep were imported from Persia and crossbred with sheep bought from the Khoi. Some sources refer to this new breed of sheep as *Afrikaanders*! The fat-tailed sheep were an important source of meat, but their fat was also used for making candles and soap. More and more farmers trekked to the interior. There were many skirmishes between the trek farmers, and the Khoi and Khoi-San. By 1730 the trek farmers reached the present Longkloof and by 1740 most of the Khoi in the Cape had no option but to become labourers.

One of the few important culinary developments during that period occurred with the arrival of Governor Ryk Tulbagh in 1751. The Cape had an established upper class and a working class, most of whom were slaves. The Dutch Reformed Church (Nederduitse Gereformeerde Kerk) enjoyed official recognition and influenced – one could almost say controlled – education. The Cape was the tavern of the seas, and sailors could gamble and carouse to their hearts' content. Prostitution flourished among the masses, as opposed to the dignity and status of the privileged. Tulbagh felt at home among the higher classes and did everything in his power to awaken an interest in science. The first library was established and the Company gardens were restructured to include a plant and animal collection. The bird cages were of particular interest to visitors. Balls and elegant dinner parties were the order of the day at the Castle. Tables groaned under the weight of spicy foods. Music was provided by slave orchestras, supplemented by Khoi *ramkies* (guitars) and a sea-bamboo trumpet. Powdered wigs

were high fashion. Tulbagh even introduced legislation against ostentation.

During this century, most housewives compiled their own, handwritten recipe books from which later food writers, like Mrs Dijkman and Hildagonda Duckitt, were able to produce the first South African cookbooks. The only other important addition to the food spectrum was in 1789 when the Cape government began importing merino sheep from the Netherlands.

British occupation and a century of wars

After Tulbagh's period of service, time ran out for the Dutch administration. In 1795 Britain occupied the Cape, only to lose it soon afterwards. It was in fact the Napoleonic wars in Europe that allowed Britain to occupy the Cape for the second time in 1806.

Meanwhile, the British administration freed the slaves in 1834, which led to the Great Trek, when white farmers shook off the yoke of the British and trekked northwards in search of freedom and a free state.

The Great Trek was preceded by the arrival, in 1820, of a large group of settlers from Britain. These people were not prepared for the *suurveld* ('sour' land) and the harsh African reality. Few of them had any farming experience and many were working class people. There were exceptions, but only the hardiest survived. What they did not know was that the Cape governor wanted them in the Eastern Cape to help the British soldiers in the wars against the black population. The settlers endured great hardship, and their petitions to their home country bore little fruit. Despite this, they did establish an infrastructure and founded a number of small towns, with Grahamstown as the centre. Fortunately, the government encouraged sheep farming in the Eastern Cape and the economy improved. Their repertoire of daily dishes included Irish stew, as well as stewed wild birds. They used maize-meal instead of oats for their daily porridge. The Xhosas learnt a lot from the settlers, and vice versa, because there was already an established tradition of more than just grinding maize and the meal to make putu.

At this time a little girl, Isabella, was born in Britain in 1836. At the age of 20 she married a neighbour, Beeton. He was a publisher, and after three years of married life the couple began publishing monthly food articles in *The Englishwoman's Domestic Magazine*. Bella Beeton's maxim was: 'The way to a man's heart is through his stomach'. These

articles were published in 1859 as *Mrs Beeton's Book of Household Management*, and to this day the book remains the greatest single seller of all cookbooks, in all languages. What do the Beetons have to do with South Africa? First of all, the notion that settlers came to South Africa carrying their Mrs Beeton's must be squashed. They couldn't have, since the book had not yet been published! The settlers and the black people with whom they came into contact together created a British-South African cuisine. The second group of settlers who arrived here in 1850 were slightly better prepared, materially speaking, than those of 1820. A few copies of books like *Modern Cookery for Private Families* by Eliza Acton, which appeared in 1845, and *New System of Domestic Cookery* by Mrs Rundell were the only books to survive the numerous times the settlers' houses were burnt to the ground. Tibbie Steyn, whose husband later became president of the Orange Free State, used 'Mrs Beeton' as a guide for the many receptions she held.

The greatest single change in terms of food during that century was, without doubt, the black population's adaptation to white cookery. Quite simply, they had to adopt the foreign flavours and cooking methods, and in the process a great deal of their own culture was forever lost. In her book *Funa*, Renata Coetzee aptly describes the development of the blacks' cookery and, in particular, their eating utensils. A wide spectrum of meat dishes peculiar to the various tribes has been recorded. For example, *bubende* is a Nguni dish in which the blood of a slaughtered goat is cooked with small pieces of fat. The Sothos also made this dish, but they added the intestines and stomach. Their predilection for 'minced' meat is demonstrated by the Sotho dish *lekgotwane*, in which goat's meat is cooked for 8-10 hours, the bones are removed, and the fat scooped off before the meat is mashed and seasoned. *Xiridza* is a Sotho version of the Free State farmers' custom of cooking biltong.

CHANGES IN FOOD PREFERENCE

As far as cuisine is concerned, the nineteenth century brought important changes. At the Cape, there was a decided change in food preference. Lady Anne Barnard – wife of the colonial secretary and hostess at the side of the governor, Lord McCartney, in the absence of his wife – made a distinct impression on the preferences of the Cape upper classes during her short stay. She found most of the dishes overspiced, and ordered that the food served at the Castle be prepared with far

less – and preferably no – spices. This was a new idea, but the inhabitants of the Cape soon followed her example. Secondly, the 1820 settlers and the later British settlers in Natal brought with them the British diet, recipes and table manners. Potatoes, golden syrup and chocolate made their appearance.

The trek farmers had to preserve meat, and so biltong became an important item in the saddlebag on treks and hunting trips and as the staple food during the war with Britain. More angora goats were slaughtered than merino sheep. The meat spoiled quickly, in spite of being salted. For this reason, large pots of meat were cooked and preserved in fat. Trekker potjies and travel food (*transportkos*) are currently being revived in the form of *potjiekos*.

Ants were a popular food ingredient on many farms in the interior. Anthills were opened, usually after a good rain shower, the ants scraped out and cooked in a little water until their stomachs burst. The ants rose to the top, floating on the fat. They were scooped out, and meat and onions were then stewed in the ant fat. According to Vivia Ferreira, termites were also prepared in this way and, after being scooped out, were fried. They were eaten on buttered bread. Her late father, Dr Steenkamp, member of parliament for Namaqualand, was particularly fond of this delicacy.

FOOD HAS ITS OWN EXPRESSION

The Indian labourers grew in numbers. Family members also came to Natal and a strong culture, with the accompanying food traditions, was established. Many people brought with them their own *lotas* (copper kettles), clay lamps, *hookahs* (water pipes) and, it goes without saying, betel leaves and nuts. After ten years as migrant labourers, the Indians could stay on as freemen, but not yet as South Africans. Most Indians were either Hindus or followers of Islam, and their religion dictated what meat they could eat. For example, Hindus may not eat beef, and Muslims may not eat pork. Many Hindus are vegetarians. An important aspect of their cooking is that dishes must be flavoured in such a way that one spice does not dominate another. A balance of flavours is characteristic of good Indian food. The combination of Indian and British flavours was excellent. There were many ex-colonials from India, and the Indians also communicated well with the Zulus – to such an extent that Zulus adopted certain Indian dishes. Dishes like *jege* were created: a large piece of risen dough cooked in salted water like a dumpling and served with sour milk and lamb curry. Although the Zulus took over the Indians' curry, they usually make it without adding ginger. *Isijababane* is another example. Crumbly porridge (*krummelpap*) is first cooked in a large three-legged pot and divided, in the pot, into three 'breads'. Beef, garlic and onions are added to the pot, flavoured with masala and cooked slowly. In the meantime, the putu swells up. A quartered cabbage is placed on top of the meat, moistened with a little water, the pot is covered and the whole lot is cooked long and slowly. The English dessert, trifle, became part of the Zulu repertoire in the twentieth century. A Zulu saying goes: 'Ukudla mtanami uyakhuluma' which, loosely translated, means: food has its own expression. They believe that you should never use foul language while you are preparing food, as the food would be cursed and lose all its nutritional value.

The twentieth century

The twentieth century began with war but, at last, a spirit of reconciliation between complex cultures is taking hold. Diversity was the chief characteristic of the cookery of the early years of this century. There was Cape cuisine, regional food, ethnic dishes and those of specific cultural groups. Let's take snoek as an example of this diversity. In the Cape Peninsula people eat braaied snoek; on the West Coast, snoek with sweet potato is preferred; the Malays prefer snoek, rather than any other fish, for making pickled fish. During the Second World War, snoek was canned and sent to Britain where, until the early fifties, it was the standby of the British working class. Yes, snoek was everywhere, right up to Sophiatown and later Soweto.

Food for the lean months and food for prosperity. Food for the poor and food for the rich. War rations. Along the Natal coast, seemingly the entire population gathered sardines when the sea deposited them on the beach. This was the time of the establishment of agricultural corporations – the KWV, NCD, SAD and many others. Royal baking powder and many petrol companies distributed books and pamphlets of recipes. In 1915, Jeanette van Duyn's *Household Science Cookery Book* appeared. Van Duyn was a vastly underrated woman. The then premier, General Louis Botha, sent her to Canada, at government expense, to study domestic science. On her return she organised the first domestic science congress. Between 1924 and 1925 she was sent to the British Empire Exhibition to run a South African food stall. When Queen Mary tasted her koesisters, she immediately asked for the recipe for the palace kitchen.

DINING OUT

During the thirties and forties, most white South Africans ate either at home or in hotels. Commercial travellers ensured that every small country town had a Royal, a Commercial or a Grand Hotel. Cafés offered mixed grills of fried lamb chops, a grilled steak, fried liver and kidneys, and crisply fried bacon with a fried egg, grilled tomato, canned peas and chips. This became the most popular meal of the period. Then came the meat braais of the sixties and seventies, and potjiekos. South Africans began to drink wine. Cheese and wine parties, where the wine was often sponsored by wine companies, became popular. Eateries on the coast served seafood platters consisting of grilled crayfish halves, prawns, calamari rings, baked fish and poached mussels. With the appliance revolution came the arrival of the electric mixer, food processor and microwave oven, followed by the shift from dining out at a hotel to dining out at a restaurant.

In the sixties there was a new wave of Italian immigrants who speedily opened eateries in every city and town. To our shame, some of these influences dominated the cooking of many Afrikaner women and this, together with the feeble excuse of lack of time, rang the death knell for many traditional dishes such as *melktert*, which is time-consuming to make because puff pastry is a major ingredient. The age of phyllo pastry had arrived. Not the phyllo that many Greek immigrants make themselves, but phyllo from a packet. Puff pastry, without butter, from a packet. Margarine instead of butter, neatly packaged as a slab. At the Belinzona Restaurant in Table View, Danny Ferris introduced a thick whisky and ice cream milkshake known as Dom Pedro. The recipe spread like wildfire throughout the country and is still one of the most popular desserts instead of a pudding. American fast-food places, pizza places, steak houses and hamburger joints with their depressing cubicles opened countrywide.

One wonderful occurrence was the establishment of home industry stores where working people, in particular, could buy home-baked goods.

The magazine, *Huisgenoot*, with its 'winning recipes' and soup powder short-cuts, took the lead in useful recipes. Women's magazines like *Sarie* and *Fair Lady* offered their readers world-class food journalism. It was *Sarie* that coined the phrase 'potjiekos', and it was also this magazine that undertook the first in-depth investigation of the regional foods of South Africa. Countrywide, regional meals followed. Restaurants improved dramatically. Some of them, full of daring, even offered mopane worms, crocodile and snake meat. The wide spectrum of women's magazines brought food styles from far and near to their readers.

Pizza and pasta from Italy, Cajun, Tex-Mex, Mediterranean and Provençal did battle with sushi and Thai for a place on the tables of South Africans. Sports-crazy South Africa discovered the importance of pasta. Vegetarianism increased. The herb gardens that were part of any Boland farm for 250 years, were revived. Parsley, basil, thyme, chives and duhnia (coriander) led, with mint, tarragon, oregano, dill, rosemary and sage close behind. From the eighties onwards, lavender and Karoo bush were combined as a herb mixture for the preparation of venison and lamb. Cheeses improved, but the choice was still limited. People ate alfresco beside the swimming pool or cooked potjies of gustatory pleasure, and slowly but surely a host of new flavours was introduced to our food. The bells rang for garlic, ginger root and chillies. The oppressive apartheid laws, which brought so much embarrassment and pain to brown and black South Africans, have disappeared, and now, at last, all South Africans can gather around the table and break bread together.

Our repertoire of recipes will change drastically in decades to come. Tastes will change. In fact, the entire agricultural industry is poised for change. A new nationhood under one African sun is being born. There will always be certain dishes that South Africans will be possessive about. This is what I, in spite of extremely limited space, have tried to record in this book. Dishes that belong to our soul and our being. A pot of gold at the end of the rainbow.

CHAPTER 1

Our daily bread

FLOUR, YEAST, SALT, and water. With these simple ingredients we have been baking bread for centuries. The history of our country is reflected in the story of how bread-making evolved.

Poor Jan van Riebeeck. The Southeaster blew away his hopes of a wheat crop and the free burghers preferred planting wine-grapes to planting wheat. Even dear Simon van der Stel had to give his bad-tempered son Willem Adriaan a notebook to remind him that bread was a prerequisite for rural development at the Cape. It was only in the years shortly before the British occupation, at the time of the periwig and of Father Tulbagh, that enough grain was cultivated to ensure that there would be bread on every table in Cape Town. Later the two northern republics, in particular the Free State, could also help feed a breadless community.

This century is encrusted with memories of hard times. Hungry months of bread with more bran than wheat germ. Quality that ranged from nutritious on the farms, to ultra-refined in the towns. Anne Martin writes in *Home Life on an Ostrich Farm* that all new South Africans or city dwellers had to travel specifically to Oudtshoorn, Ladismith, Montagu and Swellendam to learn the art of making salt-rising pot bread from the farmers' wives. Strangely, the best bread was baked in the Little Karoo and the Overberg rather than in the Swartland. As with pasta in Italy, bread brought about political change. The National Party came into power, not because of Apartheid, but because they promised the voters white bread – and then gave the nation Bremer bread. This is the century when bread was passed from the outside oven to the bakery only to become uniform, colourless and tasteless, and we lost something precious. But people were not satisfied with this kind of bread for long, and the longing for the homeliness of a farm loaf with its crunchy crust and the full flavour of salt-rising yeast persisted.

ROLLED SOWETO GREY BREAD IN FRONT, BREAD PLAIT IN THE BOWL, AND HARVEST BREAD BACK LEFT

The evolution began in the seventies when 'eat healthy, live healthy' became our credo. It was the era of whole-wheat and batter bread with a yogurt basis. In the early eighties women's organisations in the Swartland realised that bread was the showcase of their region, so they initiated an annual dinner, where regional food was served, and a bread festival. To my knowledge this is unique in our country.

The buzz word at present is fusion – world culture combined with our own. We walk down the street like Frenchmen with a *baguette* under the arm, make garlic bread to eat with our braai, and drink red Pontacq wine. We eat Indian curries, toned down with aromatic fresh coriander leaves, with *naan, chapati, parathas* and *pooris*, all flat Indian breads. In Cape Town we have discovered the tandoor, and the red, oh-so-beautiful tandoori chicken with buttered naan is as trendy as calling the President Madiba. And show me the teenager who does not enjoy pita bread from the Middle East. Especially with a filling of cucumber, yogurt and strips of smoked chicken breast.

Today we are as jovial as the Italians are, and we celebrate our renaissance with *pugliese*, that wonderful olive-oil bread with its soft crumb and very thin crust. Or we don our latest Versace and pretend that we are somewhere on Lake Como, mopping up a spoonful of virgin olive oil with *ciabata*, the Italian bread that is supposed to resemble a slipper. We enjoy our *focaccia* with a topping of herbs and black olives, or nibble a *grissini*, one of those long, hard bread-sticks, while we wait for a meal that is anything but traditional country fare. Now fruit loaves, such as *pougno* from Provençe, are as popular as our own raisin loaf, while the sweet loaves, the *pao doce* from Portugal, remind us that South Africa, second only to Portugal, has more Portuguese residents than any country in the world.

And we won't forget Africa, because we are African, after all. We have spice bread from Ethiopia or grey bread from Soweto, complete with poppy seeds.

Tomorrow I will bake salt-rising bread like my Grandmother Cilliers used to bake. I can't go to Ladismith to fetch flour from the old church, because after many years the mill there is quiet. But I can and will drive to Citrusdal where bread flour is awaiting my bread tins. And then I will bake bread, a true *internazionale*, and one for which the whole of Africa is waiting. Together we will eat it with yellow farm butter with sea-salt from the West Coast, made with cream produced by Gousblom, my favourite Jersey cow. And boldly we will march toward the turn of the century, while somewhere in an informal settlement an askoek is still baked to fulfil the need for bread.

How does yeast work?

Fortunately today the home baker can choose how he or she wants to bake: by using instant yeast, active dried yeast, fresh compressed yeast, chemical rising agents, or with a culture prepared from the natural yeast cells of flour. The best-known cultures are yeast or salt-rising leavening made from potatoes, must or dried leavened dough. When the Italian community talks about leavening they call it *biga*, while the Portuguese call it *fermento*.

Whichever yeast you use, its purpose is to break down the nutrients containing sugar and starch to release alcohol and carbon dioxide, and to stretch the gluten so that the dough will rise. Yeast is alive. It is found in the air and establishes itself on grains of wheat. Yeast threads can also be scientifically isolated and processed into compressed yeast. If the working of the yeast is slowed down by leaving the dough to prove in a cool place or even in the refrigerator, the dough will taste better and it will have a finer and smoother texture. The addition of ascorbic acid (better known as vitamin C) is essential when using instant yeast. All it does is to shorten the rising period.

Maize flour, buckwheat and oatmeal must be baked using a chemical rising agent. If natural yeast is used to bake the bread, at least half the total quantity of flour must be plain bread flour. There are two kinds of rye flour: light rye, with part of the bran layer removed; and dark rye, where the whole grain of rye is ground to produce flour with a coarse texture. Light rye, mixed with bread flour, will rise properly, while dark rye is always heavy and very dense. Pumpernickel is an example of a mixture of two parts dark rye and one part stone-ground whole-wheat flour.

If the water used to prepare a yeast plant is too hot, it will kill the yeast cells. The temperature must never exceed 43 °C.

Salt-rising yeast

For this bread you don't buy yeast; you prepare the leavening yourself. The process differs from winter to summer. During the winter months it takes longer to activate. This is how you do it: Put a kettle of water to the boil and in the meantime, prepare your yeast bucket. In earlier years these household articles were enameled and had a wire handle and tight-fitting lid. Today these buckets are display articles in the cottages of the younger generation. And what if you don't have one of these buckets? Use something similar – a container that is high in relation to its diameter, and definitely with a lid that fits properly. Wash and keep ready.

Yeast plant

750 ml (3 cups) boiled water, cooled to 43 °C or slightly lower
5 ml (1 t) salt (preferably coarse salt)
3 ml (½ t) sugar
white, brown or whole-wheat bread flour

1. Pour boiled water in bucket and sprinkle salt and sugar over top. Stir to mix. Slowly sprinkle enough bread flour on top to a depth of about 25 mm (1 inch). Using the handle of a wooden spoon, pierce a hole right through in the centre of the flour to form a 'well' through which water can ooze to the top. Cover with a clean, damp cloth, then put the lid on. Leave in a warm place for 10-12 hours to activate the mixture. In winter in a very cold region you may wrap the bucket in a dough blanket and place it in a warming oven until the mixture becomes activated.
2. Lift the lid and cloth to check. The salt-rising yeast must be well risen, bubbly and alive. If not, add another cup (250 ml) of near-boiling water and a handful of flour to the mixture and whisk through using a wire whisk. Wrap again and leave in a warm place. You may even go a step further: Peel and quarter a large potato, place it in the bucket and then add water, salt, sugar and flour as above. Complete as above. This, then, is the yeast plant, or leavening.

Salt-rising bread

(MAKES 2 LOAVES)

960 g (8 x 250 ml / 8 cups) bread flour (white, brown or whole-wheat)
2 ml (2 pinches) sugar
10 ml (2 t) salt
yeast plant
extra water, if necessary

BAKING TINS
2 greased bread tins, each 200 x 100 x 62,5 mm (8 x 4 x 2½ inches) (see Hint below)

1. Place the flour, sugar and salt in a dough basin and mix well. Make a well in the centre of the flour mixture and spoon the yeast plant into the hollow. Mix well with your hands to allow the flour to absorb the moisture of the leavening. The dough is fairly stiff and a little extra water will have to be added to achieve this effect. The dough must not be too soft. Knead 10-15 minutes until the dough is smooth and elastic.
2. Divide the dough into 2 equal parts and shape into 2 neat loaves. Place the dough in the bread tins so that it fills the tins to between half and two-thirds. Cover and leave in a warm place to prove until it has doubled in bulk. Preheat the oven to 200 °C (400 °F).
3. Bake loaves for 25 minutes, then peek into the oven. If the upper crust is darkening too fast, cover with aluminium foil, shiny side up. Bake for another 20-25 minutes and remove from oven. Test to see if bread is done.* When well baked, turn out onto cooling racks.

* TEST FOR DONENESS
Tip the baking tin to release the loaf and tap the bottom of the bread. It must have a hollow sound. If not, bake a little longer.

HINT: Smaller baking tins may also be used for salt-rising bread, and filled almost to the top. The bread will then rise above the tin, and even further during baking, giving the typical high crust of bread with a T-shaped slice.

SALT-RISING BREAD

Bread plait

(MAKES 2 LARGE
OR 3 SMALLER LOAVES)

This bread has a fine texture and a rich taste. It must be made with butter; margarine does not work. Because a three- or four-strand plaited bread looks so attractive, it should ideally be served whole and cut at the table, or as part of a bread buffet.

100 g (100 ml/8 T) butter
1,36 kg (2,85 litres/11⅓ cups) cake flour, sifted
700 ml (4 T less than 3 cups) milk
20 g (25 ml/2 T) sugar
2 eggs, beaten
1 cake of yeast (25 g), crumbled
10 g (10 ml/2 t) salt
olive oil to grease dough

TOPPING
1 egg, beaten
12,5 ml (1 T) cream

BAKING TINS
Baking trays lightly greased with margarine

1. Rub butter into flour. Mix milk, sugar, eggs and yeast and stir into the flour mixture. Do not add more water if the dough feels too stiff. Knead for 3-5 minutes. Add salt and knead to a smooth dough – about 10-15 minutes, depending on how well you knead. The dough will be stringy when ready. Form into a ball and brush with oil. Place in a greased bowl, cover, and leave to prove for 2 hours at normal room temperature, or overnight in the refrigerator, in which case the dough must first be covered with greased plastic wrap.
2. Remove dough from refrigerator and allow to reach room temperature. Knock down and divide into 2 (or 3) equal parts. Divide each piece into 3 and roll each piece into a sausage shape. Plait together 3 'sausages' to form a loaf. Repeat with rest of dough. Place on baking trays dusted with flour. Firmly press down ends of loaves (otherwise they will come undone) and fold under a small section. Cover with a damp cloth and leave to prove for 1½-2 hours or until slightly more than double in bulk. Preheat oven to 200 °C (400 °F).
3. Beat egg and cream together and carefully brush over risen loaves. Make sure that it does not drip onto the baking trays – it will burn. Place in oven and bake for 45 minutes. Test for doneness (p. 8). Do not allow the

loaves to become too dark – they should be a deep golden brown colour. Turn out onto cooling racks and leave to cool completely.

HINT: Bread plaits freeze well. Wrap the cold loaves in aluminium foil, shiny side out. Place in plastic bags, seal and freeze.

VARIATIONS
● Prepare the dough with *moskonfyt* instead of sugar. Use 50 ml (4 T).
● Knead in a packet of aniseed (28 g) with the salt. Before adding the aniseed, gently bruise the seeds in a mortar.
● The dough may also be formed into balls of 20 g each, and placed close together in two 300 mm (12 inch) baking tins. Leave to prove and bake. If the balls are increased to 30 g, you can use them for rusks. When baked, break up into individual buns, cool on a wire rack and dry in a single layer in the oven (p. 18).

Pot bread

(MAKES 2 LOAVES)

This pot bread, the best I have ever tasted, requires a lot of patience. It is baked by the South African Italian community and is their version of *pane pugliese*. Start the evening before to give the *biga* (yeast plant) enough time to activate. The long standing time ensures that the bread develops a natural yeasty taste, and that the dough has a porous texture.

YEAST PLANT
200 ml (⅘ cup) water
5 g fresh yeast
120 g (250 ml/1 cup) white bread flour
DOUGH
10 g fresh yeast
700 ml (2⅘ cups) lukewarm water
1,4 kg (3 litres/12 cups) white bread flour
20 g (18 ml/3½ t) salt
140 g (150 ml/⅗ cup) olive oil

BAKING TINS
2 flat-bottomed cast-iron pots, each ± 250 mm (10 inches) in diameter, well greased with margarine (do not dust with flour)

1. YEAST PLANT: Pour water in an upright container and stir in yeast until dissolved. Beat in flour until mixture is smooth. Cover with a damp cloth (not plastic wrap) and leave to prove overnight at normal room temperature.

2. DOUGH: Dissolve yeast in water and stir in yeast plant. Spoon flour and salt into a large kneading bowl and mix well. Using a large fork, mix in the plant mixture a little at a time. Using your hands, press the dough together. Turn out the dough onto a work surface lightly dusted with flour and knead for 12-15 minutes until elastic. The dough is fairly dry. Do not be tempted to add too much extra liquid, perhaps just a teaspoon or two of water. Form dough into a ball.
3. AND NOW FOR THE SECRET: It is all in the oil! Place the ball of dough in a large container or kneading bowl and pour over all the oil. Cover with plastic wrap and leave to prove in a cool place for about 2 hours.
4. Knock down, and even if it is difficult to do so, knead in all the oil. Form dough into balls and place in the pots. Cover with clean, damp tea towels and leave for 1-1½ hours to prove. Preheat oven to 220 °C (450 °F).
5. Bake risen loaves for 10 minutes. Reduce the temperature to 200 °C (400 °F) and bake 30-40 minutes more. Test for doneness (p. 8). Turn out on wire racks and leave to cool. Serve lukewarm with butter and grape jam, or as accompaniment to a braai.

FARM LOAF BAKED IN SMALL CLAY POTS

Maize bread

(MAKES 1 LOAF)

1 packet (500 g) self-raising flour
5 ml (1 t) salt
3 ml (½ t) baking powder
1 tin (325 g) maize kernels, well drained
25 ml (2 T) finely chopped fresh parsley
1 carton (500 ml / 2 cups) buttermilk

TOPPING
50 g (125 ml / ½ cup) finely grated
    cheddar cheese
25 ml (2 T) sesame seeds

BAKING TINS
1 greased bread tin, 200 x 100 x 62,5 mm
    (8 x 4 x 2½ inches)

1. Preheat oven to 180 °C (350 °F).
2. Sift together flour, salt and baking powder. Add maize kernels, parsley and buttermilk and mix lightly, using a two-pronged fork. Spoon into tin, sprinkle grated cheddar cheese and sesame seeds over the top and bake for 1 hour.
3. Turn out and serve with a braai.

Farm loaf

(MAKES 2 OR 3 LOAVES)

1,68 kg (14 x 250 ml / 14 cups) brown
    bread flour
30 g (25 ml / 2 T) salt
50 ml (4 T) oil
30-40 g fresh yeast (see Hint)
1,25 liters (5 cups) lukewarm water
85 g (85 ml / ⅓ cup) honey

BAKING TINS
2 tins, each 325 x 75 x 75 mm
    (13 x 3 x 3 inches) or
3 tins, each 250 x 75 x 62,5 mm
    (10 x 3 x 2½ inches)

1. Mix flour and salt and sprinkle oil over the mixture. Mix, using your hands, and make a well in the centre.
2. Dissolve yeast in 1 litre (4 cups) of the water. Stir in honey and spoon into well in flour mixture. Mix, using your hands, and add enough of the remaining water to make a sticky dough. It takes 2-3 minutes. Complete and bake as for Harvest bread.

Harvest bread

(MAKES 2 OR 3 LOAVES)

In the Swartland this thanksgiving loaf is baked when the wheat has been harvested, when it rains, or if the wheat rust has been averted. Although it is baked with fresh yeast, it involves easy mixing that takes only a few minutes. The dough is not kneaded and only has to prove once. If you don't have all four kinds of seeds, increase the ones you have accordingly.

640 g (800 ml / 3⅓ cups) crushed wheat
tap water
100 g (125 ml / ½ cup) linseeds
100 g (185 ml / ¾ cup) sunflower seeds
50 g (75 ml / 6 T) poppy seeds
50 g (75 ml / 6 T) roasted sesame seeds
37,5 ml (3 T) olive oil
840 g (1,625 litres / 6½ cups) whole-wheat
    flour
840 g (1,75 litres / 7 cups) brown bread
    flour
35 g (30 ml / 6 t) salt
30-40 g fresh yeast (see Hint)
37,5 ml (3 T) treacle or molasses
37,5 ml (3 T) honey
1,125 litres (4½ cups) off-lukewarm water
extra flour for baking tins
sesame and / or poppy seeds to sprinkle over top

BAKING TINS
2 long tins, each 325 x 75 x 75 mm
    (13 x 3 x 3 inches) or
3 shorter tins, each 250 x 75 x 62,5 mm
    (10 x 3 x 2½ inches) – oiled

1. Mix the wheat with 450 ml (4 T less than 2 cups) tap water and leave to soak overnight. All the liquid will be absorbed.
2. Mix linseeds, sunflower seeds, poppy seeds and sesame seeds, and stir, together with the oil, into soaked wheat.
3. Mix whole-wheat and brown bread flour and stir in salt. Mix in the wheat mixture. Make a well in centre of mixture.
4. Add yeast, treacle and honey to 1 litre (4 cups) of the lukewarm water, stirring until the yeast has dissolved. Pour liquid into well in flour mixture and mix with your hands to form a sticky dough. Stir in enough of the

remaining water to make a sticky, soft dough. Do not stir for longer than 2 minutes.
5. Spoon flour into tins and shake well to cover bottom and sides. Invert tins and tap lightly to remove excess flour. Divide dough among tins and neaten along the sides. At this stage more sesame and / or poppy seeds may be sprinkled over the top. Leave in a warm place for 1-2 hours until dough has doubled in bulk. Meanwhile, preheat the oven to 220 °C (450 °F). 180'
6. When ready, place in preheated oven. Reduce the heat to 200 °C (400 °F) and bake for 1 hour. Test for doneness (p. 8). Turn out onto wire racks and leave to cool completely.

HINT: Typically, this kind of bread has a fairly heavy texture, but the loaves are no bricks. You will therefore have to increase the yeast slightly in winter to get the same texture as you would in summer, when less yeast is required.

Raisin loaf

(MAKES 2 OR 3 LOAVES)

BAKING TINS
2 long tins, each 325 x 75 x 75 mm
    (13 x 3 x 3 inches) or
3 shorter tins, each 250 x 75 x 62,5 mm
    (10 x 3 x 2½ inches)

1. Follow recipe for Bread plait on p. 10.
2. Soak 1 packet (500 g) seedless raisins for at least 2 hours in warm red tea (rooibos) or honeybush tea. Spoon into a sieve and drain well. Press out remaining fluid, add to dough together with salt and knead to mix.
3. Bake 2 tins for 50-60 minutes, and 3 tins for 40-50 minutes, at 180 °C (350 °F).

GLAZE
Mix 50 g (62,5 ml / ¼ cup) sugar and 50 ml (4 T) cold water and stir over low heat until sugar has dissolved. Increase heat, bring to the boil and boil for 2 minutes. Brush over brown upper crust of loaves.

VARIATION WITH WALNUTS
Add 300 g chopped walnuts together with the raisins.

Soweto grey bread

(MAKES 2 OR 3 LOAVES)

This easy, light loaf has a springy texture. Instant yeast is used in the recipe and produces a freshly baked, aromatic loaf within two hours from the time the ingredients are measured, mixed, kneaded, left to prove twice and baked. The bread has a crisp crust and is soft inside. The only disadvantage is that it stays fresh only for a day. It may, of course, be frozen and reheated in the oven before serving, but it will be much more difficult to cut as the naturally crisp crust will be even crisper.

720 g (6 x 250 ml/6 cups) cake flour
260 g (500 ml/2 cups) whole-wheat flour
2-3 sachets (10 g each) instant yeast
15 ml (3 t) sugar
15 ml (3 t) salt
± 1 litre (4 cups) lukewarm water
50 g (50 ml/4 T) butter
extra butter to grease

GLAZE
10 ml (2 t) salt (preferably coarse salt)
10 ml (2 t) cornflour
20 ml (4 t) water

BAKING TINS
2 tins, each 325 x 75 x 75 mm
    (13 x 3 x 3 inches) or
3 tins, each 250 x 75 x 62,5 mm
    (10 x 3 x 2½ inches)

1. Mix cake and whole-wheat flours, yeast, sugar and salt and form a well in centre of mixture. First pour ± 750 ml (3 cups) of water in the well and mix using your hands. The dough must be neither sticky nor too dry, and must feel soft to the touch. If necessary, add more water, but only a teaspoonful at a time. Turn out the dough on a surface lightly dusted with flour. Some dough will stick to your hands, but will quickly come off during kneading. Butter your hands using a quarter of the butter and knead the dough. Butter hands again and continue kneading. Use all the butter in this way, kneading the dough for 12-15 minutes until smooth and elastic.
2. Lightly grease a mixing bowl with extra butter and place kneaded dough in bowl. Turn dough to cover in butter. Cover with a clean, damp tea towel and leave in a warm place to prove for 10 minutes. *The secret of the loaf:* During the first period of proving the dough must puff up just enough without doubling in bulk.

3. Knock down well. Shape into loaves or miniature loaves and place in prepared containers. Cover with a damp cloth and leave to prove for 15-20 minutes until doubled in bulk. Preheat oven to 200 °C (400 °F).
4. GLAZE: Mix salt, cornflour and water. Carefully brush over risen bread. Bake for 5 minutes. Reduce heat to 180 °C (350 °F). Bake about 20 minutes more for small, individual loaves and 40 minutes more for large loaves. Test for doneness (p. 8). Turn out onto a wire cooling rack. Serve lukewarm with butter, or leave to cool completely.

HINTS
● The recipe for grey bread uses too much yeast, therefore you must keep a watchful eye on the dough during the two proving periods to ensure that it does not rise too much.
● Ensure that the tops of the tins used for baking are cleanly cut, otherwise it will not be possible to turn out the loaves.

VARIATION
This mixture is sufficient for 18 individual loaf tins, ± 24 clay pots, 18 flat-tin loaves (use empty tuna cans), or 12 round loaves (use empty 410 g cans). Always use oil or margarine to grease the tins – butter will burn.

Whole-wheat loaf

(MAKES 1 LOAF)

This plain, healthy bread was baked during the sixties and early seventies, especially in Stellenbosch where it was soon elevated to the typical South African national whole-wheat bread.

650 g (5 x 250 ml/5 cups) whole-wheat flour
12,5 ml (1 T) oil
10 ml (2 t) salt
25 g fresh yeast
12,5 ml (1 T) soft brown sugar
    or honey
750 ml (3 cups) lukewarm water

BAKING TINS
1 oiled tin, 300 x 75 x 75 mm
    (12 x 3 x 3 inches). This size produces a
    loaf that is not too high and therefore easy to
    cut, because it has a somewhat dense and
    crumbly texture.

1. Mix flour, oil and salt. Dissolve yeast and sugar in some of the water. Spoon into the flour mixture en mix well while adding the remaining water. The dough is sticky.
2. Spoon dough into tin and smooth the top. Cover with a clean, moist tea towel and leave to prove for 1 hour until doubled in bulk. Preheat oven to 200 °C (400 °F).
3. Bake 1 hour until done. Test for doneness (p. 8). Turn out onto a wire cooling rack.

Vetkoek

(MAKES 24)

Quick and easy using instant yeast. Vetkoek made with baking powder are not traditional. Batter with baking powder is deep-fried until golden brown and the result is in fact fritters, not vetkoek.

2 sachets (10 g each) instant yeast
720 g (6 x 250 ml/6 cups) cake flour,
    sifted once
15 ml (3 t) salt
5 ml (1 t) sugar
500 ml (2 cups) lukewarm water,
    or half milk and half water
25 ml/2 T butter

1. Mix the yeast, flour, salt and sugar. Pour water (or water and milk) around the outer edge of the flour mixture and mix into flour using your hands. If using an electric mixer, attach dough hook and use a low setting. Keeping the machine running, add water in a thin stream. If you live in a dry area, a little more water may be used if necessary. Butter your hands and knead the dough for 10-12 minutes until it is smooth and elastic and forms a ball. Knead the dough for 7-8 minutes if using the mixer. Place the ball of dough in an oiled mixing bowl and turn to cover in oil. Cover with a clean, moist cloth and leave in for 15-20 minutes until the dough has almost doubled in bulk.
2. Knock down and divide dough in half. Roll each half into a long sausage. Using a sharp knife, divide each 'sausage' equally into 6-8 pieces. Arrange on baking trays, cover with a damp cloth and leave until well risen.
3. Meanwhile, heat a large frying pan or saucepan on the stove and fill to 12,5-25 mm (½-1 inch) with oil. Heat the oil until just hot, but definitely not scorching hot. Fry 2-3 vetkoek at a time in oil until golden brown on one side, turn and fry the other side. If the oil is too hot, the vetkoek will burn on the outside while still raw inside. If the oil is

too cold, the vetkoek will absorb too much oil. Remove with a slotted spoon and drain on crumpled brown or kitchen paper. Serve immediately. If the vetkoek are prepared in advance and kept warm, the wonderful crisp crust will be lost.

ASKOEK

The difference between askoek and vetkoek, both made from the same dough, lies in the fact that askoek is not fried in oil, but baked in the hot ash of a braai fire.

Naan

(MAKES 6)

Curry without naan is not curry. *Naan*, a flat, tear-shaped bread from India, is used instead of a knife and fork when the Indian community serves curry. It is traditionally baked in a tandoor. One of the unfamiliar words you will encounter in this recipe is *ghee* (clarified butter).

LEAVENING
2 ml (slightly less than ½ t) salt
15 ml (3 t) sugar
250 ml (1 cup) lukewarm water
10 g (2 t) fresh compressed yeast

BREAD
1 kg (8 x 250 ml plus 85 ml/8⅓ cups)
  cake flour
15 ml (3 t) cumin seeds
65 ml (¼ cup) lukewarm ghee*
100 g (125 ml/½ cup) sugar
2 eggs
500 ml (2 cups) milk

TOPPING
1 egg
25 ml (2 T) sesame seeds

* Ghee is prepared by cutting butter into cubes and melting it over medium heat. Lower the heat and regularly spoon off the foam that forms on top. Cook the butter for about an hour so that all impurities sink to the bottom and remain behind when the ghee is strained off.

1. LEAVENING: Mix salt, sugar and water and stir in yeast. Set aside and leave to activate. It takes about 15 minutes. If the water is too cold, the yeast will not activate, and if it is too hot the same will happen – therefore, it should be about the temperature of a baby's bottle. The mixture is ready when it foams like beer in a glass.
2. KNEAD BREAD: Sift 960 g (8 x 250 ml/ 8 cups) of the flour into a mixing bowl and stir in the cumin seeds. Make a well in the centre of the mixture.

3. Whisk the ghee, sugar and eggs together in a separate mixing bowl until light and fluffy. Spoon egg mixture and leavening into the well in the flour mixture and mix with your hands while gradually adding milk to form a soft, slightly sticky dough. Add the milk slowly, a little at a time, otherwise the dough will become too soft. Knead for 3-4 minutes. Form into a ball and place in a greased kneading bowl, turning the dough to cover it in butter all around, then cover with a clean, damp tea cloth. Leave to prove in a warm place, away from any draughts for 1-2 hours until doubled in bulk.
4. Turn out onto a floured surface and knock down. Knead for 2-3 minutes more. Divide into 6 equally sized pieces and roll each piece into a ball. Roll out flat and pull one side out to form a tear-shaped bread. Place on greased baking trays, cover again with damp tea cloths and leave to rise until doubled in bulk. Preheat oven to 180 °C (350 °F).
5. TOPPING: Beat egg, carefully brush over loaves and sprinkle with sesame seeds. Bake for 15-18 minutes in centre of oven.

Rusks

A CUP OF COFFEE and a rusk are to us what a morning *croissant* is to the French. Rusks are also a snack with tea at eleven, or with coffee at four.

A friend tells a story about a visiting Israeli student at Stellenbosch University. When offered a rusk, his guest said: 'Shame, are you so poor than you have to dry out old bread?' I remember, too, that an American guest of Mrs Maria Malan (widow of Dr D F) in Stellenbosch viewed the rusks offered her with great suspicion. Perhaps rusks are known, and loved, only in our country?

I suspect that the first rusk, baked at the Cape and known as Sedoos (southeasterly wind) to seafarers, was nothing more than home-baked bread, thickly sliced and then cut into two or three pieces before being dried. I would also like to suggest that Cape shepherds and later the Voortrekkers used rusks because they kept well on long journeys. A Dutch dictionary defines rusks as very crisp bread that is baked twice. The Dutch bake flat, round 'rusks' and enjoy them with sweet or savoury foods. *Biscotte* are French breads baked in a similar mould to the one we use for Boston bread, only much longer. They are then sliced and dried. Germany has *Zwieback*, which is not very different from toast, but rusks as we know them do not appear in any of my sources.

The French Huguenots are regarded as the ·first pastry cooks at the Cape – with which I agree – but I doubt whether they taught us how to make must buns (mosbolletjies), as Dr Anna de Villiers and Renata Coetzee assert. The French learnt how to bake bread from the Italians, but used yeasty barley beer as their rising agent. As a result, their breads had a better texture and were much lighter.

Wine and must replaced barley as a rising agent in the early seventeenth century, but it was only in 1840 that one Zang, secretary at the Austrian embassy in Paris, introduced the so-called Viennese bread to France. This method later led to the baking of the familiar, long French loaves. I suspect – but have no proof – that our famous must buns (like much of our food) were a Malay creation; perhaps based on French bread and – who knows? – perhaps elevated to the higher status they enjoy today by the bewigged governors and even the English occupiers.

HOW TO BAKE GOOD RUSKS

Making rusks consists of three processes: first the dough must be mixed and correctly kneaded; then you must understand the rising process and the shaping of the buns; and finally, the baking, cooling and drying process which is as important as the first two processes.

HINTS

● Knead the dough very well: 10-15 minutes by hand, or 8-10 minutes with the dough hook of an electric mixer.

● Do not knead too large a quantity of dough at a time. Rather divide the dough into two or more pieces and knead them separately.

● Wrap the kneaded dough well and leave it in a slightly warm, draught-free place to rise. Or wrap in cling wrap and leave overnight in the refrigerator to rise. In both cases, the dough should almost, but not quite, double in bulk.

● Punch down the dough and make balls the size of a golf ball by holding the dough in your hand, then pinching a piece between your thumb and forefinger and breaking it off. The balls must be large enough to come up to a third of the height of the tins you are using.

● Pack the balls tightly together in greased loaf tins (rather than larger tins), but do not overload the tins.

● Cover the tins and leave the balls to rise until they reach the top of the tins. Remember that the balls will rise a further 10-15% during baking.

● There is no set temperature at which rusks should be baked; the temperature will depend on the proportions.

CONDENSED MILK RUSKS

• Test with a metal skewer, or simply a knitting needle, to see if the rusk 'loaf' is cooked. If the skewer comes out dry, it's ready.

• Turn out onto a wire cooling rack and leave to rest for at least an hour until cool. Using the tip of a sharp knife, make small incisions in the crust where the buns join. Invert and break into buns. Some people prefer to slice the loaf neatly (I don't), then cut each slice into fingers.

• Pack the buns, in a single layer, on wire racks, the rack of a baking dish or directly onto the oven racks (with a pan below to catch crumbs) and dry at 50-60 °C (100-125 °F). Place a piece of crumpled paper or even a cork in the door of the oven so that it remains very slightly open to allow moist air to escape from the oven. Rusks should not brown during drying.

• Pack the rusks on a cooling rack and leave until cold. Pack in airtight containers and store in a dark place.

Condensed milk rusks

(MAKES 120 RUSKS)

The easy way out for those who can't or won't bake mosbolletjies.

1 tin (397 g) condensed milk
500 ml (2 cups) boiling water
250 g (250 ml/1 cup) butter
200 g (250 ml/1 cup) sugar
500 ml (2 cups) cold water
3 extra-large eggs, beaten
2 cakes of fresh yeast (25 g each), crumbled
1 packet (2,5 kg) cake flour
25 ml (2 T) salt
50 ml (4 T) aniseed (optional)

BAKING TINS
4 greased loaf tins

1. Mix condensed milk, boiling water, butter and sugar and stir until butter has melted and sugar has dissolved. Add cold water, eggs, yeast and half the flour. Mix thoroughly to a smooth batter. Do not be too concerned if small pieces of yeast are still visible. Cover and leave in a warm place for 1-2 hours to allow the leavening to rise and become spongy.

2. Punch back the leavening and add salt, aniseed (if used) and enough of the remaining flour to make a soft dough. Sprinkle more flour, a little at a time, onto the dough board and knead well until the dough no longer sticks to the board. Knead for 15 minutes or

until the dough is smooth and elastic. If another pair of hands is available, divide the dough into two and knead separately.

3. Read Hints (p. 17) again and complete dough by leaving it to prove, punching back, pinching into balls, packing tightly in greased baking tins and setting aside to rise again. Preheat the oven to 160 °C (325 °F).

4. Bake the rusk loaf for 40-50 minutes. Cover with aluminium foil, shiny side up, as soon as the top becomes too brown. Turn out and leave to cool. Break into rusks and dry out.

Boerbeskuit

(MAKES ± 240 RUSKS)

Boerbeskuit should be nice and big, so that two or three rusks are enough for breakfast. This recipe fills a number of tins; or rather barrels. Earlier, it was part of the packed lunch taken along when ploughing, sowing seed or working on the land, just like the apple we take to school or work today. Those were the days when the coffee left on the stove to brew was so strong that a single cup would keep you wide awake all day.

1 packet (2,5 kg) brown bread flour
1 packet (2,5 kg) cake flour
1 kg potatoes, unpeeled, washed
2 litres (8 x 250 ml/8 cups) milk
1 packet (35 g) aniseed
1 brick (500 g) butter, cubed
1 kg (5 x 250 ml/5 cups) soft brown sugar
62,5 ml (5 T) salt
12 extra-large eggs
500 ml (2 cups) oil
juice of 2 large lemons
6 sachets (10 g each) instant yeast

BAKING TINS
8 greased loaf tins

1. Mix flours. (In winter, especially inland where it can be extremely cold, it may be necessary to place the flour in a warming oven for a while to take off the chill. This will facilitate the rising process later on.)

2. Cut the unpeeled potatoes into cubes and cook until nearly done in lightly salted water. Remove potatoes with a slotted spoon, measure out 400 ml (1⅗ cups) of the cooking liquid and add to potatoes. Mash together the potatoes and liquid, using a potato masher or the machine of the day – the food processor.

3. Bring milk and aniseed to the boil, add butter, sugar and salt, remove from the heat and stir until the butter has melted and the sugar has dissolved.

4. Whisk together the eggs, oil and lemon juice. Now place all the ingredients, including the instant yeast, in a large kneading bowl and knead to a soft, pliable dough. More flour or lukewarm water may be added to achieve the desired result. Grease a large, clean kneading bowl with lard or butter and place dough in bowl. Grease dough by turning it. Cover the bowl with a clean, unperfumed black plastic bag (or, of course, your dough blanket). Set aside for a while to see if the dough rises.

5. If the dough visibly begins to rise, you may start pinching off balls of dough (see How to bake good rusks, p. 17). Get help, because it is a lot of dough. Pack about 24 balls tightly into each baking tin. Place the first four completed tins in the refrigerator to rise slowly. Repeat with the rest of the dough and let this too rise in the refrigerator. Preheat the oven to 180 °C (350 °F).

6. Bake the first half of the rusks for 25 minutes in the preheated oven. If baking on two shelves, the upper and lower tins should now be switched. Bake for another 25-30 minutes and test to see whether rusks are done. Remove from oven and allow to cool in tin for a few minutes. Repeat baking process with rest of dough. Turn out the baked rusk loaves, allow to cool slightly and break into rusks. Repeat with the rest. Dry out (see top left). Make sure that the rusks are dried right through or else they will form a hard core as soon as they are stored.

STRANGE TASTES

My dear, sweet Aunt Julia, now even more blessed, once stored a cake tin containing her delicious buttermilk rusks in a cupboard in which there were mothballs. As a child, the naphthalene taste was a new experience and I always insisted that my mother keep a small tin of rusks separately for me, and store it in a drawer in which there was a ball or two of naphthalene. Johan Odendaal relates how his mother once baked rusks while the kitchen was being painted. Well, the extra flavour was … turpentine. The moral is: keep the rusks away from strange flavours.

BOERBESKUIT AND BUTTERMILK RUSKS

Buttermilk rusks

(MAKES 72)

Because these rusks do not contain yeast, the preparation and baking are quick. They remain favourites, while out rounding up livestock, for children at boarding school, or simply to enjoy with a cup of coffee.

375 g (375 ml/1½ cups) butter
2 extra-large eggs
500 g (625 ml/2½ cups) sugar
12,5 ml (1 T) vanilla essence
1,5 kg (3 litres/12 cups) self-raising flour
30 ml (6 t) baking powder
5 ml (1 t) salt
1 carton (500 ml/2 cups) buttermilk

BAKING TINS
2 greased roasting pans, or 3 loaf tins

1. Beat the butter until fairly soft. Beat the eggs to a froth. Add the egg froth and sugar alternately to the butter, a little at a time. This way the sugar will dissolve in a jiffy. Beat in the vanilla essence.
2. Sift together the flour, baking powder and salt, and spoon into butter mixture. Using a large two-pronged fork or a spoon, mix flour mixture into butter mixture while slowly adding the buttermilk. Rinse the buttermilk carton with a little milk and add to the dough. Lightly knead mixture together. The mixture will be slightly oily and should therefore not be kneaded too much, only until the dough forms a lump. The dough is fairly soft. Preheat the oven to 180 °C (350 °F).
3. Pinch off pieces of dough and roll into balls – almost the size of golf balls. Pack tightly together into baking tins and bake for 45-55 minutes. Cover the loaf with aluminium foil before the top browns too much. Turn out and leave to cool. Break into rusks and dry out.

VARIATION: MARMALADE RUSKS
(Makes ± 36 rusks)

2 packets (500 g each) self-raising flour
5 ml (1 t) salt
5 ml (1 t) turmeric
3 ml (½ t) bicarbonate of soda
2 ml (¼ t) cream of tartar
100 g (125 ml/½ cup) sugar
2 extra-large eggs
250 ml (1 cup) sweet orange marmalade
grated rind of of 2 oranges
250 g (250 ml/1 cup) butter, melted
250 ml (1 cup) buttermilk
BAKING TINS
1 large or 2 medium loaf tins, greased

1. Sift flour, salt, turmeric, bicarbonate of soda and cream of tartar 3 times into a large mixing bowl or kneading dish. Make a well in the mixture.
2. Beat the sugar, eggs, marmalade, orange rind, butter and buttermilk together, and spoon into the well in the flour mixture. Using a large wooden spoon, rapidly incorporate until evenly mixed. Do not overmix. Preheat oven to 180 °C (350 °F).
3. Pinch off balls of dough and tightly pack them into tins. Bake for 50-60 minutes. Cover loaf with aluminium foil before the top browns too much. Turn out and leave to cool. Break into rusks and dry out.

Mosbeskuit

(MAKES ± 120 RUSKS)

Must buns (mosbolletjies) are unbeatable and definitely our best rusks. Yes, I can hear all those lazy people complaining that it's too much like hard work to bake them, or they don't have must. Calm down. I know it's only the Bolanders who can use real must in their must buns; that's why I will show you how to make must from raisins.

LEAVENING
150 g (250 ml/1 cup) unseeded raisins,
  finely chopped
625 ml (2½ cups) boiling water
¼ cake of fresh yeast (7 g), or 3 ml (½ t)
  dried yeast granules
240 g (500 ml/2 cups) cake flour
¼ cake of yeast (7 g), or 3 ml (½ t) dried
  yeast granules, dissolved in 50 ml (4 T)
  lukewarm water (optional)

DOUGH
625 ml (2½ cups) lukewarm milk
250 g (250 ml/1 cup) soft butter
3 large eggs
25 ml (2 T) salt
400 g (500 ml/2 cups) sugar
15 ml (3 t) aniseed
1 packet (2,5 kg) cake flour

BAKING TINS
4 medium 300 x 125 x 100 mm
  (12 x 5 x 4 inch) or 6-8 smaller tins

1. THE YEAST: Start preparing today, or even 2-3 days earlier, in order to bake tomorrow or the day after. Place raisins in a large screw-top jar, add boiling water and allow to stand until it reaches room temperature. Make sure that there is a fair amount of space left in the jar for the gases produced by the yeast. Add yeast and stir until dissolved. Close with lid and leave until the mixture becomes active, is nice and foamy, and all the raisins float on top. Strain through a sieve and use mixture as leavening. Remember to squeeze out all the liquid that the raisins have absorbed and add it to the rest of the yeast.
2. LEAVENING: Always prepare leavening early in the morning as it is fairly time-consuming. Measure out the strained yeast liquid. If necessary, add enough water to make 500 ml (2 cups), otherwise use as is. Sift flour into a very large mixing bowl (many people simply use a baby bath) and mix in the leavening until the mixture is smooth and without lumps. Cover and leave in a warm, draught-free place until spongy. If after 2 hours this mixture has shown no signs of fermenting, dissolve another ¼ cake of yeast and put aside to activate. Add it to the leavening, mix, cover and leave to stand until the mixture becomes active.
3. THE DOUGH: Stir leavening well, add milk and stir again. Beat butter into mixture. Beat in eggs one at a time. Add salt, sugar and aniseed and mix. Keep the flour at hand. Sift a cup of flour over the leavening and knead to mix. Repeat until a soft but pliable dough is obtained. Divide dough in half. Sift a cup of the remaining flour onto a dough board, place 1 piece of soft dough on top and knead until flour has been absorbed. Set aside and repeat with the other piece of dough. Continue by kneading the 2 pieces of dough in turn, using the remaining flour. Knead each piece of dough for 10-15 minutes at a time. The dough must be smooth and elastic. Note that in certain parts of South Africa, using enough flour for the right consistency would mean that about a cup of flour will remain. In other

parts it may be necessary to knead in a little more flour. Cover the dough and leave it in a slightly warm place to rise until almost doubled in bulk. This will take 2-3 hours. Punch down, cover and again leave to rise until almost doubled in bulk. This time it will take 1-2 hours. *Do not* punch down again.

4. Lightly grease baking tins with butter.

5. MAKING UP THE BATCH: Preheat the oven to 160 °C (325 °F). Pinch off balls of risen dough as described in How to bake good rusks (p. 17) and pack them tightly in the tins. The tins must be nearly half full. Cover and leave to rise until doubled in bulk. Handle carefully and place in oven. Bake for 40-50 minutes or until golden brown and firm. Turn out one of the bun loaves and test for doneness (p. 8). If not done, return the loaf to the tin and bake a little longer. Turn out, allow to cool and dry (see top of p. 18). I think it is a shame to dry out all the rusk loaves. I always keep one to enjoy with butter and a piece of melon preserve.

VARIATION: RUSK BREAD
(Makes 1 loaf)

Set aside one half of the rusk dough. Lightly grease a loaf, round or *brioche* baking tin and shape the dough into a loaf. Place in prepared baking tin and leave to rise until dough has doubled in bulk. Bake as you would for rusks until cooked, turn out onto a wire rack and leave to cool. Serve with butter and preserves or jam. This tasty loaf quickly becomes dry and stale, so it is best to eat it immediately.

Breakfast rusks

(MAKES 72 RUSKS)

Fitness and healthy eating habits gained popularity in the seventies, and even more so in the eighties. Balanced meals and the importance of breakfast have always been some of my many self-taught 'food causes', about which I tried, in many publications, to inform people. If there isn't enough time in the morning for a balanced breakfast, this dried muesli bar is the answer. It's particularly suitable for children who refuse to eat porridge. Very healthy. Any other flavour of yoghurt may be used.

1 large packet (1 kg) self-raising flour
5 ml (1 t) baking powder
500 ml (2 cups) muesli
75 g (125 ml/½ cup) bleached sultanas
75 g (125 ml/½ cup) dried apricots
  or pears, chopped
1 packet (100 g) nuts,
  preferably walnuts
  or pecan nuts,
  lightly chopped
80 g (250 ml/1 cup) coconut
250 ml (1 cup) sunflower seeds
50 ml (4 T) sesame seeds
300 g (375 ml/1½ cups) brown sugar
2 extra-large eggs
1 carton (500 ml/2 cups) yoghurt, preferably
  pineapple or guava flavour
500 g (500 ml/2 cups) butter, melted,
  skimmed and cooled

BAKING TINS
3 medium loaf tins, greased with margarine

1. Mix flour, baking powder, muesli, sultanas, apricots, nuts, coconut, sunflower and sesame seeds, and sugar in a large mixing bowl or kneading dish. Make a well in the centre. Preheat the oven to 180 °C (350 °F).

2. Beat eggs and yoghurt together and stir in cooled butter. Spoon yoghurt mixture into the well in the flour mixture and mix rapidly but thoroughly, using a large two-pronged fork or a wooden spoon.

3. Divide mixture between two baking tins. Smooth the top and bake for 1 hour. Check loaves in oven after 40 minutes: If the top browns too quickly, cover with aluminium foil, shiny side up.

4. Remove from oven and leave to cool in tins for 5 minutes. Turn out, allow to cool completely and cut loaves into thick slices and then into fingers. Dry out.

CHAPTER 3

From putu to polenta

ONCE, LONG AGO, two crows, a male and a female, went to Mexico in search of maize, but could only find *atole* (wild maize). Frustrated, they decided to fly eastward in search of delicious, plump kernels. They flew and flew, past Cape Point, and eventually changed course northward. Somewhere in the Eastern Cape they rested, exhausted from their long trip. And so they dropped the seeds from their country of origin. Thus, according to Xhosa legend, the first maize became established in our country, long before Jan van Riebeeck first set foot here.

We know that, in 1655, Jan received some maize from his home country, but it could not be grown successfully at the Cape. Cape stock farmers trekking towards the eastern border became acquainted with maize through the established Nguni farmers. I suspect that maize was established there from seed obtained from the Portuguese seafarers, or perhaps from the Arabs from North Africa trading in the region.

It was only with the arrival of the British Settlers in 1820 that maize was cultivated on a larger scale in the Eastern Cape. The Celts can be regarded as the inventors of porridge and, long before the British first set foot here, the people from England, Scotland and Wales were already eating oats for breakfast. The British Settlers had more success cultivating maize than grain. Maize-meal had to be mixed with wheat flour to bake bread – not too successfully, it may be added. The need for a solid breakfast encouraged the Settlers to start making porridge. I am still searching for proof that the black tribes were already making putu at the time, or whether it is something the British taught them to do. What we do know is that porridge has been a staple diet in our country for more than 150 years.

That is why we now move to the Eastern Cape, the source of our porridge culture. Not the most important maize region, but without a doubt the place where maize is treated in an old-fashioned way. Not machine-ground flour, but the real, fresh, stone-ground meal. During the summer months the maize is harvested, the cobs tied in bundles and hung in huts to dry. A hut is swept and the cleaned area becomes the threshing floor. The maize is packed on the floor and thrashed with knob-kieries to strip the kernels. Sometimes it is stripped entirely by hand, but it is common practice to strip by hand only those kernels left behind after the thrashing. Part of the harvest is kept as seed for the next season, and the rest is stored in baskets, clay pots, or even in underground wells smeared with aloe ash.

The kernels are broken by pounding them in a pounding block, using a wooden pestle of more than a metre (3 ft 3 in) in length. This is done with a steady rhythm. When the pounder tires, she may take a short break to add a little water to the maize to soften the hard husks. Once pounded, the kernels are placed on a flat basket and winnowed against the wind to remove the husks. The next step is to grind the kernels. They are placed on a flat grinding stone, pounded with a second round stone, and then ground to the consistency of flour.

But it is not quite so simple. Every tribe has its own customs. Women do the grinding. The Tsonga women place a *guyo* (grinding stone) at an angle on three supporting stones so that the broken or ground maize kernels can slip into a basket. The Pedi women, bound by a strong communal tradition, use one grinding stone, which is guarded at night by a watchwoman. She only goes to sleep in the morning after the women responsible for grinding the meal have arrived. Each woman uses her own millstone. In the Xhosa community the grinding stones are placed on a clay elevation in the cooking hut. Using a small broom, the Sotho women brush the meal onto a densely woven mat. It is every young

KRUMMELPAP

girl's duty to know how fine or how coarse to grind the meal. This is a skill learnt from her mother, because each traditional dish requires meal of a specific texture. A good *pap* is to the rural Eastern Cape community what puff (flaky) pastry or jars of preserves are to the farmer's wife. And a good *pap* can only be made from freshly ground meal. A connoisseur will immediately taste the difference between shop-bought and freshly ground meal. The *pap* is cooked, or rather steamed, at moderately low heat over an open fire.

Interaction between the nineteenth century immigrants and the locals soon led to the spreading of maize to the Free State and Transvaal. It is here that the Voortrekkers were introduced to maize and *pap*. Maize cultivation in the interior with its summer rain was also more successful than in the winter rain regions. With the discovery of diamonds and gold the demand for maize increased, and this led to the establishment of a successful maize industry in this country. In South Africa between 40 per cent and 50 per cent of cultivated land is planted with maize annually. In fact, maize is the largest agricultural industry in the country!

Mieliepap
(Maize porridge)

This breakfast food is made in many different ways. Described below are methods for making milk-rich *slap pap* (breakfast porridge), as well as *stywe pap* and *krummelpap*.

Slap pap

(MAKES 2 SERVINGS)

For those who did not grow up with a tradition of eating porridge, this is by far the best way to enjoy *pap* for breakfast.

75 g (125 ml/ ½ cup) maize-meal
400 ml (1⅗ cups) milk
1 ml (pinch) salt
10 ml (2 t) butter

1. Mix maize-meal with 100 ml (8 T) milk and add salt. Bring the rest of the milk to the boil. Spoon teaspoonfuls of maize-meal mixture into the warm milk. Stir constantly to prevent it from sticking to the bottom of the saucepan.
2. Reduce heat and cook for 15 minutes or slightly longer. The pap must be cooked, but still runny. Whisk in butter. Serve with milk and sugar.

PAP TART

Deep-fried maize-meal balls

(MAKES 6 SERVINGS)

1 litre (4 x 250 ml/4 cups) milk
240 g (500 ml/2 cups) maize-meal
salt to taste
50 g (50 ml/4 T) butter
150 g (375 ml/1½ cups) grated cheddar cheese
3 ml (½ t) cayenne pepper
3 ml (½ t) mustard powder
3 ml (½ t) turmeric
freshly ground pepper*
freshly grated nutmeg
oil for frying
1 egg, beaten
250 ml (1 cup) dried white breadcrumbs

* Use freshly ground white pepper, black pepper or, for something different, crushed Madagascan green peppercorns. We tend to forget that Madagascar is part of Africa.

1. Bring milk to the boil, add maize-meal, season with salt and stir to mix. Reduce heat to low and simmer until cooked. Whisk in butter and remove from heat. The *pap* must be smooth and stiff.
2. Stir in cheese and season with cayenne pepper, mustard powder and turmeric, as well as pepper and nutmeg to taste. Leave mixture to cool until lukewarm. Take spoonfuls of the mixture and roll in the palms of your hands to form small balls. Line a shallow container, Swiss roll tin or tray with greaseproof paper. Arrange the balls in the container, cover with plastic film and refrigerate until required.
3. Fill a small, deep, stainless steel saucepan with oil up to at least 200 mm (8 inches) deep. Heat to 180 °C (350 °F). Bread cube test: Place a cube of white bread in the oil. If after a few seconds it rises to the surface and gradually turns golden brown, the oil is ready. If the bread turns black, the oil is too hot. If the bread takes more than 5 seconds to rise to the surface, the oil is too cold.
4. Dip some of the balls in beaten egg, allowing excess egg to drain off. Roll in breadcrumbs and shake off excess. Using a slotted spoon, lower 3 balls at a time into hot oil. Fry until golden brown, remove with the slotted spoon and drain on kitchen towels. Keep warm and repeat with the rest. Serve with boerewors cooked over hot coals (p. 58).

Stywe pap

(MAKES 6 SERVINGS)

This breakfast porridge may be used in recipes such as Pap tart (below) instead of prepared polenta.

1 litre (4 cups) water
10 ml (2 t) salt
600 g (4 x 250 ml/4 cups) maize-meal
25 ml (2 T) butter

1. Bring water and salt to the boil. Spoon all the maize-meal into a heap in the centre of the saucepan. Reduce heat to low. Cover and simmer for 5 minutes.
2. Using a large two-pronged fork, stir until porridge becomes crumbly. Cover again and steam or simmer for 30-45 minutes over low heat. Stir in butter. Serve with milk, sour milk, or even buttermilk, and also sugar or golden syrup.

Krummelpap (Putu)

(MAKES 6 SERVINGS)

This multi-purpose breakfast porridge is also a traditional accompaniment with a braai, sometimes topped with Sheba (see p. 27).

500 ml (2 cups) water
10 ml (2 t) salt
450 g (750 ml/3 cups) maize-meal

1. Bring water and salt to the boil. Spoon all the maize-meal into a heap in the centre of a saucepan and stir rapidly to mix.
2. Reduce heat and stir often, at least every 5 minutes. Keep covered in between stirring so that the *pap* will steam rather than simmer. No butter is added to *krummelpap*.

Pap tart

(MAKES 6-8 SERVINGS)

This tart is made with polenta, but *stywe pap* works equally well. You may make as many layers as you wish. They may be thick or thin, depending on how much polenta or *pap* you wish to use. If you are serving the tart to people who do not normally eat *pap*, it will be wise to concentrate on the filling. Serve lukewarm or warm, but never cold.

POLENTA
300 g (500 ml/2 cups) polenta
1 litre (4 cups) boiling water
10 ml (2 t) salt
5 ml (1 t) cumin seed
3 ml (½ t) cayenne pepper
25 ml (2 T) butter

FILLING
1 quantity Sheba (p. 27)

TOPPING
brinjal, sliced and fried (p. 142)
whole, unpeeled cloves of garlic, fried
thin Parmesan shavings
chopped chillies
fresh coriander or basil leaves

1. Gradually sprinkle polenta onto boiling water and stir in salt, cumin and cayenne pepper. Cover with plastic film and pierce 3 holes into plastic. Microwave 2 minutes at 50% (medium) power. Remove from microwave, remove plastic film and stir. Cover again with plastic film and repeat the process of microwaving and stirring 14 more times so that the polenta is microwaved 30 minutes until cooked. Stir in butter. Leave to cool.
2. Line a square baking tin of about 250 x 250 mm (10 x 10 in) with Bakewell paper, with the paper extending beyond the rim of the tin. Afterwards it is easier to lift the crust out using the paper. Grease your fingers with butter, press a layer of polenta into the baking tin and smooth the top. Spread some Sheba over and repeat the layers of Sheba and polenta until all the ingredients have been used. End with a layer of polenta. Spread a little extra butter over the top layer and cover tightly against the surface with plastic wrap. Refrigerate for at least 1 hour to set. The tart may also be prepared in individual bowls.
3. Remove tart from refrigerator. Place in a preheated oven at 160 °C (325 °F) for 20 minutes, or until heated through. Top with brinjal, garlic, cheese, chillies and coriander leaves. Serve with a braai.

Putu is made with maize-meal and has a crumbly texture. It is a staple food traditionally eaten with meat or vegetables, but may also be eaten with milk and sugar.

Stywe pap is maize-meal porridge with a consistency that is similar to that of bread dough, but without the elasticity, and it has a coarse, almosty grainy, texture.

Sheba
(Braised tomato and onions)

(MAKES 750 ML/3 CUPS)

2 large onions, peeled, halved lengthwise,
    and sliced
1 cinnamon stick
5 ml (1 t) cumin seed
25 ml (2 T) oil
3 plump cloves of garlic, bruised,
    peeled and crushed with:
10 ml (2 t) salt
freshly ground black pepper
250 ml (1 cup) water
1 kg ripe, deep red tomatoes, peeled
    and chopped (see Hint)
250 ml (1 cup) red wine
    or tomato juice
50 ml (4 T) tomato concentrate
salt and cayenne pepper to taste

OPTIONAL FRESH HERBS
50 fresh basil leaves, washed, rolled up and
    shredded finely
10 ml (2 t) fresh thyme or origanum
3 ml (½ t) chopped fresh lavender

1. In a large saucepan, sauté onions, cinnamon and cumin in oil over medium heat
until soft and translucent, but not brown.
Season well with garlic, salt and pepper. Add

HINT: Drop tomatoes in boiling water,
refresh in ice water, and remove skins.
Remove stem end, cut flesh into quarters
and remove seeds.

---

water and bring to the boil. Add tomatoes,
wine and tomato concentrate and simmer,
uncovered, until mixture has thickened. Stir
from time to time.
2. Taste and add more salt if necessary. Season with cayenne pepper and stir in herbs (if
used). Keep warm for 1 minute and serve
with Krummelpap (p. 26), Fish cakes (p. 49)
and Fried brinjal slices (p. 142).

Couscous salad

(MAKES 6 SERVINGS)

Prepare this salad on the day it is served.

COUSCOUS
250 ml (1 cup) water
5 ml (1 t) olive oil
5 ml (1 t) salt
250 g (½ packet) couscous
15 ml (3 t) butter

SALAD
50 ml (4 T) olive oil
grated rind of 1 lemon
10 ml (2 t) lemon juice
salt and freshly ground black pepper to taste
1 plump clove of garlic, bruised,
    peeled and crushed
1 red and 1 green chilli, seeded
    and finely chopped
1 baked red pepper (see p. 146), skinned
    and finely chopped, or 6 peppadews, chopped
25 ml (2 T) chopped fresh coriander leaves

1. Bring water, oil and salt to the boil.
Sprinkle couscous over, a little at a time, stirring after each addition. Remove from heat
and leave for 3 minutes to swell out.
2. Put couscous back on stove over very low
heat. Using a large, two-pronged fork, stir in
butter. Stir for 5 minutes to loosen the
grains. Leave to cool.
3. SALAD: Whisk oil, lemon rind and juice
together and season with salt, pepper, garlic
and chillies. Stir into couscous to moisten it.
Using the two-pronged fork, stir in peppers
and coriander. Store in refrigerator and serve
within hours. The salad may also be spooned
into an oiled mould and then inverted.

VARIATION
Mix the cooked couscous with Marinated
vegetables (p. 153) and serve.

CHAPTER 4

Bountiful soup

LOOKING AT THE progress of the soup pot in the twentieth century – symbolically speaking – you can discern something of the nature of our country and its peoples.

At the start of the century, vegetable and meat soups were the food of rich and poor. Both had a strong economical streak. All leftovers were simmered in the soup pot to make a nutritious family meal. Soup and bread was the staple diet of many families, and there was nothing else on the table. Lentil, dried bean, barley and split pea soup were, together with vegetable soup, the best known then, as they are now. Among the soups popular at the turn of the century which are very seldom made now is *swartsuursop* (blood soup), prepared from chicken blood and finished with chicken dumplings. In some regions the same name is used for lentil soup with vinegar. Other once-popular soups are *hemel-en-aarde* (heaven and earth), made from cracked maize and beans, and Jerusalem artichoke and pork soup.

Flour soup, the humiliating alternative to vegetable soup with soup bones, was made when there were no soup bones and so few vegetables available that the thin, watery soup had to be thickened with flour. It was eaten especially just after the Anglo-Boer War, in the Western Transvaal and elsewhere, where people were impoverished.

The opposite was true of cattle and sheep farmers. Their meat soup contained hardly any vegetables, but an excess of meat, which led to the 'potato, rice and meat' (*aartappel-rys-en-vleis*) syndrome. A slice of salt-rising yeast bread was placed in a large soup bowl, covered with the liquid part of the soup and eaten as soon as the bread had 'swollen'. The meat was then dished into the same bowl and eaten; and to end proceedings, the marrow was sucked from the bone.

By the thirties, urbanisation had begun. First came the white population and the accompanying poor white status; then the coloured farm labourers who, particularly in

BUTTERNUT AND MANGO SOUP

the fifties, flocked to the cities in search of a better future; and lastly the blacks to the townships, that gradually grew into black cities like Soweto.

Family meals were vastly different then. Soup was the most important and – most of the time – the only first course served. Bones, especially meaty ones, and even tortoises (in the days before they were protected) found their way into the soup pot. There was also oxtail and offal soup. Starters like Avocado Ritz, seafood or fruit cocktails only came into circulation after the Second World War. That was also when French onion soup appeared on the scene. Clear soups (consommés) were only prepared in households with large kitchen staffs, and therefore were popular among the foremost hostesses. From 1936 onwards, good sherry was available too. And then there was Campbell's canned consommé. One of the most popular 'secrets' of smart hostesses was a spoonful of ice-cold jellied consommé, with a glass of sherry poured over, followed by a thin layer of lightly flavoured smooth cottage cheese, finished with a spoonful of caviar and shredded chives. Hotels, restaurants and the foremost hostesses served beef consommé with blocks of baked savoury custard (consommé royale). Consommé was always prepared from beef rather than, as Leipoldt wrote, sometimes from mutton.

Cream soups have been part of the repertoire since the Cape's *belle époque*. Asparagus and mushroom soup came mainly from cans, while chicken, tomato, mussel and crayfish cream soups were made at home. When the first mushrooms were grown in the Boland and Natal, cream of mushroom soup came into its own. By the sixties, fresh asparagus – mainly from Natal and the Free State – was quite widely available.

Men were, in every sense, the head of the family, chauvinistic and dominant. South African men were meat eaters who disliked gimmicks or delicate little nibbles. Thick soup – one could almost call it soup bredie or stew – satisfied male expectations of filling food. Chowder became established with fish chowder, in which fried bacon played an important role.

Maize (corn on the cob) was served as an informal starter or used in corn chowder. In the townships, there was an interesting angle: leftover cracked maize and beans were supplemented with fresh mealie kernels, water and chillies and served as soup. This was sometimes curried and supplemented with pieces of fried sausage. Leftover offal also made its way to the soup pot, and often, too, a whole sheep's head.

In the sixties and seventies, thinnish soup was often thickened with egg yolk. This was the time when waterblommetjies regained their former popularity. As a result, acquaintance was renewed with the 200 or so species of sorrel (*Oxalis* spp, or *surings*) that grow in our country. The best known are the yellow-flowered *Oxalis pes-caprae* that grow in marshlands, or the scarcer broad-leaved ones that grow in the mountains. The first Cape soup was made from broad-leaved sorrel and thickened with egg yolk. This kind of soup enjoyed a brief revival, only to virtually disappear later. Cultivated sorrel soup with spinach added to it, and the Greek *avgolemono* soup, made from stock and lemon juice and thickened with egg, are the only two from this group still to be found today.

Traditional pea soup has become slightly German with the addition of Eisbein, as has bean soup with sliced frankfurters. The wintertime week-long soup pot became increasingly popular. A myriad flavours invaded our tables with the curry nuances of mulligatawny, and the Italian *minestras* of which minestrone is best known. Sixties authors, André P Brink in particular, introduced us to French countryside cuisine. The Provençal *soupe au pesto*, redolent with the aromas of garlic and basil, was served in many an intellectual's home, along with French bread and wine. One is inclined to forget that we were not, at that stage, a wine-drinking country.

Cold soups like vichyssoise and cucumber soup became fashionable along with the miniskirt. Yoghurt and fresh herbs were most commonly used. The middle seventies saw the introduction of creamier soups, but still with a white sauce base.

In the eighties, we staged a small rebellion against the health craze by leaving out the white sauce in cream soups and making the soup richer with reduced cream. We also learned to cook with extracts. Thinly sliced mushrooms were baked in the oven to release the natural liquid. These exotic juices were collected and spooned into small soup bowls with thin slices of fresh mushroom, covered with puff pastry and frozen – enough to try the patience of a saint! The result was baked in a hot oven until done, and the puff pastry with all its layers opened up a new world. The

mushroom extract was also used as flavouring, or the flavour was intensified by reducing it until almost nothing remained at the bottom of the French copper saucepan. Wine and fortified wine were cooked to a syrup before litres of cream were incorporated into it, cup by cup, to offer the tastebuds a foretaste of heaven after a sweaty session on the modern apparatus in a gym.

The last decade of this century bears witness, on the one hand, to a more boring approach with the advent of packet soup; but on the other hand to a search for new flavours by, for example, combining fruit and vegetables. A good example is Butternut and mango soup (p. 34) with Coriander leaf purée (p. 34). Worldwide, there has been a rediscovery of the magical flavours of Eastern spices. We know them here, at the Cape of Good Hope, and at last are starting to use them.

Recipes are exchanged on the Internet, creative cooks chat to one another and the world becomes a multi-braided loaf. Italian pesto, traditionally made with basil and pine nuts, is adapted by using fresh coriander leaves and almonds. Spanish gazpacho with a hint of chilli and a dash of tequila from Mexico is followed, in full African glory, by harissa and savoury maize ice cream. Russian borscht rises in status with the red roots of Africa, fortified with witblits and topped with a layer of lightly flavoured crème fraîche, then baked until golden brown (p. 34).

At last, soups have come into their own.

Marrowbone soup

(SERVES 8 GENEROUS HELPING)

You cannot hurry this flavoursome dish. Rub a flat-bottomed cast-iron pot well with garlic beforehand. The soup is slowly simmered over low heat. The longer it takes, the better the end result.

1 kg beef shin with plenty of meat on the bone, cut into 37,5 mm (1½ inch) thick slices
1 kg marrow bones with hardly any meat or fat, sliced
50 ml (4 T) oil
5 litres (20 cups) water
2 onions, halved lengthwise, peeled and sliced thickly
2 celery stalks (with leaves), washed, stringed and coarsely chopped
4 carrots, scraped and sliced thickly
1-2 turnips, peeled, quartered and sprinkled with lemon juice
6 cloves

1 small cinnamon stick
2-3 bay leaves
6 stalks of parsley, rinsed throroughly
6 whole allspice
15 ml (3 t) black peppercorns
salt to taste

1. Wipe the shin clean and make sure that there are no bone shavings on the bones or meat. In a large saucepan, bring water to the boil. Place meat and bones in saucepan, bring to the boil and remove from water. With a clean tea towel, pat shin and bones dry. Discard water used for blanching.

2. Heat oil in a cast-iron pot or large stockpot and brown shin long and slowly on both sides over medium heat. Remove and drain off excess fat. Pour 250 ml (1 cup) water in saucepan in which meat was browned, and scrape and stir to dissolve all the solid bits sticking to the bottom in the water. Place marrow bones and shin in saucepan and add rest of water. Bring to the boil and skim. Add the rest of the ingredients and simmer, uncovered, for 2-3 hours. Add more water if necessary. Slow cooking and patience are the passwords. The soup must constantly simmer with just a hint of a swell.

3. The shin should now be tender. Taste the liquid: it must have a rich, meaty flavour. Season with more salt and pepper if necessary. Remove marrowbones and carefully remove the marrow.

4. TO SERVE: Place 1-2 slices of bread, preferably Salt-rising bread (p. 00), in soup plates and ladle the hot, thin liquid over the bread so that it can absorb the liquid and swell out. The guests eat this, and then more soup, including the shin meat and marrow, is dished up in each plate.

HINT: The marrowbones may be served before the soup. Serve on toast.

MARROWBONE SOUP

Snoek head soup

(SERVES 6)

There are literally hundreds of versions of this sought-after West Coast soup. Some, unfortunately, resemble rainwater in a farm dam, but my version is rich and full of flavour. There are basically two kinds: the lazy housewife method in which the cooked fish is flaked, added to the fish stock and served; and the one where the fish heads are first baked and then processed, one step at a time, into a soup. Snoek head soup is a meal in itself and is served with bread and sweet potatoes, especially those baked in their jackets. Some West Coast inhabitants also serve home-made grape jam (korrelkonfyt) with it. I do not recommend this.

2 kg snoek heads, flecked, gills removed, and washed well
freshly ground pepper
1 kg hake fillets, skin removed
2 carrots, scraped and thinly sliced
1 large onion, halved lengthwise, peeled and thinly sliced
leaves of a sprig of fresh thyme
2 bay leaves
10 ml (2 t) fennel seeds
500 g tomatoes, peeled, seeded and chopped (see Hint, p. 27)
12,5 ml (1 T) tomato concentrate
1,5 litres (6 cups) strong Fish fumet (p. 46)
salt and pepper to taste

CROUTONS
2 slices white bread, crusts removed, diced
25 ml (2 T) olive oil
1 chilli, seeded and chopped
25 ml (2 T) Parmesan cheese
finely grated rind of 1 orange and 1 lemon
25 ml (2 T) finely chopped fresh parsley
2 cloves of garlic, bruised, peeled and crushed

SAUCE
1 red chilli, seeded and finely chopped
10 ml (2 t) tomato concentrate (not tomato paste)
4 plump cloves of garlic, bruised, peeled and crushed
2 egg yolks
125 ml (½ cup) olive oil
salt and freshly ground pepper
lemon juice to taste

1. Arrange snoek heads, skin down, in a single layer in a deep casserole. Season with pepper. Place hake fillets between the heads. Sprinkle carrots and onion over the fish. Sprinkle with thyme and arrange bay leaves on top. Sprinkle with fennel. Spoon tomatoes and tomato concentrate over and add the stock. Cover with aluminium foil, shiny side down, and bake for 40 minutes in a preheated oven at 180 °C (350 °F).
2. Strain cooking liquid through a sieve into a large saucepan. Leave fish mixture in oven to cool. Remove all bones and unsightly 'bits'. Pulp fish, carrots, onion and tomato, together with a little fish liquid, and stir into rest of fish liquid in saucepan. Reduce until mixture has the consistency of thick cream. Taste and season with salt and pepper. Pour soup into a soup tureen and keep warm while preparing the croutons.
3. CROUTONS: Spoon bread cubes into a casserole, sprinkle oil and chilli over and bake in oven until bread is golden brown. Using a spoon, turn the cubes over after a few minutes. Remove from oven and spoon into a mixing bowl. Add cheese, rind, parsley and garlic to croutons and mix. Set aside.
4. SAUCE: Spoon chilli, tomato concentrate and garlic into the bowl of a food processor and blend for 10 seconds. Keep the machine running and add egg yolks one at a time. Blend for 1 minute. Keeping the machine running, add the oil in a thin stream to make a thick mayonnaise. Taste and season with salt, pepper and lemon juice.
5. TO SERVE: Spoon sauce in equal quantities in middle of soup plates. Ladle soup into plates and garnish with croutons.

VARIATION
Add 500 ml cream to soup before it is reduced, then reduce. Chopped, fresh dill may also be used as flavouring. Or add a tot of Pernod instead of the dill.

Mussel soup

(SERVES 4 AS A LIGHT MEAL, OR 6-8 AS A STARTER)

1 carrot, scraped and coarsely grated
1 onion, halved lengthwise, peeled and finely chopped
2 plump cloves of garlic, bruised, peeled and crushed
12,5 ml (1 T) butter
500 ml (2 cups) Fish fumet (p. 46)
1,5 kg mussels, shells well scrubbed
250 ml (1 cup) Velouté sauce (p.34)
500 ml (2 cups) cream
12,5 ml (1 T) Pernod
5 ml (1 t) grated lemon rind
salt and lemon juice to taste
cayenne pepper to taste

GARNISH
reserved mussels (see method)
sprigs of fresh dill
chopped chives

1. Place carrot, onion, garlic and butter in a large saucepan and cover with a sheet of buttered wax paper, the buttered side tightly against the vegetables. Cover and place over low heat. Braise vegetables for 30 minutes until completely soft. Remove paper, add stock and bring to the boil. Add mussels about 20 at a time, cover and steam until they open. As they open, remove them with a slotted spoon. Repeat with the rest of the mussels. Discard those that do not open. Reserve about 12-24 mussels in double shells for garnishing. Remove the rest of the mussels from the shells and return to the saucepan with the vegetables and stock.
2. Spoon velouté in and return to medium heat. Bring to the boil and then immediately remove from heat. Blend soup in a food processor until smooth and strain through a sieve into a clean saucepan.
3. Add 125 ml (½ cup) of the cream, place over medium heat and reduce mixture by half without increasing the heat. Stir well from time to time. Once again add 125 ml (½ cup) cream and continue cooking until the soup has the consistency of cold cream. Add the rest of the cream, Pernod and lemon rind and bring to the boil. Taste and season with salt (if necessary), lemon juice, and cayenne pepper to taste. Keep warm. Just before serving, spoon reserved mussels into soup to heat through.
4. TO SERVE: Ladle soup into warmed soup bowls and garnish each bowl with three or more mussels (in the shell), sprigs of dill chopped chives.

MUSSEL SOUP

Velouté sauce

(MAKES 250 ML / 1 CUP)

25 ml (2 T) butter
37,5 ml (3 T) cake flour
250 ml (1 cup) Court bouillon (p. 44)
  or Fish fumet (p. 46)
salt and freshly ground white pepper to taste
1 ml (pinch) cayenne pepper
2 ml (¼ t) grated nutmeg

Melt the butter, stir in flour and stir-fry for 1 minute. Remove from heat and whisk in stock. Whisk thoroughly to prevent any lumps from forming. Return to heat and stir continuously. Bring to the boil, reduce the heat and simmer for 2-3 minutes. Taste and season with salt, pepper, cayenne pepper and nutmeg. Remove from heat and cover with a sheet of greased wax paper, with the greased side touching the surface of the sauce to prevent a skin from forming on top.

Beetroot soup

(SERVES 6)

4 large or 6 medium beetroot, baked
  (see p. 141)
500 ml (2 cups) vegetable or chicken stock
250 ml (1 cup) cream or Crème fraîche
  (this page)
milk
5 ml (1 t) cayenne pepper
salt to taste
25 ml (2 T) witblits or Swedish vodka (Absolut)

GARNISH
125 ml (½ cup) sour cream
  or Crème fraîche (this page)
25 ml (2 T) capers, chopped
25 ml (2 T) chopped pickled cucumbers
sprigs of fresh dill

1. Cut baked beetroot into smaller pieces and pulp with the stock. Strain. Cool and refrigerate until an hour or so before serving. This beetroot base will keep for up to 3 days in the refrigerator.
2. Spoon half of the beetroot purée and cream into a saucepan and bring to the boil. Add the rest of the beetroot purée and dilute with just enough milk to bring it to the consistency of pouring cream. Bring to the boil and do not simmer too long, as the soup will lose its colour. Taste and season with cayenne pepper and salt. Whisk in the witblits just before serving.

3. TO SERVE: Ladle warm soup into warmed soup plates and garnish with a spoonful of sour cream, capers, pickled cucumbers and dill.

VARIATION
Whip enough cream until it forms the first stiff peaks. Ladle beetroot soup into small bowls and spread whipped cream on top. Place under the preheated element of the grill for a minute or so to brown slightly.

Crème fraîche

Mix 250 ml (1 cup) cream and 25-37,5 ml (2-3 T) buttermilk. Spoon the mixture into a sterilised jar, cover and leave at room temperature until the cream is the consistency of soft butter. Refrigerate and use as ordinary fresh cream.

Butternut and mango soup

(SERVES 6)

2 very large, ripe butternuts (skin should not be
  green), halved lengthwise and seeded
125 g (125 ml/½ cup) butter
salt and cayenne pepper
6 fresh curry leaves (optional)
500 ml (2 cups) mango or orange juice
1 onion, halved lengthwise, peeled and finely
  chopped
2 cloves of garlic, bruised, peeled and crushed
12,5 ml (1 T) oil
25 ml (2 T) Sri Lankan spice blend (p. 100)
2 ripe mangoes, peeled, coarsely grated and
  juices reserved
500 ml (2 cups) cream (potatoes)
milk (optional)

GARNISH
37,5 ml (3 T) Coriander pesto (this page)
50 ml (4 T) cream

1. Arrange butternuts, hollow side up, in a single layer in an oven-roasting pan greased with a little butter. Dot with rest of butter. Season lightly with salt and cayenne pepper to taste (less cayenne pepper if you do not like it hot, and more if you do). Place curry leaves on top and spoon 250 ml (1 cup) mango juice over. Cover with aluminium foil, shiny side down, and bake for 90 minutes in a preheated oven at 160 °C (350 °F). (Do not bake at a higher temperature.) Remove from oven and cool.

2. Sauté onion and garlic in oil until onion is soft and translucent, but not brown. Sprinkle with spice blend and stir-fry for 2-3 minutes more. Remove from heat and stir in grated mango and natural mango juice. Mix through and cool.
3. Remove butternut flesh from skin; discard skins and curry leaves, but reserve pan juices. Combine butternut and onion and mango mixture and blend in a food processor. Add rest of mango juice to aid the process, as well as reserved pan juices. Rub mixture through a sieve. The cold soup base may be stored in a container in the refrigerator until required. It will keep well for up to 3 days.
4. TO COMPLETE THE SOUP: Bring half the cream to the boil, reduce heat and cook for 6-8 minutes while stirring continuously. Add butternut base and mix through. Heat over low heat and gradually add the rest of the cream. Taste and season with more salt and cayenne pepper, if necessary. If you wish, you may dilute the soup with milk or, for a more pronounced mango flavour, with more mango juice.
5. TO SERVE: Mix coriander pesto and cream to a runny mixture. Ladle warm soup into warmed soup bowls and garnish with remaining pesto.

Coriander pesto (Dhania pesto)

(MAKES 125 ML / ½ CUP)

50 g (125 ml/½ cup) pine nuts
  or blanched almonds
50 ml (4 T) olive oil
3 ml (½ t) salt
freshly ground white pepper to taste
250 ml (1 cup) fresh coriander leaves,
  removed from stalks,
  rinsed thoroughly and patted dry
grated rind of 1 lemon
5 ml (1 t) lemon juice

Place pine nuts in a food processor and pulse until finely ground. Turn machine on and add oil in a slow drizzle. Add salt and season with pepper. Allow machine to run another 2 minutes or so. The mixture will be fine, but not smooth. Add half the leaves and pulse 15 seconds. Repeat with rest of leaves. Add rind and juice and pulse for another 15 seconds. Do not leave machine running longer, otherwise the pesto will discolour. Spoon into a container, cover close to the surface with plastic wrap and close with lid. Store in refrigerator until required.

Lentil and vegetable soup

(SERVES 6)

1 packet (500 g) brown lentils
25 ml (2 T) oil
1 onion, halved lengthwise, peeled
   and coarsely chopped
1 carrot, scraped and coarsely grated
1 kg soup bones, immersed in boiling water
   for 1 minute and drained
1,5 litres (6 cups) water
4 tomatoes, peeled and chopped
   (see Hint, p. 27), or a
   410 g tin tomatoes
10 ml (2 t) fresh thyme
salt and freshly ground black pepper
3 ml (½ t) grated nutmeg
2 ml (¼ t) ground cloves
3 bay leaves
wine vinegar

GARNISH
25 ml (2 T) chopped fresh parsley
25 ml (2 T) chopped chives

1. Cover lentils with boiling water and soak for at least 1 hour.
2. Heat oil in a stockpot, add onion, carrot and bones, and braise for 10 minutes over low heat. Meanwhile, drain lentils. Add lentils, water and tomatoes to vegetables and bones in stockpot and bring to the boil. Skim from time to time. Season with thyme, salt, pepper, nutmeg, cloves and bay leaves. Reduce the heat and simmer for 1½-2 hours. Add more water if necessary. Skim regularly.
3. Taste and season with more salt and pepper if necessary. Add a dash or two of wine vinegar and ladle into warmed soup plates. Sprinkle with parsley and chives.

Pea soup

(SERVES 6-8)

½ packet (250 g) split peas,
   soaked overnight in water
2,5 litres (10 cups) water
15 ml (3 t) salt
5 ml (1 t) freshly ground pepper
5 allspice
5 cloves
2 bay leaves
2 onions, halved lengthwise, peeled
   and coarsely chopped
1 celery stalk, washed, threaded and thinly sliced
1 large carrot, scraped and thinly sliced
1 large turnip, peeled and grated
1 large potato, peeled and grated
1 kg soup bones or beef shin with plenty
   of meat on the bone
1 Eisbein (smoked pork shank)

TO SERVE
dry, medium or medium cream sherry (optional)
4 slices white bread, diced and fried
   in oil until golden brown
12,5 ml (1 T) chopped fresh mint

1. Rinse peas under running water. Drain. Place all soup ingredients in a large saucepan and bring to the boil; reduce the heat and cook for 3 hours. Skim and stir regularly to prevent it from burning. Add more water if necessary. The meat must be tender and come away from the bone. Remove meat, cut into smaller pieces and return to the saucepan. Taste and season with more salt and pepper if necessary.
2. This soup is thick, reasonably smooth and tends to be somewhat salty. A glass or two of sherry may be stirred in at this stage. Ladle soup into a warm soup tureen or soup plates and sprinkle with croutons and mint.

Bacon and bean soup

(SERVES 6-8)

1 packet (500 g) dried beans (preferably red
   sugar beans), covered with boiling water
   and soaked overnight
125 g smoked speck, diced, or back bacon,
   shredded
2 pig's trotters, immersed in boiling
   water for 2 minutes, removed and
   rinsed thoroughly
2,5 litres (10 cups) water
1 large onion, halved lengthwise,
   peeled and sliced
50 ml (4 T) tomato concentrate
2 bay leaves
3 cloves
salt and freshly ground pepper
25 ml (2 T) Worcestershire sauce
5 ml (1 t) cayenne pepper or 1 whole chilli

GARNISH
chopped fresh parsley (optional)

1. Wash beans under running water. Drain. Fry speck in a large saucepan over low heat until crisp. Remove from saucepan. In the same saucepan, brown pig's trotters on all sides. Add beans and water and bring to the boil. Skim from time to time.
2. Add rest of soup ingredients, bring to the boil and leave to simmer for 2-3 hours until the beans are tender and the soup has thickened. Taste and season with more salt and pepper if necessary.
3. Ladle soup into warmed soup plates and sprinkle with parsley (if used).

VARIATION
Ten minutes before serving, slice 8 frankfurters diagonally. Add to the soup and heat through. Serve in warmed, deep soup plates.

SRI LANKAN SPICE BLEND

25 g coriander seed
15 g cumin seed
15 ml (1 tbsp) fennel seed
5 ml (1 tsp) fenugreek
small stick cinnamon
6 green cardamom seeds
6 cloves
6 curry leaves
15 ml turmeric
5 ml cayenne pepper

Place coriander, cumin, fenugreek, fennel, cinnamon, cardamom & cloves in large saucepan & stir over moderate heat til spices release their odour. Remove from heat taking care not to burn. Add curry leaves, turmeric & cayenne. Stir to mix. Spread out in shallow pan & cool. Grind to fine powder & sift thru fine sieve. Discard what's left behind. Store in airtight container. For deeper flavour, spices should be roasted a bit longer, but don't allow to burn.

Cold cucumber soup with herbs

(SERVES 8)

4 leeks, rinsed thoroughly and thinly sliced,
    or 2 onions, peeled and finely chopped
50 ml (4 T) olive oil
3 ml (½ t) ground aniseed, fennel
    or cumin seeds
grated rind of 1 lemon
4 cloves of garlic, bruised, peeled
    and crushed with:
5 ml (1 t) salt
75 ml (6 T) dry white wine
250 ml (1 cup) chicken stock
2-3 English cucumbers (depending on size),
    halved lengthwise, seeded and sliced
ice cubes
cayenne pepper to taste
125 ml (½ cup) chopped fresh coriander leaves
lemon juice to taste

TO SERVE
125 ml (½ cup) mascarpone, cream cheese
    or creamed cottage cheese
extra coriander leaves
chopped chives

1. Sauté leeks in oil in a large saucepan until soft. Add cumin, lemon rind and garlic and stir-fry for 1 minute. Add wine and stir-fry until only 25 ml (2 T) of the wine remains. Add stock and cucumber, cover, reduce heat to low and simmer for 15-20 minutes or until the cucumber is soft. Remove from heat and cool.

2. Blend in a food processor and add a few ice cubes. Season with cayenne pepper and pulp coriander leaves into cucumber mixture. The colour of the soup will now be green. Strain through a sieve into a suitable freezer container and place in freezer for 30 minutes.
3. Remove from freezer and taste. Season, if necessary, with salt and lemon juice. Refrigerate until just before serving.
4. TO SERVE: Ladle cold soup into chilled soup bowls (leave bowls in fridge for about 30 minutes) and place one or two spoonfuls mascarpone onto each portion of soup. Garnish with coriander leaves and chives.

Chilled gazpacho

(SERVES 12-18 AS A STARTER)

This soup is placed in an African context by serving it with Couscous salad (p. 27).

2 kg ripe red tomatoes, quartered and seeded
1 large onion, peeled and quartered
1 English cucumber, peeled and cut into chunks
8 plump cloves of garlic, bruised and peeled
2 small or 1 large green pepper, halved, seeds
    and pith removed, and chopped
2,5 litres (10 cups) tomato juice
    or tomato cocktail
salt and freshly ground black pepper
cayenne pepper to taste
24-36 fresh basil leaves, washed,
    rolled and shredded
6 slices of white bread, crusts removed
125 ml (½ cup) olive oil
25-50 ml (2-4 T) balsamic vinegar
10 ml (2 t) Worcestershire sauce (optional)

GARNISH
maize kernels, cucumber slices and/or red
    and/or yellow cherry tomato slices

1. Blend half of tomatoes, onion, cucumber, garlic and green pepper and add a quarter of the tomato juice. Repeat with rest of tomatoes, onion, cucumber, garlic, and green pepper and add another quarter of juice. Season with salt, black pepper, cayenne pepper and basil. Strain mixture through a sieve and stir in rest of juice. Naughty cooks may stir in 1-2 t (5-10 ml) red food colouring.
2. Blend bread and slowly drizzle in olive oil. Pulse in some of the tomato mixture until it is runny. Whisk into tomato mixture. Stir in the vinegar and Worcestershire sauce (if used). Taste and season with more salt, pepper and cayenne pepper. The soup must have a strong flavour when you taste it, because it will forfeit some of its flavour during freezing.
3. Ladle soup into suitable freezer containers and place in freezer until almost frozen. Remove from freezer and whisk well until soup is runny, but still well chilled. Ladle into chilled bowls and garnish with maize kernels, and sliced cucumber and/or cherry tomatoes. Serve with chilled tequila or witblits.

GAZPACHO AND COUSCOUS SALAD (P. 27)

Melkkos for supper

NOTHING REFLECTS the spirit of this century better than *snysels* (milk noodles) and 'prayer' milk … which came and went; were loved and ignored; rediscovered and eventually incorporated into our diet.

Snysels, I suspect, are a German inheritance from the time of the first settlement at the Cape: none other than the *spätzle* of the Austro-Hungarian-German alliance. There, the dough was rubbed through a special sieve to make small dumplings that could be cooked in a saucepan of boiling water. The dumplings were carefully spooned out, dotted with butter, moistened with cream and served as an accompaniment to meat. The Dutch also knew this kind of dish. Because the special sieve was not available here, the dough was made slightly stiffer and cut into strips or *snysels*.

We should not lose sight of the fact that most of the food that preceded this century was dominated by the Malay influence. Malay cooks who had to make *snysels* were always aware of their own traditions of *gedatmelk* and *boeber*. For this reason, they could not resist adding cinnamon, replacing the water with milk, and adding lemon or naartjie peel – so creating an inexpensive, easily digested supper of *snysels*.

Up to the fifties, *melkkos* was known as *Slinger-om-die-smoel* (milk soup). *Melkkos* is the same as *snysels*, except that the dough is slightly stiffer. It was rolled out and cut into long strips (*slingers*), rather like tagliatelle. These strips were then cooked in water with a pinch of salt, drained and served with milk and cinnamon sugar. Most cooks preferred to cook them long and slowly in milk until a thick porridge was formed, and that is how they were usually served, with cinnamon sugar. With time, vermicelli, sago or even elbow macaroni replaced the dough strips! *Melkkos* gradually took on the flavour of *gedatmelk* – a cultural cross-pollination. During the economic boom of the sixties and seventies, *melkkos* gradually disappeared, making room for *melksopkos*, found especially in the north of the country. At present,

BOEBER

especially among the younger generation, there is a strong demand for fusion food, so dishes like *melkkos* have resurfaced.

Gedatmelk, or 'prayer' milk, got its name from a special prayer said on certain nights after a funeral, and from the milk drunk then. In Java, *boeber*, a sweet milk drink with the consistency of a thin, liquid porridge, was made from coconut milk. During Ramadan, the Muslim month of fasting, they prepared this dish towards sundown on the fifteenth day of the fast. A portion was sent to the neighbours to celebrate the halfway mark of the fast. It is such a delicious winter drink that it has become a tradition during the winter months. Some Malays, influenced by *melkkos*, prefer the *boeber* to be thicker, so that it can be eaten with a spoon. As a result they thicken it with sago, vermicelli or cornflour. The traditional flavourings of this delicacy are cardamom, cinnamon and rose water.

Both *melkkos* and *boeber* appear these days on the menus of some local restaurants, as well as on those of some of the famous international chefs who have visited Cape Town over the past few years.

Milk soup

(SERVES 6)

1,5 litres (6 cups) milk
1 cinnamon stick
1 packet (500 g) letters and numbers noodles
37,5 ml (3 T) cornflour slated in:
50 ml (4 T) water

TO SERVE
30 ml (6 t) golden syrup
cinnamon sugar to taste

1. Heat milk and cinnamon sticks over medium heat and infuse until the milk has a strong cinnamon flavour. Remove cinnamon. Increase heat and bring milk to the boil. Gradually add noodles and cook until soft. Remove from heat and gradually stir in cornflour mixture. Return to heat, bring to the boil and simmer for 5-8 minutes until thickened.
2. Spoon into 6 soup plates and drizzle a spoonful of golden syrup over each portion. Serve with cinnamon sugar.

Traditional milk noodles (Melkkos)

(SERVES 4)

120 g (250 ml / 1 cup) cake flour
3 ml (½ t) salt
2 extra-large eggs
water
1 litres (4 cups) milk
2 cinnamon sticks

TOPPING
cinnamon sugar

1. Sift flour and salt. Make a well in the centre of the flour mixture. Beat eggs and pour into well. Stir and add enough water to make a stiff dough. Knead until elastic – this takes about 8 minutes. Roll out the dough on a floured surface to about 6 mm (¼ inch) thick. Cut into narrow strips. Roll strips in extra flour to cover all round. The secret lies in this extra flour – it thickens the *melkkos* as it cooks.
2. Meanwhile, heat milk and cinnamon over medium heat so that the cinnamon can infuse the milk. The longer the better. Reduce the heat if the infusion has to take longer. As soon as the milk has a strong cinnamon flavour, you may go ahead.
3. Remove cinnamon sticks and bring milk to the boil. Add strips of dough a few at a time and cook over medium heat until done.

Spoon into deep soup plates and serve with cinnamon sugar.

VARIATION
Add a piece of dried naartjie peel, 1-2 strips of orange peel or even 2-3 bruised cardamom seeds to the milk with the cinnamon. Some cooks omit the cinnamon and use a vanilla pod as flavouring.

Boeber

(SERVES 6)

Cass Abrahams, connoisseur of Cape Malay food, prepares the best *boeber* I have ever tasted. Here is her recipe.

100 g (100 ml / 8 T) butter
250 ml (1 cup) vermicelli
2-3 cardamom seeds
2 cinnamon sticks
1 litre (4 cups) milk
50 ml (4 T) sago, soaked in:
125 ml (½ cup) lukewarm milk
sugar to taste
150 g (250 ml / 1 cup) bleached sultanas
10 ml (2 t) rose water

TOPPING
1 packet (100 g) blanched almonds
   or almond flakes, lightly roasted
ground cinnamon

1. Melt butter in a large saucepan. Add the vermicelli, cardamom and cinnamon and stir-fry over medium heat until vermicelli is golden brown.
2. Add milk, increase heat and bring to the boil. Reduce the heat and simmer until the vermicelli is cooked.
3. Add the soaked sago, sugar to taste, and sultanas. Stir continuously and simmer until the sago is translucent. Add rose water and spoon into soup bowls.
4. Sprinkle with almonds and garnish with ground cinnamon. Serve hot.

Gedatmelk (Prayer milk)

(MAKES 6 SMALL DRINKS)

1 litre (4 cups) milk
12 cardamom seeds, bruised
2 cinnamon sticks
sugar to taste
5-10 ml (1-2 t) rose water

1. Place the milk in a saucepan and add the cardamom and cinnamon. Place over low heat and infuse for 1 hour.
2. Remove from the heat and remove the cardamom and cinnamon. Add sugar to taste and bring mixture to the boil. Remove from heat and cool slightly.
3. Add rose water and serve in small cups.

CHAPTER 6

Fish and seafood

OVER THE PAST century, the ocean – from the cold salty seas of the West Coast to the warmer waters of the East coast – has brought a great variety of foods to our tables. Hake, sole, angelfish and monkfish, kabeljou (cob), geelbek, elf, yellowtail, baardman, barracuda, seventy-four, musselcracker, white and red steenbras, red and white stumpnose, galjoen, bonito, snoek, tuna, mackerel, harders, pilchards, calamari (chokka), octopus, crayfish, mussels, periwinkles (alikreukel) and abalone (perlemoen) are the best known.

In Saldanha Bay, on the West Coast, lies one the world's best natural harbours, where millions of oyster shells nestle deep in the sand and shipwrecks tell tales of piracy. Seaweed is harvested from the seabed to make gelatine or agar-agar. A number of factories can fish here, or freeze it, so that the rest of the country can also enjoy it. Crayfish, the king of seafood, is sent out into the wider world from Saldanha, as are pilchards, harders and tuna. Mussels and oysters are also cultivated and harvested here.

If you want to experience the West Coast at its best, however, you have to go to Paternoster. Make sure that you're on the beach at noon to experience the arrival of the fishing boats and their catch. During the crayfish season, the fishermen's baskets swarm with clawing crayfish. Back home, later, you'll associate Paternoster mainly with the bunches of bokkems against the walls of the white-washed houses that stand, all higgledy-piggledy, wherever there's space.

Harders are the staple food of the West Coast. Inhabitants say there are two kinds: the red harder which lives in the deep sea, and the ordinary harder. It really doesn't matter which you eat. Locals eat them entrails and all, throwing them, alive and salted, directly onto the coals. The salt pops off by itself during braaiing (barbecueing). They can also be fried in butter on both sides and flavoured with lemon juice. Serve with mashed potatoes or new potatoes brushed with parsley (and chive) garlic butter.

COURT BOUILLON

HOW TO PREPARE HARDERS

Non-experts should restrict themselves to cleaned harders. Butterfly the harders like galjoen, remove the entrails, wash them and place them, skin side down, in a single layer in a large enamel baking pan. Sprinkle coarse salt over to cover the fish completely. Leave for 30 minutes, then rinse them under cold, running water. Wind-dry the harders by fastening them to the washline with a peg and leaving them for 1-24 hours. The flesh must be firm.

Bokkems are harders that are dried like biltong. Start by pulling off the skin from the tail end – it comes off easily because of the fat under the skin. Strip the meat off the backbone towards the sides with your fingers and eat like biltong. The head is dessert: suck out the contents.

Fishermen of both the West and East Coasts know how to prepare fish or seafood in such a way that the flavour and taste are not spoilt. The natural taste is all; additions are taboo. In the past, wine was seldom, if ever, used in the preparation of fish dishes. Vinegar and spices were; but it had to be nutmeg with abalone (perlemoen) and masala with pickled fish.

No other fish is as delicious braaied as galjoen (see page 44), except, perhaps, elf. The galjoen must be bled after it is caught. Many fish-braaiing experts believe it will braai better if the scales are left on.

During the twentieth century, the preparation of fish and seafood underwent radical changes. At the start of the century there was an abundance of fish; at its end, far less. Restaurateurs can no longer specify kinds of fish like kabeljou (from the French *cabbellaud*), geelbek, stumpnose or steenbras by name on menus, but have to resort to the collective name 'linefish' and inform their guests day by day. This scarcity is the direct result of large-scale fishing enterprises, especially from the East, which obtained unlimited fishing rights from the former government.

A relic of the Victorian era is kedgeree. This creamy mixture of haddock, rice and hard-boiled eggs flavoured with garam

HOW TO BRAAI GALJOEN

Cut open the galjoen along one side of the backbone and open it out, without cutting through the stomach side. Remove the entrails and rinse the fish. Rub in coarse salt and finely ground white pepper and wind-dry it by hanging it in the wind, in a shady place, for 4-6 hours. Place the fish, skin side down, on a grid brushed with oil. Braai at least 45 cm above the coals. The fish must braai very slowly. If the skin shows any sign of blackening, it is being braaied too quickly, or the coals are too hot. The skin must become a parchment brown colour. Don't spread butter, oil or anything else over the fish, because a galjoen has enough of its own fat. Catch up some of the natural oil that runs out during braaiing with a long-handled spoon and spoon it over the fish. Turn the grid and braai the flesh side of the fish very briefly, close to the coals, just until golden brown. A little lemon juice may be squeezed over the fish before serving. If you have enough galjoen, serve it without any accompaniments; if you have only one, serve it with bread and salad.

masala was a popular breakfast dish up to the late thirties. Then poached haddock took over. Haddock mousse was considered very smart in the fifties and sixties, as was haddock roulade in the eighties – only to be replaced in the nineties by haddock salad.

Avocado Ritz came here from England in the twenties. Only places that live in the past still serve it.

Fish roe spread (tarama) was made into a pâté in the smart sixties, only to reappear in the late eighties as part of the Mediterranean renaissance.

One of the most popular party dishes served by the elegant hostess in the sixties was the fish mousse, prepared mainly from canned salmon and neatly set in fish-shaped moulds, then turned out and surrounded with cucumber rings. The dish became even smarter in the eighties by setting the mousse in individual moulds lined with smoked salmon.

Sole was undoubtedly the showpiece of prominent and wealthy people. It is not our best fish; it fares much better in the northern hemisphere. We nevertheless *bonne femme*-ed it with béchamel sauce, mushrooms and white wine. In sole Colbert, the bone was removed and the top fillets were folded over before being crumbed and fried.

Fried bananas were spooned into the folded-out part of the fish as a garnish. The first, still slightly sour, grapes of the season were used in sole Véronique.

In the seventies, all the other fish varieties were known only to anglers and to food fundis. General knowledge about fish got a boost in 1979 with Lannice Snyman's *Fresh from the Sea* and Peter Veldsman's *The South African Seafood Banquet*. These two books (and others by the same writers which followed later) taught most South Africans how to cook fish correctly.

The best-known South African fish has to be hake, which is available countrywide today, frozen and packed in packets. This is the fish most often used for fish and chips, as well as for the classic dishes of the first half of the century: fish Portugaise, in which it was topped with fried onions and tomatoes; and fish Mornay, in which it was covered with cheese sauce.

Once the scales have been removed, linefish is filleted (with the skin still on), cut into flat slices without removing the skin, then poached, fried, baked, grilled or steamed. Fish is microwave-friendly and good results are obtained at 70% power. Calculate 1 minute's cooking time for every 100 g fish.

The fashion for serving fish on a plate, with the crisply fried skin uppermost, has not yet been generally accepted. This is a pity, as the crisp skin is a pleasant eating experience. Many South Africans prefer not to fillet fish, but to cook them as cutlets. This method is particulary suitable for fish that is to be poached.

Smoked fish is very popular. The fish is smoked according to the heat method, in a drum or other household container, over ignited oak shavings.

The serving of cured fish is uncommon. Place the fillets on a layer of coarse salt in a stainless steel dish. Cover with coarse salt and leave for 5-6 hours. Rinse well, pat dry, cut into paper-thin slices and serve. Our version of the Scandinavian *gravad* process has increased in popularity since the eighties, and Japanese sushi has appeared over the past few years.

Up to and including the Second World War, most South Africans did not eat crayfish or mussels. After the war it was a different story and today our salt-water crayfish is extremely expensive. And talking about expense, it's only people in the Far East who are prepared to pay exorbitant prices for our abalone. Fortunately, the law allows us to harvest a limited quantity of crayfish, periwinkles and abalone ourselves.

With the exception of trout, fresh-water fish is not that popular. Fresh-water crayfish are available in the Boland these days, but have not yet proved their worth.

Court bouillon

(MAKES 2,5 LITRES/10 CUPS)

Although seafood and fish can be poached in fresh or sea water, they taste much better if they are cooked in a flavoursome liquid. Court bouillon is one such liquid, in which a mixture of water, wine and vinegar is used. Fish fumet is a fish stock prepared from wine, water and the fish heads and bones. It will taste even better flavoured with herbs, spices and aromatic vegetables. It's possible always to have court bouillon available, as it freezes well.

400 g carrots, scraped and sliced
150 g celery stalks, threaded and sliced
250 g pickling onions, peeled and sliced
40 g spring onions, chopped
1 head of garlic, halved horizontally
1 bouquet garni, made from 1 leek,
  halved lengthwise, 1 sprig of fresh thyme,
  2 bay leaves, 2-3 sage leaves, 1 sprig of
  tarragon and 10 sprigs of parsley,
  tied together with a piece of string
1 whole red chilli
1-2 sprigs of dill or fennel
25 ml (2 T) salt
3 litres (12 cups) liquid, made up
  of half dry white wine and half water,
  or at least 500 ml (2 cups) dry white wine
10 ml (2 t) white peppercorns
10 ml (2 t) scorched coriander seed
  (see Hint, p. 60)
2 pieces star anise
2-3 cloves

1. Mix carrots, celery, pickling and spring onions in a large saucepan. Add garlic, bouquet garni, chilli, dill or fennel, and salt to the vegetables. Add enough of the liquid to just cover the vegetables.
2. Bring to the boil and cook for 4 minutes. Reduce heat and simmer for 15 minutes. Add the rest of the ingredients and again bring to the boil. Immediately reduce heat and simmer for another 15 minutes. Strain through a sieve.

FISH AND CHIPS

VARIATIONS: COURT BOUILLON

- Instead of 500 ml (2 cups) water, use the same quantity wine vinegar. The acidity in this variation gives the flesh of freshwater fish such as trout a delicate blue tinge, therefore this method is known as *au bleu*.
- COURT BOUILLON FOR HADDOCK: Peel and core 4 lemons so that the pips are removed, and slice. Add to 500 ml (2 cups) milk, 2 litres (8 cups) salted water, 5 coriander seeds, 5 white peppercorns, 2 pieces star anise, and 2 cloves. Place fish in mixture without cooking it first and slowly bring to the boil. Immediately reduce heat and poach fish following instructions in the recipe.

Fish fumet

(MAKES 2 LITRES/8 CUPS)

Fish fumet is a more concentrated version of court bouillon. To make fumet, prepare a court bouillon with only half the water, and use it to poach filleted and skinned fish. Remove the fish and reduce the remaining liquid to 2 litres (8 cups) by cooking it uncovered. Another method, and one needed for strongly flavoured fish sauces, is to add 500-700 g chopped fish bones, without skin, and 3 flecked fish heads to a court bouillon. Bring the liquid to the boil and skim. Simmer for 15 minutes and strain through a colander into a deep saucepan.

Garlic butter and other savoury butters for fish

(MAKES 250 G)

Most South Africans prefer to eat fried fish with sauce tartare, and grilled or braaied fish with lemon butter. More refined tastes prefer neat slices of savoury butter gradually melting in the heat of the cooked fish. Such butter is prepared by creaming it together with wine, mustard, herbs, egg yolks, shellfish or nuts, rubbing it through a sieve, shaping it or rolling it into a sausage, and cooling it.

- GARLIC BUTTER: Crush 50 g peeled garlic in a mortar, mix with 250 g butter and rub through a fine sieve.
- LEMON BUTTER: Add grated rind of 1 lemon and 50 ml (10 t) lemon juice to 250 g butter. Shape and refrigerate.
- MAÎTRE D'HÔTEL BUTTER: Add 25 ml (5 t) finely chopped fresh parsley, freshly ground white pepper and lemon juice to taste to 250 g butter.

- ANCHOVY BUTTER: Soak 10 anchovy fillets in warm milk. Remove as soon as the milk is cold, pound and add to 250 g butter.
- BASIL BUTTER: Finely chop or process in a food processor 24 large basil leaves and add to 250 g butter.

HINT: Leftover savoury butter may be frozen for use at a later date, but each flavour should be marked clearly to prevent confusion.

Baked roman with mushroom stuffing

(SERVES 4)

FISH
1 red roman of ± 1,5 kg, gutted
salt and freshly ground white pepper

STUFFING
1 onion, halved lengthwise, peeled and chopped
25 ml (2 T) oil
2 cloves of garlic, bruised, peeled and crushed
1 punnet (250 g) brown mushrooms
salt and freshly ground black pepper
50 g (50 ml/4 T) butter
10 ml (2 t) fresh lemon juice
1 ml (pinch) each cayenne pepper and mustard powder
250 ml (1 cup) fresh bread crumbs
1 egg, beaten
5 ml (1 t) finely chopped fresh dill, or 10 ml (2 t) Pernod
5 ml (1 t) finely chopped fresh coriander leaves (optional)

TO FINISH
250 ml (1 cup) late harvest or dry white wine
1 onion, halved lengthwise, peeled and chopped
Sauce bonus (p. 49) (optional)

1. Make sure that the fish is washed well without any blood or membranes remaining in the cavity. Pat dry and season inside and out with salt and white pepper.
2. STUFFING: Sauté onion in oil until soft and translucent but not brown. Stir in garlic and remove from heat.
3. Peel mushrooms and slice. Arrange in a single layer in a roasting pan and season with salt and black pepper. Dot with butter and sprinkle with lemon juice. Lightly season with cayenne pepper and mustard powder. Bake 6-8 minutes in a preheated oven at 200 °C (400 °F). Remove from oven and allow to cool. Remove mushrooms with a slotted spoon and chop finely. Stir onion mixture into mushrooms, then bread crumbs. Beat the

mushroom juices remaining in the pan and egg together and and use to moisten the mushroom mixture. Stir in dill and coriander (if used), and more salt and pepper if necessary. Stuff the fish with the mixture and sew closed using a needle and thread. Place tin the pan in which the mushrooms were baked and pour over the wine. Top with onions. Cover with aluminium foil, shiny side down, and bake at 180 °C (350 °F) for 30 minutes. Increase baking time if fish weighs more than 1,5 kg. Serve with Sauce bonus (p. 49).

Mayonnaise for fish

(MAKES 250 ML)

For a succesful mayonnaise all the ingredients must be at room temperature. The mayonnaise will keep a number of days if 10 ml (2 t) boiling water is whisked into the mixture after adding the lemon juice.

yolks of 2 extra-large eggs
salt and freshly ground white pepper
3 ml (½ t) prepared mustard
few drops white wine vinegar
250 ml oil, preferably 200 ml (¾ cups) sunflower oil and 50 ml (10 t) local olive oil
25 ml (5 t) lemon juice

Whisk or process egg yolks, salt, peper, mustard and vinegar. Continue whisking or processing and gradually add 75 ml (5 T) oil, a drop at a time. Whisk or pulse in half the lemon juice. Add remaining oil in a very thin, even stream while whisking or processing continuously. Taste and adjust seasoning if necessary, then stir in the rest of the lemon juice.

VARIATIONS

- EASY AÏOLI: Add 3 large cloves of garlic, crushed, to egg yolks.
- WATERCRESS MAYONNAISE: Process 100 ml (8 T) chopped fresh watercress. Add 5 ml (1 t) chopped fresh dill and half an onion, grated. Process and add to mayonnaise.
- SAUCE TARTARE: Add 4 finely chopped gherkins, 3 finely chopped chives or 1 finely chopped medium onion, chopped yolk of 1 hard-boiled egg, 15 ml (1 T) chopped capers, 12,5 ml (2½ t) chopped fresh tarragon (or 3 ml [½ t] dried tarragon) to mayonnaise. Mix, taste and also add 5 ml (1 t) French mustard, 5 ml (1 t) lemon juice and 5 ml (1 t) sugar.

BAKED ROMAN WITH MUSHROOM STUFFING

Sauce bonus

(MAKES ± 250 ML)

If preferred a tasty sauce may be prepared to go with the baked roman (p. 46). Transfer the whole, baked fish from the roasting pan to a serving dish and keep warm in the warming drawer while preparing the sauce. Place the roasting pan with the remaining juices on top of the stove, bring to the boil and cook for about 2-3 minutes. Add 125 ml (½ cup) cream, increase the heat and cook while stirring continuously. Add another 125 ml (½ cup) cream and continue cooking until the sauce thickens. Taste and season to taste with salt and cayenne pepper. Pour sauce through a sieve and stir in 12,5 ml (1 T) finely chopped fresh parsley or freshly chopped coriander leaves and 12,5 ml (1 T) finely chopped chives.

Fish cakes

(SERVES 4)

The most basic recipe for the whole country.

2 potatoes, peeled and cubed
500 g cooked fish fillets, skinned,
  deboned and flaked
1 small onion, peeled and finely chopped
37,5 ml (3 T) finely chopped fresh parsley
2 eggs, lightly beaten
salt, pepper and grated nutmeg
grated rind and juice of 1 lemon
fresh bread crumbs, dried slightly in the oven
oil

1. Boil potatoes in salted water until cooked. Drain and mash. Add fish, onion and parsley. Stir in eggs. Season well with salt, pepper and nutmeg and add lemon juice and rind. Using a two-pronged fork, lightly mix all the ingredients. Divide mixture into 12 portions

GRILLED LINEFISH WITH
SEAFOOD TOPPING

and shape each into a patty. Cover each fish cake in crumbs seasoned with salt and pepper. Refrigerate.
2. Pour oil into a frying pan, so that it is about 6 mm (¼ inch) deep. Heat oil and fry 4 dish cakes at a time until golden brown on both sides. Drain on a paper towel. Serve with Sauce tartare (p. 46), Sheba (p. 27) or Quince sambal (p. 156).

Grilled linefish with seafood topping

(SERVES 4)

This fairly intricate dish is an example of how fish and seafood are currently being combined and is representative of what is now considered to be food for entertaining.

SEAFOOD TOPPING
500 ml (2 cups) cream
salt and cayenne pepper
25 ml (2 T) fresh lemon juice
12,5 ml (1 T) Pernod
12,5 ml (1 T) Martini
1 packet (200 g) frozen prawns, thawed,
  shelled and veins removed
  and coarsely chopped
20 poached mussels, removed from shells
  and coarsely chopped
5 ml (1 t) finely chopped dill

CRAYFISH SAUCE (OPTIONAL)
shells and legs of 2 crayfish, finely pounded
1 small onion, peeled and chopped
1 carrot, scraped and grated
½ stick of celery, stringed and chopped
12,5 ml (1 T) tomato concentrate
25 ml (2 T) brandy
250 ml (1 cup) Fish fumet (p. 46)
250 ml (1 cup) cream
ice-cold butter

FISH
4 portions, each ± 275-300 g, fresh white
  linefish such as cob, Cape salmon (geelbek),
  or red or white steenbras
well-seasoned flour
oil
butter

TO FINISH
1 tin (410 g) red kidney beans, drained and rinsed
12 fresh basil leaves, rinsed, stacked together,
  rolled up and finely shredded
freshly ground black pepper
1 container (50 g) salmon roe or other caviar
sprigs of fresh dill

1. SEAFOOD TOPPING: Place half the cream in a small saucepan and bring to the boil. Reduce heat and simmer until cream thickens. Add rest of cream and repeat the process. Season with salt, cayenne pepper, lemon juice, Pernod and Martini. Simmer until the sauce is nice and thick. Set aside until just before it is required.
2. CRAYFISH SAUCE: Place crayfish shells, onion, carrot and celery in a saucepan and stir over low heat until the shells are deep pink. Add the tomato concentrate and then stir-fry for 1 minute. Add brandy and allow it to evaporate completely. Now add the stock, bring to the boil, reduce heat and simmer for 10 minutes. Allow to cool and pour though a muslin cloth. Place stock in a small saucepan and cook on high until the liquid is reduced to 50 ml (4 T). Add half the cream, bring to the boil and cook for 3 minutes. Add the rest of the cream and cook until the sauce thickens slightly. Set aside until just before it is required.
3. THE FISH: Cover the fish in seasoned flour and shake off all excess flour. Heat enough oil, about 5 mm (± ¼ inch) deep, in a heavy-based frying pan until hot but not smoking. Place one portion of fish, skin side up, in the oil and seal for about 10 seconds. Turn and repeat on the skin side. Remove and place in a baking tray or roasting dish. Repeat with the other portions of fish. Preheat the grill. Brush a little butter over each portion of the fish and place it under the hot element for 2-3 minutes. Remove and again brush with butter. Repeat until the fish, when lifted at one corner, breaks to almost against the skin. Do not overcook the fish – it must be brown and crispy on top and tender and juicy inside. Keep the fish warm while adding the finishing touches to the topping and the sauce.
4. Bring the seafood topping to the boil. Stir in the prawns, simmer for 30 seconds and stir in the mussels and dill. Heat through and keep warm. Bring crayfish sauce to the boil and whisk in small lumps of ice-cold butter until the sauce has thickened. Taste and add a dash of lemon juice if necessary. Do not make the sauce too salty.
5. TO SERVE: Place grilled fish on 4 warmed plates. Using a slotted spoon, place seafood topping on each portion. Spoon crayfish sauce around the sides of the plates so that it spreads right up to the seafood topping.
6. GARNISH: Flavour kidney beans with basil and pepper and sprinkle on top. Place teaspoonfuls of caviar on top and finish with sprigs of dill. Serve immediately. This dish does not require any side dishes – it is a meal in one.

Poached crayfish

Never poach more than 2 crayfish at a time, even if the guests have to wait. Weigh crayfish and calculate the cooking time, allowing 6 minutes for every 500 g. Place 1-2 crayfish, shell side down, in a large fish kettle and cover with cold Court bouillon (page 44). Heat to boiling point over moderate heat and calculate the cooking time from the moment that the liquid begins to boil. When the liquid starts to bubble, reduce the heat immediately. The temperature must never be more than 90 °C (175 °F). Halve crayfish as for Grilled crayfish.

Crayfish salad

(Serves 4 as a starter, or 2 as a main course)

During the first half of the century, the sauce for *slaphakskeentjies* (onion salad) was used in this salad, instead of mayonnaise. It was the custom to serve crayfish slices on shredded lettuce leaves in a glass dish and to garnish it with hard-boiled egg. Pickled nasturtium seeds were sometines also added. Very occasionally, strips of fresh pineapple were used in the cocktail. This was the exception, because pineapple was extremely scarce at the time. In the nineties, mango became a popular ingredient

4 poached crayfish tails (see above)
lettuce leaves
1 ripe mango, peeled, first sliced
*   and then cut into strips*
halved cherry tomatoes
shredded red cabbage
fresh coriander leaves
snipped chives
cooked crayfish legs (optional)
50 ml (4 T) Mayonnaise for fish (p. 46)

1. Remove crayfish flesh from the shells and slice diagonally.
2. Arrange the crayfish on cold plates and arrange lettuce leaves in between. Place the mango, tomatoes, red cabbage and coriander on the plates. Sprinkle with snipped chives. Garnish with crayfish legs (if used) and spoon a little mayonnaise onto each crayfish slice. Serve cold.

Grilled crayfish

(Serves 2)

Traditionally, freshly caught live crayfish are cooked in sea water at the beach and eaten right there. It's delicious, exceptionally good, and the only place where crayfish should be prepared like this. Undoubtedly, the best method is to cut open the live crayfish lengthways and cook it in lemon or maître d'hôtel butter. Crayfish tails, fresh or frozen, are excellent cold in a salad with mayonnaise, or as part of a seafood cocktail or as a white fricassée. This recipe is for large crayfish; for smaller ones, the grilling time will be shorter. Crayfish harvested at Kommetjie in Cape Town, as well as the large deep-sea crayfish, should be grilled with lemon butter.

2 very large crayfish
coarse salt
30 ml (6 t) oil
salt to taste
1 ml (pinch) cayenne pepper
125 g (125 ml/½ cup) Maître d'hôtel or
*   Lemon butter (p. 46), melted*

1. Place the crayfish on their backs on a wooden board. Insert the point of a sharp knife where the hard and soft section of the shell is joined and cut in half lengthwise by first cutting towards the head and then towards the tail. Wipe clean and remove the digestive tract.
2. Place 4 crayfish halves, cut side up, on a layer of coarse salt in a roasting pan. Lightly brush with oil and season with salt and cayenne pepper. Place the pan in the middle of the oven under the preheated grill and grill for 5 minutes. Remove the pan and take the crayfish out. Butter the dull side of a sheet of aluminium foil and place it, shiny side down, on the salt. Place the crayfish, shell side up, in the pan and grill 5 minutes more. Turn and spoon half the butter over the crayfish flesh. Grill 5-8 minutes longer, depending on the size of the crayfish, and spoon more of the remaining butter over every 2 minutes. Serve the crayfish immediately.

CRAYFISH SALAD

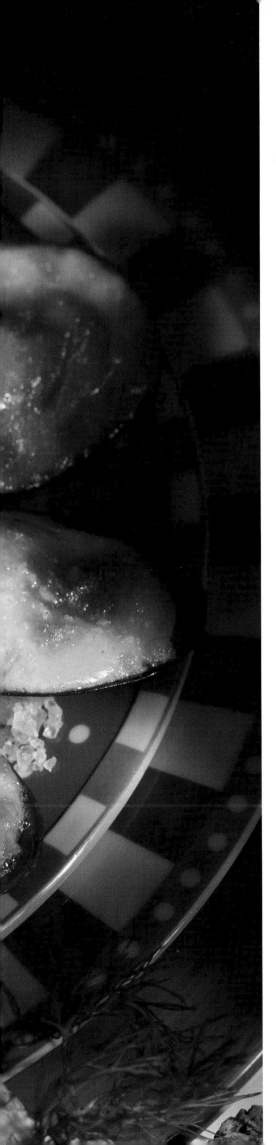

Baked mussels

(SERVES 4)

Baked mussels, smothered in hollandaise sauce, has become a classic South African dish.

24 poached mussels,
*   cooked (p. 32)*

HOLLANDAISE SAUCE
250 g (250 ml/1 cup) butter, cubed
3 extra-large egg yolks
1 ml (pinch) turmeric
salt, pepper and cayenne pepper
fresh lemon juice

TO SERVE
grated Parmesan, Grana
*   or any other hard cheese*

1. PREPARE THE SAUCE: The sauce may be prepared up to 1 hour in advance. Place butter in a small saucepan or microwave jug. Place over medium heat or microwave 2 minutes at 100% power. Skim. Meanwhile, place egg yolks and turmeric in the bowl of a food processor and process for 1 minute. Reheat the butter or microwave on 100% power until bubbly. Keep the food processor running, and add the bubbling hot butter to the egg yolks by pouring it in a thin stream through the feeder of the food processor. Reheat the butter if it stops bubbling. The idea is that the hot butter should cook the egg and form an emulsion similar to that of mayonnaise; now you know how thick the sauce should be. Season to taste with salt, pepper and cayenne pepper. Taste and add enough lemon juice for a slightly tangy taste – a sauce that is too tangy will destroy the delicate flavour of the mussels.
2. Open the mussel shells, remove the mussels and discard one half of each shell. Clean the shells. Arrange the shells, hollow side up, on a layer of coarse salt or maize-meal in a roasting pan. Place mussels in shells and cover each mussel with sauce.
3. Preheat the oven grill. Sprinkle a little of the cheese over each mussel and brown. (Take care not to place the oven shelf too close to the element.)

BAKED MUSSELS

VARIATIONS
• Replace the mussels with oysters. Open the fresh oysters and carefully remove from the shell. Reserve the juices. Rinse the shells and arrange them on coarse salt as decribed above. Place oysters in the shells, spoon over the reserved juices, cover with the sauce, sprinkle with cheese and brown.
• Use a combination of mussels and oysters.
• Cut a ripe avocado in half, remove the pip and peel. Chop flesh finely. Lightly season with salt, pepper and cayenne pepper and moisten with a little wine vinegar or lemon juice. Spoon a little avocado in each shell and add mussels and/or oysters as above. A grated fresh mango may also be used.
• Sauté 1 small, finely chopped onion in 12,5 ml (1 T) oil until soft and translucent. Sprinkle with 12,5 ml (1 T) Sri Lankan spice mix (p. 100) and stir-fry for 1 minute. Add 1 large, fresh pineapple, peeled and chopped, and stir-fry until all the liquid has evaporated. Chill. Spoon into shells, top with mussels and/or oysters and complete as above.

Periwinkles (Alikreukel)

You can find hellishly expensive periwinkles all along the South African Strandloper coast – from the Strand right up to KwaZulu-Natal. Divers collect them mainly from underwater rocks, but sometimes – just sometimes – you can find them in shallow rock pools at low tide. Make sure that the periwinkles are still alive before you cook them: the little door or lid at the shell's opening must snap closed when you disturb them. Rinse in fresh water and cook the periwinkles for 15-20 minutes in fresh water or Court bouillon (page 44). The little lid comes off easily once they are cooked. Remove the periwinkles from the shells, discard the soft intestines and rinse well. Slice the flesh thinly and fry quickly in Maître d'hôtel butter or Lemon butter (page 46). My farmer friends don't agree with this cooking method. They throw the periwinkles against a rock, remove the flesh from the broken shells, discard the intestines and slice the raw flesh before frying it lightly in garlic butter. The slices can also be crumbed before frying.

Smoorsnoek (Braised snoek)

(SERVES 8)

The snoek are running and people are excited. In the Cape Town of years ago, you knew when this happened because the fishermen went from suburb to suburb, blowing their fish horns. Snoek should be handled as little as possible. Open it out butterfly fashion and inspect it thoroughly. Those who know what I'm talking about will know what I mean, and those who don't know don't need to know. Inhabitants of the West Coast are so fond of snoek that they preserve it in salt for the days when fresh snoek is not available. The butterflied snoek is covered with coarse salt or cut into portions and stored for months in the pickle barrel. Salted snoek must be refreshed in fresh water for about an hour. Replace the water at least once, or more often. Then it's ready to be braised to make *smoorsnoek*.

Fresh snoek can also be smoked and the result, once it's been flaked and the bones removed, is served on salt-rising yeast bread. It can also be made into a spread: mix 1 kg smoked snoek, skinned and the bones removed, with lemon juice and freshly ground pepper (both to taste). Add a 250 g container of chive cream cheese, as well as 25 ml finely grated onion, 50 ml finely chopped fresh parsley, 10 ml grated lemon rind, 10 ml finely chopped capers and 125 ml home-made mayonnaise and mix – it's

heavenly on whole-wheat bread. Those who don't know better refer to snoek spread as snoek pâté.

A savoury tart or flaked smoked snoek with a custard topping is one or the most delicious light lunches imaginable, especially served with a crisp green salad.

This recipe for smoorsnoek originates from the Sandveld, near the West Coast.

2 kg dried, salted snoek, or filleted,
*   fresh snoek*
25 ml (2 T) oil
25 ml (2 T) butter
4 large onions, halved lengthwise,
*   peeled and sliced*
1 kg potatoes, peeled,
*   cooked and cubed*
1 small red pepper, halved,
*   seeds and membranes removed,*
*   chopped (optional)*
1 red chilli, halved, seeds and membranes
*   removed, shredded*
salt and freshly ground white pepper
a little fresh lemon juice
*   or vinegar*

1. Refresh the salted snoek by soaking for about 8 hours in fresh water; replace the water 1-2 times during soaking. Drain. Place the fish (or fresh snoek) in a large saucepan and add enough water to just cover the fish. Bring to the boil, reduce heat and simmer for about 10 minutes until tender and cooked. Using a fork, flake the fish and remove all the bones.

2. Heat oil and butter in a saucepan, add onions and sauté until soft and translucent but not brown. Stir in potatoes and fish. If the mixture is too dry, add a little of the liquid in which the fish was cooked. Add red pepper and chilli and season with salt and pepper. Heat through. Sprinkle with lemon juice and serve with white rice.

VARIATIONS

● TRADITIONAL MALAY SMOORSNOEK: Use 4 or more chillies without removing the seeds.
● Add 4 ripe tomatoes that have been peeled, seeded and chopped (see Hint, p. 27), 5 ml (1 t) sugar and a few freshly chopped basil leaves to the onions when adding the fish and potatoes.
● Reduce the potatoes to 750 g and add 500 ml (2 cups) cooked sugar beans to the mixture when adding the potatoes.
BACALAO: This Spanish version of our *smoorsnoek* is always prepared from refreshed salted snoek. Onions, tomatoes and red peppers are cooked together to a thick sauce. It is then layered with the fish in a earthenware dish and baked in the oven.
● *BACALHAU:* This Portuguese version of *smoorsnoek* may also be prepared from refreshed snoek. Different versions are popular in the Portuguese community: *bacalhau à brás*, in which the snoek is braised together with roast potatoes and garlic and then covered with beaten egg, and most popular of all, *bacalhau à gomes de sá*, where hard-boiled egg replaces the omelet-type mixture and it is moistened with white wine.

Abalone (Perlemoen)

Abalone or *perlemoen*, also known as 'klip-kous' or, to a lesser extent, as 'see-oor', is one or our country's oldest foods. The Khoi and San inhabitants of the coastal regions packed it in freshly cut seaweed and braaied it over the coals long before the white man reached these shores. Today, Hermanus is our abalone mecca.

It's best to remove the flesh from the shell immediately after the abalone has been collected and is still alive. Force the shell open, beat it on the 'mouth' with a stone and cut it loose from the shell. Remove the dark alimentary canal and discard it. Scrub the flesh with a hard brush or pot scourer under cold running water. Cut off the edge, also known as a 'frill'. Cut out the mouth and slice the flesh very thinly, but not thinner than 5 mm (thinner than ¼ inch). Place the slices between layers of waxed paper and beat with a meat mallet until the flesh is soft but not crushed.

If ever a food has been mistreated, it's minced abalone. Lack of knowledge led to most cooks trying to cook this expensive, tough, univalve mollusc as long as possible in an effort to tenderise it. Some commit murder by mincing it and then cooking it in a pressure cooker. The real fools, who enjoy explosions, try to cook the whole abalone in a pressure cooker. Abalone should rather be eaten raw, like carpaccio.

If you prefer it cooked, fry it very quickly in melted ordinary, Maître d'hôtel or Lemon butter (page 46). The slices can be crumbed, then cooked literally for seconds on either side in sizzling hot butter. Remove and serve immediately.

Calamari and prawn salad

(SERVES 6)

300 g large prawns,
    shelled and veins removed
300 g calamari rings
500 ml (2 cups) Court bouillon
    (p. 44)
salt and freshly ground black pepper
variety of salad greens,
    broken into pieces
2 celery stalks, julienned
12 spring onions, sliced
½ English cucumber, halved lengthwise,
    seeded and thinly sliced
melon balls from ½ a winter melon
18 large basil leaves, rinsed, stacked,
    rolled up and shredded

SAUCE
50 ml (4 T) mayonnaise
12,5 ml (1 T) Dijon
    mustard mayonnaise
5 ml (1 t) hot prepared mustard
50 ml (4 T) joghurt
50 ml (4 T) chopped, fresh fennel
5 ml (1 t) finely chopped peeled
    fresh ginger
3-5 ml (½-1 t) Tabasco sauce

1. First blanch the prawns, then the calamari, in court bouillon. Remove, cool and lightly season with salt and pepper. Mix with salad greens, celery, spring onions, cucumber, melon and basil.
2. Reduce court bouillon to 50 ml (4 T), cool and mix with mayonnaise, mustard mayonnaise, mustard and joghurt. Stir in fennel, ginger and Tabasco sauce. Spoon over salad just befor serving and toss gently.

Boerewors, braais and biltong

WITHOUT A DOUBT, meat is the most popular food in South Africa: venison (small and large game), beef, veal, lamb, mutton, goat or pork – it makes no difference. We braai meat over coals, braise it in a potjie, stew it to a delightful bredie and make biltong from it – and each cut has a specific cooking method. Boerewors is an indigenous sausage, bredies (stews) are a Cape contribution to international cookery, and offal is a delicacy to some people and some cultures. In short: meat is the one important factor that binds together the black, Coloured and white inhabitants of this country. Afrikaners enjoy roast beef and Yorkshire pudding just as much as a born and bred Brit, a Zulu enjoys curry just as much as – if not more than – an Indian, and a Xhosa braais meat exactly the same as any Yuppie in the City of Gold.

Can one make any sense of such a hotch-potch of food preferences? I will explain step by step. First we look at braaiing, sample a potjie, slice a piece of biltong, and then investigate the various meat cuts (chapter 8) and their cooking methods. Bredies and stews are such important, characteristic dishes that they also deserve a separate chapter (chapter 9), as do offal (chapter 10) and curry (chapter 11).

Braais

The braai ritual is taken very seriously by most braaiers. First of all, you have to relax, sit on your stoep, a glass of beer in hand, and thoughtfully, pleasurably, meditatively drain it, sip by sip. This is called planning.

BOEREWORS BRAAIED OVER THE COALS

You contemplate who to invite. You take a walk to see if you have rooikrans for firewood. That's in the Boland; elsewhere you might use camelthorn. You compile your menu. Choose the wine. Not the best or the oldest, but the most suitable. Perhaps you will serve an ice-cold gamay noir. Years ago, Verdun and Muratie, estates just outside Stellenbosch, marketed such wines. Oh, well. Or perhaps Tassies, the wine of Stellenbosch students. Or pinot noir or pinotage. Or simply a nouveau wine.

THE PRELIMINARIES

Braaiing is an adventure, a sensory, physical experience. Sometimes a braai begins with bread; basically, two slices of bread with slices of cheese, tomato and onion, clamped in a grid and braaied until golden brown – a little something to whet the appetite. Pot bread, freshly baked, served with smoked snoek spread is an alternative. Avocado mascarpone, lightly beaten with a touch of lemon juice; taramasalata; or marinated mozzarella and tomato slices with rocket can replace the snoek spread. Pot bread with marinated, grilled vegetables; tapenade, or anchoïade are other possibilities. Karoo oysters (raw testicles of buck) wrapped in caul fat, *vlermuisies* (liver in caul fat), even pofadder or fried large intestine, are traditional nibbles. Rule: These should be a nibble, not a course or a meal. Such starters should be an introduction to conversation while the real reason for such a gathering wafts silently towards you through the air: the heavenly aroma of meat braaiing slowly over the coals.

A FISH COURSE

Fish as a first course is, for obvious reasons, not always possible. But who can resist slowly braaiing a simple, butterflied, wind-dried galjoen (or elf), high above the coals, skin side down (p. 44). The skin is what it's all about. Just as the Chinese do not eat duck for its meat but for its crisp skin, so too for galjoen. That skin! As crisp yet tender as a sea anemone, as rich and brown as roasted chestnuts – a sensuous taste experience. Again, serve just a small portion with only a slice of lemon as accompaniment. That is the secret of eating: relaxed, moving forward gradually, step by step.

MEAT

Now the meat. One step at the time: you may have to take a small spadeful of glowing coals from a second fire to add to the braai fire – yes, it is important to have two fires. And you must have more than one level, for fish grids and meat grids, which should be easy to move higher or lower. Steak needs fierce heat close to the coals for a minute or so before it is cooked to the desired degree of doneness further away from the coals.

Lamb loin chops should be cooked over moderate heat. Snip the fat beforehand and cut off the sinew connecting the meat to the T-bone. Saratoga chops, made from boned lamb ribs and loin, threaded onto skewers, are a highlight at any braai. Sosaties, slightly smoky, must braai long and slowly high above the coals, and boerewors should be cooked slowly, far from the coals. I often braai boerewors on a grid in which a few bay leaves have been clamped – it improves the flavour.

There are two approaches to braaiing butterflied chicken: basting with olive oil, either constantly while high above the coals, or beforehand; and meat that gets that final smoky flavour and colour in the centre position above the coals. Quail, butterflied and braaied slowly, fairly high above the coals, became the fashion in the nineties. Sometimes chicken, poussins and other birds are basted with tomato sauce. This must be done carefully, because the meat can easily become black and bitter.

Choose only one or, at the most, two kinds of meat for a braai.

If you have braaied a whole saddle of lamb, or beef fillet or loin, leave it on the grid beside the coals for at least 20 minutes, at warming drawer temperature, for the juices to settle. If you don't do this, sensitive guests may be put off at the sight of the bloody water. Slice the meat and arrange about four or five slices of varying sizes on a slightly warmed plate for each guest.

Bake new potatoes at the edge of the fire, cut a cross in the top of each and press the potato so that it opens out like a flower, top with herb butter and serve with the meat. Baked whole heads of garlic is a must. A crisp green salad could also be a welcome addition.

HOW TO COOK BOEREWORS
• Braai the sausage slowly and for a long time *high* above the coals until golden brown. Turn the grid only once during the braaiing time.
• *Do not* cook sausage in a pan of water.
• If you roast sausage in an oven, it is best to place the pan fairly far from the preheated element of the oven.
• Sausage may also be fried in a ridged pan over medium heat on top of the stove. Do not use any oil. As soon as the sausage no longer sticks to the pan, turn it over. Fry the other side until just cooked.
• Sausage should *never* be overcooked. The meat must be tender and juicy on the inside and crisp on the outside.

Braaied lamb chops can be served with the traditional *sousbone* (sweet and sour bean salad) or grilled vegetables.

Lovers of T-bone steaks enjoy two worlds in one. Snip the fat and baste the meat with rosemary oil or herb butter during braaiing. Serve the steaks with crumbly maize porridge (*krummelpap*) topped with sweet pepper and tomato concassée.

Pork is ideal for braaiing. Chops or Kassler rib chops should be braaied high above the coals so that the snipped fat will crisp.

DESSERT
Dessert usually consists of fruit and coffee. I prefer ice-cold fresh fruit arranged on crushed ice in a large dish. A dessert of watermelon and sweet melon slices, or red and green grapes – especially hanepoot – is simplicity itself; and simplicity is a sign of good taste. Ice cream and/or sorbet with fresh fruit coulis (ice-cold, slightly reduced fruit purée), moistened with liqueur, is another possibility. Another popular choice is Dom Pedro, a dessert 'drink' which Danny Ferris introduced to Cape Town in the sixties. And finally, serve strong black coffee, without cream or milk or sugar – because life is not life without a taste of bitterness.

Boerewors

(MAKES 3,5 KG)

2 kg boned beef, cut into 50 mm (2 in) cubes
1 kg boned pork, cut into 50 mm (2 in) cubes
12,5 ml (1 T) black peppercorns
50 ml (4 T) coriander seed
4 cloves
75 ml (6 T) wine vinegar
25 ml (2 T) sweet wine, port or muscadel
2 bay leaves
20 ml (4 t) salt
5 ml (1 t) freshly grated nutmeg
250 g speck, finely diced or coarsely minced
100 g intestines, soaked thoroughly in salted water

1. Mix beef and pork.
2. Place peppercorns, coriander and cloves in a heavy-based saucepan and heat over medium heat until coriander begins to brown and gives off a slight aroma. Remove from heat and set aside to cool slightly. Spoon mixture into a spice mill and grind until fine. Shake through a sieve. Sprinkle the spice mixture over the meat, then add vinegar and wine. Combine well with your hands. Break the bay leaves into small pieces and press into the mixture. Cover and place in the refrigerator overnight.
3. Remove mixture from the refrigerator and sprinkle salt and nutmeg over the meat. Mix thoroughly. Mince to a rough texture and add the speck.
4. Some people sprinkle water over the meat mixture before stuffing the sausage. Stuff the casings lightly but smoothly.

BLACK POT OF THE FUTURE

Spare ribs

(MAKES 4-6 SERVINGS)

2 kg fresh or smoked pork short ribs
pepper
SAUCE
2 large onions, halved lengthways,
    peeled and chopped
2 plump garlic cloves, bruised,
    peeled and crushed
25 ml (2 T) oil
125 ml (½ cup) vinegar
250 g (250 ml/1 c) tomato sauce
25 ml (2 T) Worcestershire sauce
250 ml (1 cup) chutney
10 ml (2 t) mixed spice
125 ml (½ cup) brown sherry
    (Old Brown Sherry)
salt
pepper

1. Place ribs in a large enamel dish, season with pepper and set aside.
2. SAUCE: Fry onions and garlic in oil until onions are soft and transparent, but not browned. Add vinegar and simmer until it evaporates. Add tomato sauce, Worcestershire sauce, chutney and spices and simmer over moderate heat to make a thick sauce. Allow to cool. Purée in a food processor or rub through a sieve. Add sherry.
3. Spoon the sauce over ribs and mix. Cover the dish with cling wrap and marinate overnight in the refrigerator. The ribs can even be marinated for 2-3 days in the refrigerator before cooking.
4. Place the ribs on a grid, season lightly with salt and pepper and braai very slowly, high above the coals, so that meat takes about 1½ hours to cook. Baste often with the marinade.

HINT: To cook the ribs in the oven, preheat the oven to 200 °C (400 °F). Arrange the meat on the oiled rack of a roasting pan, bake for 1 hour and baste often with the marinade. Switch on the grilling element in advance and grill the meat, not close to the element, for about 10 minutes until nicely browned. Turn the ribs so that the meat browns on both sides.

Salted ribs (Soutribbetjie)

(MAKES 6 SERVINGS)

Salted ribs (*soutribbetjie*) are an example of trekkers food born out of the necessity to preserve meat. This dish was adopted so wholeheartedly in the nineteenth century that it still survives today. This doesn't surprise me in the least, as most South Africans only got refrigerators in the fifties, and millions still have to manage without one. The ribs are salty. If you prefer them less salty, soak them in cold water before wind-drying them.

1 breast of mutton (separated from shank),
    ± 1,5 kg
15 ml (3 t) brown sugar
225 g (200 ml/⅘ cup) coarse salt
2 ml (slightly less than ½ t) saltpetre
50 ml (4 T) roasted coriander seed (see Hint)
5 ml ground allspice

1. IN ADVANCE: Ask your butcher to saw through the breast bone, so that you can easily cut the meat into portions later.
2. Mix sugar, salt, saltpetre, coriander and allspice and rub into the meat. Place meat in an enamel dish, cover with a muslin cloth and leave in the refrigerator for 2-3 days. Rub salt mixture into meat 2-3 times a day.
3. Suspend meat in a cool, well-ventilated place to dry.
4. Place meat in a saucepan, cover with cold water and heat to boiling point. Cover, reduce heat and simmer for 1 hour. Remove from the liquid and allow to cool. Hang meat up again to wind-dry. Braai over moderate coals until browned and crisp. Cut into portions and serve.

HINT: Stir-fry coriander seed in a heavy-based saucepan over moderate heat until a fairly strong coriander aroma can be detected. Spoon immediately into a spice mill and grind the seeds finely, or crush them with a mortar and pestle. Shake through a sieve. Do not rub them through, otherwise the hard shells will also get through, which will make the spice bitter. Do not roast coriander days in advance, as it loses its flavour.

Sosaties

(MAKES 6 SERVINGS)

The word 'sosaties' comes from the Malay word *sesate*, which means 'meat on skewers'. Sosaties are a unique example of an original Muslem dish which did not contain pork, but did contain sheep-tail fat. Over the years, sosaties have become typically South African, and today non-Muslems prefer using speck. Sosaties should be prepared three days in advance, and should always contain lamb. There are no other ingredients apart from meat, onions, bacon, apricots and bay or lemon leaves. When any other kind of meat, or a mixture of meats, is threaded onto skewers, it is called a kebab. When sweet peppers or marinated prunes are added, you also have a kebab. The recipe below is the original sosatie recipe, written by hand in the recipe books of the Roux family of Stellenbosch. I prefer this method to the custom of serving sosaties with a sauce which was popular during the sixties and seventies. A too sweet sauce simply spoils the meaty flavour.

MARINADE
1 onion, halved lengthways, peeled and chopped
10 ml (2 t) oil
2 plump garlic cloves, bruised, peeled and crushed
4 lemon leaves, shredded
freshly ground pepper
250 ml (1 cup) buttermilk

SOSATIES
1,5 kg leg of lamb, thick rib or shoulder,
    deboned and cut into 25 mm (1 in) cubes
12 skewers, soaked in water overnight
500 g speck, first cut into strips and then into
    25 mm (1 in) cubes, or 500 g sheep-tail fat,
    cut into slices
2 medium onions, halved lengthways, peeled and
    blanched in boiling water for 5 minutes,
    refreshed in ice water and the rings separated
24 fresh lemon leaves (optional)
100 g (170 ml/⅔ cup) dried apricots,
    soaked in onion water

BASTING MIXTURE
1 large onion, halved lengthways, peeled
  and chopped
12,5 ml (1 T) oil
12,5 ml (1 T) Indian spice mixture (p. 100)
1 piece (12,5 mm / ½ in) fresh ginger, peeled
  and finely chopped
1 red chilli, finely chopped with seeds
3 ml (½ t) turmeric
2 bay or lemon leaves, crushed
125 ml (½ cup) brown vinegar
50 ml (4 T) apricot jam
50 ml (4 T) chutney
salt and freshly ground pepper

1. MARINADE: Fry onion in oil until soft and transparent, but not browned. Add the garlic and lemon leaves and stir-fry for 1 minute. Remove from heat and allow to cool. Season with pepper and stir buttermilk into onion mixture.

2. SOSATIES: Spoon meat into a large enamel or glass bowl. Pour marinade over. Mix well and cover with cling wrap. Marinate overnight in the refrigerator.

3. Remove meat from refrigerator and drain, a little at a time, in a colander. Pat dry with kitchen paper and thread onto soaked skewers, alternately with speck, onion, 2 lemon leaves per skewer and soaked apricots. Cover and store in the refrigerator.

4. BASTING SAUCE: Fry onion in oil until softened and transparent, but not browned. Sprinkle spice mixture over and stir-fry for 2 minutes. Add ginger, chilli, turmeric and bay leaves. Stir, then gradually add vinegar. Stir in apricot jam and chutney, remove from heat and allow to cool.

5. Spread a thin layer of sauce in a large enamel dish. Pack in sosaties, in a single layer. Spread the rest of the sauce over. Cover with cling wrap and marinate for 2 days in the refrigerator. Turn once or twice.

6. TO BRAAI: Remove the sosaties from the basting sauce marinade and season with salt and pepper. Arrange on a grid and braai long and slowly, very high above the coals. Moisten frequently with the remaining basting sauce.

Potjiekos

Potjiekos has been part of our lives since the first settlement at the Cape. In those days, food was cooked in an open hearth in the *keuken* (kitchen), in a black cast-iron pot with legs so that the coals could be scraped under the pot. The flat-bottomed pots stood on a wrought-iron triangle or square, or were suspended on a hook above the kitchen fire. Round-bellied, three-legged pots only made their appearance in the nineteenth century.

Let's take a look, for a moment, at those first Cape kitchens. The hearth was the focal point of the kitchen. In large manor houses, the hearths stretched across the width of the kitchen. The houses of the poor had smaller hearths. At the front was a beam that carried the chimney breast. The chimney stretched upwards, alongside the gable, ending high above the thatched roof to minimise the danger of fire from sparks. This was not always the case, however. Most of the old chimneys were badly constructed and often caused fires. In the centre of the chimney one or more wrought-iron hooks, about a metre apart, were built into the front and back walls. Two thick iron bars were positioned on the hooks with a ring (sometimes called an eye). A long iron rod with a hook at either end rested on these bars. The rod could move forwards or backwards. The hooks could be hoisted up or down to increase or decrease the heat. For this reason people did not refer to cooking food, but to hanging it. This expression gradually disappeared with the arrival of the black range, and if you were to ask a young lady about it today, she would not have the slightest idea what you were talking about.

The black range is undoubtedly the best way to cook. Unfortunately, it needs many hands to scrub the outside of the pots. It is interesting how our ancestors solved the soot problem. They smeared a porridge made of fine ash on the outside of the pots, and this could later simply be scraped off and the pots rubbed until shiny.

Modern houses no longer have a hearth or an Aga, and great-grandmother's pots have become a showpiece in many homes.

But how did potjiekos get its name? In the seventeenth and eighteenth centuries it was called *spys*. The potjie made its appearance in the nineteenth century, along the route of the Great Trek, as the trekkers'

outdoor food. Most of the time, venison was stewed in the hunters' pots. Sometimes an old ox, which was fairly tough, was cooked this way, and sometimes it was goat or mutton. The meat was cooked in large pots and simply loaded onto the wagons again, or hooked under them, as the trekkers moved on. The fat that set on top sealed the meat and prevented it from spoiling. When they stopped and formed a laager, the potjie was placed over the fire again and a meal was enjoyed. Then came the transition from trekkers' food to trek food, when farmers trekked with their sheep in search of better grazing. These potjies consisted of mutton, onions and potatoes, strongly seasoned with pepper to keep flies and other insects away.

Food fusion took place when the 1820 Settlers settled on the East Coast, as a result of their contact with black people and the planting of maize. New ingredients were added to the porridge pot. Spring hares, east coast crayfish and marog found their way into the cooking pot. Potjiekos was later introduced to the people in Zululand and then to people living in the central northern region, where mopane worms were fried. One of the interesting potjies made by the Zulu people consisted of snake cooked in the fat of the large, flying termites to which *kohwe* (large, flat field mushrooms which tasted like fried beef when cooked) were added. In ordinary households, leg of lamb was cooked until meltingly tender in flat-bottomed pots on the Aga stove. Bredies were cooked in cast-iron pots, as was pot bread.

In the sixties and early seventies of the twentieth century, South Africans really took to braaiing. This was the era of the Kellerprinz braai competitions. Prosperity declined, and a nostalgia for the cooking methods of long ago prompted us to return to the potjies of our ancestors. In the Boland, on the West Coast and in the game camps of the north, the three-legged potjie was hauled out of the cellar and all sorts of dishes were concocted. Late in the seventies, I recorded this on paper and gave the phenomenon the name *potjiekos*. Before long, the entire country was crazy about potjiekos. All kinds of silly rules surfaced. Excess and non-complementary flavours abounded. Some believed that potjiekos had to consist of layer upon layer of ingredients. Nonsense! Potjiekos is braised food, which should not be stirred unnecessarily. It is an outdoor food for everyone to enjoy.

Curried flat rib and fruit potjie

(MAKES 6 SERVINGS)

Stewed, sun-dried fruit with meat is characteristic of our cooking. This clever recipe uses coconut as a binding agent as well as a flavour enhancer. It not only allows us to relive the trekking tradition; it also marries a whole array of Malay flavours – a symbol of our new, unfolding food culture. A few sambals (chapter 17) paint the rest of the rainbow.

- 2 kg flat rib, sawn into portions   *lamb*
- 25 ml (2 T) oil
- 1 large onion, halved lengthways, peeled and thinly sliced
- 6 plump garlic cloves, bruised, peeled and crushed with:
- 12,5 ml (1 T) salt
- 1 piece (50 mm / 2 inches) fresh ginger root, peeled and chopped
- 3 red chillies, halved and seeded
- 25 ml (2 T) Indian spice mixture (p. 100) or other hot curry powder
- 500-750 ml (2-3 cups) hot beef stock
- 125 ml (½ cups) desiccated coconut
- 75 g (125 ml/ ½ cups) each bleached sultanas, dried apricots and pitted prunes
- 1 stick cinnamon

TOPPING
3 apples, peeled and quartered
37,5 ml (3 T) wine vinegar
5 ml (1 t) turmeric

1. Using a No 3 potjie, brown meat, a little at a time, in oil. Remove each batch and repeat process with remaining meat.
2. Pour off excess fat. Fry onion in the same potjie until softened and lightly browned. Add garlic and salt, ginger and chillies and stir-fry for 1 minute. Sprinkle spice mixture over and stir-fry for 2-3 minutes. Add a little of the hot stock to the onion and spice mixture if it begins to stick to the base of the potjie. Now add half the stock and heat to boiling point. Return the meat to the liquid and sprinkle the coconut over. Spoon the sultanas, apricots and prunes on top and place the stick of cinnamon on top. Add more stock, to almost cover the ingredients. Cover and simmer for 1½-2 hours, or until meat is tender.
3. TOPPING: Peel the apples, remove the cores with an apple corer and quarter the flesh. Mix vinegar and turmeric and roll apple quarters in it until covered all over. Reserve remaining liquid. Remove the lid from the potjie and arrange the apples on top. Sprinkle the remaining vinegar mixture over. Cover and simmer for a further 15 minutes, or until apples are tender but not mushy. Serve with sambals (chapter 17), into which a generous amount of chopped fresh coriander leaves has been stirred.

Beef shin and bean potjie

(MAKES 8 SERVINGS)

250 g (250 ml/1 cup) haricot beans
500 ml (2 cups) water
25 ml (2 T) oil
2 kg beef shin slices, rinsed and patted dry
250 g smoked pork flank, cut into pieces without removing fat
1 large onion, halved lengthways, peeled and chopped
10 ml (2 t) salt
freshly ground pepper
1 tin (410 g) tomatoes
25 ml (2 T) tomato concentrate
500 ml (2 c) beef stock
3 red chillies, halved and seeded
1 piece (25 mm / 1 inch) fresh ginger root, peeled and coarsely grated
250 g green beans, trimmed and sliced diagonally

TOPPING
1 tin (410 g) red kidney beans, rinsed
25 ml (2 T) chopped fresh parsley
25 ml (2 T) chopped chives

1. Rinse haricot beans and place in a No 2 potjie. Add water, heat to boiling point and cook for 3 minutes, then remove from heat and leave over cool coals for 1 hour to keep warm.
2. Meanwhile, heat oil in a No 3 potjie. Place beef in the potjie, a few slices at a time, and brown on both sides. Remove with a slotted spoon. Repeat with remaining slices. Do the same with the pork flank. Pour off excess fat, leaving one spoonful in the potjie, and fry the onion in it until tender and lightly browned. Season meat with salt and pepper and place in the potjie. Drain haricot beans and spoon on top of meat.
3. Place tomatoes, tomato concentrate, stock, chillies, ginger and its liquid in the potjie. Cover and simmer for 2-2½ hours or until meat is almost tender.
4. Spoon green beans on top, cover and simmer for 15 minutes. Add kidney beans and sprinkle herbs over. This one-dish meal does not need accompaniments.

CURRIED FLAT RIB AND FRUIT POTJIE

Lamb and brinjal potjie

(MAKES 6 SERVINGS)

4 brinjals, prepared as described on p. 00 and
*   cut into 25 mm (1 inch) thick slices*
salt
2 red and 2 yellow sweet peppers,
*   halved lengthways, seeded and membranes*
*   removed, then halved lengthways again*
50 ml (4 T) olive oil
2 kg breast of mutton, sawn into slices,
*   or lamb leg chops*
25 ml (2 T) oil
2 onions, halved lengthways, peeled and sliced
4 plump garlic cloves, bruised, peeled and
*   crushed*
salt and freshly ground black pepper
1 kg ripe, red tomatoes, skinned, seeded and
*   coarsely chopped (see Hint, p. 27),*
*   or 2 tins (410 g each) tomatoes, chopped*
6 young baby marrows, scrubbed under cold
*   running water and halved lengthways*
10 ml (2 t) fresh lemon thyme
5 ml (1 t) chopped fresh rosemary
50 ml (4 T) snipped chives

1. Arrange brinjals and sweet peppers on an oiled grid and brush with olive oil. Braai over the coals, but not too close to them, until the skins of the sweet peppers blacken and blister. Remove vegetables from the coals, allow to cool and pull off the skins of the sweet peppers.
2. Arrange unseasoned meat slices on the grid and braai both sides until nicely browned. Do not braai too close to the coals.
3. Heat the oil in a No 4 potjie. Add the onions and fry until softened and transparent, but not browned. Add garlic. Season meat on one side with salt and pepper and place, seasoned side down, on top of the onions. Season the other side with salt and pepper. Season the brinjal slices on one side with salt and pepper and place them on top of the meat, seasoned side down. Season other side with salt and pepper. Spoon sweet peppers and tomatoes into the potjie, cover and braise for 1 hour over low heat. Add the baby marrows and simmer, uncovered, for 30 minutes. Make sure that the heat is not too high. The longer and slower the potjie cooks, the better.
4. Taste and season with salt and pepper if necessary. Sprinkle thyme, rosemary and chives over and serve with Krummelpap (p. 26) or Couscous salad (p. 27).

BILTONG

Biltong

Various kinds of biltong were made from the round of beef. Round strips of biltong called *predikantsbiltong* (minister's biltong) was made from the silverside. Topside and thick flank were also used. The most sought-after biltong, known as *garingbiltong* (chine biltong), was cut from the eye muscle on either side of the backbone. *Ouma se biltong* (grandmother's biltong) was cut from the fillet. Farmers of old also used thick rib, but the biltong was thin and it took too long to remove the connective tissue. The younger the animal, the better. The layers of fat should be very thin, because thick fat quickly becomes rancid. Fatty meat also takes too long to absorb salt. Biltong made from an old carcass is tough and sinewy. In the Free State biltong was wind-dried, sliced to form 'ears' and fried with eggs instead of bacon for breakfast. Today, biltong is a snack often served with drinks. Together with *droëwors* (dried sausage), and peanuts and raisins, it has become a popular spectator snack at rugby matches. Earlier generations liked to make very dry biltong, then pulverise it with a hammer and eat the powdery meat, with fat, on bread.

Droëwors

To make this dried sausage, fill small casings with the Boerewors mixture (p. 58) and hang them from a chrome or copper pipe – not wire – in a cool, dry place. Use an electric fan to cool the sausage if you wish, in which case it will be ready within five to seven days.

Tangy beef biltong

(MAKES ± 6 KG)

The biltong recipe below has a strong, zesty coriander flavour, which is inclined to dominate the meaty flavour. If you prefer a stronger meat flavour, halve the quantity of coriander throughout and omit the pepper that is rubbed in afterwards. I prefer the stronger pepper taste, particularly as it keeps the flies away during the drying process. If you are drying the biltong in an area where there are plenty of flies and midges, it is a good idea to wrap the biltong in mosquito netting. Some people like to use aniseed, allspice and garlic salt; I strongly advise against this. Biltong should be biltong, so don't overdo the seasoning. Over the past ten years, chilli bites, those thin pieces of biltong made

from off-cuts and which burn your palate like long, dry nails, have become popular.

about 12 kg whole beef silverside
150 g (185 ml/¾ cup) brown sugar
15 g (15 ml/3 t) saltpetre
15 g (22,5 ml/4½ t) bicarbonate of soda
62,5 ml (¼ cup) freshly ground black pepper
75 g (185 ml/¾ cup) roasted coriander seed
*   (see Hint, p. 60)*
415 g (415 ml/1¾ cups) coarse salt
375 ml (1½ cups) vinegar

DIPPING MIXTURE
375 ml (1½ cups) vinegar
5 litres (20 cups) boiling water

TO RUB IN
25 g (62,5 ml/¼ cup) roasted coriander seed
15 ml (3 t) finely ground black pepper

1. Inspect the meat and cut out all visible connective tissue. Cut meat into long strips, each ± 25-50 mm (1-2 inches) thick. Do not cut meat into strips thinner than 25 mm (1 in).
2. Mix sugar, saltpetre, bicarbonate of soda, pepper and coriander and rub into the meat. Layer meat in a large dish, sprinkling salt and vinegar over each layer. Cover with a muslin cloth and leave overnight in a cold room, the refrigerator or any cold place.
3. DIPPING MIXTURE: Mix the vinegar and boiling water. Hang each strip of meat on a piece of wire bent into an S-shape, or on biltong hooks. Holding the strip of meat by the hook, dip it in the dipping mixture for 2 seconds and hang it up to dry in a cool, well-ventilated place, where the floor is covered with newspaper. After a day, rub the roasted coriander and pepper onto the meat. Biltong should hang for about 10-14 days, depending on the thickness of the meat; or longer for drier biltong.

VARIATION: VENISON BILTONG
The tastiest venison biltong is the long chine biltong which is cut from the fillets on both sides of the backbone. It can also be cut from the leg, along the sides of the muscles. Don't cut it too thickly. Messy pieces and edges must be trimmed. Venison biltong is treated in the same way as beef biltong, except that the meat is sometimes first rubbed with juniper berries. A little finely ground allspice is rubbed in during drying, along with extra ground coriander and pepper. Remember, however, that small quantities should be used. Dried biltong should be wrapped individually in cling wrap, then packed into a large plastic bag, before freezing.

CHAPTER 8

Other meat dishes

DURING THE FIRST half of the twentieth century, mutton and lamb were everyday food, eaten throughout the week. Only lamb pie was good enough to serve with chicken on Sundays.

In the fifties, the tables were turned. Chicken became everyday food, and lamb and beef were elevated to pride of place. The easy way was to serve a leg of lamb. Saddle of lamb was roasted whole in the oven, or the backbone was sawn in half and the two parts were placed facing each other so that the cleaned rib parts interlocked and the fat side of the meat faced outwards. Sometimes this cut – or guard of honour, as it was called – was given a stuffing, but most of the time it was cooked just as it was. For special occasions, a crown rib roast was prepared. Two sets of ribs, each with eight rib bones, were tied together with the fat facing inwards, to make a crown. Towards the end of the cooking time a meat stuffing was usually added. This dish has largely disappeared. Over the past few decades, the most popular cuts have been roast rack of lamb with a herb, pepper, nut or crumb crust; and noisettes – boned rib of lamb rolled up (the flank, which was not needed, was cut off) and tied with string, then sliced. The slices were grilled and served with savoury butter.

Braising meat long and slowly until it falls off the bone is one of the oldest cooking methods around. It has been used for centuries and is currently enjoying great popularity again. Finely minced meat is needed for mutton, rabbit and venison pies. *Denningvleis* and *pienangvleis* were traditionally served with the bones, but lately this method has been replaced with the use of mince, so that most of the fat can be removed. Both are also served as pies today. Miniature meat pies are the most important snacks at South African cocktail parties.

When it comes to beef, most South Africans immediately think of steakhouses and grilled steak: T-bone, Porterhouse, entrecôte and rump steak, and a ladies' fillet – with chips and fried onion rings as accompaniments. Then comes Sunday's roast beef, beef Wellington, corned beef and the ever-popular minced beef in all its guises. After the Second World War, Italian restaurateurs contributed greatly to the popularisation of veal. Later, the pasta revolution reached us, particularly in the form of lasagne verdi and spaghetti bolognaise (see chapter 13). Mediterranean and Provençal flavours became our favourite taste sensation in the eighties. Garlic, wholegrain mustard and chopped fresh herbs like thyme, rosemary and lavender were rubbed thoroughly into sirloin and fillet. Sometimes a little tarragon and marjoram were added. Take care, though, that the herbs do not overpower the flavour of the meat.

Not much pork was available at the start of the twentieth century. Farmers slaughtered pigs in the winter months and used the meat mainly for sausage, mince mixtures, salted rib and other dishes containing ribs. The English community and the Zulu monarchy both enjoyed roast pork and served it with fruit jelly and *amatangula* (num-num) jelly respectively. In Natal and the Cape, leg of pork was processed to make bacon and ham. In fact, bacon – streaky, back or shoulder – is still very popular for breakfast today; which is not strange, as many people follow the British diet. And ready-cooked ham sells like hotcakes. Pigs do not develop strong muscles like other animals, and as a result their meat can be prepared in any way you please.

Pork chops, smoked shin (better known here by its German name, *Eisbein*), rolled rib, grilled fillets, chippolata sausages as an accompaniment to the Christmas turkey, roast leg and, especially, pork strips for stir-fries, today make up the range, along with schnitzels, cordon bleu and Kassler chops. Pork combines particularly well with fresh and dried fruit.

The collective name, game, is divided into large game, small game and feathered game. Buffalo, nyala, zebra, kudu, gemsbok, hartebeest, wildebeest and eland are large game.

ROAST BEEF AND YORKSHIRE PUDDING

Duikers, steenbuck, springbok, impala, rhe-buck, bushbuck and blesbuck are small game. Wild pigs, like the bushpig and warthog, are also considered to be game. Wild hares and rabbits – the mountain rabbits are larger and tastier than those of the plains – provide for one of the truly traditional dishes in our cui-sine: rabbit pie. Wood pigeons, doves, quail, partridge, pheasant, guineafowl, wild ducks, Muscovy ducks, Egyptian geese, ostrich and kori bustards are the most important of the feathered game.

Game should, in general, be fairly young and should preferably not be marinated because this spoils the flavour. The meat of game older than six months should be mar-inated, larded or barded. Young venison should be well matured. A fully grown ewe's meat is generally juicier than that of a ram of the same age. Delicious sausage and salami can be made from venison, especially warthog. The bones are suitable for stock. The offal can be prepared in exactly the same way as described in chap-ter 10; the meat can be braaied according to the instructions in the braai section; it can also be used to make potjiekos, as described on p. 61.

But the most common use of venison in South Africa probably remains the making of biltong (p. 63). Men still go on hunting expeditions in the winter months to collect a year's supply of biltong. Rina Pont's book gives complete information on the process-ing of venison. The accompaniments to venison are pearl wheat or crumbly porridge (krummelpap), baked sweet potatoes and stewed dried fruit. In many respects, we fol-low the British tradition of serving fruit jelly with roast venison. The European custom of serving poached fruit as an accompaniment is gaining popularity, and gourmets relish fried field mushrooms.

HOW TO COOK RED MEAT
Each animal and each cut has its own method; one would not, for instance, potroast a young leg of lamb, but rather roast it on the rack of a roasting pan in the oven so that air can circulate around it. This is an example of the dry-heat method. Beef bolo should be stewed – an example of the moist-heat method. When making bredies, braising, potroasting, stewing, cooking in cooking bags or in aluminium foil, follow the moist-heat method. On the other hand, grilling, roasting and braaiing are dry-heat methods.

Mock leg of venison
(MAKES 4-6 SERVINGS)

This is one of the most popular dishes from the first seven decades of the twentieth century.

1 leg of mutton, ± 2 kg
5 ml (1 t) ground cloves
25 ml (2 T) ground, roasted coriander seed
 (see Hint, p. 60)
25 ml (2 T) soft brown sugar
25 ml (2 T) salt
5 ml (1 t) freshly ground black pepper
3-5 ml (½-1 t) grated nutmeg
3 ml (½ t) ground allspice
250 ml (1 cup) vinegar,
 preferably wine vinegar
250 g speck, cut into strips 6 mm (¼ in) thick
 and 50-75 mm (2-3 in) long
125 ml (½ cup) sweet wine, such as hanepoot
 or muscadel

TO SERVE
apple or quince jelly, heated

1. Wipe meat well and remove bone.
2. Mix cloves, coriander, sugar, salt, pepper, nutmeg and allspice and stir in the vinegar. Spread the spice mixture over the prepared speck and marinate for ± 1 hour.
3. Remove speck from the marinade and reserve the marinade. Freeze the speck strips for ± 20 minutes until stiff – this makes it easier to lard the leg.
4. Lard the leg with speck, by making deep incisions in the meat with a boning knife, widening the incisions slightly with your little finger and pressing the marinated speck strips into them. Place meat in an enamel or ceramic container and spread the remaining spice mixture over. Turn often and spread marinade over frequently.
5. Remove the meat from the marinade. Heat a piece of fat in a heavy-based saucepan until the saucepan is hot. Pat the meat dry and fry on all sides until golden brown. Add a little water, cover and potroast for 1½ hours, frequently adding a little water. Add sweet wine and potroast for a fur-ther 30 minutes. Remove from the saucepan and brush with melted jelly.

Butterflied leg of mutton with ginger
(MAKES 4 SERVINGS)

The mixing of sweet and savoury is charac-teristic of the Afrikaner's food, and this recipe is one example. A little extra ginger – once the hottest of spices – reminds us of the days when pepper was worth its weight in gold.

1,25-1,5 kg leg of mutton or lamb (or even
 smaller), boned and butterflied
 (ask your butcher to do this)
5-10 ml (1-2 t) salt
3-5 ml (½-1 t) freshly ground black pepper

MARINADE
50 ml (4 T) oil
25 ml (2 T) soft brown sugar
10 ml (2 t) ground ginger
75 ml (6 T) chutney
50 ml (4 T) wine vinegar
50 ml (4 T) finely chopped preserved ginger

1. Fold meat flat and beat lightly with a meat mallet, so that it is about the same thickness throughout.
2. Mix the marinade ingredients and spread them on both sides of the meat. Place in an enamel or a ceramic container, cover and marinate for 2 hours in the refrigerator.
3. Remove the meat from the container. Using your palm, wipe off excess marinade into the dish. Reserve marinade. Season meat all over with salt and pepper.
4. Lightly oil the rack of a roasting pan. Place the meat, fat side up, on the rack. Roast in the oven (see How to oven roast beef, p. 73). Brush meat often with reserved marinade during cooking. Leave in a pre-heated warming drawer for 30 minutes before carving. Serve with a potato dish and at least one green and one yellow vegetable.

Goat and mutton are from older animals and should preferably be cooked according to the moist-heat method. On the other hand, there are two options for lamb and kid:
DRY-HEAT METHOD: shoulder, leg, chops, saddle and loin
MOIST-HEAT METHOD: all other cuts.

Bobotie

(MAKES 4 SERVINGS)

Mince and forcemeat are used in dishes like bobotie and shepherd's pie. There are more recipes for bobotie than spots on a guineafowl. The original recipe called for cooked leftover leg of mutton. Some cooks use beef, but then it is no longer bobotie and should be called beef bobotie. Recipes containing 'stretchers' of dried fruit and cooked leftover vegetables do nothing for this prince among recipes. Bobotie can also be made from uncooked minced lamb, but then it needs a slightly longer baking time.

2 thick slices white bread, crusts removed
250 ml (1 cup) milk
2 onions, halved lengthways,
    peeled and finely chopped
25 ml (2 T) oil
3 plump garlic cloves, bruised,
    peeled and crushed
1 piece (25 mm/1 in) fresh ginger root,
    peeled and finely chopped,
    or 8 ml (1½ t) ground ginger
25-50 ml (2-4 T) Sri Lankan spice mixture
    (p. 100) or other mild curry powder
    (depending on how spicy you like it, but do
    not use too much curry powder)
12,5 ml (1 T) smooth apricot jam
1 extra-large egg, beaten
50 ml (4 T) cream (optional)
salt and pepper to taste
1 kg cooked minced lamb, preferably leg of lamb
25 ml (2 T) lemon juice
finely grated rind of 2 lemons
12 almonds, bruised
8 fresh lemon or 4 bay leaves, wiped clean

TOPPING
3 extra-large eggs, beaten
375 ml (1½ cups) milk
2 ml (2 pinches) turmeric
salt and pepper to taste

1. Place bread in a shallow container and pour the milk over slowly. Leave to soak for 10 minutes. Mash with a fork.
2. Fry the onions in oil until softened and transparent but not browned. Add the garlic and ginger and stir-fry for 1 minute. Sprinkle the spice mixture over and stir-fry for 2-3 minutes. If the spice mixture sticks to the base of the saucepan, add a little water. Stir in the apricot jam. Remove from the heat and allow to cool.
3. Beat the egg and the cream (if using) and season well with salt and pepper. Place the meat in a mixing bowl and spoon the soaked bread over. Add the onion mixture, then pour the egg mixture, lemon juice and rind over. Mix together thoroughly but lightly with a large, two-pronged fork. Spoon the meat mixture into a greased pie or other shallow baking dish and smooth the top. Press the almonds evenly into the meat. Roll up the lemon leaves and press them into the mixture. Bake for 15 minutes in a preheated oven at 160 °C (325 °F).
4. PREPARE THE TOPPING: Beat the eggs and stir in the milk. Add turmeric and season well with salt and pepper. Remove the dish from the oven and pour the egg mixture over. Return to the oven and bake for a further 25-30 minutes, until the egg mixture sets. Serve with Funeral rice (p. 122), Stewed dried fruit (chapter 14) and/or Sambals (chapter 16).

Denningvleis

(MAKES 6 SERVINGS)

2,5 kg mutton or lamb chops
4-6 large onions, halved lengthways,
    peeled and thinly sliced
25 ml (2 T) butter
24 garlic cloves, bruised, peeled and crushed

SPICE MIXTURE
2 large or 3 smaller whole nutmeg, grated
12 cloves
3 bay leaves
15 ml (3 t) black peppercorns
15 ml (3 t) salt
125 ml (½ cup) tamarind water

TO SERVE
extra grated nutmeg
a little balsamic vinegar

1. IN ADVANCE: Rinse meat well and pat dry. Place in the refrigerator.
2. Place onions in a saucepan and dot with butter. Place a sheet of greased waxed paper tightly on the surface of the onion mixture

It is best to potroast a leg of mutton and to oven roast a leg of lamb. When potroasting, a spoonful or two of oil is heated in a large, flat-based, cast-iron pot. The leg is seasoned with salt, pepper and herbs, and sometimes garlic is rubbed in. It is browned all over, then braised in stock and vegetables until cooked (as for mock venison, p. 68). The recipe for butterflied leg of mutton illustrates the oven-roasting method.

and cover. Heat over low heat and braise ± 30 minutes or until the onions are tender. Remove from the heat and allow to cool. Stir in half the garlic. Spoon the rest of the garlic into a small dish, cover with cling wrap and store in the refrigerator until needed. Remove the meat from the refrigerator and arrange in a single layer on a smooth surface. Spread the onion mixture over.
3. SPICE MIXTURE: Grind the nutmeg, cloves, bay leaves and peppercorns finely in a spice mill. Shake through a sieve. Add salt and mix. Sprinkle the spice mixture over the meat and onions. Arrange spiced uncooked meat in layers in a large enamel or ceramic container. Cover well with cling wrap and marinate overnight in the refrigerator.
4. Spoon the contents of the container into a large saucepan and cover. Heat to boiling point over moderate heat. Do not add any liquid at this stage. As the meat heats up, it will make its own liquid. Stir from time to time. Remove the lid once the meat reaches boiling point. Reduce the heat and simmer for ± 2 hours, until meat is tender.
5. Stir in reserved garlic and simmer for a further 15 minutes. Turn out into a flat pan and allow to cool. Refrigerate. The fat will set on top. Spoon off all the set fat with a large spoon. Remove bones.
6. Spoon the jellied liquid into a saucepan and boil until only about 125 ml (½ cup) of the liquid remains.
7. Spoon the boned meat into the saucepan and heat thoroughly, stirring constantly with a large fork. Add tamarind water, a little at a time, when the mixture becomes dry, to give the meat its characteristic dark colour and slightly sour taste.
8. TO SERVE: Make sure that the denningvleis is spicy. Taste and season with a little more nutmeg and a few drops of balsamic vinegar, if desired. Spoon onto plates and serve with Funeral rice (page 122) and Sambals (chapter 16).

Lamb and lentils

(MAKES 4-6 SERVINGS)

The older generation had a passion for lentils, which can be ascribed to their fascination with foods mentioned in the Bible, especially among Afrikaners. Lentils and chickpeas are currently in fashion again.

500 ml (2 cups) brown lentils, rinsed
25 ml (2 T) tomato concentrate
10 ml (2 t) coarsely chopped
 fresh rosemary
25 ml (2 T) melted mutton fat,
 lard or oil
1,25-1,5 kg breast of lamb,
 sawn into portions
10 ml (2 t) salt
2 onions, halved lengthways,
 peeled and coarsely chopped
4 plump garlic cloves, bruised,
 peeled and coarsely chopped
2 large or 4 medium carrots,
 scraped and sliced
freshly ground black pepper to taste
2 bay leaves, crushed
1 small stick cinnamon
a few springs of fresh thyme (optional)
500 ml (2 cups) hot, strong beef stock
37,5 ml (3 T) vinegar or lemon juice

TO SERVE
grated rind of 1 orange and 1 lemon
250 g smoked sausage, sliced

1. Spoon lentils into a small saucepan and cover with cold water. Add tomato concentrate and rosemary and heat to boiling point. Boil for 3 minutes, covered, remove from the heat and allow to stand for 1 hour.
2. Spoon half the fat into a heavy-bottomed saucepan and heat until hot but not smoking. Fry a few pieces of meat at a time until browned all over. Spoon out with a slotted spoon. Pour off fatty liquid from saucepan and add remaining fat to the saucepan. Heat until hot and brown the rest of the meat. Spoon out, season with half the salt and set aside.
3. Fry the onions until tender in the saucepan in which the meat was browned. Add the garlic and carrots and stir-fry for 3 minutes. Season with the remaining salt, lots of freshly ground pepper, bay leaves, cinnamon and thyme. Increase heat and add stock, which should be hot to ensure that meat mixture does not lose heat. Add the contents of the lentil saucepan. Reduce

the heat to very low, cover and simmer for 1½-2 hours until meat is tender.
4. Taste and season with salt if necessary. Sprinkle rind over and place sausage slices on top. Cover and simmer a further 8-10 minutes, until sausage is heated through. Serve with mashed potatoes.

Pienangvleis

(MAKES 8 SERVINGS)

2,5 kg mutton chops, wiped clean to remove
 any scraps of sawn bone
oil
salt and freshly ground pepper
12 garlic cloves, bruised, peeled and crushed
250 ml (1 cup) strong beef stock

CURRY
2 large onions, halved lengthways,
 peeled and finely chopped
25 ml (2 T) oil
1 piece (50 mm/2 in) fresh ginger root,
 peeled and finely chopped
6 garlic cloves, bruised, peeled and crushed
2-3 chillies, halved, seeded and chopped
100 ml (8 T) Sri Lankan spice mixture
 (p. 100) or mild curry powder
10 ml (2 t) turmeric
75 ml (6 T) tamarind water or plain water

1. Heat water to boiling point in a large saucepan. Add meat to water and remove immediately. Pat dry. Heat oil in a heavy-based saucepan and fry a few chops at a time until golden brown all over. Remove each batch and drain on kitchen paper. Season with salt and pepper. Spoon meat and garlic into a large saucepan, add hot stock and heat to boiling point over moderate heat. Reduce heat, cover with the lid and simmer until the meat is tender and falls off the bone – 2-2½ hours. Allow to cool. Refrigerate overnight.
2. Remove the fat congealed on the meat. Jug the meat and remove the bones.
3. CURRY: Fry the onions in oil until softened and transparent. Stir in the ginger, garlic and chillies and stir-fry for 2-3 minutes. Sprinkle the spice mixture and turmeric over and stir-fry for 2 minutes. Moisten frequently with a little tamarind water. Spoon boned meat into spice mixture and mix with a large two-pronged fork. Simmer over low heat until the meat is hot and fairly dry. This dish is a dry curry, not one with a sauce.
4. TO SERVE: Spoon a portion of meat per person into a ring mould and unmould on to a plate. Garnish with moulded Funeral rice (p. 122) and Sambals (p.156-157).

Ouvrou onder die kombers (a variation of toad-in-the-hole)

(MAKES 4 SERVINGS)

In the Karoo, Kalahari and former South-West Africa, mutton was traditionally used in this recipe. It's a sort of lazy-housewife recipe, because a batter replaces the pie crust. As time went on, many variations made their mark on this recipe and beef replaced mutton in other parts of the country. The dish is an example of something made from whatever is available: mutton, and yet more mutton, flavoured with whatever you have and covered with a batter. This is a slightly better flavoured version.

MINCE (OUVROU)
1 large onion, halved lengthways,
 peeled and finely chopped
25 ml (2 T) melted mutton fat or oil
1 kg minced mutton, uncooked
25 ml (2 T) vinegar
10 ml (2 t) salt
freshly ground black pepper to taste
grated nutmeg to taste
3 ml (½ t) ground cloves
5 ml (1 t) ground coriander

BATTER (KOMBERS)
250 ml (1 cup) cake flour, sifted
3 ml (½ t) salt
5 ml (1 t) baking powder
2 eggs, beaten
250 ml (1 cup) water
125 ml (½ cup) milk
125 g (125 ml/½ cup) melted mutton fat,
 lard or butter

1. MINCE: Fry the onion in the fat in a flat-based, cast-iron pot until softened and transparent, but not browned. Stir in meat, a little at a time, but make sure that meat is loose and not lumpy before adding the next batch. Season with vinegar, salt, pepper, nutmeg, cloves and coriander. Taste. Add more vinegar, if desired. Spoon meat into a baking dish, or leave it in the saucepan, and flatten it slightly with the back of a spoon.
2. BATTER: Sift the flour, salt and baking powder together. Beat the eggs, water and milk together and stir into the flour mixture. Stir in the fat and mix to a runny, smooth batter. Pour carefully over the meat. Cover and bake for 20-30 minutes in a preheated oven at 180 °C (350 °F).

DENNINGVLEIS

Potatoes, rice and meat

(MAKES 4-6 SERVINGS)

This is one of my favourite dishes from the Little Karoo, where I grew up. Once again, it is a combination of simple ingredients available to the cook. The potatoes brown deliciously, because the flavoursome stock is absorbed. This dish typifies the kind of food many Afrikaners enjoyed. Cook it in a three-legged pot, like the Voortrekkers used to do.

37,5 ml (3 T) rendered sheep-tail fat or oil
2 large onions, halved lengthways,
*   peeled and finely chopped*
1,5 kg neck of lamb, sawn into slices,
*   rinsed, patted dry and fat snipped*
4 plump garlic cloves, bruised,
*   peeled and crushed with:*
15 ml (3 t) salt
freshly ground pepper to taste
8 medium-sized potatoes, peeled and quartered
5 ml (1 t) grated nutmeg
500 g (625 ml/2½ cups) uncooked rice
2,5 litres (10 cups) hot beef stock

1. Heat fat in a large heavy-bottomed saucepan and fry onions until softened and transparent, but not browned. Spoon out and set aside. In the same saucepan, fry the meat slices, a few at a time, until golden brown on both sides. Remove each batch and set aside. Do not add to the onion mixture. Repeat with remaining meat. Season meat with garlic, salt and enough pepper.
2. Spoon the meat into the base of a saucepan or a large roasting pan. Arrange the potatoes on top of the meat and season with nutmeg. Spoon the onion mixture on top of the potatoes and sprinkle the rice over. Spoon the hot stock over slowly and season lightly with more salt. Cover and simmer for 2 hours over low heat or stew for 3-4 hours in a preheated oven at 160 °C (325 °F). The liquid will be absorbed by the rice by the time the stew is ready.

VARIATION

I sometimes spoon a layer of pitted prunes over the meat before arranging the potatoes on top. That is the way the Huguenots liked it.

Roast beef and Yorkshire pudding

(MAKES 6 SERVINGS)

The way you make Yorkshire pudding is a matter of interpretation, or reinterpretation – perhaps rather translation. Yorkshire pudding is a savoury batter, traditionally served in Yorkshire as a separate dish before the main course of meat – the reason was probably to fill stomachs and get away with having only a small quantity of meat. In South Africa, during the sixties and seventies, the rules for cooking meat were thrown overboard, and the pudding rather than the meat was cooked at a high heat. For this reason, it was baked on a rack just below the meat, so that the fat and juices from the meat dripped onto the batter during cooking.

Today, Yorkshire pudding is baked separately, this time in a muffin pan. The reason is self-explanatory. We have learnt that meat should rest before being carved. A new fashion has appeared on the scene: first, a starter is served, then a vegetable course and then, in this case, the meat with Yorkshire pudding and gravy. Yorkshire pudding may also be spooned into a rich brown onion soup, and served as a starter. I interpret the recipe as follows: spoon a rich meat gravy flavoured with onions and sweet wine onto a plate, then arrange slices of sirloin over the gravy, with the Yorkshire pudding at the centre, topped with a small garnish of fried onions. Finally, spoon an eighth of a teaspoonful of horse-radish cream onto each slice of meat.

1,5-2 kg chined wing rib or sirloin
salt and pepper
a little mustard powder and cayenne pepper
YORKSHIRE PUDDING
120 g (250 ml/1 cup) cake flour, sifted
3 ml (½ t) salt
2 extra-large eggs, beaten
250 ml (1 cup) milk
30 ml (6 t) pan juices

1. Season meat with salt, pepper, mustard powder and cayenne pepper (see p. 74).
2. Sift the flour and salt into a mixing bowl and make a hollow in the mixture. Pour the eggs and half the milk into the hollow. Gradually work the flour into the egg mixture with a fork. Using an electric hand beater or a wire whisk, beat the mixture for 5-10 minutes until bubbles form. Stir in the rest of the milk, cover the batter and allow to stand for 30 minutes. Preheat the oven to 220 °C (450 °F).

3. Spoon 5 ml (1 t) of the pan juices into each hollow of a 6-hollow muffin pan. Place the pan in the preheated oven until boiling hot. Remove from the oven, then divide the batter among the hollows, working quickly. Return to the oven immediately and bake for 20 minutes until the puddings have risen and are browned on top. Serve immediately. The baking time is the same as the resting time for meat in the warming drawer.

Chateaubriand with béarnaise sauce

(MAKES 4 SERVINGS)

During the good old days, South Africa could boast of an unusual number of good hotels, some of them world-class. Most hotels imported chefs from France, England, Holland and, to a lesser extent, Italy. The Mount Nelson in Cape Town and the Carlton Hotel in Johannesburg consequently built up an enviable reputation for quality service and excellent food. Those were the days of Russian tea and the silver service. With a few exceptions, this peak of perfection began to wane in the fifties and sixties, and by the seventies the Holiday Inns and Sun hotels with their buffet meals took over. If I'm not mistaken, it was between 1960 and 1961 that Urbaniac, general manager of the last of the world-class city hotels, the Grand Hotel in Adderley Street, invited Raymond Oliver to come to Cape Town as guest chef. Oliver was the first French chef to become a television star and was the owner of the famous Grand Véfour restaurant in Paris. The main dish at the gala dinner was chateaubriand with béarnaise sauce and château potatoes – most innovative for the time.

Chateaubriand is more English than it is French, because the French chef Montmireil got to know it in England, where the meat was cut from the sirloin, not the fillet. It was not, naturally, known by this name. A French writer, Viscount Chateaubriand (1768-1848) learnt it from his chef, Montmireil. The chef developed his own, juicier version by using the eye fillet, tying it between two thick sirloin steaks and then grilling it over the fire. The blackened sirloin steaks on either side of the fillet were discarded and the juicy fillet carved and served – in honour of his employer, Chateaubriand, with château sauce and château potatoes (a tarragon-flavoured meat sauce and roast baby potatoes respectively).

It was the great French chef Auguste Escoffier who, at the beginning of the century, specified that chateaubriand should be served with Colbert sauce and *pommes château* (Château potatoes, p. 138) and that the fillet should not be more than 500 g. Colbert sauce is a rich meat sauce into which lots of butter, parsley, tarragon and lemon juice are beaten. By the fifties it was served with Béarnaise sauce, a rich egg and butter sauce flavoured with tarragon leaves and tarragon vinegar. That is how I got to know it at the Grand Hotel. For the next two decades, it was the favourite dinner choice for upper-crust South Africans.

2 pieces chateaubriand (upper, thick part
of beef fillet), each ± 500 g
salt and freshly ground black pepper
12,5 ml (2 T) oil mixed with:
15 ml (3 t) melted, clarified butter

SAUCE
2 spring onions or 1 small onion,
peeled and chopped
50 ml (4 T) tarragon vinegar
50 ml (4 T) dry white wine
3 ml (½ t) finely chopped fresh tarragon leaves
(reserve stripped stems)
5 white peppercorns, crushed
3 extra-large egg yolks
250 g (250 ml/1 cup) ice-cold butter, cubed
5 ml (1 t) chopped fresh chervil or parsley
5-10 ml (1-2 t) lemon juice
grated rind of 1 lemon
salt and freshly ground white pepper
pinch cayenne pepper

1. Tie the meat at 25 mm (1 in) intervals with string. Season meat with salt and pepper, place on the oiled rack of a roasting pan and roast for 45-60 minutes in a preheated oven at 160 °C (325 °F). Baste from time to time with the oil and butter mixture. Allow to rest in the warming drawer for at least 20 minutes.

2. SAUCE: Spoon the spring onions, vinegar, wine, tarragon stems and pepper into a small saucepan, heat to boiling point and boil over moderate heat until the liquid has almost evaporated. Rub the mixture through a sieve into a large glass mixing bowl and allow to cool slightly. Add egg yolks and beat until mixed. Place the mixing bowl over a saucepan of slowly simmering water. Add the butter, cube by cube, beating constantly until each cube has been thoroughly incorporated before adding the next. Stir in the chopped tarragon leaves, chervil, lemon juice and rind. Taste and season with salt, pepper, cayenne pepper and more lemon juice, if necessary.

3. TO SERVE: Carve the meat and serve with the sauce and fried potatoes or Château potatoes (p. 138).

HINT: Remove tarragon stems from the evaporated liquid and spoon the contents of the saucepan into a food processor. Add the egg yolks and switch on the machine. Leave it switched on for 2-3 minutes. Meanwhile, melt the butter and skim off the froth. Heat the butter to boiling point over moderate heat until it begins to bubble. Add to the egg yolk mixture in a thin stream, with the machine running. Complete recipe.

Beef olives

(MAKES 4 SERVINGS)

This dish was first served at the beginning of the nineteenth century, during the Second British Occupation, with the name 'olives of birds'. Cooks to the Cape's high society changed it to beef olives, and the Dutch named it 'blindevinke'. In rural areas, sausage meat is often used as a filling.

12 thin slices veal or beef, cut from the topside
salt and pepper
12 fresh sage leaves (optional)

FILLING
1 small onion, peeled and finely chopped
25 ml (2 T) butter
500 g minced pork
50 ml (4 T) fresh breadcrumbs, lightly toasted
25 ml (2 T) sweet sherry
5 ml (1 t) chopped fresh or 3 ml (½ t) dried
mixed herbs
15 ml (3 t) chopped fresh parsley
salt and freshly ground pepper
1 small egg, lightly beaten

TO COOK
30 ml (6 t) oil
1 large onion, peeled and thinly sliced
lengthways
1 large carrot, scraped and thinly sliced
1 celery stalk, rinsed, strings removed,
and sliced
15 ml (3 t) tomato concentrate
50 ml (4 T) sweet wine, muscadel or port
250 ml (1 cup) hot beef stock

TO SERVE
25 ml (2 T) snipped chives

1. Place a slice of meat between 2 layers of waxed paper and beat lightly with a meat mallet to flatten. Roll out thinly with a rolling pin. Repeat with remaining meat. Trim loose pieces at sides. Season lightly with salt and pepper and place a sage leaf (if used) on each slice.

2. FILLING: Fry the onion in butter until softened and transparent, but not browned. Remove from the heat, allow to cool and mix with pork, crumbs, sherry, herbs and parsley. Season well with salt and pepper. Add egg and mix with a large two-pronged fork. Divide filling into 12 portions and spread one quantity over each slice of meat. Roll up and tie securely with thin string. Repeat with remaining filling and meat.

3. TO COOK: Heat the oil in a large flat-bottomed saucepan or cast-iron pot. Fry 4 beef olives at a time until golden brown all over and remove. Place the onion, carrot and celery in the same saucepan in which the meat was fried and stir-fry until softened. Add the tomato concentrate, sweet wine and stock. Return the meat to the pan, heat to boiling point then reduce the heat, cover and simmer for 1½-2 hours until the meat is tender. Remove the beef olives, discard the string and spoon the sauce over. Sprinkle chives on top. Serve with Creamed potatoes (p. 140).

HOW TO COOK VEAL AND BEEF
Veal and beef are cooked according to two basic heat methods:
MOIST-HEAT METHOD: bolo, hump, shin, neck, thick and flat rib, brisket, thin and thick flank, topside, silverside and aitchbone.
DRY-HEAT METHOD: steaks, prime and wing rib, flank, fillet and rump.

Beef Wellington

(MAKES 8 SERVINGS)

A South African hostess of the sixties and seventies who did not have Beef Wellington – or *boeuf en croûte*, as it was known in the original French – in her repertoire was considered uncultured. There were many versions. The generally accepted version was the one in which fried mushrooms and duck liver were spread over the fillet before it was wrapped in the pastry and baked. It was served with Madeira sauce – a rich meat sauce prepared with sweet wine, especially muscadel.

PASTRY
750 g (6 x 250 ml / 6 cups) cake flour, sifted
5 ml (1 t) salt
250 g (250 ml / 1 cup) salted butter,
*   coarsely grated and chilled until ice cold*
250 g (250 ml / 1 cup) vegetable fat,
*   cubed and chilled until ice cold*
1 egg, lightly beaten
± 125 ml (½ cup) ice-cold water

FILLING
50 ml (4 T) butter
1 large, prepared fillet, eye cut out and the
*   bottom, pointed end folded back before being*
*   tied, weighing ± 1,2 kg*
50 ml (4 T) brandy
6-8 rashers streaky bacon, chopped
250 g brown mushrooms,
*   peeled and sliced across*
salt and freshly ground black pepper
1-2 ml (1-2 pinches) each cayenne pepper
*   and mustard powder*
50 ml (4 T) finely chopped fresh parsley
*   and/or chives*
1 egg, lightly beaten
250 g Chicken liver pâté (p. 88)
*   or spread (see Hint)*

SAUCE
100 g (100 ml / 8 T) butter
1 large onion, halved lengthways,
*   peeled and finely chopped*
10 ml (2 t) chopped fresh thyme
750 ml (3 cup) strong beef stock
150 ml (⅗ cup) white or red muscadel
50 ml (4 T) sweet sherry or port

1. PASTRY: Sift the flour and salt into a large mixing bowl. Add butter, fat, egg and water and mix with a spatula to a coarse, lumpy dough. Turn out onto a floured surface and complete as for pastry for Steak and kidney pie (p. 94).

2. FILLING: Melt the butter in a large frying pan and heat until very hot and on the point of browning. Place the fillet in the frying pan and fry until golden brown all over. Pour brandy over and ignite. Remove fillet from the pan, allow to cool on a wire rack and place in the freezer until ice cold. Take care that the meat does not freeze; remove it after ± 10 minutes and place it in the refrigerator.
3. Fry the bacon in the same frying pan over low heat until crisp. Add the mushrooms and fry over low heat until all the liquid has evaporated. Season well with salt, black pepper, cayenne pepper and mustard powder. Remove from the heat and stir in the herbs. Spoon into a colander to drain, and set aside to cool.
4. Divide the pastry into 2 pieces and roll each out into a rectangle ± 200 mm (8 in) wide and ± 100 mm (4 in) longer than the length of the fillet. Brush one rectangle with egg and spoon the mushroom mixture in the centre, over the entire length of the pastry. Remove the string with which the fillet was tied, season meat well with salt and pepper and place it on top of the mushroom mixture.
5. Slice the liver pâté thinly and arrange slices on top of the fillet. Fold the long edges of the pastry rectangle up against the sides of the fillet and press to secure. Brush egg on the outside of the pastry.
6. Cut the second pastry rectangle smaller and reserve the long strips for decoration. Place the second rectangle on top of the fillet, so that the sides hang over those of the

first rectangle and almost reach the bottom. Press to secure. Make 3 diagonal incisions ± 37,5 mm (1½ inches) long in the top layer to allow steam to escape during baking. This ensures that the pastry touching the surface of the meat will not soften. Attach reserved pastry strips to top of pie – drape them, criss-cross them or cut them in leaves and attach them with egg. Brush the remaining egg over the pastry and decorations. Place on a baking sheet and place in the freezer until ice cold. Preheat the oven to 220 °C (460 °F) and roast meat for 30 minutes.
7. MEANWHILE, PREPARE THE SAUCE: Melt 25 ml (2 T) butter in a frying pan and fry the onion until softened and transparent, but not browned. Add the thyme, stock and wine and heat to just under boiling point. Reduce the heat and simmer until the sauce has reduced by half. Remove from the heat and pour through a sieve. Beat in the remaining butter, a little at a time, and finish with sherry.
8. Place the meat on a wooden carving board with a broad silver rim and pour the sauce into a heated sauce boat. The host carves the meat and each guest spoons sauce onto his or her plate. Traditionally, this dish is served with grilled tomatoes and steamed broccoli, seasoned with butter and nutmeg.

HINT: Buy chicken spread and spread over fillet, or simply fry chicken or duck livers marinated in sweet wine, and arrange on top of fillet. Ready-made puff pastry or sour cream pastry may, of course, also be used.

HOW TO GRILL A STEAK
Choose well-ripened, good-quality meat and ripen, uncovered, on a rack in the refrigerator for a further 2-3 days. This is the first step towards serving a good steak. The steaks should be about 50 mm (2 in) thick. Heat a ridged cast-iron grilling pan until very hot. Pour in a little oil and heat until smoking. Grill fillet steak first on one side, then on the other, until browned and cooked to the desired degree of doneness. It is preferable not to keep on turning the steaks. Fillets will cook more quickly than T-bones or rump and should not be cooked to more than medium done. It's at its best rare. Place grilled meat on the rack of a roasting pan and keep warm in a warming drawer. Do not keep warm for longer than 20 minutes, otherwise the meat will cook further. Season now – never before cooking – with salt and pepper and serve.

Corned beef

The name 'corned beef' is used for virtually any pickled beef cut. The most popular cuts are the breast and, especially, silverside. Cook it like Pickled tongue (p. 94) and calculate the cooking time at 25-30 minutes for every 500 g meat. Serve with peeled potatoes, cooked in salted water, then covered with melted butter and flavoured with chopped parsley, and with braised cabbage and boiled carrots or parsnips.

Osso buco

(MAKES 6 SERVINGS)

The Milanese version of osso buco was popularised here by Italian prisoners of war. South Africa has a close-knit Italian community, many of whom work in the food industry.

3-4 veal shanks, sawn into 50 mm
   (2 in) thick slices
salt and pepper
± 50 ml (4 T) cake flour
50 ml (4 T) olive oil
25 ml (2 T) butter
1 large onion or 2 medium-sized onions,
   halved lengthways, peeled and chopped
3 garlic cloves, bruised,
   peeled and crushed with:
5 ml (1 t) salt
1 large or 2 small carrots,
   scraped and coarsely grated
1 celery stalk, washed, strings removed,
   and coarsely chopped
250 ml (1 cup) meat stock
500 ml (2 cups) dry white wine
75 ml (6 T) tomato concentrate
5 ml (1 t) chopped fresh sage
   or 3 ml (½ t) dried sage
5 ml (1 t) chopped fresh rosemary
   or 3 ml (½ t) dried rosemary

TOPPING
1 quantity Citrus herb mixture (p. 85)

1. Rinse shanks under cold running water and pat dry. Season with salt and pepper. Season flour with salt and pepper. Roll meat in flour and shake off the excess.
2. Place the oil and butter in a large, heavy-bottomed saucepan and heat over high heat until the butter has melted. Fry the shanks quickly, a few slices at a time, in the oil mixture until browned all over, and remove. If the oil mixture is not hot enough, the flour will remain in the oil and stick to the saucepan.
3. Place the onion, garlic and salt, carrot and celery in the same saucepan in which the meat was fried, and stir-fry for 2-3 minutes. Add 50 ml (4 T) of the stock and stir. Cover, reduce heat and simmer for 10 minutes until the vegetables are tender.
4. Meanwhile, heat the remaining stock, the wine and tomato concentrate to boiling point in a separate, small saucepan. Add the meat to the vegetables and pour the boiling stock mixture over. Sprinkle the sage and rosemary over. Cover, heat to boiling point, then reduce the heat and simmer for ± 2 hours until the meat is meltingly tender.
5. Spoon the shanks into an attractive serving dish and sprinkle citrus herb mixture over liberally. Serve with Risotto (p. 123) or buttered noodles.

Frikkadels

A frikkadel or rissole is only as good as the meat from which it is made, the way it is seasoned, how the balls are shaped and, last but not least, how it is cooked. Some swear by a mixture of minced beef and pork. Sprinkle with roasted coriander, shaken through a sieve, and season with salt, freshly ground pepper and thyme. Do not mix. Cover with cling wrap and leave overnight in the refrigerator. Mix lightly but thoroughly and shape into balls. Some cooks use an ice-cream scoop; others drop a spoonful in a cup and shake the cup, turning it at the same time, to form rissoles. Do not knead or press the meat mixture – that is when you get heavy-as-lead frikkadels.

If baking frikkadels in the oven, preheat the oven to 160 °C (325 °F). Do not bake for too long, because the meat juices evaporate and the frikkadels will be hard.

Frikkadels cooked in liquid on top of the stove should simmer long and slowly over low heat. Small frikkadels fried in a frying pan should be cooked over moderate heat, so that they will be golden brown and crisp all over and just cooked inside.

Drain on kitchen paper and serve.

Curried banana frikkadels

(MAKES 12 LARGE FRIKKADELS)

In the mid-nineties, readers of my food column in *Rapport* voted for the Frikkadel of the Decade. This recipe, one of thousands, won. It is a national asset.

FRIKKADELS
1 large onion, peeled and finely chopped
12,5 ml (1 T) oil
75 ml (6 T) milk
2 thick slices day-old white bread,
   crusts removed
1-2 carrots, scraped and coarsely grated
1 extra-large egg, beaten
800 g minced lean beef
50 ml (4 T) chutney
25 ml (2 T) vinegar
15-20 ml (3-4 t) salt
freshly ground pepper and grated nutmeg to taste
1 ml (pinch) ground cloves
Worcestershire sauce to taste (optional)

SAUCE
15 ml (3 t) oil
15 ml (3 t) butter
3 onions, halved lengthways, peeled and sliced
2 garlic cloves, bruised,
   peeled and crushed with:
5 ml (1 t) salt
12,5 ml (1 T) Indian spice mixture
   (p. 100) or other hot curry powder
12,5 ml (1 T) turmeric
3 ml (½ t) each ground ginger and cinnamon
1 ml (pinch) cayenne pepper or to taste
75 ml (6 T) vinegar
50 ml (4 T) smooth apricot jam
50 ml (4 T) chutney
25 ml (2 T) soft brown sugar
freshly ground pepper to taste
500 ml (2 cups) water
6-10 very ripe, almost over-ripe, bananas,
   peeled, sliced and covered with lemon juice

1. FRIKKADELS: Fry the onion in oil until softened and transparent, but not browned. Set aside to cool. Meanwhile, pour the milk slowly over the bread and leave to soak thoroughly. Squeeze out the excess milk and mash the soaked bread with a fork. Spoon the cold onion, bread, carrot and egg over the meat. Do not mix. Spoon the chutney and vinegar over and season with salt, pepper, nutmeg, cloves and Worcestershire sauce (if used). Mix all ingredients lightly but thoroughly with a large, two-pronged fork. Do not knead or press the mixture. Shape 12 frikkadels as described above. Arrange the frikkadels in a single layer in a lightly greased baking dish, cover and place in the refrigerator.
2. SAUCE: Heat oil and butter in a deep saucepan over moderate heat until butter has melted. Add onions and fry until softened and transparent, but definitely not browned. Add garlic and salt and stir-fry for 1 minute. Sprinkle the spice mixture and turmeric over and stir-fry until a strong aroma is released. Stir in the ginger, cinnamon and cayenne pepper and add the vinegar, a little at a time. Stir, scraping the base of the saucepan to loosen any pieces that adhere. Take care: the mixture should not stick to the saucepan. Add the jam, chutney, sugar, pepper and half the water. Heat to boiling point. Reduce heat and simmer for 5 minutes. Add remaining water, increase the heat, heat to boiling point again and boil for 10-15 minutes. Stir from time to time.
3. Remove the sauce from the heat and stir in the banana slices. Remove the frikkadels from the refrigerator and spoon the hot sauce over. Bake for 40-45 minutes in a preheated oven at 160 °C (325 °F) until the meat is cooked. Serve with rice.

Hamburgers

(MAKES 8 PATTIES)

The American influence on South Africa is far greater than most people realise. Our favourite entertainment is television with its American soaps, we prefer drinking Coca-Cola to home-made ginger beer, and hamburgers and chips are our favourite fast food.

500 g minced lean beef
1 onion, halved lengthways, peeled and chopped
1 thick slice white bread, soaked in:
125 ml (½ cup) milk
salt and freshly ground pepper to taste
12,5 ml (1 T) chopped fresh mixed herbs, like thyme, tarragon, basil, marjoram, parsley and chives
1 egg, beaten (optional)
75 ml (6 T) oatmeal (optional)
oil

1. Mix all the ingredients lightly with a fork. If egg is used, oatmeal must also be used – it 'stretches' the meat mixture.
2. Shape 8 flat hamburger patties and sift a little flour over both sides of the patties. Place on a tray lined with waxed paper, cover with cling wrap and refrigerate for 30 minutes.
3. Heat a little oil in a frying pan and fry 2 patties at a time on both sides until cooked. Keep warm in the warming drawer. Serve on buttered hamburger rolls with lettuce leaves, slices of pickled gherkins, tomato and onion slices, cheese slices or thin slices of fresh or canned pineapple rings.

Venison pie

(MAKES 6 SERVINGS)

MARINADE
50 ml (4 T) apple, quince or marula jelly
25 ml (2 T) wine vinegar
125 ml (½ cup) muscadel
1 small onion, peeled and sliced
1 fresh sprig thyme or 5 ml (1 t) dried thyme
3-5 juniper berries, crushed
freshly ground black pepper
    and grated nutmeg to taste
2 kg venison shoulder or leg,
    cut into 25 mm (1 in) cubes
500 g pork, cubed

TO COOK
30 g (30 ml/6 t) butter
20 ml (4 t) olive oil
125 g streaky bacon, shredded
1 onion, halved lengthways, peeled and chopped
2 plump garlic cloves, bruised, peeled and crushed
100 g speck or sheep-tail fat, minced
salt, pepper and nutmeg
2-3 cloves
50 ml (4 T) brown vinegar
2 bay leaves
250 ml (1 cup) meat stock
puff pastry
1 egg, beaten with:
1 ml (pinch) salt

1. MARINADE: Melt the jelly and allow to cool. Add the vinegar and muscadel and mix. Add the onion, thyme and juniper berries and season with pepper and nutmeg. Pour the marinade over the venison and pork, mix, cover with cling wrap and marinate overnight in the refrigerator.
2. TO COOK: Remove the meat from the marinade. Pour the marinade through a sieve and reserve the liquid. Pat the meat dry. Melt the butter in a large frying pan, add oil and heat until very hot. Fry the meat, a little at a time, until browned all over. Transfer each batch to a large saucepan or flat-bottomed, cast-iron pot, using a slotted spoon. Fry the bacon in the same pan until cooked and nearly crisp. Add onion, garlic and speck and fry until onion has softened and the speck begins to crisp. Remove with a slotted spoon and add to the meat. Season well with salt, pepper and nutmeg and add cloves, vinegar and bay leaves.
3. Pour off the excess fat from the saucepan in which the meat and onion were fried. Heat the pan over high heat, add the reserved marinade and boil until the marinade is reduced by half. Add the stock and heat to boiling point. Scrape off pieces adhering to the base of the pan, stirring until they dissolve in the liquid. Pour over meat. Heat the saucepan containing the meat to boiling point, reduce the heat and simmer for 3-4 hours. Add more meat stock or water if it cooks dry.
4. Allow to cool, shred the meat and spoon it into a baking dish. Preheat the oven to 230 °C (450 °F).
5. Roll out the pastry (see Chicken pie, p. 108) and place on top of meat (see Steak and kidney pie, p. 94). Bake for 15 minutes. Reduce oven temperature to 180 °C (350 °F) and bake for a further 30-35 minutes. Serve with stewed dried fruit (chapter 14).

Potroast leg or shoulder of venison

(MAKES 4 SERVINGS)

1 small leg or shoulder of venison, larded with speck (see Mock leg of venison, p. 68)
1 carton (500 ml/2 cups) buttermilk
500 g mixed dried fruit
375 ml (1½ cups/½ bottle) white or red muscadel, port or Old Brown Sherry
2 cloves
1 cinnamon stick
salt and freshly ground black pepper
10 juniper berries, bruised
30 ml (6 t) oil
1 onion, halved lengthways, peeled and sliced
2 plump garlic cloves, bruised, peeled and crushed
1 carrot, scraped and thinly sliced
2 bay leaves
250 ml (1 cup) meat stock
fresh or dried naartjie peel

1. Place the meat in an enamel casserole dish and pour the buttermilk over. Cover with cling wrap and marinate overnight in the refrigerator.
2. Spoon the dried fruit, wine, cloves and cinnamon into a mixing bowl. Cover with cling wrap and leave to stand overnight.
3. Remove the meat from the marinade, wipe it clean and pat dry with kitchen paper. Season well with salt and pepper and rub juniper berries in all over.
4. Heat the oil in a large, heavy-based saucepan and fry the onion, garlic and carrot for 3 minutes. Remove with a slotted spoon and set aside.
5. Fry the meat in the same saucepan until browned all over. Return the onion mixture and add the bay leaves.
6. Pour off the liquid, if any, from the dried fruit and add it to the stock. Add the stock mixture to the meat, cover and simmer for 2 hours. Add a little water or more stock, if necessary. Add the soaked fruit, cinnamon, cloves and naartjie peel and potroast, uncovered, for a further 30 minutes. Serve with Game chips (p. 138).

Suckling pig

Suckling pigs are not freely available, and must be ordered from a butcher in plenty of time. They can be braaied over the coals or cooked in the oven – provided the pig will fit in your oven. Many cooks prefer to bone the breast cavity and fill it with a stuffing. Pork sausage pressed out of the skin and mixed lightly with chopped fried onion, chopped fresh pineapple, pineapple sage and macadamia nuts, makes an excellent stuffing. Rub salt, freshly ground pepper and mustard powder thoroughly into the meat. Stuff the breast cavity lightly and close the opening with thread or secure it with skewers. Cut a diamond pattern lightly in the rind, without cutting into the meat. A few cloves – not too many – can be inserted here and there. Preheat the oven to 160 °C (325 °F). Rub olive oil over the pig and roast it for 25 minutes for each 500 g, plus an extra 25-30 minutes. Test if the meat is done: insert a skewer in the thickest part of the leg, without touching the bone, and remove it. Press the meat. If pink liquid comes out, the meat must be cooked for longer. Serve with baked quinces, baked apples or any other fruit, or fruit jellies like Kei apple, marula, quince or apple jelly.

Glazed Kassler rib

(MAKES 8 SERVINGS)

1 Kassler rib, ± 3 kg
100 ml (8 T) apple juice
25 ml (2 T) brandy
1 tin (410 g) apricots, drained
5 ml (1 t) peeled, finely chopped,
   fresh ginger root
5 ml (1 t) finely grated lemon rind
10 ml (2 t) sugar

1. Place a large sheet of aluminium foil, shiny side up, on a smooth surface. Place the meat on it and pull up the sides of the foil to make a 'dish' around the meat. Sprinkle the apple juice and brandy over. Close the foil and place meat in a baking dish. Bake for 2 hours in a preheated oven at 160 °C (325 °F) or until meat is tender.
2. Purée the apricots, ginger root and lemon rind. Open the foil and spread the glaze over. Switch on the grilling element of the oven. Sprinkle sugar over the meat and allow to melt under the grill. Serve with boiled potatoes and red cabbage.

Pork baked in milk

(MAKES 6 SERVINGS)

A simple and really delicious dish, served with baked sweet potatoes.

1,5 kg boned pork thick rib, rolled and tied

MARINADE
125 ml (½ cup) virgin olive oil
   (sunflower oil will also do)
15 ml (3 t) vinegar
3 plump garlic cloves, bruised,
   peeled and crushed
1 sprig fresh rosemary

TO BAKE
salt and pepper
1 litre (4 cups) milk

1. Mix the marinade ingredients in a baking dish. Place the meat in it, cover and marinate for 24 hours in the refrigerator. Turn once or twice.
2. Remove the meat and season with salt and pepper. Return to the marinade and add the milk. Do not cover the baking dish. Bake for 1 hour in a preheated oven at 180 °C (350 °F) and turn meat from time to time. Increase temperature to 200 °C (400 °F) and bake for a further 20-30 minutes. Baste meat often. Remove the string and slice the meat. Pour the sauce remaining in the baking dish through a sieve, over the meat and serve with baked sweet potatoes, Candied sweet potatoes (p. 135) or apples.

Loin of pork with mango purée

(MAKES 6 SERVINGS)

± 2 kg boned pork loin
salt and freshly ground pepper

BASTING SAUCE
12,5 ml (1 T) butter
12,5 ml (1 T) oil
2-3 plump garlic cloves, bruised and peeled
125 ml (½ cup) dry white wine
125 ml (½ cup) freshly squeezed orange juice
10 ml (2 t) grated orange rind
5-10 ml (1-2 t) salt
freshly ground black pepper to taste
10 ml (2 t) chopped fresh tarragon
   or sage or 5 ml (1 t) dried tarragon or sage
1 kg pickling onions, peeled
25 ml (2 T) soft brown sugar

MANGO PURÉE
2 ripe mangoes, peeled
5 ml (1 t) lemon juice
5 ml (1 t) grated orange rind
125 ml (½ cup) orange juice
salt and cayenne pepper

1. Cut the rind off the loin, season meat lightly with salt and pepper, roll up and secure with string.
2. BASTING SAUCE: Place the butter and oil in a small saucepan and add the garlic. Fry for 5 minutes over low heat, until the butter mixture has a strong garlic aroma. Add the white wine, juice and rind, heat to boiling point, boil for 30 seconds and remove from the heat. Preheat the oven to 160 °C (325 °F).
3. Season the meat on the outside with salt, pepper and tarragon. Place the meat, fat side up, on the rack of a roasting pan and roast 25-30 minutes for every 500 g, plus an extra 25 minutes. Baste the meat often with the basting sauce.
4. About 45 minutes before the end of the cooking time, spoon the onions into the pan, under the meat. Sprinkle the sugar over. Stir from time to time and baste with pan juices.
5. Meanwhile, make the mango purée: Cut the mango flesh off the stone and place it in a food processor. Add the orange juice and rind and purée. Taste and season with salt and cayenne pepper. Place the purée in the refrigerator until ice cold.
6. TO SERVE: Slice the meat and serve with onions, mashed potatoes and ice-cold mango purée.

Festive ham

(MAKES 18-24 SERVINGS)

This meat dish has become part of the Christmas table, and no buffet would be complete without a glazed ham. Ham can be cooked in various ways, but the best method remains poaching it until cooked and then glazing it. Modern pickling methods make it unnecessary to soak ham overnight in cold water before cooking it. Make sure that you have a saucepan large enough to cook the ham in.

5-8 kg ham
2 carrots, scraped and thickly sliced
1 celery stalk, washed and
    cut into 3 pieces
1 turnip, peeled, quartered and
    covered with water to which
    lemon juice has been added
1 large onion, peeled, studded with 6 cloves
1 Bouquet garni (p. 44)
12 black peppercorns

GLAZE
250 ml (1 cup) apple juice
37,5 ml (3 T) soft brown sugar
37,5 ml (3 T) honey, golden syrup
    or smooth apricot jam
12,5 ml (1 T) mustard powder

TOPPING
cloves
extra sugar

1. Place ham in a large saucepan and cover with water. Add the carrots, celery, turnip, onion, bouquet garni and peppercorns. Heat to boiling point, skim off froth and cover. Reduce heat and simmer as follows: 30 minutes for every 500 g meat or until a strip of skin is easy to pull off. Remove from the liquid and reserve liquid. Cool slightly. Pull off the rind (outer skin) and return the ham to the liquid to cool completely. This ensures that the ham will be succulent.
2. GLAZE: Mix the juice, sugar, honey and mustard powder and stir over low heat until the sugar has dissolved. Remove the glaze

from the heat and set aside. Preheat the oven to 160 °C (325 °F).
3. Cut a diamond pattern in the fat layer, using a sharp knife. Press a clove in the centre of each diamond. Brush half the glaze over the ham and bake for 30-45 minutes. Brush the ham often with the remaining glaze during baking. Sprinkle the last quantity of sugar over and allow to melt under the grill. Remove the ham from the oven. Slice thickly and serve hot. The ham can also be served cold, but then the slices must be thin. Serve with Slaphakskeentjies (p. 150).

Beef and pork frikkadels with sesame seeds

(MAKES 6 SERVINGS)

This recipe dates from the seventies, when pizza cheese and sesame seeds were new on the scene.

FRIKKADELS
60 g (250 ml / 1 cup) fresh breadcrumbs,
    well seasoned
125 ml (½ cup) milk
1 small onion, peeled and chopped
10 ml (2 t) oil
250 g minced beef
250 g minced pork
salt and pepper
15 ml (3 t) chopped fresh herbs, e.g. rosemary,
    oregano, basil and thyme
175 g mozzarella or pizza cheese,
    cut into 18 cubes
50 ml (4 T) cake flour
2 egg whites, lightly whisked
1 packet (100 g) sesame seeds

TO FRY
50 ml (4 T) oil

TO SERVE
fried chippolata sausages

1. Place the crumbs in a large mixing bowl. Add the milk and set aside. Fry the onion in oil until softened and transparent, but not browned. Allow to cool and add to

crumbs. Add the meat and season with salt and pepper. Sprinkle the herbs over and mix with a large, two-pronged fork. Shape into 18 frikkadels and flatten lightly. Place cube of cheese on each frikkadel and roll the frikkadel to enclose the cheese. Roll frikkadels in flour and dip first in egg whites and lastly in sesame seeds.
2. Heat the oil in a large frying pan until fairly hot and place the frikkadels in the pan. Fry on both sides until golden brown. Thread 3 frikkadels onto kebab sticks alternately with hot chippolata sausages, and serve with fried sweet pepper strips.

Sweet and sour pork stir-fry

(MAKES 4 SERVINGS)

The Chinese sweet and sour stir-fry was popular among South Africans long before the arrival here of the electric frying pan, the wok and stir-fried meals at home. In the large cities, Chinese restaurants were always packed, mainly because their food was affordable.

30 ml (6 t) oil
800 g boned pork thick rib, cut into thin strips
1 onion, halved lengthways,
    peeled and sliced very thinly
1 celery stalk, rinsed, strings removed and cut
    diagonally into 50 mm (2 in) lengths,
    and each slice cut into 4 strips
1 small pineapple, peeled, sliced
    and cut into thin strips
25 ml (2 T) brown sugar
25 ml (2 T) wine vinegar
25 ml (2 T) soy sauce
25 ml (2 T) dry sherry
salt and freshly ground pepper

Heat oil until smoking in a wok or frying pan. Add the meat and stir quickly to blend. Add the onion and stir-fry for 1 minute. Add the celery and pineapple and stir-fry for 2 minutes. Add the sugar, vinegar, soy sauce and sherry and season with salt and pepper. Stir to blend and serve with fried rice.

BEEF AND PORK FRIKKADELS WITH SESAME SEEDS AND CHIPPOLATAS, SERVED WITH STIR-FRIED SWEET PEPPERS

Bredie is a blessing

 THE VINE LEAVES have turned pontacq red and the first rains of winter have arrived. Blush-pink and bright yellow *surings* appear in the *vlei* (marshes). The boer pumpkins are on the roof, and in the avenue the quinces are bright yellow. Ouma's black, flat-bottomed pot has been cleaned and rubbed with garlic. It's time to make one of our timeless recipes, so dear to our hearts. We are dealing with bredies, for centuries a unique South African culinary creation.

If you don't have common sense, you will never understand a bredie. If you don't have the time, you should never cook it; and if you do not possess the gift of hospitality, don't ever serve it. Bredies are meant for the wise, but not everyone is wise.

Bredies are simply mutton cooked long and slowly with fruit or vegetables and flavourings, so that the result is neither meat nor vegetable but a delectable mingling of flavours. In short: a new flavour, a new taste experience.

There are bredies – and then there are bredies. The best-known are undoubtedly tomato bredie or green-bean bredie. Wild asparagusbush (*veldkool*) bredie – which I would prefer to call by its old name, *hotnot-skool* – and waterblommetjie bredie are Cape regional foods. But bredies have a wider repertoire than this. Asparagus, artichokes, wild sorrel (oxalis, *suring*), beetroot, beans, maize, cauliflower, broccoli, Brussels sprouts, baby marrows and all the different kinds of

pumpkin, particularly boer pumpkins. And fruit: dried apricots, peaches and prunes; fresh fruit like mangoes, bananas, quinces, apples, pears, pineapple … bright yellow quinces are closest to my heart.

First, we have to choose the meat. Mutton with a true Karoo-bush flavour; merino rather than dorper. Short ribs, neatly sawn and all connective tissue wiped with a vinegar-soaked cloth. A piece of neck sawn into slices and cleaned well and, for those with an unbridled desire for meat, boned shoulder, neatly cubed. Ouma's pot is heated and a piece of sheep-tail fat slowly rendered, for the fat. The *kaiings* (crackling) are removed, the fat is poured off, leaving only enough to brown the meat long and slowly, a little at a time. All the fat is again poured off. The meat returns to the pot. An onion or two, peeled and sliced, is added, as well as a little crushed garlic. The lid is put on and the slow braising begins. The meat must not be rushed; wait until a thin layer of 'marmite' forms on the base of the pot, then add a tea-spoonful of sugar, a stick of cinnamon, cloves, grated nutmeg, bay leaves, shelled cardamom seeds and bruised peppercorns. One or two whole chillies are added, but no potatoes – they belong to other kinds of bredie, like greenbean bredie. Add the same quantity of quinces – peeled and neatly sliced, pips and all – as the quantity of meat; first a quarter, later another quarter, and later still the remainder. The only liquid added is water, a little from time to time. A pulpy mess or runny affair is not a bredie. Stir through to mix. And now for my great secret: chop a few rosemary leaves finely and mix them with the freshly grated rind of one lemon and two garlic cloves, peeled and fine-ly chopped. Add a handful of chopped fresh coriander leaves. Taste your bredie; perhaps it needs a little salt? Stir in the rosemary mix-ture and …

The moment of truth has finally arrived – judging whether the bredie is cooked. If you cook it too long, it's like a young woman tired of flirting. If you cook it too quickly, it's like a precocious girl – of whom one quickly tires. But if you cook it just right, it's like a good woman – a blessing.

STILL LIFE OF INGREDIENTS
FOR QUINCE BREDIE

Although the cooking time is 2-3 hours, bredies can be cooked for longer. A slow cooker, set at the lowest temperature, works well. The slower a bredie cooks, the better. Take care that the bredie is, indeed, cooking and not fermenting; if there are tomatoes in the bredie, it may begin to ferment while cooking over low heat and the result will be a sour bredie.

Green bean bredie

(MAKES 6-8 SERVINGS)

2 kg mutton (see p. 81)
25-50 g (25-50 ml/2-4 T) rendered sheep-tail
    fat or butter
10 ml (2 t) ground ginger
5 ml (1 t) ground cloves
10 ml (2 t) freshly ground pepper
5 allspice berries
1 stick cinnamon
6 plump garlic cloves, peeled and crushed with:
10 ml (2 t) salt
3 large onions, halved lengthways,
    peeled and sliced
4 large potatoes, peeled, halved lengthways and
    each half again halved lengthways,
    and all then halved once across
grated nutmeg
1-2 whole chillies
2-4 bay leaves
1,5-2 kg green beans, trimmed and sliced
15 ml (3 t) dried savory, oregano or marjoram
grated rind and juice of 1-2 lemons

1. Fry the meat, a little at a time, in fat or butter in a flat-bottomed, cast-iron pot over moderate heat until nicely browned. Do not try to hurry it. Set meat aside. Pour off all the excess fat, pour ½ cup water into the pot and loosen all the fried bits adhering to the base with a wooden spoon. Return the fried meat to the pot. Sprinkle the ginger, cloves, pepper, allspice, cinnamon, garlic and salt over the meat and cover the pot. Braise for 30 minutes over low heat.
2. Add the onions and potatoes and grate a little nutmeg over. Add the chillies and bay leaves. If necessary, add a little water too. Cover and braise for 30 minutes. Add ⅓ of the green beans, cover and braise. Stir thoroughly. Check pot and add a little water if necessary. Add next ⅓ of green beans and braise again for 30 minutes. Check pot and add a little water if necessary. Add remaining green beans, savory, lemon rind and

juice. Cover and simmer until cooked. Remove chillies. Taste for seasoning and add more salt and pepper if necessary. Serve with rice.

Waterblommetjie bredie

Follow the recipe for Green bean bredie, using very well-rinsed waterblommetjies. Cut off the bottom, hard parts, slice them like green beans and cook these first with the meat. The soft, white, flower part is added last. Add a bunch of sorrel (oxalis, suring) with the lemon juice, as well as some broad-leafed sorrel, cut into strips, if you can find them. If this sour herb is not available, add a peeled sour apple or two with the second addition of waterblommetjies. At the end, stir in extra grated lemon rind to revitalise the pot. Many people add a cup of vaaljapie (rough wine) – taboo to me.

Quince and ginger bredie

(MAKES 6 SERVINGS)

1,5 kg mutton breast and shoulder, cubed
10 ml (2 t) grated nutmeg
3 ml (½ t) ground cloves
salt and freshly ground black pepper
25 ml (2 T) oil
2 large onions, halved lengthways,
    peeled and chopped
1,5 kg quinces, peeled, sliced and covered in
    water to which lemon juice has been added
5 ml (1 t) turmeric
5 ml (1 t) ground ginger
5 ml (1 t) allspice
1 stick cinnamon
1 piece (50 mm/2 in) fresh ginger root, sliced
6 plump garlic cloves, peeled and crushed

1. Season the meat cubes with nutmeg, cloves, salt and pepper. Set aside for 30 minutes.
2. Heat a little oil in a heavy-bottomed saucepan and fry a few meat cubes at a time until browned. Remove and set aside. Repeat with a little more oil and meat.
3. Place the onions in the saucepan in which the meat was fried and fry until softened. Return half the meat to the saucepan. Remove the quinces from the water and drain them. Season the quinces with turmeric, ground ginger and allspice. Spoon half the quinces and the stick of cinnamon on top of the meat in the saucepan, then the rest of the meat and the rest of the

quinces. Sprinkle ginger root and garlic over. Add a little water, reduce the heat, cover and simmer for about 2 hours or until the meat is tender and cooked. Add more water frequently, a little at a time.

Tomato bredie

(MAKES 6-8 SERVINGS)

2 kg mutton (see introductory paragraph)
25-50 g (25-50 ml/2-4 T) rendered sheep-tail
    fat or butter
15 ml (3 t) salt
10 ml (2 t) freshly ground pepper
5 ml (1 t) ground allspice
5 ml (1 t) grated nutmeg
3 ml (½ t) turmeric
3 onions, halved lengthways, peeled and chopped
2 potatoes, peeled and diced
2 kg tomatoes, skinned, seeded and coarsely
    chopped (see Hint, p. 27)
10 ml (2 t) sugar
2 whole chillies
125 ml (½ cup) fresh basil leaves
    or 15 ml (3 t) dried basil
5 ml (1 t) caraway seed

1. Brown the meat in the fat as for green bean bredie.
2. Sprinkle salt, pepper, allspice, nutmeg and turmeric over the meat. Braise the meat uncovered, for 30 minutes. Add the onions, potatoes, tomatoes, sugar and chillies and stew for about 2½ hours or until the meat and tomatoes are so well combined that they can no longer be identified separately. The bredie should, by this time, have cooked dry.
3. Stir in the basil and caraway seed and serve with rice.

HINT: Unlike most other bredies, tomato bredie is cooked uncovered, because the tomatoes draw a lot of water. All the liquid must evaporate during cooking.

GREEN BEAN BREDIE

Basic citrus herb mixture

(ENOUGH FOR 8 PORTIONS)

12,5 ml (1 T) finely chopped fresh parsley
12,5 ml (1 T) finely chopped chives
2 plump garlic cloves, bruised,
  peeled and crushed
5 ml (1 t) finely chopped fresh rosemary
5 ml (1 t) grated lemon rind
10 ml (2 t) grated orange rind

Mix all the ingredients.

VARIATIONS FOR DIFFERENT BREDIES

● TOMATO BREDIE: Increase the quantity of lemon rind to 10 ml (2 t) and orange rind to 15 ml (3 t). Omit rosemary and use 12 large, fresh basil leaves, chopped, instead.
● GREEN BEAN OR WATERBLOMMETJIE BREDIE: Remains the same.
● PUMPKIN BREDIE: Use half the mixture.
● QUINCE AND GINGER BREDIE: Omit chives and rosemary and replace with chopped fresh coriander leaves.

Pumpkin bredie

(MAKES 4 SERVINGS)

1,5 kg lamb, cut into portions
15 ml (3 t) oil
2 large onions, halved lengthways,
  peeled and chopped
salt and freshly ground pepper
kaiings (crackling) (optional)
250 ml (1 cup) water
1 kg pumpkin, peeled, seeded and cubed
1 green chilli, chopped (with seeds)
3 cloves
1-2 sticks cinnamon
12,5 ml (1 T) soft brown sugar
25 ml (2 T) butter

1. Place the meat in the heated oil in a saucepan and cook over moderate heat until browned. Pour off all the fat. Add the onions, mix to combine and stew the meat for a further 5-10 minutes. Season with salt and pepper. If the lamb is lean, a few *kaiings* (crackling) can be added.

CITRUS HERB MIXTURE

2. Add water and heat to boiling point. Add half the pumpkin, reduce the heat, cover and simmer for 30 minutes.
3. Add the chilli, cloves, cinnamon, sugar and butter, cover and simmer for 1 hour.
4. Add the remaining pumpkin, season with salt and pepper, cover and simmer for about 1 hour, until last addition of pumpkin is tender but not mushy.

Flemish stew

(MAKES 6 SERVINGS)

Stews are just as much a part of our food repertoire as bredies are. Flemish stew, with beer, from the cultural heritage of the Lowlands, and Irish stew, from the British, have stood the test of time.

1,5 kg beef thick rib, cubed
15 ml (3 t) oil
2 onions, halved lengthways,
  peeled and thinly sliced
2 plump garlic cloves, bruised,
  peeled and crushed
15 ml (3 t) cake flour
salt and freshly ground pepper
125 ml (½ cup) boiling water
1 tin (340 ml) beer, poured into a mixing bowl
  and stirred until all the gas has escaped
25 ml (2 T) tomato concentrate
10 ml (2 t) fresh or 5 ml (1 t) dried thyme
2 bay leaves
grated nutmeg
5 ml (1 t) sugar
5 ml (1 t) wine vinegar
25 ml (2 T) snipped chives

1. Fry the meat, a little at a time, in oil in a saucepan until browned all over. Remove each batch and set aside.
2. Reduce heat and fry the onions in the same saucepan until softened. Stir in the garlic and flour, season well with salt and pepper and stir-fry for 2 minutes. Stir in the boiling water and scrape off all the bits adhering to the saucepan until they have dissolved in the gravy. Simmer until about 25 ml (2 T) liquid remains. Return half the meat and season with more salt and pepper. Return the remaining meat to the saucepan and season again with salt and pepper. Add the beer, tomato concentrate, thyme, bay leaves and nutmeg. Heat to boiling point, reduce heat, cover and simmer for 2 hours.
3. Remove the lid and stir in the sugar, vinegar and chives. Serve with Creamed potatoes p. 140).

Irish stew

(MAKES 6 SERVINGS)

18 mutton chops
salt and pepper
2 sprigs fresh thyme or 10 ml (2 t) dried thyme
15 ml (3 t) oil
4 large carrots, scraped and thickly sliced
4 turnips, peeled, cubed and placed in water to
  which lemon juice has been added
3 leeks, washed and sliced, or 3 medium-sized
  onions, peeled and sliced
2 plump garlic cloves, bruised,
  peeled and crushed
6 potatoes, peeled and sliced
grated nutmeg
750 ml (3 cups) hot beef stock
37,5 ml (3 T) butter
15 ml (3 t) cake flour

GARNISH
50 ml (4 T) chopped fresh parsley

1. Season chops with salt and pepper and rub thyme into the meat. Heat the oil in a large, heavy-based saucepan and fry chops until golden brown all over. Remove each batch and set aside. Pour off excess fat each time.
2. Place the carrots, turnips, leeks and garlic in the same saucepan and fry for 2 minutes. Return meat to the saucepan.
3. Arrange a layer of potatoes on top. Season with nutmeg and more salt and pepper. Repeat with the rest of the potatoes and season again. Add the stock, reduce the heat immediately, cover and simmer for 1½ hours.
4. Melt the butter in a smaller saucepan. Sprinkle flour over and stir-fry for 1 minute over moderate heat. Remove from the heat. Pour off all the liquid in the meat saucepan and add it, a little at a time, to the flour mixture. Return the gravy saucepan to the heat and stir until thickened. Taste and season again with salt, pepper, grated nutmeg and half the parsley. Add to the meat, stir to combine and heat through. Spoon into a heated serving dish, sprinkle the remaining parsley over and serve. No accompaniments are needed.

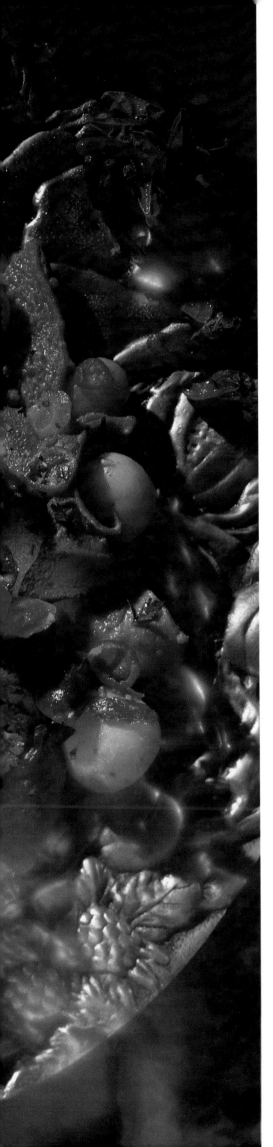

Offal

I DON'T KNOW if our love of offal stems from our French heritage; what I do know is that the French, like the Chinese, favoured pork offal. Think of the many variations of pâtés in which pork liver, and especially pork fat, are the main ingredients. South Africans, with their great love of beef, prefer meat loaf to pâtés, any day. Perhaps this is because the goose liver that is required for pâté is not readily obtainable in our country, and because many South Africans have an inborn aversion to pork. However, coarse pâtés, known as country pâtés, do have a place on our tables.

Fried chicken livers are a contribution of the Portuguese community to South African cuisine. Chicken liver spread, today a convenience product, is popular with most people. So are chicken liver pâtés. Many people have recently begun making duck pâté, or a mixture of duck and chicken liver pâtés. One thing I do regret is that we did not get to know *andouillettes*, a delicious offal sausage sliced like salami before serving. Blood sausages were part of the Little Karoo's British heritage, but these days no one knows the art of making them. Extinct … as is blood pudding. On the other hand, there is probably not a single butchery in the country that does not make liver sausage.

Steak and kidney pies have almost become the staple food of the young. They buy the worst pies, with the palest, most revolting 'army gravy' which, made from synthetic thickeners, surrounds the few hard pieces of beef and the even harder pieces of kidney with tough, fatty dough. When well prepared, this pie is one of the best legacies from Britain.

Offal was, to us, an essential part of slaughtering day. Today it remains only a reminder of the agricultural heritage from which the greater part of our population stems, and for which we yearn. If you visit a farm in Bushmanland or Namaqualand, you can take part in the ritual of slaughtering day. Large intestines braaied just as they are over the coals, or stuffed with liver as 'pofadder'. *Pofadder* can be stuffed with literally any part of the offal or the pluck (heart, liver, kidneys, lungs, windpipe). Then there's liver in caul, known as 'skilpad' or tortoise. *Skilpad* can also be made like this: minced liver, lungs and kidneys, flavoured with minced onions, coriander, salt and pepper, stewed with water in a flat-bottomed pot in the oven. In the northwestern Free State, where maize is king, *skilpad* is baked in an oval Pyrex dish so that the result has the shape of a tortoise. It is served warm with mashed potatoes and braised onions or cold, sliced, on bread. In the eastern Free State, *skilpad* means something completely different: it is two pieces of flank sandwiched together with a bobotie-like stuffing, sewn up and then potroasted. The diamond-shaped incisions on the roasted flank look like the shell of a tortoise. 'Vlermuise' (bats) are pieces of liver covered with caul and then braaied over the coals. Hunters of large and small game eat the liver immediately after caramelising it with chopped onions and Old Brown Sherry. And talking of hunters, I dare not forget the food of the true connoisseur. The baptism of fire for a hunter is to swallow the raw testicles of the first buck he shoots. In cookery they are known as Karoo oysters, which are thrown directly onto the coals and, after a few minutes, scraped out and peeled. They don't look all that marvellous, but the taste is definitely moreish.

The dish known as 'Namaqualand offal' is more than just offal. First the offal and all parts of the pluck are soaked separately in basins of salted water to remove any bloodiness. The pluck is minced and flavoured with grated nutmeg, salt and pepper. Oatmeal is added as a thickener, as well as grated onions and extra beef suet. The offal is then stuffed with this mixture. The offal 'cushion' is then given a covering of caul, which is fastened to the offal with toothpicks, and is placed in a flat-bottomed pot, covered with water and slowly stewed.

Most South Africans know two versions of offal: plain and curried. The recipes below make further clarification unnecessary.

CURRIED OFFAL WITH NEW POTATOES

My story would not be complete without mentioning brawn, also known as head cheese. It is made from three kinds of meat – such as sheep offal with a cowheel, pig's head with trotters, or beef shin with cowheel – cooked until glutinous. It can be curried, or left as it is; you can mince it or cut it finely, it makes no difference, but it must be cooked long and slowly so that the sinews will provide enough gelatine to make it set later. Remove all the bones. Add the flavourings, and set the mixture in a loaf pan. And if you throw any of the liquid away, you haven't read the recipe!

No visitor to the Karoo will ever forget their first experience of baked sheep's head. In her book *Afval en Afvalligheid*, Dine van Zyl describes as follows how to clean, cook and eat a sheep's head. First the head is scraped clean with a blade. Then it is rinsed thoroughly, again and again; especially the mouth. Then follows an hour's soaking in salted water, and it is rinsed well again. A small axe is used to chop out the nasal bones. It is rinsed again. All that remains to be done is to put salt in the mouth. Then the baking, at a low oven temperature, begins; and continues all night. The cutlery consists of a Joseph Rogers or an Oom Paul penknife, honed until razor-sharp. First the lips are cut off and eaten, then the cheek meat, which melts like marrow in your mouth. After that the tongue is eaten, and then comes the highlight: the portion that stretches past the eyes to behind the ear. Dessert is the brain. The latest method is to season the cleaned head with salt, pepper and a tiny bit of thyme (or a sprig in the mouth) and to bake it inside a cooking bag in a baking dish for 4 hours at 160 °C (325 °F). Delicious! If you prefer the skin to be browned, bake the head in the same way, but use a paper bag.

We have to go to the Tswanas to learn about the traditions of meat eating. 'Old-fashioned belief' is the name of one of their festive dishes, which they prepare about three years after the death of a parent. A number of things are needed: specially brewed beer, snuff, tobacco and meat. Mutton for a woman and beef for a man. All parts of the animal – except the intestines, stomach (offal), hooves, head, kidneys, liver, lungs and heart – are cut into chunks and braised with water, salt, pepper and a little onion until the meat falls from the bone. The liver and kidneys are cooked in a three-legged pot. A flat-bottomed pot is lined with the offal. The heart is cut open and layered on top of the intestines. The lungs (cut open and rinsed) come on top of the heart. The whole lot is seasoned with salt and pepper and a little chopped onion is sprinkled over.

Then the offal is folded around everything, the pot is covered and the offal cooked over moderate coals for hours. Special scissors are used to cut everything finely. Meanwhile, the head and hooves are scraped clean. The nasal bones in the head are chopped out with an axe and checked for maggots; if there are any, these bones are discarded. The cheeks and ears are cut out. All the glands are cut out and thrown away. The head, cheeks, ears and hooves go into a three-legged pot; they're covered with water and stewed until tender. The meat is spooned out first onto a large piece of scrubbed corrugated iron, then the offal, and the glutinous juices are poured over the meat so that everything on the corrugated iron takes on an offal flavour. The mourners can now indulge in the feast of 'old-fashioned belief'. One ritual has still to be observed: all the bones that have been picked clean must be spread on a special cloth, and all the eaters must clean their hands with the cloth. Then the bones are wrapped in the cloth and burnt in the fire. The ceremony has come to an end.

Portuguese chicken livers

(MAKES 4-6 SERVINGS)

The large Portuguese community in South Africa introduced this dish to our country. They believe it was born of necessity, as chicken features prominently in their cookery and the offal quickly piles up and has to be processed somehow. The spices that are used form part of the wealth of exotic flavours which had already been taken by Portuguese seafarers from the East to the land of their birth. There should be a fair amount of sauce. Crusty bread that is soft inside is part of the tradition. The livers are eaten with a fork, leaving the other hand free to mop up the juices with pieces of bread.

4 tubs (250 g each) chicken livers, prepared as
    for Easy chicken liver pâté below
25 ml (2 T) olive oil
3 ml (½ t) ground cumin
1 ml (pinch) ground cloves
5 ml (1 t) paprika
salt and pepper
2 bay leaves
cayenne pepper to taste, but not less
    than 5 ml (1 t)
2 onions, halved lengthways, peeled and chopped
4-6 garlic cloves, bruised and peeled
100 ml (8 T) dry white wine

1. Stir-fry the livers ± 3 minutes in hot oil in a large, heavy-bottomed frying pan or saucepan over high heat until browned.
2. Sprinkle cumin, cloves and paprika over and season with salt and pepper to taste. Add bay leaves and season with cayenne pepper to taste. Stir for 1 minute. Add onions and garlic, reduce heat and stir-fry for 5 minutes. Add wine and simmer for a further 2-3 minutes.

Easy chicken liver pâté

(MAKES 12-18 SLICES)

2 tubs (250 g each) chicken livers, a mixture of
    chicken, duck or guineafowl liver,
    or only duck or goose liver
125 ml (½ cup) milk
25 ml (2 T) sweet wine, port or muscadel
25 ml (2 T) Van der Hum
12,5 ml (1 T) brandy
2 sprigs fresh thyme or 5-10 ml
    (1-2 t) pinch of herbs
500 ml (2 cups) cream
3 extra-large eggs
5 extra-large egg yolks
salt and freshly ground black pepper to taste
3-5 ml (½-1 t) cayenne pepper
10 ml (2 t) green peppercorns, crushed
    (optional)
5 ml (1 t) red food colouring
    or 1 ml (pinch) saltpetre (optional)

1. Place completely thawed livers in a mixing bowl. Heat milk to lukewarm, pour over livers and set aside for 30 minutes to draw bitterness from livers. Place in a sieve and drain. Rinse under slowly running cold

Delectable sheep's kidneys

(MAKES 2 SERVINGS)

This delicacy is becoming more popular by
the day, and can now be found on most
menus. It was, and still is, a popular breakfast dish.

8 sheep's kidneys, prepared as described in
   the box, top left
salt and pepper
50 ml (4 T) cake flour
4 chopped fresh sage leaves
   or 3 ml (½ t) dried sage
25 ml (2 T) butter
25 ml (2 T) oil

1. Season halved kidneys with salt and pepper.
Season flour with salt, pepper and sage. Roll
kidneys in the flour and shake off the excess.
2. Heat the butter and oil in a frying pan and
fry the kidneys until cooked but not overcooked. They should still be light pink inside.

VARIATIONS
● Most South Africans fry kidneys in butter
and oil in a frying pan. If you have a good
supply of lard, it would be better to roast
them in the lard.
● Use tarragon instead of sage.
● Stir 5 ml (1 t) prepared mustard into the
butter in which the kidneys are fried.
● Fry a chopped onion with the kidneys.
● Flame kidneys with brandy before serving.
● Snipped chives are the perfect finish for
any kidney dish.
● Risotto (p. 123) is a delicious accompaniment to kidneys served as a main course. So
are Fried mushrooms (p. 145) or potato
slices baked in cream. And don't forget
about Potato balls (p. 138) with garlic and
parsley butter.
● Follow the same method to make devilled
kidneys, but omit the sage and season the
cake flour with 5 ml (1 t) cayenne pepper.
First fry a finely chopped onion in the pan
until softened and transparent, then stir in
2-3 chopped, seeded chillies, add kidneys
(covered with flour mixture) and continue
to stir-fry. Sprinkle a little Tabasco sauce
over and serve. If you like a really strong
taste, do not remove the seeds from the
chillies. Use bird's eye chillies. The kidneys
can be threaded crosswise onto kebab sticks
before serving.

Offal

(MAKES 4 SERVINGS)

Offal is a truly regional dish; every area has
its own method. In Namaqualand it is
cooked with salt, pepper and vinegar and
served with samp. In the Sandveld, more
spices are added and it is served with pearl
wheat. In the Eastern Cape the accompaniment is Samp and beans (p. 124), but in the
Stormberg offal is fried in goose fat. In the
irrigation area alongside the Lower Orange
River, offal is served with steamed new potatoes, just as it is in certain parts of France.
Traditionally, in most parts of our country,
potatoes are cooked in the sauce. KwaZulu-
Natal and the townships curry it until it is so
hot that your mouth burns and your eyes
water. Offal has roots that wind through the
Free State and Western Transvaal right up to
the Bushveld. But the very best recipes come
from the Little and Great Karoo.

1 pair brains, wrapped in
   honeycomb offal
remaining offal, cut into 50 mm
   (2 in) cubes
1 sheep's head
4 sheep's trotters
2 pork trotters, each cut
   into 3 pieces
salt and freshly ground black pepper
4-6 cloves
6 allspice berries
5 ml (1 t) grated nutmeg
2-3 bay leaves
25 ml (2 T) white vinegar
grated rind and juice of 1 lemon
4 sheep's tongues

1. Set aside brains in offal. Place remaining
meat in a large saucepan, cover with tap
water, heat to boiling point, reduce the heat
and boil for 1 hour.
2. Pour off and discard the water. Add the
remaining ingredients to the offal and add
enough water to cover them. Heat to boiling
point, reduce heat and simmer for 8 hours.
Add the tongues and simmer for 3-4 hours
or until the offal is meltingly soft and the
tongues are cooked.
3. Taste and season with salt and pepper if
necessary. Remove the tongues from the
offal and pull off the skins. Leave the
tongues whole, or slice them, and serve with
the tripe.

water. Place livers in a glass or ceramic container and pour the sweet wine, Van der
Hum and brandy over. Add thyme or herbs.
Cover with cling wrap and marinate for 2-24
hours in the refrigerator. (The Portuguese
simply remove the unwanted skin and membranes, rinse the livers and pat them dry.)
2. Place the cream in a saucepan and heat
to boiling point over high heat. Turn the
heat down slightly and reduce, stirring constantly, until cream has thickened and half
has evaporated.
3. Remove the liver mixture from the refrigerator and discard the thyme (if you used it).
Strip thyme leaves from the stalks and place
the livers, marinade, thyme leaves and cream
in a food processor. Purée for 5 minutes. Add
first the whole eggs and then the egg yolks,
one by one. Process for another minute. Pour
through a sieve into a clean mixing bowl.
Season with salt, pepper and cayenne pepper. Taste, then stir in green peppercorns (if
used), as well as food colouring. Refrigerate.
4. Use 8-12 ramekins or other small, heat-
proof glass dishes or containers, or a 1,5 litre
terrine or bread pan. Grease dishes with butter
and place a round of baking paper on the base
of each. (Line a terrine/bread pan with baking
paper.) Choose a baking pan large enough to
take all the dishes or the terrine/bread pan and
place the dishes/pan in it.
5. Carefully spoon the cold liver mixture
into the dishes or pan until almost full. Preheat the oven to 150 °C (300 °F). Boil a kettleful of water. Pour the water into the pan
and place the pan in the oven. Bake small
dishes of pâté for 25-30 minutes and pâté in
a terrine or bread pan for 50-60 minutes.
Test the pâté with the tip of a finger: it
should be firm. Remove from the oven and
allow to cool in the water. Remove from the
water and cool completely. Place cling wrap
tightly on surface and refrigerate.
6. Turn out and slice. Serve the pâté with a
green salad.

Curried brawn

(MAKES 12 SERVINGS)

2,5 kg beef shin, washed
1 cowheel, washed
3 bay leaves
12 peppercorns
3 plump garlic cloves, bruised and peeled
3 large onions, halved lengthways,
    peeled and chopped
25 ml (2 T) oil
50 ml (4 T) Sri Lankan curry powder (p. 100)
375 ml (1½ cups) vinegar
ground pepper to taste
10 ml (2 t) ground coriander
± 25 ml (2 T) salt
10 ml (2 t) turmeric
25 ml (2 T) soft brown sugar
25 ml (2 T) smooth apricot jam

1. Heat water to boiling point in a large saucepan. Blanch the shin and cowheel in it, and pat dry.
2. Place the meat and cowheel in a large saucepan and cover with cold water. Add the bay leaves, peppercorns and garlic. Heat to boiling point, reduce the heat, cover and simmer for 3-4 hours or until tender. Allow to cool, remove meat and cowheel and cool completely. Reserve liquid.
3. Fry the onions in the oil until softened and transparent, but not browned. Sprinkle the curry powder on top and stir-fry for 2-3 minutes. Add a little vinegar from time to time, if it looks as if the curry powder is going to burn. Add the remaining ingredients, heat to boiling point, reduce heat and simmer for 5 minutes.
4. Remove the bones. Cut the meat into smaller pieces, or chop it, or mince it, depending on how coarse or fine you prefer the brawn to be. Add the meat to the curry mixture and add some of the liquid in which the meat was cooked, to just cover the meat with the liquid. Simmer for 1 hour, stirring from time to time. If necessary, more of the reserved liquid can be added.
5. Pour the mixture into an oiled mould and refrigerate to set. Turn out and cut into slices. Serve with tomato or cucumber sambal and bread (Farm bread, p. 13, or Wholewheat bread, p. 14).

Curried offal

(MAKES 4 SERVINGS)

2 large onions, halved lengthways,
    peeled and sliced
25 ml (2 T) oil
cooked offal, prepared as on p.89
12 plump garlic cloves,
    peeled and crushed
1 piece (25 mm/1 in) fresh ginger root,
    peeled and finely chopped
1 stick cinnamon
2 pieces star anise
12-24 new potatoes

CURRY MIXTURE
6 dried red chillies, halved,
    seeded and chopped
25 g (40 ml/8 t) roasted coriander seeds
    (see Hint, p. 60)
10 ml (2 t) cumin
3 ml (½ t) mustard seeds
5 ml (1 t) black peppercorns
5 ml (1 t) fenugreek
5 ml (1 t) ground ginger
15 ml (3 t) turmeric
5 ml (1 t) ground cinnamon
1 ml (pinch) ground cloves
10 ml (2 t) fresh curry leaves

1. PREPARE THE CURRY MIXTURE: Crush the chillies, coriander, cumin, mustard, peppercorns and fenugreek together, or grind them finely in a spice mill. Add the ground ginger, turmeric, cinnamon and cloves and mix well. Stir in the curry leaves.
2. Fry the onions in oil until softened and transparent, but not browned. Sprinkle the curry mixture over the onions and stir-fry for 1 minute. Add the curry mixture to the offal and add garlic, ginger root, stick cinnamon and star anise. Heat to boiling point, reduce heat and add potatoes. Simmer for 1 hour, until glutinous.

EASY CHICKEN LIVER PÂTÉ

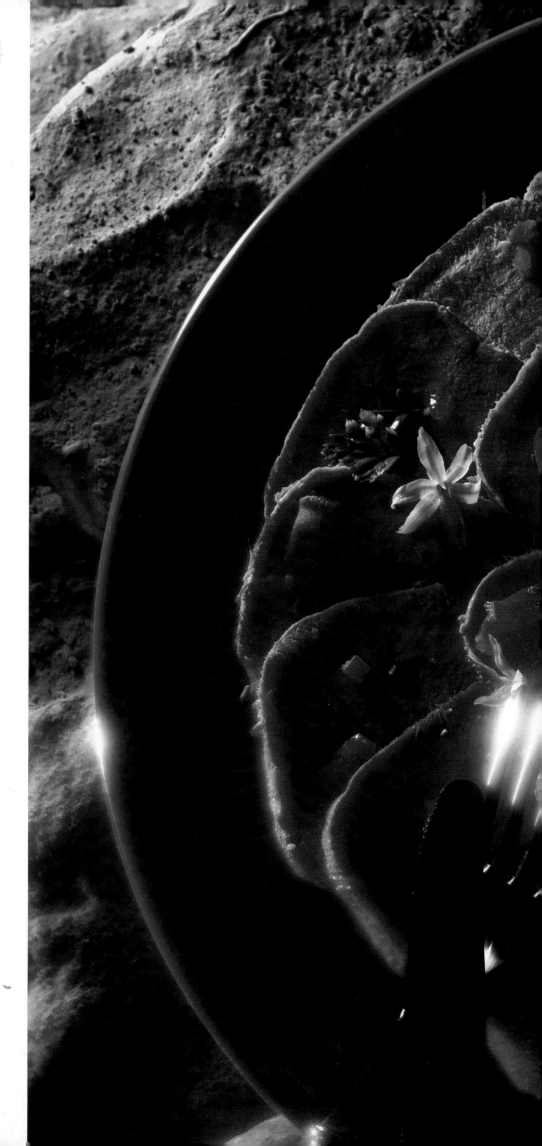

Pickled tongue

(MAKES 6 SERVINGS)

TO PICKLE
1-1,5 litres water
700 g (625 ml / 2½ cups) salt
150 g (187,5 ml / ⅔ cup) brown sugar
14 g (12,5 ml / 1 T) saltpetre
1 ox tongue
garlic clove, bruised and peeled (optional)

TO COOK
cold water
5 ml (1 t) salt in 1 litre water (fresh tongue)
5 ml (1 t) black peppercorns
5 ml (1 t) allspice berries
2 fresh bay leaves
6 sprigs fresh parsley
1 sprig fresh thyme
2 carrots, scraped and thickly sliced
1 large onion, halved lengthways,
   peeled and thickly sliced
1 celery stalk, washed and threads removed,
   then coarsely chopped

1. Heat water, salt, sugar and saltpetre and boil for 10 minutes. Allow to cool.
2. Pour cold pickling liquid over the tongue, covering it completely. It would be best to roll the tongue up in a small, conical earthenware dish. Place a heavy plate on top of the tongue to keep it under the pickling liquid.
3. Leave in a cool place for ± 3 days. Add garlic (if used), heat and boil for a few minutes. Remove tongue from pickling liquid.
4. Cover tongue with cold water and add salt, if tongue is fresh. No salt is added to pickled tongue. Add remaining ingredients. (In grandma's day, a peeled and thickly sliced turnip was also added.)
5. Heat mixture to boiling point, reduce heat and simmer for 3-4 hours. When the tongue is tender, place it in ice-cold water. Pull the skin off immediately and cut off the root. Slice and serve hot or cold with Slaphakskeentjies (page 150) and Raisin sauce.

RAISIN SAUCE
Mix 100 g (125 ml / ½ cup) brown sugar, 10 ml (2 t) mustard powder, 25 ml (2 T) cornflour mixed to a paste with 25 ml (2 T) lemon juice, grated rind of 1 orange and 1 lemon, 250 ml (1 cup) grape juice, salt, pepper and cayenne pepper. Stir over low heat until the sugar has dissolved. Add 75 g (125 ml / ½ c) seedless raisins and simmer until thickened. Taste and season with salt, pepper and cayenne pepper. Serve hot.

PICKLED TONGUE

Steak and kidney pie

(MAKES 6 SERVINGS)

In the past, the meat was fried in fat rather than butter – even goose fat. The pastry was made with half butter and half suet. For the first seventy years of the twentieth century, the pie was served with mash and gravy; these days it is served with salad.

PASTRY
180 g (375 ml/1½ cups) cake flour, sifted
3 ml (½ t) salt
3 ml (½ t) mustard powder
3 ml (½ t) cayenne pepper
150 g (150 ml/⅗ cup) cold butter,
    grated
37,5-50 ml (3-4 T) ice-cold water

FILLING
1 kg stewing beef,
    cut into 25 mm (1 in) cubes
250 g kidneys, prepared as described
    on p. 89 and diced
25 ml (2 T) cake flour
salt and freshly ground pepper
50 g (50 ml/4 T) butter
1 onion, halved lengthways,
    peeled and chopped
325 ml (1⅓ cups) hot beef stock
15 ml (3 t) Worcestershire sauce
25 ml (2 T) tomato paste
50 ml (4 T) mixed chopped fresh herbs
    (chives, tarragon or sage)

GLAZE
1 egg, beaten

1. PREPARE THE PASTRY: Sift the flour, salt, mustard powder and cayenne pepper together once. Stir in the grated butter until it is covered with flour mixture. Make a hollow in the flour mixture and add 37,5 ml (3 T) of the water. Mix, cutting in butter and adding more of the remaining water to make a stiff, lumpy dough. Turn out on to a floured marble slab, press together and roll out into a rectangle. Fold in three and turn pastry so that the open end is facing you. Roll out again into a rectangle and fold into three. Repeat once more. On a hot day, you will have to refrigerate the pastry for 30 minutes between rollings. Cover the pastry with cling wrap and refrigerate the rolled-out pastry until cold.
2. FILLING: Place the meat, kidneys, flour, salt and pepper in a large mixing bowl and mix well.
3. Melt half the butter in a large saucepan.

Fry the onions in it until softened and transparent, but not browned. Add the rest of the butter and heat to boiling point. Add the meat mixture, a little at a time, and brown each batch before adding another one. Boil, uncovered, until any extra liquid that may have formed, evaporates. Gradually add hot stock. Add Worcestershire sauce and tomato paste. Reduce the heat, cover and simmer for 2 hours until the meat is meltingly tender. Remove from the heat and stir in the herbs. Place a pie funnel or an inverted egg cup in the centre of a pie dish. Spoon the filling into the dish and allow to cool.
4. Preheat the oven to 220 °C (450 °F). Roll out the cold pastry on a lightly floured marble slab, to 25 mm (1 in) larger than the pie dish. Trim the edges of the pastry, then cut off a strip 15 mm (± ½ inch) wide all round. Moisten the edge of the pie dish with water and press the pastry strip securely onto it. Roll the large piece of pastry over a rolling pin and roll it out over the pie dish. Pinch around the edge of the pastry with your fingers. Cut a cross above the funnel. Brush the beaten egg over. Press the leftover pastry pieces together and roll them out. Cut out shapes, like leaves or other decorations, and affix to the pastry with the remaining beaten egg. Brush the pastry decorations with egg. Bake for 10 minutes. Remove from the oven and brush the remaining egg over. Return to the oven, reduce the temperature to 180 °C (350 °F) and bake for 20-25 minutes.

Skilpadjie

(MAKES 6 SERVINGS)

1 sheep's liver, prepared as for
    Sweet and sour liver
6 sheep's kidneys, prepared as described
    on page 89
2 eggs, beaten
1 large onion, halved lengthways,
    peeled and finely chopped
5 ml (1 t) ground coriander
1 ml (pinch) ground cloves
salt and freshly ground pepper
75 g (125 ml/½ cup) currants or shredded
    bleached sultanas
caul
1 large intestine (chitterling), washed, turned
    inside out and washed again, then turned
    right side out

1. Mince the liver and kidneys. Add the eggs, onion, coriander, cloves, salt and pepper. Stir in the currants.

2. Line a greased baking dish with caul, extending over the sides of the dish. Spoon in the meat mixture. Fold the caul fat in towards the centre, over the meat mixture. Use the large intestine to secure the caul.
3. Place the dish in a pan of hot water and bake for 1½ hours in a preheated oven at 180 °C (350 °F).

Sweet and sour liver

(MAKES 4 SERVINGS)

Rinse the liver under cold running water. Holding the membrane in your right hand, pull the meat from it with your left hand. If the membrane is difficult to remove, soak the liver for a while in cold water to which 10 ml (2 t) vinegar has been added. Slice thinly and remove all the large glands. Ox liver must be soaked for 1-2 hours in milk, buttermilk or salted water to remove the strong flavour. Venison liver can be soaked in perlé wine (wine with a slight sparkle). Rinse, pat dry and cook.

500 g liver, prepared as described
    above and cubed
freshly ground black pepper
3 ml (½ t) cayenne pepper
25 ml (2 T) lard or oil
1 large onion, peeled and coarsely grated
125 ml (½ cup) boiling water
25 ml (2 T) lemon juice
grated rind of 1 lemon
15 ml (3 t) cornflour
10 ml (2 t) sugar
15 ml (3 t) vinegar
salt to taste

1. Season the liver with the pepper and cayenne pepper.
2. Heat lard or oil in a frying pan until hot. Fry the onion in the lard until softened and transparent, but not browned. Add the liver and stir-fry for 3-4 minutes. Mix the water and lemon juice and add. Simmer for 8 minutes over low heat.
3. Mix the rind, cornflour, sugar and vinegar. Make sure that the cornflour has dissolved completely. Remove the pan from the heat and stir in the cornflour mixture. Return to the heat and simmer until the sauce is thick and clear. Taste, then season to taste with salt. Serve hot with pearl wheat, rice or Krummelpap (p. 26).

Sheep's tongues with coconut milk

(MAKES 6 SERVINGS)

24 sheep's tongues
1 onion, peeled and quartered
1 carrot, scraped and cut into pieces
1 celery stalk, rinsed and threads removed,
    then coarsely chopped
4 cloves
12 black peppercorns
2 bay leaves
10 ml (2 t) salt

CURRY SAUCE
3 large onions, halved lengthways,
    peeled and finely chopped
25 ml (2 T) oil
6 plump garlic cloves, bruised,
    peeled and crushed
1 piece (25 mm / 1 in) fresh ginger root,
    grated
25 ml (2 T) curry powder
5 ml (1 t) cayenne pepper
    (optional, if you don't like it too hot)
1 tin (410 g) Indian tomatoes
250 ml (1 cup) coconut milk
    (see Hint)
liquid in which tongue was cooked
2 bananas
12 pickling onions, peeled

1. Wash tongues and set aside. Place the onion, carrot, celery, cloves, peppercorns, bay leaves and salt in a large saucepan and fill halfway with water. Heat to boiling point, and skim off the froth. Add the tongues to the liquid, heat to boiling point, skim off the froth that forms on the surface, and reduce the heat to moderate. Cover and boil for ± 1½ hours or until tongues are tender and the skin comes off easily. Immediately remove from the liquid and pull off the skins while the tongues are still hot – it will be easier to do so. If the tongues are cold, you will have difficulty removing the skins. Return the tongues to the liquid and set aside.
2. MAKE THE CURRY SAUCE: Fry the onions in oil until softened and transparent, but not browned. Add the garlic and ginger and stir-fry for 3 minutes. Sprinkle the curry powder and cayenne pepper (if used) over and stir-fry for a further 1-2 minutes.

Add the tomatoes and heat to boiling point. Add the coconut milk, reduce the heat and simmer for 30 minutes, or until thickened. Pour some of the liquid in which the tongues were cooked through a sieve, and add about 500 ml (2 cups) to the sauce. Add the bananas and onions and cook for 30 minutes. Halve the tongues lengthways, add to the curry sauce and cook for 15 minutes. Serve with Funeral rice (p. 122) and Spiced peaches (p. 135).

HINT: You may also use coconut cream, available these days in supermarkets. If it is not available, place 250 ml (1 cup) coconut in a saucepan and add 400 ml (1⅗ cup) milk. Heat to boiling point, remove from the heat and leave to draw for 1 hour. Pour through a sieve and squeeze all the liquid from the coconut pulp. It should make 250 ml (1 cup).

Oxtail

(MAKES 6 SERVINGS)

25 ml (2 T) oil
2 ox tails, cut into joints
1 kg meaty beef shin slices,
    blanched and patted dry
250 g smoked pork, cubed
salt and freshly ground pepper
50 ml (4 T) cake flour, well seasoned with
    salt and pepper
6 medium carrots, scraped
    and thickly sliced
2 celery stalks (leaves and all),
    washed and threads removed,
    then chopped
3 onions, peeled and coarsely chopped,
    or 6 leeks, rinsed and sliced
12 large, ripe red tomatoes, skinned,
    seeded and coarsely chopped
    (see Hint, p. 27)
50 ml (4 T) tomato paste
6 whole medium-sized red chillies
6 bay leaves
6 cloves, tops removed
1 litre (4 cups) hot, strong beef stock
375 ml (½ bottle / 1½ cups) dry red wine
4 sprigs fresh thyme
15 ml (3 t) coarsely chopped fresh
    rosemary

1. Heat the oil until hot, but not smoking, in a large flat-bottomed saucepan or cast-iron pot. Brown the oxtail, a few pieces at a time, removing each batch with a slotted spoon. Brown the shin slices on both sides and remove. Pour off all the excess fat. Place the pork in the saucepan and fry long and slowly over moderate heat until crisp. Pour off the excess fat.
2. Season oxtail with salt and pepper. Roll the segments in flour and shake off the excess flour. Add to the pork in the saucepan. Season the shin with salt and place on top of the oxtail. Add the carrots, celery, onions, tomatoes, tomato paste, chillies, bay leaves and cloves. Add the stock and heat to boiling point. Add the wine gradually, and add water (if necessary) to cover the meat completely. Add the thyme and rosemary. Reduce the heat, cover and stew for 4 hours.
3. Spoon into a serving dish and sprinkle a little Citrus herb mixture (p. 85) over. Serve with Dumplings (see Variations), mashed potatoes, pearl wheat or, as in the nineties, with tagliatelle liberally seasoned with pepper and moistened with olive oil.

VARIATIONS

● WITH DUMPLINGS (6 servings): Sift 180 g (375 ml / 1½ cups) cake flour, 7,5 ml (1½ t) baking powder, 5 ml (1 t) salt, 5 ml (1 t) mustard powder, 1-2 ml (1-2 pinches) cayenne pepper. Grate 100 g (100 ml / 8 T) butter over and rub in until mixture resembles breadcrumbs. Stir in 25 ml (2 T) chopped fresh parsley with a large, two-pronged fork. Add enough soda water to make a soft dough (like that of scones). Dip a spoon in boiling water and drop spoonfuls of dough on top of the oxtail. Cover and simmer for 30 minutes, without removing the lid.
● WITH PIG'S TROTTERS (8 servings): Make basic recipe, but brown 4 pig's trotters with the oxtail. Add 1 tin (410 g) tomatoes and 250 ml (1 cup) dry white wine. Cover and simmer until cooked. Spoon 250 ml (1 cup) uncooked pearl wheat in a thin layer over the cooked meat, cover and simmer for about 45 minutes, until the pearl wheat is cooked.

Curry

IN OUR COUNTRY, there's curry, and then there's curry. The word 'curry' comes from the Tamil word 'kari' which means saucy, spicy food. Curry is truly curry when various spices are cleverly blended, just like the ingredients of a good perfume.

Spices have been part of our cuisine from the time of Jan van Riebeeck. This fondness for spicy food reached a peak in the bewigged era of Ryk Tulbagh. The liberal use of spices became less popular during the nineteenth century. In the twentieth century, however, spiceless food became unacceptable, and as a result five distinct curry styles evolved in South Africa: Malay, Indian, township, Zulu and farm-style. English-speaking South Africans adopted the Indian style, especially in Natal. On the Rand, the townships made curry that was so hot that even the most hardened eater's eyes watered. The Zulus and Xhosas were influenced by the cuisine of the Natal Indians, but – unlike those with religious constraints – they concentrated on pork curry. White and Coloured Afrikaners increasingly prepared curry using potatoes and prepacked curry powder. The Tswanas copied them, especially when it came to offal. Balti and many south-east Asian influences became noticeable from the eighties onwards.

A curry meal consists of one or more red meat, poultry, fish, seafood or vegetable dishes. Rice, lentils (or a mixture of the two), relishes and one or two kinds of bread are served with them. The stronger the curry dish, the more important it is to serve fairly neutral relishes with it. There is always a rich dish and a lighter one. All the dishes are brought to the table at once and the guests make their choice. There is a difference in the taste and preparation of Indian and Malay curry. Indian curry contains fewer ingredients, and usually no sweet ones; Malay curry is sweeter and often contains fresh or dried fruit.

The 'Rijstafel' (rice table) was particularly popular in Cape Town and vicinity during the eighteenth and nineteenth centuries and up to the Second World War. The last time I experienced it was in the seventies, at the Dutch Club (Nederlandse Klub). It is a great pity that the rice table has disappeared. A feast of twenty to thirty curry dishes, where many flavours mingle, is placed on the table with a large bowl of rice and many, many relishes like fresh pineapple, fresh and fried bananas, dried prawns, peanuts and pistachio nuts, fresh coconut, cucumber, mango chutney, a choice of sambals and kroepoek (finely crushed dried prawns fried in boiling hot olive oil so that they separate into flakes). Dishes like saté, clear chicken or vegetable soup, a hot curry, a strongly spiced fish dish and nasi goreng must always be part of a rice table. Nasi goreng consists of fried rice mixed with chicken, prawns, vegetables, spices, and sometimes ham. Fried eggs are often used as a garnish.

Typical relishes currently served with a curry are chutney, atchar, pickles, toasted coconut, yoghurt, poppadums, and sambals of chopped tomato (with or without onions), carrots, dates, mangoes, quinces, kiwi fruit, sour figs and lots of other fresh fruit – all of them given that extra bite with chilli, really fresh, and usually perfumed with fresh coriander leaves. At Malay and Indian feasts, samoosas, dhaltjies and savoury vetkoek, potato and sweetcorn puffs and small fish frikkadels are often served as appetisers. Butternut soup, especially combined with mango, has become the norm at Eurocentric meals. Puris or chapatis are flat Indian breads served with a curry dish. Malays serve roti, and Afrikaners serve vetkoek. Curry is eaten with a fork, a spoon or with the hands.

One aspect that is still not clearly understood is how strong, or hot, a curry should be. The cook determines the strength. The eater tastes, and decides how much is needed in the way of accompaniments to make each mouthful hot, mild or weak. Each mouthful should consist not of only a single item, but of a combination of curry, rice and the accompaniment so that flavours, tastes and textures can melt together in the mouth.

At a curry buffet, the relishes and accompaniments are often served on banana leaves. Bowls containing the various dishes are placed on large copper trays, as a symbol of

SPICE MIXTURES

the golden bowls in which curry was served to royalty in India.

Dessert usually consists of fresh fruit, but also includes ice cream, frozen yoghurt, boeber, sago, trifle, puffs, milk tart and even potato or sweet potato pudding.

Alcohol is a problem when it comes to curry meals. Muslims are prohibited from drinking alcohol, and so are adherents of many other Eastern religions. There are very few 'ex-India' families in this country. In the early colonial years of the twentieth century, many of them came to South Africa from India, establishing themselves particularly in Natal and in the former Rhodesia. By retaining their traditions and lifestyle, this group introduced one of the many curry 'identities' to South Africa. They were great beer drinkers, and practised the custom of serving beer before and during a curry meal. By contrast, the farmers of the Boland advocated the serving of sweet wine, or even vermouth. By the forties, sherry had replaced the sweet wine. Today the approach is simpler: wine before the meal, fresh fruit juice, yoghurt or other dairy drinks during the meal, and fortified wine afterwards. Late harvest wine, especially gewürztraminer, may also be served. The strangest thing I've ever come across was a wine named 'Curry', made from riesling, which was displayed on the spice shelf in a large chain store. Perhaps a glass of ice-cold milk would be the best drink with curry? Or perhaps – nothing!

Three spice mixtures are particularly popular in our country, and are available under literally thousands of names. I prefer to name them for their country of origin: Sri Lanka (Ceylon), India and Malaysia. Before making a spice mixture, you need a spice mill or coffee grinder.

Pickled fish

(MAKES 6 SERVINGS)

The earliest reference to this very popular dish comes from the handwritten recipe book of Marie Cloete of Groot Constantia. The Klooten family had this book in the eighteenth century. (The original surname was South Africanised to Cloete.) This is the family who made the famous Constantia wine for which Napoleon yearned on his deathbed; they also catered for the Dutch taste for Curaçao with Van der Hum. Yellowtail, kingklip or kabeljou (cob) are popular choices, but snoek remains the tastiest. The dish can be served cold or hot.

*1 kg snoek, washed, filleted and cut
   into portions*
salt and freshly ground white pepper
grated rind and juice of 2 lemons
sheep-tail fat, butter or oil

PICKLING SAUCE
*2 large onions, halved lengthways,
   peeled and sliced*
100 g (125 ml / ½ cup) soft brown sugar
50 ml (4 T) smooth apricot jam
*25 ml (2 T) Garam masala (p. 100)
   or Indian spice mixture (p. 100)*
10 ml (2 t) turmeric
2 ml (2 pinches) cayenne pepper
750 ml (3 cups) brown vinegar
6 fresh lemon leaves
*1 piece (50 mm / 2 in) fresh ginger root,
   peeled and finely chopped*
*20 ml (4 t) roasted coriander seed
   (see Hint, p. 60)*
100-125 ml (± ½ cup) water

1. Season the fish with salt and pepper and rub it into the fish with the lemon juice and rind. Heat the fat in a frying pan and fry a few pieces of fish quickly on both sides until just cooked (see Hints). Remove and repeat with remaining fish.
2. PICKLING SAUCE: Place all the ingredients in a saucepan, heat to boiling point, reduce the heat and simmer for 20-25 minutes. Spoon a little sauce into a sterilised container and place a layer of fish in it. Cover the fish with a layer of hot sauce. Repeat with the remaining fish and sauce, allow to cool and seal. Store for at least 2-3 days in a cool place or in the refrigerator before eating.

HINTS
● The seasoned, uncooked fish can also be placed in a greased baking dish. Sprinkle a little water over, cover and bake for 10-15 minutes in a preheated oven at 180 °C (350 °F).
● The fish can also be cooked in the sauce. Make sure that the seasoned, uncooked fish is covered completely with the cooked sauce and simmer for ± 20 minutes. Or spoon the hot, cooked sauce over the seasoned, uncooked fish in a greased baking dish and bake for 20 minutes in a preheated oven at 180 °C (350 °F).

PICKLED FISH

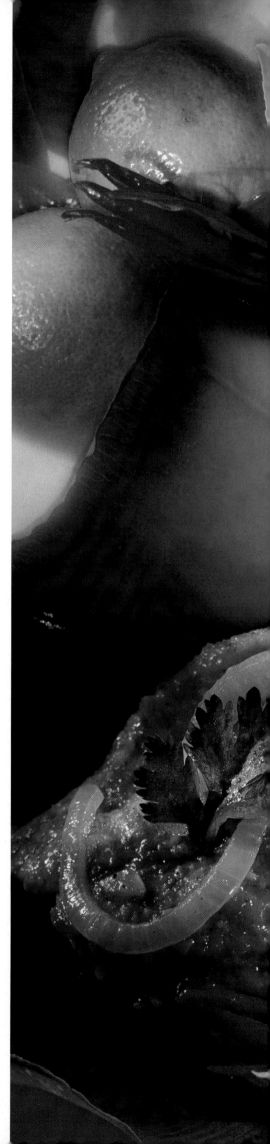

Sri Lankan spice mixture

Sri Lankans roast the spices longer than usual before grinding them, which gives their indigenous dishes a characteristic 'darker' flavour than the traditional Indian dishes. If the spices are roasted until you can only just smell them, the result will be a very light, flavoursome curry mixture. This lighter Sri Lankan spice mixture is used in the preparation of curried brawn. Don't make too much spice mixture at a time, unless you are going to use it constantly. The mixture will retain its delicious flavour for six to eight weeks at the most, if stored in an airtight container. It can be doubled or trebled successfully. In other words: rather make a smaller, fresh supply every two months than a large quantity that will stand, unused, on the shelf for months.

- 25 g coriander seed
- 15 g cumin seed
- 15 ml (1 T) fennel seed
- 5 ml (1 t) fenugreek
- small stick cinnamon
- 6 green cardamom seeds
- 6 cloves
- 6 fresh curry leaves
- 15 ml (3 t) turmeric (optional)*
- 5 ml (1 t) cayenne pepper

*TURMERIC: Turmeric is not an essential ingredient in this curry mixture, but if you prepare the lighter variation, it is needed to make the mixture slightly more bitter and yellower. That's why I recommend the turmeric.

1. Place the coriander, cumin, fennel, fenugreek, cinnamon, cardamom and cloves in a large, heavy-bottomed saucepan and stir over moderate heat until the spices begin to release their aroma. For a lighter spice mixture, the saucepan should be removed from the heat immediately. For a 'darker' flavour, the spices must be roasted longer, but take care not to burn them. Remove from the heat and add the curry leaves, turmeric (if used) and cayenne pepper. Stir to mix, spread out in a shallow pan and allow to cool.
2. Grind all the ingredients to a fine powder and sift through a fine sieve. Discard everything that remains behind. Store the spice mixture in an airtight container.

Garam masala

When one thinks of North Indian cooking, one thinks of garam masala. There are about the same number of variations as there are cooks. It varies from hot to aromatic. Sometimes, some of the spices are left whole, and variations to the more refined cuisine call for expensive ingredients, like dried rose leaves, to be added to the basic mixture. Cinnamon and black peppercorns are an important ingredient in the mixture, and colour it brown.

- 2 sticks cinnamon
- 3 bay leaves
- 40 g cumin seed
- 25 g coriander seed
- 20 g black peppercorns
- 15 g cloves
- 15 g grated nutmeg

1. Break the cinnamon and bay leaves into pieces. Place the cinnamon, bay leaves, cumin, coriander, pepper and cloves in a large, heavy-based saucepan. Stir-fry the mixture over moderate heat until the spices release a strong, spicy aroma. Remove from the heat and allow to cool.
2. Stir in the nutmeg. Grind the mixture finely in a spice mill and sift through a fine sieve. Discard everything that remains in the sieve. Store garam masala in an airtight container to preserve the flavour.

HINT: For a stronger flavour and taste, add chopped, dried chillies (seeds and all) before the mixture is ground.

Indian spice mixture

- 4 dried red chillies
- 25 g coriander seed
- 10 ml (2 t) cumin seed
- 3 ml (½ t) mustard seed
- 5 ml (1 t) fenugreek seed
- 5 ml (1 t) black peppercorns
- 12 fresh curry leaves
- 3 ml (½ t) ground ginger
- 15 ml (3 t) turmeric
- 5 ml (1 t) cinnamon
- 1 ml (pinch) ground cloves

1. Fry chillies, coriander, cumin, mustard and fenugreek with peppercorns and curry leaves until they emit a strong aroma. Remove from the heat and allow to cool.
2. Grind the mixture finely and shake through a sieve. Add the ginger, turmeric, cinnamon and cloves and mix well. Store the spice mixture in an airtight container in a dark place.

Sambal oelek

Malay flavours are a combination of ginger, turmeric, ginger root, lemon grass and other aromatic leaves and herbs; but, above all – chillies! This sambal is served separately, but is also sometimes stirred into dishes during cooking, with garam masala. Take care – it is *really* hot!

250 g shredded fresh red chillies*
5 ml (1 t) salt
5 ml (1 t) soft brown sugar

*Remove the seeds if a milder mixture is preferred.

Heat a heavy-bottomed saucepan until hot and place chillies in it. Reduce the heat to moderately low and stir-fry with a wooden spoon until the chillies are dry. Remove from the heat, chop finely and grind in a spice mill with the salt and sugar.

Samoosas

(MAKES 36)

Traditionally, minced beef is used in the filling, but chicken or vegetable fillings are equally popular today. Many people add cooked potato cubes to stretch the filling.

FILLING
1 onion, halved lengthways,
    peeled and chopped
65 ml (¼ cup) oil
10 ml (2 t) ground cumin
10 ml (2 t) ground coriander
2 ml (slightly less than ½ t) cayenne pepper
350-500 g minced beef
salt and white/black pepper to taste
3 plump garlic cloves, peeled and crushed
1 piece (25 mm/1 in) fresh ginger root,
    peeled and finely grated
2 ripe red tomatoes, skinned,
    seeded and chopped
    (see Hint, p. 27)
50 ml (4 T) chopped fresh
    coriander leaves
grated rind of 1 lemon

PUR (PASTRY)
5 ml (1 t) lemon juice
250 ml (1 cup) cold water
360 g (750 ml/3 cups) cake flour, sifted
1-2 ml (1-2 pinches) salt
oil for brushing
extra flour for sprinkling

1. PREPARE THE FILLING: Stir-fry the onion in oil until softened and transparent, but not browned. Sprinkle the cumin, coriander and cayenne pepper over and stir-fry for 1-2 minutes. Add the meat, a little at a time. Loosen constantly with a large fork and stir-fry until the meat is lightly browned. Season with salt and pepper. Add the garlic and ginger and stir to mix. Add the tomatoes, reduce the heat and simmer until the mixture is thick and dry. Take care that it doesn't burn. Remove from the heat and allow to cool. Stir in the coriander leaves and lemon rind and cool completely.

2. PUR (PASTRY): Mix the lemon juice and water. Sift flour and salt together 3 times. Add water mixture to flour mixture and knead, mixing to a stiff dough. Divide the dough into 12 equal parts and roll each part into a ball the size of a table tennis ball. Roll each ball out with a rolling pin into a round ± 75 mm (3 in) in diameter. Set 6 rounds aside, and start with the first of the other 6 rounds. Brush the top of the first round with oil. Sift the flour over. Brush 4 rounds on both sides with oil, one at a time. Place the second round on the first and sift flour over. Repeat with round 3, then with rounds 4 and 5. The last round is brushed with oil on one side only and then placed on the pastry stack, oiled side down. In other words: the bottom and top of the pastry stack are not brushed with oil. Using a rolling pin, roll the pastry stack slightly flatter, into a round 200-225 mm (8-9 inches) in diameter. Repeat with the other 6 pastry rounds. Preheat the oven to 200 °C (400 °F).

3. Place 2 large rounds on baking sheets and bake for 3-5 minutes, so that the layers will separate again.

4. Remove from the stove and allow to cool slightly. Cut the pastry into strips ± 37,5 mm (1½ in) wide. Pull layers apart and cover with a damp cloth. Fill samoosas as shown in the sketch. Seal the ends with a paste of flour and water to prevent the filling coming out during deep frying, or unnecessary oil running into the filling. Deep-fry (see Deep-fried maize-meal balls, p. 26) until golden brown. Drain on kitchen paper. Serve lukewarm with lemon wedges.

HINT: If you're short of time, you can use phyllo pastry instead of the pur, although it will not have the same result. Brush phyllo layers with oil and use only 2 layers on top of one another. Cut into 37,5 mm (1½ in) strips and complete as shown in the sketch. The strips should not be too long, or the filling will be enclosed by too much pastry when folded; the pastry will not cook completely and the filling will still be cold when the samoosas are already golden brown outside.

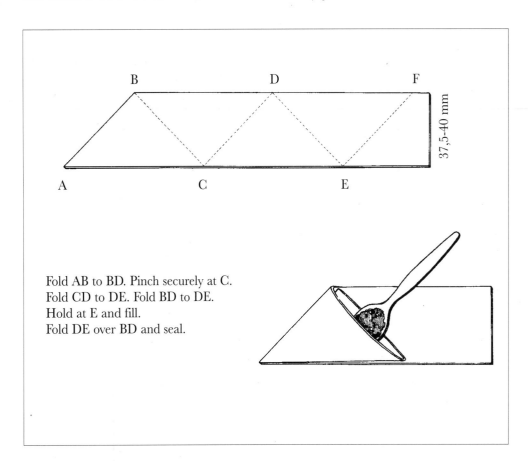

Fold AB to BD. Pinch securely at C.
Fold CD to DE. Fold BD to DE.
Hold at E and fill.
Fold DE over BD and seal.

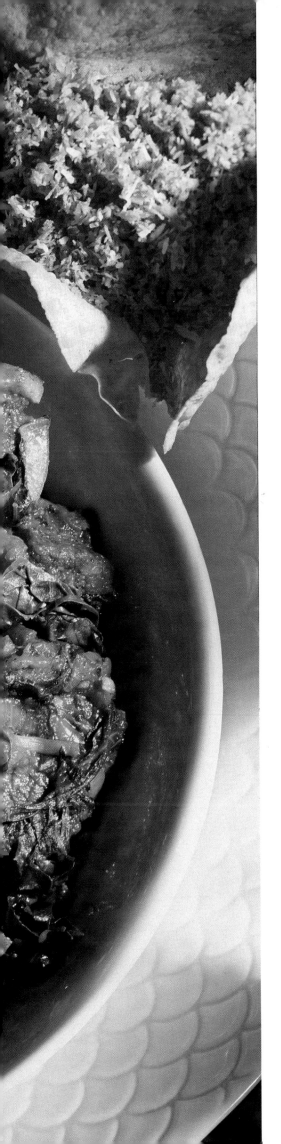

Seafood curry

(MAKES 6 SERVINGS)

These days, unlike at the beginning of the century, this dish is served hot as a party dish.

CURRY
12,5 ml (1 T) oil
2 onions, halved lengthways, peeled and chopped
25 ml (2 T) tomato concentrate
15 ml (3 t) Sri Lankan spice mixture (p. 100)
    or mild curry powder
5 ml (1 t) turmeric
5 ml (1 t) paprika
5 ml (1 t) ground coriander
3 ml (½ t) finely ground cardamom seed
2 bay leaves
500 ml (2 cups) Fish fumet (p. 46)
salt and freshly ground white pepper

SEAFOOD
12,5 ml (1 T) oil
6 langoustines, shells and alimentary
    canals removed
18 prawns, shells and alimentary
    canals removed
400 g firm-fleshed white fish, preferably
    yellowtail, skinned and cut into
    20 mm (± 1 in) cubes
200 g North Sea calamari rings
24 mussels in the half shell (p. 53)

GARNISH
bunches of fresh coriander leaves

1. CURRY: Heat the oil in a large saucepan and fry onions until softened and transparent, but not browned. Add the tomato concentrate and stir-fry for 5 minutes. Sprinkle the spice mixture of turmeric, paprika, coriander and cardamom over and stir-fry for 1 minute. Add the bay leaves and stock and simmer for 5 minutes. Taste and season with salt and pepper.
2. SEAFOOD: Heat the oil in a large frying pan and fry the langoustines for 1 minute. Add to the curry sauce. Fry the prawns for 1 minute and add to the sauce. Fry the fish on all sides and add to the curry sauce. Add the calamari, place the saucepan over moderate heat and simmer for 5 minutes. Add the mussels and heat through. Spoon into a heated serving dish, garnish with coriander leaves and serve with rice.

LAMB CURRY WITH SPINACH

Cold curried chicken

(MAKES 4 SERVINGS)

800 g-1 kg chicken breast fillets
salt and pepper
1 bottle (200 ml) apple juice
1 onion, halved lengthways, peeled and chopped
15 ml (3 t) oil
25 ml (2 T) spice mixture
    or curry powder
5 ml (1 t) turmeric
250 ml (1 cup) thick mayonnaise (p. 46)
1 ml (pinch) cayenne pepper
25 ml (2 T) chopped fresh parsley
    and/or chives and/or coriander leaves

SALAD
500 ml (2 cups) cooked rice
25 ml (2 T) sour cream
1 small pineapple or 1 large mango,
    peeled and finely chopped, or 3 bananas,
    peeled and sliced
1 tub (250 g) smooth cottage cheese
125 ml (½ cup) cream
salt and pepper

GARNISH
cherry tomatoes, halved
fresh coriander leaves

1. Place chicken in a large saucepan, season with salt and pepper and add apple juice. Heat to boiling point, reduce heat and simmer over low heat until chicken is cooked. Remove from heat and allow to cool in liquid.
2. Fry the onion in oil in a frying pan until softened and transparent, but not browned. Sprinkle the spice mixture and turmeric over and stir-fry for 1 minute. Add the liquid in which the chicken was cooked and simmer over low heat until all the liquid has evaporated. Purée in a food processor or blender. Stir half the curry mixture into the mayonnaise and reserve the remainder. Season the mayonnaise with a pinch of cayenne pepper and taste to see if it needs salt. Stir in the parsley/chives/coriander leaves. Cut the chicken into bite-sized pieces and stir it in. Place the chicken mixture in a shallow dish.
2. SALAD: Moisten the rice with the sour cream and spoon it over the chicken. Spread evenly. Arrange the pineapple/ mango/ bananas on top of the rice. Stir the remaining curry mixture into the cottage cheese. Spread cottage cheese mixture over the fruit. Beat cream until soft peaks start to form and season with salt and pepper. Spread over the cottage cheese. Garnish with cherry tomatoes and coriander leaves.

HOW MUCH MEAT SHOULD BE ALLOWED FOR CURRY?

Determining how much meat to allow for a curry can be a headache for cooks. The quantities are given in grams per eater:

Beef, with bone	250-500 g
Beef, without bone	200-300 g
Mutton, with bone	250-400 g
Mutton, without bone	200-300 g
Pork, with bone	250-400 g
Pork, without bone	200-300 g
Chicken, with bones	250-500 g

Chicken curry

(MAKES 4 SERVINGS)

This curry is best served hot and is very light. Take care not to overcook the chicken: it will get hard and the coconut milk will separate.

MARINADE
5 ml (1 t) turmeric
25 ml (2 T) light Sri Lankan spice mixture
  (p. 100)
12,5 ml (1 T) vinegar
12,5 ml (1 T) oil
150 ml (⅗ cup) water

CHICKEN
800 g chicken breast fillets,
  cut into bite-sized pieces
50 g (50 ml/4 T) salted butter
15 ml (3 t) cumin seed

OTHER INGREDIENTS
1 onion, halved lengthways, peeled and chopped
1 green chilli, seeded and chopped
250 ml (1 cup) coconut milk
5 ml (1 t) cayenne pepper
3 fresh curry leaves

1. MARINADE: Mix the turmeric and the spice mixture. Heat the vinegar and oil to boiling point in a saucepan. Stir in the curry mixture and stir-fry for 1 minute. Add the water, a little at a time, and bring the mixture just to boiling point. Remove from the heat and allow to cool.
2. Spoon the marinade over the chicken and stir to blend. Cover with cling wrap and marinate for at least 4 hours.
3. Remove the chicken from the marinade and wipe off the excess marinade. Reserve the marinade.

4. Heat the butter in a large frying pan until it begins to foam. Skim off the foam. Add the chicken, sprinkle cumin seed over and stir-fry for 5 minutes. Remove the chicken from the pan, using a slotted spoon, and add the onion and chilli to the pan. Stir-fry for 2 minutes. Add the coconut milk, cayenne pepper and curry leaves. Add the reserved marinade and return the chicken to the pan. Simmer over low heat until cooked. Serve with dhal rice (lentils and rice) and a selection of sambals (chapter 17) and accompaniments. Fried bananas (p. 141) are a must.

Mutton and cabbage curry

(MAKES 8 SERVINGS)

This recipe comes from the townships, where fiery food is appreciated. Note that a fairly small quantity of meat is used, and that the dish is stretched with cabbage and potatoes without adversely affecting the flavour.

1,5 kg stewing mutton, cubed
25 ml (2 T) Indian spice mixture (p. 100)
  or hot curry powder
5 ml (1 t) turmeric
salt and pepper to taste
3 plump garlic cloves, peeled and crushed
2 large onions, halved lengthways,
  peeled and chopped
50 ml (4 T) oil
750 ml (3 cups) boiling water
10 ml (2 t) Sambal oelek (p. 101)
  or 4 red chillies (optional)
6-8 potatoes, peeled and halved
1 cabbage, quartered and core removed,
  then shredded
1 tin (410 g) Indian tomatoes
12,5 ml (1 T) Garam masala (p. 100)
  or mild curry powder

1. Rub a mixture of spice mixture, turmeric, salt, pepper and garlic into the meat. Cover with cling wrap and refrigerate for 2-3 hours to allow the flavourings to be thoroughly absorbed.
2. Fry the onions in the oil in a large saucepan over moderate heat until softened and slightly browned. Remove and set aside. Fry meat in the same saucepan, a little at a time, until browned all over. Return all the meat and onions to the saucepan. Heat to boiling point, reduce the heat to low, cover and braise for 20 minutes.
3. Add the boiling water and sambal oelek, heat to boiling point, reduce the heat and simmer for 1 hour.

4. Place the potatoes on top of the meat, then half the cabbage. Mix to blend. Place the remaining cabbage on top, then the tomatoes. Sprinkle the garam masala on top. Cover and simmer for 30 minutes. Remove the lid and stir the mixture. Cover and simmer for a further 20-30 minutes or until the meat is meltingly tender and the sauce has thickened. Serve with rice and a selection of sambals (chapter 17).

Basic curry for four

(MAKES 4-6 SERVINGS)

Because there are literally thousands of recipes for curry dishes, the recipe below is a basic method, leaving room for cooks to improvise.

37,5 ml (3 T) Ghee (p. 15)
25-50 ml (2-4 T) spice mixture
  or curry powder
  (depending on how hot you prefer it)
6 plump garlic cloves, peeled and crushed
1 piece (25-50 mm/1-2 in) fresh ginger root,
  peeled and finely grated (depending on how
  hot you prefer it)
2 large or 3 medium-sized onions,
  halved lengthways, peeled and chopped
1 tin (410 g) Indian tomatoes
1,2-1,5 kg meat
boiling water
2 pieces cassia
4-6 fresh curry leaves (optional)
2 bay leaves

GARNISH
chopped fresh coriander leaves

1. Heat the ghee to moderately hot and sprinkle the spice mixture over. Fry for 15 seconds, then add garlic and ginger. Stir-fry for 30 seconds. Add the onions, reduce the heat and stir-fry until the onions have softened. Add the tomatoes and heat to boiling point.
2. Add the meat and just enough boiling water to cover the meat halfway. Add the cassia, curry leaves and bay leaves, cover and simmer over low heat until the meat is tender. Garnish with coriander leaves.

ADDITIONS
• Two bunches of spinach, washed and ribs removed, then rolled up and cut into thin strips. Season the spinach with 3 ml (½ t) finely ground fenugreek seed and spoon on top of curry 30 minutes before the end of cooking time.

• Six carrots, scraped and thickly sliced. Add to the curry 45 minutes before the end of cooking time.

• Four to six potatoes, peeled and quartered. Add to the curry 45 minutes before the end of cooking time.

• For a sweeter curry, add 4 ripe bananas and 250 ml (1 cup) cream to the curry 30 minutes before the end of cooking time and simmer, uncovered, over low heat until the sauce thickens.

• Add 500 ml (2 cups) almost-cooked lentils or chickpeas to the curry 30 minutes before the end of cooking time.

• Add 2 brinjals (prepared as described on p. 142) to the curry 45 minutes before the end of cooking time. Brinjals should be used with tomatoes in a curry dish and, if necessary, more water should be added because brinjals become mushy with cooking and make the sauce very thick. If you do not want the brinjals to become mushy, add them to the curry 20-30 minutes before the end of cooking time.

• Add 2-3 celery stalks to the curry with carrots and potatoes.

• Break 1 cauliflower into florets and add to the curry about 20 minutes before the end of cooking time. Sprinkle 5 ml (1 t) turmeric over the cauliflower florets so that they will turn yellow during cooking and enhance the appearance of the curry.

• Soak 225-300 g (375-500 ml/1½-2 cups) dried fruit – such as apples, apricots, prunes, pears or peaches – beforehand in water or rooibos tea and add to the curry 30-40 minutes before the end of cooking time. Because apricots tend to make the curry a bit sour, it may be necessary to add 12,5 ml (1 T) soft brown sugar. The quantity of fruit called for here will make a true fruit curry. If you prefer a more meaty fruit curry, reduce the quantity of fruit. Serve fruit curry with a strong-flavoured chutney and toasted coconut.

Vetkoek with curried mince

Prepare the mince mixture as for Samoosas (p. 101) and keep warm. Use one of the bread recipes – especially Braided loaf (p. 10) for finely textured white vetkoek, Soweto grey bread (p. 10) for a light, slightly coarse texture, or Pot bread (p. 10) for a denser texture with an olive oil flavour – and shape flat, round vetkoek from dough that has risen once. Cover with a damp cloth and leave to rise until the vetkoek have doubled in volume. Deep-fry until done (see p. 15). Halve the vetkoek horizontally and fill with the curried mince. Drop a spoonful of tomato or cucumber sambal on top. Banana slices, sprinkled with lemon juice, and/or toasted coconut can also be sprinkled on top of the meat in the vetkoek.

VARIATION
Halve butternut squash lengthways and bake as for Butternut and mango soup (p. 34). Spoon the mince into the hollows of the butternut and serve with a spoonful of Coriander pesto (p. 34).

MORE CURRY RECIPES
Frikkadels (p. 75), Curried tripe (p. 90), Brawn (p. 90), Pienangvleis (p. 70), Bobotie (p. 69) and Butternut and mango soup (p. 34).

Feathered Food

POULTRY, SO THE old hands say, is to the cook what a canvas is to a painter. Chickens, wood pigeons, pheasant and guineafowl were cooked in the pot or used for making 'ragoe' and pies during the governorship of Simon van der Stel.

Whether the indigenous peoples ate chickens before the arrival of the Europeans in South Africa has yet to be researched. Chickens, ducks, Muscovy ducks, peacocks and turkeys were available as early as the seventeenth century. Quail, wood pigeons, guineafowl and pheasant were indigenous to our country. The Sothos often cooked them and served them mainly with maram nuts, a typical Bushveld nut cooked in the ashes of the braai fire. Infinitely better than peanuts!

The trek farmers came into contact with ostriches, but did not eat the meat. The feathers, however, were sold from the eighteenth century onwards. It was only in the 1970s that ostrich meat appeared on the menu. These days it is very popular, especially because – like most game – it is very low in cholesterol.

Chicken is undoubtedly the most popular poultry, and chicken pie, with its characteristic puff pastry crust, is the principal poultry dish. The art of making puff pastry is still ascribed to the French Huguenots, but I doubt the validity of this claim, as the pastry was not yet known in France at that time. In fact, it was only after the French Revolution that the quality of flour in France improved to the point where it could have made a contribution to a more refined baking art. A group of Viennese bakers established themselves in Paris in 1840, and only a decade later was puff pastry, as we know it today, recorded by Anton Carême.

Chicken farming expanded dramatically during the 1960s. Many people complained about the so-called fishy taste, but with the ever-rising price of red meat, chicken became increasingly more popular – just as margarine did at the expense of butter. The first fried chicken eateries also made their appearance during that decade. Sometimes fried chicken was served in a basket, but most of the time it was served on a plate with chips. Guests ate

POUSSINS WITH GRAPES

the chicken with their hands, rinsing their fingers in a finger bowl afterwards and drying them on a small cloth. Chicken, once a favourite Sunday food, became an everyday meal. Feeding and housing of chickens have improved since then, but a free-range chicken remains special, although the current generation will probably find it very difficult to chop off the head!

Goose fat was an important ingredient in the kitchens of the first half of the twentieth century. Ducks, Muscovy ducks and geese wandered around every farmyard in the country. Up to the end of the 1940s, poultry was preserved for months by salting the flesh and then storing it in its own fat, or in a mixture of fat and lard, in dishes or jars. Salted goose was served in the winter months and a freshly slaughtered, fattened goose was served instead of turkey at Christmas. This kind of preserving is called a 'confit', and is currently in fashion again. The older generation salted, cooked and preserved; the new generation parcooks, removes the bones, covers the flesh with the rendered fat and later cooks it in its own fat. Goose was served at the Cape, but the birds only really became food on our tables with the arrival of the second group of British settlers, especially those from Ireland. The Irish continued their tradition of serving goose on St Michael's Day (29 September) in their adopted country to ensure that, so the saying goes, they would have money in their pockets all year round. The goose should weigh at least 4,5 kg (10 lb) and is given a potato stuffing, which absorbs a large part of the fat. The liver is carefully removed and fried separately, or used to make an excellent pâté.

Ostrich meat is treated in exactly the same way as beef, but should first be marinated in yoghurt or buttermilk. The fillet, or fillets, cut from the leg are fried over high heat in a ridged grilling pan and served sliced. The rest of the meat is stewed, especially the neck, shin and offal. I prefer to serve only the fillet fried, and to marinate the leg and then stew it until cooked. One exception is the butterflied leg, which is prepared with a salsa from 'Patataland', as the region from Ladismith to Knysna was once called. This recipe exemplifies the freedom of the new generation of cooks – they have no fear of strong flavours.

Chicken pie

(MAKES 8-10 SERVINGS

Grandma's recipe book calls for a 'book-muslin' cloth in which to tie the herbs, but ordinary muslin will do.

STOCK

2 onions, halved lengthways, peeled and sliced
1 large carrot, scraped and sliced
1 small celery stalk, washed and threads
removed, then thinly sliced
2 whole red chillies
3 plump garlic cloves, bruised and peeled
3 litres (12 cups) water
1 bottle (750 ml) dry white wine
6 bay leaves
12 black peppercorns
6 allspice berries
6 cloves

FILLING

2 large chickens, halved, rinsed well
and patted dry
25 ml (2 T) vermicelli, soaked overnight
in 125 ml (½ cup) water
25 ml (2 T) sago, soaked overnight
in 125 ml (½ cup) boiling water
2 extra-large egg yolks
25 ml (2 T) lemon juice
50 ml (4 T) butter
4 hard-boiled eggs, shelled and
coarsely chopped
250 g cooked ham, diced
salt, pepper and grated nutmeg

CRUST

500 g puff pastry
1 egg, separated
12,5 ml (1 T) milk

1. Place stock ingredients in a large saucepan. Heat to boiling point, reduce the heat and simmer for 1 hour. Pour through a sieve.
2. Add the chickens to the stock, cover and simmer for 1-1½ hours until the flesh is just tender and is easy to remove from the bones. Do not overcook the chicken, as it will be mushy when flaked. Remove the cooked chickens from the saucepan and allow to cool. Reduce the stock to 500 ml (2 cups) and spoon it into a large baking pan so that it cools quickly. Place in the freezer until ice cold, so that all the fat gathers at the top. Skim off the fat.
3. Meanwhile, remove the flesh from the bones, making sure that there are no small bones. Cut the flesh into bite-sized portions and place in the refrigerator.

4. Boil the vermicelli and sago in two separate saucepans until cooked and completely transparent. You may have to add more water. Stir constantly, to prevent sticking. Heat the stock to boiling point and skim off any froth immediately. Add vermicelli and sago. Simmer for a few minutes. Taste and season with salt and pepper if necessary.
5. Mix the egg yolks and lemon juice. Remove the saucepan containing the sago mixture from the heat and quickly stir in the egg yolk mixture. Add the chicken, hardboiled eggs and ham. Taste and season with more salt, pepper and nutmeg to taste. Spoon the filling into a greased, shallow pie dish, level the top and refrigerate to cool completely.
6. MAKE THE CRUST: Roll out the dough to extend 25 mm (1 in) beyond the rim of the pie dish. Wrap the dough over a rolling pin and then roll over the pie filling. Cut the pastry edge to fit the filling, and press it in around the sides. Using an apple corer, press 2-3 holes in the centre of the crust. Cut out decorative motifs from the leftover pastry and affix them to the crust with lightly whisked egg whites. Place the pie in the freezer for 1 hour. Preheat the oven to 220 °C (450 °F).
7. Beat the egg yolk and milk. Remove the pie from the freezer and brush the top lightly with the egg yolk mixture, taking care that it does not form 'tears'. Make 2-3 funnels from aluminium foil and press them into the pie, through the holes, to allow steam to escape.
8. Bake the pie for 35-45 minutes, or until the crust is nicely browned and puffed up. Serve the pie with Funeral rice (p. 122), Old-fashioned green-beans, Sweetened pumpkin (p. 134), Sweet potatoes (p. 135) and/or stewed dried fruit (chapter 14).

Fried chicken

South Africans like to fry meat in a saucepan and then to braise it until tender, especially large free-range chickens, duck, guineafowl and wood pigeons. The bird, whole or cut into portions, is fried in a little oil in a black flat-bottomed pot until golden brown. All the excess fat is poured off, and the meat is then seasoned with salt and pepper. A little coriander and ground ginger is rubbed into duck, and wood pigeons are rubbed with coriander, ground cloves and ground ginger. Sometimes one or two bay leaves are also added to the saucepan. Often a small sliced onion and a scraped carrot, cut into rings, are added. And lastly, a little stock or water is added. The saucepan is covered and the

bird braised for about another half hour, over low heat. Today's chickens cook very quickly. Sometimes peeled potatoes, halved lengthways, are also added: to free-range chickens after about 30 minutes of cooking time have elapsed, and from the start for supermarket chickens. Duck, guineafowl and wood pigeons have 500 ml (2 cups) chicken stock added, and no potatoes. Sometimes mushrooms are added to guineafowl and wood pigeons, and olives to duck. The chicken is served with white rice, over which the cooking juices are spooned.

Butterflied chicken

Another way to grill chicken is to butterfly it first. Place the chicken, breast side down, on a board and cut out the entire backbone with poultry scissors. Turn the chicken over so that the breast is uppermost and press it flat with both palms. Cut incisions through each flank and push the tips of the leg bones (shins) through them to ensure that the cooked chicken will have a neat shape. Insert butter under the skin, especially on the breast. Place the chicken, skin side up, on the oiled rack of a roasting pan, place on the lowest rack in the oven and grill for 12-20 minutes under the preheated grilling element. Insert a skewer in the thick part of the leg: if a pinkish liquid comes out, it must be grilled longer. Turn the chicken over and grill for 5 minutes. Turn again and grill the chicken for another 5 minutes. Test again.

A butterflied chicken may also be grilled with bricks on it. Do not insert butter under the skin, but season well with salt and pepper. Heat 125 ml (½ cup) olive oil in a large flat-bottomed saucepan until hot but not smoking and place the chicken in it, skin side down. Cover two bricks with aluminium foil and place them on the chicken in the saucepan. Cover and grill for 12 minutes. Remove the lid and bricks, and turn the chicken carefully without tearing the skin. Grill for 12 minutes without the bricks. Test for doneness. Keep on grilling until no more watery blood flows from the legs. Place the chicken, breast side down, on a large, heated serving dish and push a small plate halfway up under the tail end of the chicken. The meat juices will then flow towards the breast and keep it succulent. Cover lightly with aluminium foil and bake for 10-20 minutes in a preheated oven at 160 °C (325 °F).

Halve the chicken and serve one half per person, with chips and lemon wedges. Serve a green salad separately.

Fried chicken wings

Chicken wings are one of the tastiest of snacks. They are served at cocktail parties, but especially as a snack at large family get-togethers, before the meat is braaied over the coals outside. The recipe may look long, but it has the advantage that you can start it on one day and complete it the next.

24 chicken wings, rinsed thoroughly
   and patted dry
3 large egg whites
180 g (375 ml/1½ cups) cornflour
5 ml (1 t) cayenne pepper
oil

MARINADE
2 plump garlic cloves, bruised,
   peeled and crushed
50 mm (2 in) piece fresh ginger root, peeled and
   finely chopped, or 25 ml (2 T) ground ginger
50 ml (4 T) soy sauce
30 ml (2 large T) brandy

SAUCE
250 ml (1 cup) chicken stock
finely grated rind of 2 lemons
50 ml (4 T) lemon juice
30 ml (2 large T) sugar
20 ml (4 t) soy sauce
5 ml (1 t) ground ginger
10 ml (2 t) cornflour, dissolved in:
15 ml (3 t) cold water
salt

1. MAKE THE MARINADE: Mix all the ingredients in a large mixing bowl and place in the freezer for 20 minutes until well chilled. Remove from the freezer, add the wings and mix to blend, cover with cling wrap and place in the refrigerator.
2. Remove the dish of wings from the refrigerator, remove the cling wrap and pour off the marinade. Place the wings in a colander, and make sure that they are fairly dry.
3. Whisk the egg whites lightly with a fork. Sift the cornflour and cayenne pepper together. Roll each wing first in the egg white, then in the cornflour mixture. Shake off excess cornflour and deep-fry 6 wings at a time in hot oil until golden but not browned. Reserve the oil. If you are making the wings for a party, they may be left to cool. Store in the refrigerator. Reheat in the oil just before serving.
4. Meanwhile, mix all the sauce ingredients, except the salt, heat and boil for 2 minutes. Fry the wings, this time 12 at a time, for 2 minutes in hot oil. Remove with a slotted spoon and drain on crumpled kitchen paper. Season lightly with salt, keep warm and repeat with remaining 12 wings. Pour the sauce into a bowl and place it on a large serving plate. Arrange the wings around the sauce bowl and serve with paper serviettes.

Tandoori chicken

(MAKES 2 SERVINGS)

This recipe is not the real thing, because it is not cooked in a tandoor. The dish is often cooked in a clay pot buried under hot coals next to the braai fire. The chicken may also be cooked on the spit in the oven (see Variations).

1 large broiler chicken, rinsed thoroughly
   and patted dry
1 large onion, peeled and quartered
3 plump garlic cloves, bruised and peeled
25 mm (1 in) piece ginger root,
   peeled and sliced
10 ml (2 t) finely ground roasted coriander seed
   (see p. 60)
10 ml (2 t) cumin seed, roasted and finely
   ground, like coriander seed
3 ml (½ t) chilli powder
10 ml (2 t) salt
125 ml (½ cup) yoghurt
10 ml (2 t) wine vinegar
10 ml (2 t) Worcestershire sauce
grated rind and juice of 2 lemons
50 g (50 ml/4 T) butter
5 ml (1 t) Garam masala (p. 100)

1. Make 3 diagonal cuts in each leg and 3 diagonal cuts in each breast, down the sides of the chicken.
2. Pulse the onion, garlic and ginger in a food processor. Add the coriander and cumin seeds to the onion mixture. Add the chilli powder and salt and mix to a smooth paste. Stir in the yoghurt, vinegar, Worcestershire sauce, lemon rind and juice. Place the chicken in a mixing bowl, pour the yoghurt mixture over and rub it into the chicken. Cover with cling wrap and marinate for at least 6 hours in the refrigerator. Preheat the oven to 160 °C (325 °F).
3. Melt the butter in a baking pan. Sprinkle the garam masala over. Place the chicken in the pan and cover with aluminium foil, shiny side in. Bake for 40 minutes.

VARIATIONS
● If a clay pot is to be used, first soak it in water for 24 hours. Follow the recipe above. Make a large fire on the ground and draw coals to one side with a spade. Make a hole in the ground and place some of the coals in the hole. Place pot containing the chicken on top, cover with the rest of the coals and bake for 40-60 minutes.
● If the rotisserie in the oven is to be used, it must be inserted through the chicken. Baste the chicken constantly with melted Ghee (p. 15) mixed with garam masala. Halve the chicken and serve a half per person with Naan bread (p. 15).

HINT: Tandoori chicken is traditionally coloured red. Stir red food colouring into the marinade to achieve this. If red food powder is available, rub it into the skin.

Soweto chicken

(MAKES 6 SERVINGS)

2 onions, halved, peeled and chopped
25 ml (2 T) oil
3 plump cloves garlic, bruised,
   peeled and crushed
10 ml (2 t) ground cinnamon
10 ml (2 t) cayenne or chilli pepper
5 ml (1 t) turmeric
15 ml (3 t) curry powder
salt and pepper
1,5 kg chicken portions
1 can (410 g) tomatoes, chopped
2 red sweet peppers, halved, seeds
   and membranes removed,
   then cut into strips
6 bay leaves
2 red chillies, halved lengthways
   and seeds removed, then shredded

GARNISH
1 bunch spring onions, trimmed diagonally
   and green parts shredded with scissors

1. Fry the onions in the oil in a large, flat-bottomed, cast-iron pot until softened and transparent, but not browned. Add the garlic and stir.
2. Meanwhile, mix the cinnamon, cayenne pepper, turmeric, curry powder, salt and pepper to taste. Rub into the chicken portions. Arrange the chicken in the pot, cover and simmer for 15 minutes over low heat. Turn the chicken, add the tomatoes, sweet peppers, bay leaves and chillies and simmer, uncovered, for 45 minutes over low heat.
3. Place the chicken in a serving dish, sprinkle shredded spring onion greens over and arrange the stems on top. Serve with Pearl wheat (p. 127) or Samp and beans (p. 124).

Stuffed poussins with grapes

(MAKES 6 SERVINGS)

This is a delicious dish for summer entertaining, and is especially suitable for the buffet table. The grapes create a convivial atmosphere and represent our cornucopia of fruit.

STUFFING
250 ml (1 cup) cooked brown rice
1 packet (250 g) streaky bacon,
    chopped and fried until crisp
25 ml (2 T) homemade grape jam (with pips)
1 packet (100 g/250 ml/1 cup) walnuts,
    coarsely chopped
3 hard-boiled eggs, finely chopped
10 ml (2 t) peeled, grated, fresh ginger root
50 g (50 ml/ 4T) butter, melted and foam
    skimmed off
2 apples, peeled and coarsely grated
150 g (250 ml/1 cup) seedless raisins,
    soaked in: 75 ml (6 T) grape juice
250 g pork sausages, meat squeezed from
    the casings
grated rind of 2 lemons
5 ml (1 t) lemon juice
salt, pepper and grated nutmeg to taste

POUSSINS
about 25 ml (2 T) salt
freshly ground pepper to taste
5 ml (1 t) ground ginger
6 petits poussins, rinsed thoroughly
    inside and out, and patted dry
12 rashers streaky bacon

SAUCE
125 ml (½ cup) dry white wine
250 ml (1 cup) chicken stock
25 ml (2 T) each butter and cake flour
250 ml (1 cup) cream
salt, pepper and grated nutmeg to taste
grated rind and juice of 1 lemon
25 ml (2 T) brandy
500 ml (2 cups) peeled,
    halved and pitted grapes

GLAZE
50 ml (4 T) smooth apricot jam
12,5 ml (1 T) brandy
5 ml (1 t) prepared strong mustard
10 ml (2 t) lemon juice

1. STUFFING: Mix all the stuffing ingredients, except the flavourings, lightly but thoroughly with a large, two-pronged fork. Taste and season with salt, pepper and nutmeg to taste. Cover with cling wrap and refrigerate until needed. Preheat the oven to 180 °C (350 °F).
2. Mix the salt, pepper and ginger and use to rub the poussins inside and out. Divide stuffing into 6 portions and use to stuff the cavities. Tuck the neck skin under each chicken and secure it, front and back, with toothpicks or skewers. Place the poussins next to one another on the greased rack of a roasting pan, and arrange 2 bacon rashers over the breast of each. Roast until the skin begins to brown and the bacon is crisp. Remove the bacon and set aside. Roast the poussins for a further 10 minutes or so. Remove the rack from the oven, place it on another pan and keep poussins warm.
3. SAUCE: Pour off the fat from the pan in which poussins were roasted. Add wine to pan and heat over moderate heat. Chop crisp bacon finely and add to pan. Using a wooden spatula, loosen all the bits sticking to the base so that they can dissolve in the liquid. Pour liquid through a sieve into a clean saucepan and add stock. Heat until hot, but not boiling. Meanwhile, mix butter and flour to a beurre manié (smooth paste). Remove stock from heat and beat in the beurre manié, a little at a time. Return to the heat and stir until the sauce thickens and starts boiling. Stir in cream, heat to boiling point and boil to required thickness. Taste and season with salt (if necessary), ground pepper and nutmeg. Lastly, stir in lemon peel, juice and brandy and keep sauce warm.
4. GLAZE: Switch on the grill and place a rack low in the oven. Mix jam, brandy, mustard and lemon juice in a small saucepan and heat until runny. Brush over poussins and return them to the oven. Check after a few minutes, brush more glaze over and grill until golden brown and shiny.
5. TO SERVE: Arrange the poussins in a large, heated serving dish. Add the grapes to the hot sauce and serve separately. You could also arrange one whole – or halved lengthways – poussin on each of 6 heated plates. Spoon the sauce on to the plates and sprinkle the grapes over. Serve with Creamed potatoes (p. 140), mangetout and baby squash.

Chicken Maryland

(MAKES 4 SERVINGS)

This dish unleashes a nostalgic 'fifties' feeling. Remember those kitchens with chrome-legged Formica tables and matching chairs; the food cupboard with glass panes that you could shift back and forth … Those were the days before KFC, when chicken Maryland was a luxury to ordinary people, and chicken Kiev or cordon bleu appeared as very 'with-it' dishes at elegant parties. Elvis Presley, 'Jailhouse Rock' and ducktails on one side, and Marlene Dietrich and Maurice Chevalier on the other.

CHICKEN
37,5 ml (3 T) milk
30 g (65 ml/¼ cup) cake flour, seasoned with:
salt and pepper
1 egg, lightly beaten with:
5 ml (1 t) water
100 g (375 ml/1½ cups) fresh beadcrumbs,
    lightly toasted in the oven and crushed
4 large chicken breast fillets,
    flattened between 2 sheets of waxed paper
50 g (50 ml/4 T) butter
37,5 ml (3 T) oil

FRIED BANANAS
50 ml (4 T) sugar
25 ml (2 T) butter
2 bananas, peeled, halved lengthways
    or sliced and sprinkled with:
12,5 ml (1 T) lemon juice

1. Place milk, flour, egg mixture and crumbs in separate mixing bowls. Season each bowl, and the chicken breasts, with salt and pepper. Dip the breasts, one at a time, in the milk, allow the excess milk to drip off and then dip the breast in the flour. Shake off excess flour and place the chicken on a wire rack over a baking sheet. Refrigerate for 10 minutes.
2. Dip the breasts, one at a time, in the egg mixture and allow the excess egg mixture drip off. Dip in the crumbs, press them in lightly and shake off excess crumbs. Return to the refrigerator for 10 minutes.
3. Preheat the oven to 160 °C (325 °F). Place the butter and oil in a heavy-bottomed saucepan and heat until hot. Skim off the foam and fry the chicken, 2 breasts at a time, on both sides until golden brown. Place on the rack of a roasting pan and roast for 20 minutes.
4. MEANWHILE, FRY THE BANANAS: Place the sugar and butter in a frying pan and stir over moderate heat until sugar has melted. Add the bananas and fry them until golden brown and cooked. Turn the bananas often, to prevent their sticking.
5. TO SERVE: Place the cooked chicken on a serving plate, arrange sweetcorn fritters around them and finish with the fried bananas, cherry tomatoes and parsley.

CHICKEN MARYLAND

Chicken Tetrazzini

(MAKES 8 SERVINGS)

This dish was introduced to South Africa, and popularised, by Lesley Faull of the Silwood Kitchen. Along with lasagne verdi it was, in the 1970s, the most common party dish.

1 very large or 2 small chickens,
    rinsed thoroughly and patted dry
1 litre (4 cups) weak chicken stock
2 celery stalks, rinsed and threads removed,
    then chopped
1 large or 2 medium-sized onions,
    halved lengthways, peeled and sliced
4 large carrots, scraped and sliced
5 ml (1 t) dried tarragon
1 packet (500 g) spaghetti or, preferably,
    tagliatelle (bought or home-made),
    cooked and treated with oil (p. 127)
50 g (50 ml/4 T) butter
2 punnets (500 g) button mushrooms,
    wiped clean and sliced
12,5 ml (1 T) lemon juice
1 ml (pinch) each mustard powder,
    grated nutmeg and cayenne pepper
salt and pepper
½ packet (50 g/125 ml/½ cup) blanched
    almonds, lightly bruised

SAUCE FOR CHICKEN
37,5 g (37,5 ml/3 T) butter
12 g (25 ml/2 T) cake flour
1 ml (pinch) each grated nutmeg,
    mustard powder and ground cloves
salt and pepper
250 ml (1 cup) cream
75 ml (6 T) dry sherry or herbed wine
    such as vermouth

TOPPING
250 ml (1 cup) finely grated cheese:
    a mixture of mature Cheddar,
    Parmesan, Gruyère and/or
    Emmenthaler cheese
paprika

1. Place the chicken(s) in a large saucepan, add the stock, celery, onions, carrots and tarragon and simmer until just tender. Remove the chickens from the saucepan and leave until cold. Pour the stock through a sieve, allow to cool and place in the freezer.
2. Spoon the cooked pasta into a baking dish.
3. Melt the butter in a frying pan and add the mushrooms. Season with lemon juice, mustard, nutmeg and cayenne pepper. Fry until cooked and stir in the almonds. Using a slotted spoon, spoon the mixture on top of the pasta and mix to blend. Cut the chicken into bite-sized pieces, place on top of the pasta and mix lightly. Preheat the oven to 180 °C (350 °F).
4. SAUCE: Melt the butter in the pan in which the mushrooms were fried and sprinkle the flour over. Stir-fry for 1 minute. Remove from the heat. Season with nutmeg, mustard and cloves. Remove stock from the freezer and skim off the fat on the surface. Stir the stock gradually into the roux (flour mixture in the pan) and return to the heat. Stir until the sauce is cooked and has thickened. Taste and season with salt and pepper. Stir in the cream. Stir in the sherry, very slowly. Simmer for 1 minute and spoon the sauce over the pasta and chicken mixture.
5. Sprinkle the cheese over, season lightly with paprika and bake for 30-45 minutes. Serve with a green salad.

Chicken à la king

(MAKES 4 SERVINGS)

The great favourite of the middle of the twentieth century is back again.

8 chicken breasts, skinned
250 ml (1 cup) dry white wine
1 small onion, peeled and chopped
25 ml (2 T) butter
15 ml (3 t) oil
1 large yellow and/or red sweet pepper, halved,
    seeds and membranes removed,
    then thinly sliced
1 punnet (240 g) button mushrooms,
    wiped and thinly sliced
salt and freshly ground white pepper
3 ml (½ t) cayenne pepper
3 ml (½ t) mustard powder
15 ml (3 t) chopped fresh marjoram
SAUCE
50 g (50 ml/4 T) butter
15 ml (3 t) cake flour
250 ml (1 cup) chicken stock,
    made from 1 stock cube
250 ml (1 cup) cream
25 ml (2 T) dry sherry
salt and freshly ground white pepper
chopped fresh parsley

1. Place the chicken breasts in a saucepan and pour the wine over. Place a sheet of buttered waxed paper on top, cover and heat to boiling point. Reduce the heat, remove the lid and simmer for 30 minutes until the liquid has evaporated and the chicken is cooked.
2. Fry the onion in butter and oil until softened and transparent, but not browned. Add the sweet pepper and fry for 1 minute. Add the mushrooms and fry until the liquid has evaporated. Season with salt, pepper, cayenne pepper, mustard and marjoram.
3. SAUCE: Melt the butter in a saucepan, stir in the flour and cook for 1 minute. Remove from the heat and beat in the stock. Return to the heat and cook for 3 minutes. Stir in the cream and sherry, taste and season with salt and pepper. (If the sauce is very thick, it can be thinned with a little milk.) Slice the chicken breasts and mix them with the sauce. Add the vegetable mixture and stir to blend. Heat through. Spoon chicken mixture onto rice in a large serving dish and garnish with parsley.

Coq au vin

(MAKES 6 SERVINGS)

This dish was preceded by various versions, from C Louis Leipoldt and others, but it was in the 1960s that the Burgundian version came our way. We first had to become wine drinkers. Before this, chicken was cooked in vaaljapie (rough wine), but that was a long, long way from coq au vin. If we adopt something from the French, it must be done correctly.

COQ AU VIN ROODEBERG
There is no such dish as coq au vin in France. There is, however, coq au vin rouge (with red wine) or coq au riesling. The name of the wine in which the chicken is cooked should, preferably, be added. So chicken cooked in red wine would, for example, be coq au vin Roodeberg and the white wine version would be, for example, coq au vin La Gratitude. The red wine version follows.

125 g lean bacon, cut into 25 x 6 mm
    (1 x ¼ in) cubes
30 g (30 ml/2 large T) butter
1 large chicken, cut into portions
salt and freshly ground black pepper
75 ml (6 T) brandy
1 bottle (750 ml/3 cups) matured red wine
300 ml (1⅓ cups) hot, strong
    chicken stock
10 ml (2 t) tomato paste
2 plump garlic cloves, bruised,
    peeled and crushed
3 ml (½ t) dried thyme
2 bay leaves
24 braised small onions (p. 147)
250 g fried button mushrooms (p. 145)
30 g (60 ml/3 large T) cake flour
30 g (30 ml/2 large T) butter

1. Cover the bacon with water and simmer for 10 minutes. Refresh under cold running water and pat dry. Melt the butter in a large, heavy-bottomed saucepan. Add the bacon and fry until lightly browned. Remove with a slotted spoon and set aside. Fry ½ of the chicken portions in the same saucepan until golden brown all over. Add to the bacon. Repeat with the remaining chicken portions. Pour off the excess fat.

2. Return the chicken and bacon to the saucepan and season with salt and pepper. Cover and simmer for 10 minutes over low heat. Remove the lid, add the brandy and ignite it. Shake the saucepan until the flames die. Add the wine, stock, tomato paste, garlic, thyme and bay leaves. Cover and heat to boiling point. Immediately reduce the heat and simmer, uncovered, for 30 minutes. Test for doneness. Continue to simmer, if necessary.

3. Meanwhile, prepare the onions and mushrooms (p. 145 and 147).

4. Place the cooked chicken in a large, heated serving dish and keep warm. Heat the sauce in the saucepan to boiling point and skim off any fat that rises to the surface. Reduce the sauce to 500 ml (2 cups). Taste and season with more salt and pepper if necessary. Remove the bay leaves. Mix the flour and 30 g butter to a paste. Remove the saucepan from the heat and beat in the flour paste, a little at a time. Return to the heat and boil for 2-3 minutes, stirring constantly with a wooden spoon (see Hint). Add the chicken to the sauce and simmer for 2-3 minutes. Add the onions and mushrooms and simmer for a further 2-3 minutes. Spoon into an attractive serving dish and sprinkle the parsley over. Traditionally, parslied potatoes are served with this. If you want to serve vegetables, buttered mangetout are perfect.

GOLDEN RULE: Never use poor quality wine for cooking, and make sure that the wine you use for cooking is good enough to be drunk with the meal.

HINT: This dish may be made in advance. Remove the saucepan containing the sauce from the heat and add the chicken, onions and mushrooms. Allow to cool and refrigerate overnight. Do not refrigerate for longer than 12 hours, as the onions will begin to ferment. If you want to keep it for longer, or to freeze it, leave out the onions and cook them just before serving. Remove from the refrigerator and skim off any fat.

Settlers' goose

(MAKES 6 SERVINGS)

1 goose of at least 4,5 kg
salt, white pepper and ground ginger
neck, heart and stomach, covered
*   with lightly salted water*
*   and cooked separately – retain stock*
*   (do not cook liver)*

STUFFING
1 medium-sized onion,
*   halved lengthways,*
*   peeled and chopped*
125 g back bacon, shredded
750 g (3-4) cooked potatoes, mashed
uncooked goose liver, chopped
salt and freshly ground pepper
grated nutmeg
1 ml (pinch) ground cloves
15 ml (3 t) finely chopped fresh parsley
15 ml (3 t) finely chopped fresh sage

ONION SAUCE
2 large onions, halved lengthways,
*   peeled and sliced*
100 ml (8 T) milk
1 large turnip, peeled and sliced
25 g (25 ml / 2 T) butter
salt and freshly ground pepper
grated nutmeg
250 ml (1 cup) cream

APPLE SAUCE
4 apples, preferably Golden Delicious,
*   peeled, cored and sliced*
100 ml (8 T) white muscadel
2 cloves
25 g (25 ml / 2 T) butter
25 ml (2 T) sugar
grated nutmeg
1 ml (pinch) salt

1. STUFFING: Heat the onion and bacon in a pan over moderate heat. Stir-fry until the bacon crisps. Pour off the fat and place the onion and bacon mixture in a mixing bowl. Add the potatoes and liver and season with salt, pepper, nutmeg, cloves, parsley and sage. Preheat the oven to 200 °C (400 °F).

2. Season the goose, inside and out, with salt, pepper and ground ginger. Spoon the stuffing into the cavity and secure with a skewer. Place the stuffed goose in a roasting pan and add the stock from the offal. Cover with aluminium foil, shiny side in, and roast for 30 minutes. Reduce the heat to 160 °C (325 °F) and roast for 25 minutes per 500 g goose – ± 3 hours. Spoon a little of the stock over the goose from time to time to ensure it stays moist. Remove the goose from the oven, place on the rack of a roasting pan and return to the oven, on the lowest rack. Switch on the grill and brown the skin for ± 15 minutes.

3. MEANWHILE, MAKE THE ONION SAUCE: Place the onions in a saucepan and pour the milk over. Add the turnip and simmer until the onion is soft. Purée in a food processor and rub through a sieve into a saucepan. Stir in the butter and season with salt, pepper and nutmeg. Add the cream and simmer until the sauce resembles thick, liquid cream. Keep warm.

4. MEANWHILE, MAKE THE APPLE SAUCE: Place the apples in a saucepan and pour the wine over. Add the cloves, heat and boil over high heat until the liquid has evaporated. Remove from the heat and spoon out the cloves. Add the butter and sugar and mash the mixture. Season with nutmeg and salt and beat with a wooden spoon.

5. TO SERVE: Place the goose on a large, heated meat board and arrange the watercress around it. Serve with the two sauces, glazed carrots and green beans with nut butter, and Jerusalem artichokes.

Duck

(MAKES 2 SERVINGS)

This recipe may also be used for Muscovy duck. Muscovy ducks are larger, and make six servings. Do not cut up Muscovy duck afterwards in the same way as the duck in this recipe. Cut off its drumsticks, then the thighs. Cut off both wings and cut the breast downwards, from the centre. Two eaters will get wings, two thighs, two drumsticks and the breast is divided among the six.

duck of ± 2 kg, wing tips cut off

SPICE MIXTURE
10 ml (2 t) salt
5 ml (1 t) freshly ground white pepper
3 ml (½ t) ground ginger
1 ml (pinch) ground cloves
1 ml (pinch) ground allspice (optional)

SPREADING MIXTURE
1 plump garlic clove, bruised,
  peeled and crushed
5 ml (1 t) finely grated fresh ginger
grated rind of 2 oranges

OTHER INGREDIENTS
pith removed from 2 oranges,
  and oranges reserved
3 rhubarb stalks, rinsed and cut into 50 mm
  (2 inch) pieces
50 ml (4 T) Van der Hum

GLAZE
250 ml (1 cup) litchi juice
50 ml (4 T) honey
5 ml (1 t) chicken stock powder
5 ml (1 t) cornflour

1. Rinse the duck thoroughly, inside and out, under slowly running tap water. Make sure that there is no bloodiness inside. Do not cut off the neck skin.
2. SPICE MIXTURE: Mix all the spices. Rub ⅔ of the mixture into the outside of the duck, and ⅓ on the inside. Mix ingredients for spreading mixture and rub inside of duck with mixture. Place 2 peeled oranges and rhubarb in the cavity and sprinkle Van der Hum over. Fold the neck skin over the neck cavity and under the duck and secure with a skewer or toothpicks. Prick the breast. Roast for 30 minutes at 220 °C (450 °F), pricking the breast every 10 minutes.
3. Reduce the oven temperature to 180 °C (350 °F). Remove the pan from the oven, pick up the rack and place it over a mixing bowl. Pour the fat from the pan. Add the litchi juice to the pan and place the duck in it. Roast for 1 hour. Remove the duck from the pan and allow to cool.
4. GLAZE: Heat pan containing the liquid quickly to boiling point. Using a wooden spatula, loosen sticky bits in the pan so that they can dissolve in the liquid. Pour through a sieve into a small saucepan and reduce by half. Add the honey and stock powder and stir until dissolved. Meanwhile, mix the cornflour to a smooth paste with a little water. Remove the small saucepan from the heat and beat in the cornflour mixture. Return to the heat and stir until the sauce thickens and reaches boiling point. Taste and season with more salt and pepper.
5. TO SERVE: Halve the cooled duck lengthways (easy if you have poultry scissors). Cut the drumstick and thigh from the carcass, then the breast. You now have two breast and two drumstick and thigh portions. Heat the grill. Brush some of the glaze over the duck and place on the rack of a roasting pan. Grill for 5-6 minutes, remove and brush more glaze over. Grill until crisp and browned. Serve a breast portion and a leg portion to each person, with tagliatelle and braised red cabbage.

Braised pigeon

(MAKES 4 SERVINGS)

Braised pigeon is one of the oldest recipes we have. They were prepared as a pie with steak and mushrooms, to which raisins or dried pears were added. Generally, the pigeons are braised and served on their own.

4 pigeons, rinsed thoroughly and patted dry
salt and freshly ground pepper
4 cloves
250 g streaky bacon

VEGETABLES
250 g (250 ml / 1 cup) butter
1 large carrot, scraped and thinly sliced
1 onion, halved lengthways,
  peeled and thinly sliced
1 celery stalk, washed and threads removed,
  then thinly sliced
2 garlic cloves, bruised, peeled
  and crushed
2 bay leaves
leaves of 1 fresh thyme sprig
125 ml (½ cup) strong chicken stock
125 ml (½ cup) sweet wine,
  preferably muscadel

1. Season the pigeons, inside and out, with salt and pepper and place 1 clove in the cavity of each. Wrap 2 bacon rashers around each pigeon. Shred the remaining bacon.
2. Place the shredded bacon in a large, flat-bottomed, cast-iron pot and fry over low heat until crisp. Pour off the fat. Place the butter in the saucepan and spread it over the base. Add the remaining ingredients and place the pigeons on top. Cover with a sheet of buttered waxed paper and cover with the lid. Simmer for 30 minutes.
3. Remove the lid and waxed paper. Test for doneness and continue to simmer, if necessary. Place the pigeons in a deep serving bowl and spoon the vegetables over them, using a slotted spoon. Taste the liquid in the saucepan and season with more salt and pepper, if necessary. Reduce rapidly by half and pour over the pigeons. The sauce can be thickened with 5 ml (1 t) cornflour, mixed to a paste with 25 ml (2 T) water.

HINT: Dried fruit such as apples, pears, prunes or even a handful of raisins, may be cooked along with the pigeons.

DUCK WITH TAGLIATELLE
AND RED CABBAGE

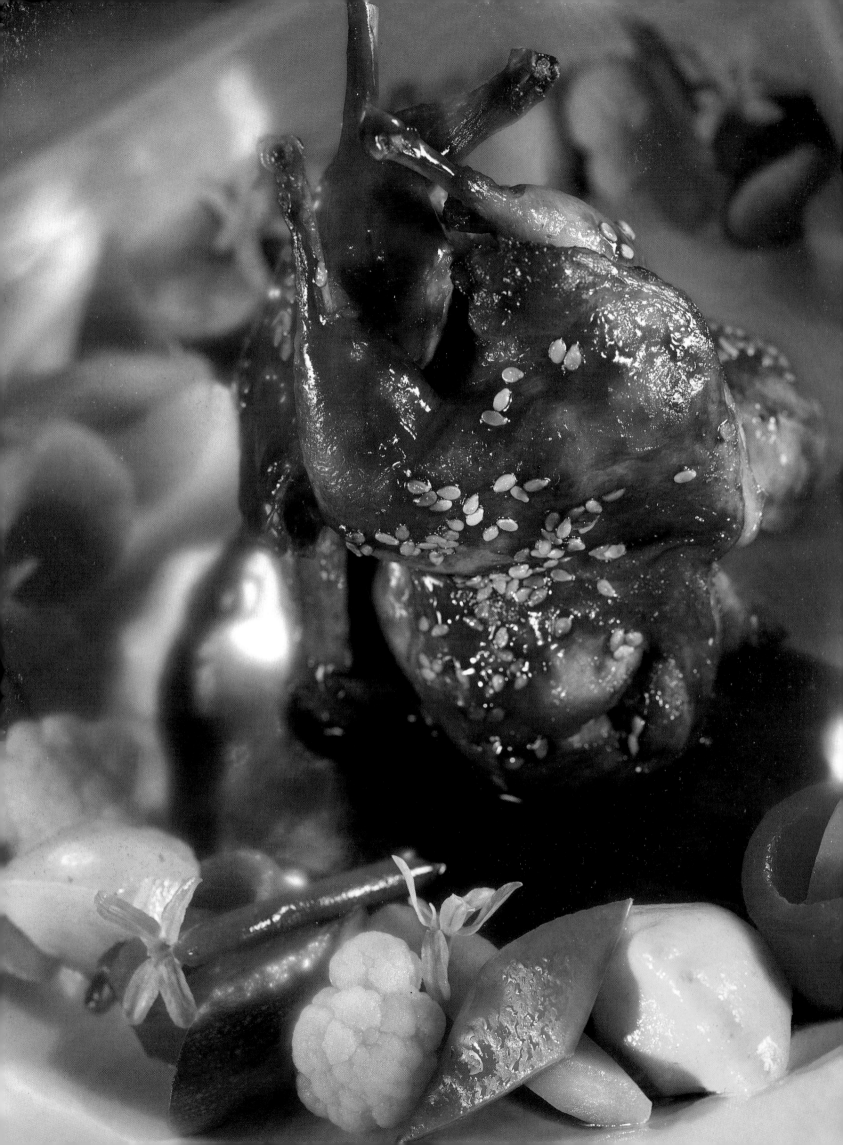

Pheasant

(MAKES 2 SERVINGS)

Pheasant hens are smaller than the cocks, but the flesh is more tender and juicier. Thick bread sauce is traditionally served with pheasant.

pheasant, cleaned thoroughly,
*   rinsed and patted dry*
25-50 ml (1-2 T) Lemon butter (p. 46)
salt and pepper

BREAD SAUCE
250 ml (1 cup) milk
1 thick slice onion
2 cloves
2 bay leaves
3 ml (½ t) grated nutmeg
75 ml (6 T) fresh breadcrumbs
25 ml (2 T) butter
salt and pepper

1. Fill the cavity with lemon butter and season the flesh well with salt and pepper. Roast at 200 °C (400 °F) for 1 hour.
2. BREAD SAUCE: Heat the milk, onion, cloves, bay leaves and nutmeg for at least 30 minutes in a small saucepan over low heat. Pour the mixture through a sieve and stir in the breadcrumbs. Return to the heat and beat in the butter, a little at a time. Taste and season with salt and pepper. Serve the pheasant and bread sauce with roast celeriac or ordinary celery.

Quail

(MAKES 6 SERVINGS)

9 quail, rinsed thoroughly and patted dry
salt, freshly ground pepper (preferably white
*   pepper) and ground ginger to taste*
250 ml (1 cup) apple juice
25 ml (2 T) brandy
2 cloves
18 fresh sage or pineapple sage leaves

GLAZE
500 ml (2 cups) veal stock
freshly ground pepper
50 ml (4 T) honey
10 ml (2 t) cornflour

TOPPING
lightly toasted sesame seed

1. Place the quail, breast side up, on a wooden board and cut through the breast bone, from the neck to the tail. Pull the carcasses open and place the quail skin side down. Lightly press them flat, using your palm. Cut loose from the backbone on both sides. Reserve backbones. Cut off all loose skins and bits of meat. Season the quail halves with salt, pepper and ground ginger. Place in a baking pan. Pour the apple juice and brandy into the pan and add the cloves. Place a sage leaf on each quail half. Cover with aluminium foil, shiny side in, and bake for 20 minutes in a preheated oven at 160 °C (325 °F). Remove pan from the oven, remove the quail from the pan and cool them on a cooling rack. Reserve pan juices.
2. GLAZE: Place the backbones in a flat-bottomed saucepan and fry them until golden brown, without adding any oil. Add the stock and simmer for 1 hour. Pour the sauce through a sieve, taste and season with pepper, but no salt. Add the pan juices, heat to boiling point and reduce by half. Stir in the honey, taste and season with more salt if necessary. Mix the cornflour to a smooth paste with a little water. Remove the glaze from the heat and stir in the cornflour mixture. Return to the heat and stir until the mixture reaches boiling point and thickens. Boil for 1 minute.
3. TO SERVE: Place the quail halves on the rack of a roasting pan and roast for 5 minutes at 180 °C (350 °F). Meanwhile, reheat the glaze to boiling point, brush half lavishly over the quail and roast for a further 10 minutes. Remove quail from the oven and brush the rest of the glaze over. Sprinkle sesame seed over each quail half and return to the oven for a further 5 minutes. Serve 3 quail halves a person with mashed potatoes and steamed, fresh, young vegetables.

Guineafowl with honey

(MAKES 2 SERVINGS)

MARINADE
1 guineafowl, rinsed thoroughly,
*   patted dry and wing tips removed*
250 ml (1 cup) buttermilk

TO FRY
50 g (50 ml/4 T) butter
25 ml (2 T) oil

TO COOK
salt and pepper
1 onion, halved lengthways, peeled and chopped
1 celery stalk, rinsed and threads removed,
*   then chopped*
50 ml (4 T) finely chopped fresh parsley
4 slices ham, finely chopped
10 ml (2 t) mustard powder
50 ml (4 T) soft brown sugar
50 ml (4 T) honey
250 ml (1 cup) strong, hot chicken stock

TO SERVE
2 apples, peeled, cored, quartered
*   and covered with lemon juice*
3 ml (½ t) turmeric
chopped chives

1. Place the guineafowl in a mixing bowl and pour the buttermilk over. Cover with cling wrap and refrigerate overnight.
2. Remove the guineafowl, wash under cold running water and pat dry. Season thoroughly, inside and out, with salt and pepper. Crisscross the legs and secure with string. Tie the wings to the carcass with string.
3. Heat the butter and oil to boiling hot in a heavy-bottomed saucepan and fry the guineafowl until golden brown on all sides. Remove the guineafowl from the saucepan. Add the onion, celery, parsley, ham, mustard and sugar and stir-fry until sugar begins to caramelise. Return the guineafowl to the saucepan and fry on all sides until covered with pan juices. This takes ± 10 minutes. Dissolve the honey in the stock and pour it over the guineafowl. Cover and braise for 1½ hours over low heat.
4. Add the apples and sprinkle the turmeric over. Stir lightly, cover and braise for a further ± 15 minutes or until the apples are just tender.
5. TO SERVE: Do not try to cut through the wishbone. Cut into portions as for Muscovy duck (p. 114, introducton to Duck recipe) and serve with Pearl wheat (p. 127). Spoon some of the apple mixture and juices over. Sprinkle the chives over and serve. Fried breadcrumbs were traditionally served too.

ROAST QUAIL

Turkey

(MAKES 10-12 SERVINGS)

apricot stuffing for breast
pork stuffing for cavity
1 turkey of ± 4,5 kg, wing tips removed
salt and freshly ground pepper
250 g (250 ml/1 cup) Maître d'hôtel butter
*   (p. 46)*
500 ml (2 cups) strong, hot poultry stock

CHRISTMAS BREAD SAUCE
250 g maize bread, coarsely chopped
salt and pepper
15 ml (3 t) chopped fresh thyme
25 ml (2 T) chopped fresh parsley
250 ml (1 cup) hot milk
50 ml (4 T) medium cream sherry
75 ml (6 T) cream
grated nutmeg to taste

TO SERVE
500 g chippolata sausages
oil
watercress

1. Make both stuffings.
2. Make a lengthways slit in the shin of both legs and pull out the sinews with pliers. Season the turkey well, inside and out, with salt and pepper. Lift up the neck skin with your right hand. Wiggle the fingers of your left hand over the meat on the carcass and pull the skin over your left hand, using your right hand, so that the skin over the breast loosens. Press half the butter under the skin and over the breast. Spread it out further, using both hands. Spoon the apricot stuffing into the crop, pull the skin over and secure it under the wing tips with a skewer. Secure the wings to the carcass with string. Place spoonfuls of meat filling in the stomach cavity. Do not stuff it too tightly. Fold the legs over one another and secure with string. Preheat the oven to 230 °C (450 °F).
3. Place the turkey in a roasting pan and add half the stock. Spread the rest of the butter onto a doubled sheet of butter paper or aluminium foil, place it, buttered side down, on the turkey and press at the sides to secure. Roast for 10 minutes, reduce the temperature to 160 °C (325 °F) and roast for a further ± 3 hours. Baste every 20 minutes with the pan juices and the rest of the stock. Use more stock if necessary. Test for doneness: insert the sharp point of a knife into the thigh and pull it out immediately. The liquid that runs out should be as clear as water. If it is bloody, roast the turkey longer.

4. Keep the cooked turkey warm and make the sauce. Purée the bread, salt, pepper, thyme and parsley and gradually add the hot milk. Place in a saucepan and stir in the sherry. Add the cream and heat gradually. Season with nutmeg.
5. TO FINISH: Shake the sausages in oil in a frying pan to coat them with oil. Heat over low heat and fry slowly until golden brown. Shake the pan from time to time to turn the sausages, so that they will cook evenly to a golden brown. *Do not* fry them over high heat – they will burst. Keep warm.
6. TO SERVE: Remove the string and skewer and place the turkey on a large, heated meat platter. Surround with browned chippolata sausages and garnish with watercress. Serve with roast potatoes, baked pumpkin, peas and Christmas (or traditional English) bread sauce.

APRICOT STUFFING
75 g (125 ml/½ cup) dried apricots, shredded
250 ml (1 cup) port
10 ml (2 t) finely chopped fresh ginger root
25 ml (2 T) butter
1 onion, halved lengthways,
*   peeled and finely chopped*
1 celery stalk, rinsed and threads removed,
*   then thinly sliced*
375 ml (1½ cups) fresh breadcrumbs
15 ml (3 t) finely chopped fresh parsley
5 ml (1 t) ground ginger
5 ml (1 t) ground coriander
1 ml (pinch) ground cloves
salt and pepper
1 packet (100 g/250 ml/1 cup) walnuts,
*   coarsely chopped*
3 ripe, fresh apricots, halved and stoned

1. Place the dried apricots in a saucepan and add the port and ginger root. Heat to boiling point, remove from the heat and leave to stand overnight.
2. Melt the butter in a frying pan and fry the onion until softened and transparent, but not browned. Add the celery and stir-fry for 1 minute. Remove from the heat and stir in the crumbs, parsley, ginger, coriander and cloves. Taste and season with salt and pepper. Add the dried apricot mixture, walnuts and fresh apricot halves. Mix well with a large, two-pronged fork.

PORK STUFFING
25 ml (2 T) butter
1 onion, halved lengthways, peeled and chopped
25 ml (2 T) chopped fresh parsley
15 ml (3 t) chopped fresh thyme
15 ml (3 t) chopped fresh sage or pineapple sage
250 ml (1 cup) fresh breadcrumbs

750 g pork sausage, meat squeezed from casings
1 egg, lightly beaten
salt, freshly ground pepper and grated
*   nutmeg to taste*
3 ml (½ t) cayenne pepper

1. Heat the butter in a frying pan, add the onion and fry until softened and transparent, but not browned.
2. Remove the pan from the heat and stir in the parsley, thyme, sage and crumbs. Add the sausage meat and mix with a large, two-pronged fork. Add the egg, season with salt, pepper, nutmeg and cayenne pepper. Mix well with the fork without making the mixture clumpy.

Stewed leg of ostrich

(MAKES 4 SERVINGS)

1,2 kg ostrich leg, after muscles have been cut
*   into fillets and membranes removed*

MARINADE
1 litre (4 cups) yoghurt or buttermilk
1 carrot, scraped and thinly sliced
1 small onion, halved lengthways,
*   peeled and sliced*
4 sprigs fresh thyme
8 sprigs parsley
2 bay leaves
10 ml (2 t) roasted whole coriander seeds
2 cloves

TO COOK
olive oil
salt and pepper
3 ml (½ t) aniseed
4 garlic cloves, bruised, peeled and
*   coarsely chopped*
1 carrot, scraped and sliced
500 ml (2 cups) hot beef stock
250 ml (1 c) heated red wine
1 punnet (240 g) button mushrooms,
*   wiped clean and halved*
8 small onions
12 pitted prunes

GARNISH
25 ml (2 T) finely chopped fresh parsley
25 ml (2 T) snipped chives

1. MARINADE: Place the meat in a mixing bowl. Pour the yoghurt over. Add the carrot, onion, thyme, parsley, bay leaves, coriander and cloves and mix to blend. Turn the meat in the marinade to cover all sides. Cover with cling wrap and refrigerate for 12-48 hours. Turn 2-3 times.

2. Remove the meat from the marinade, wipe clean and pat dry. Cut the meat into bite-sized portions.

3. Heat the oil and fry the meat, a little at a time, until browned all over. Remove each batch with a slotted spoon and keep warm. Repeat until all the meat is browned. Pour off excess fat. Return the meat to the pan and season well with salt and pepper. Sprinkle the aniseed over. Add the garlic, carrot, stock and wine. Heat to boiling point, reduce the heat, cover and simmer for 1 hour.

4. Add the mushrooms, small onions and prunes and simmer, uncovered, until the onions are tender. Place in a serving dish and sprinkle parsley and chives over. Serve with Pearl wheat (p. 127) or buttered noodles.

Roast leg of ostrich

(MAKES 8 SERVINGS)

I created this recipe specially to bring together the flavours of the Little Karoo.

ostrich leg of ± 3,5 kg, boned and butterflied
15 ml (3 t) crushed juniper berries
olive oil
salt and freshly ground black pepper
24 garlic cloves, bruised, peeled and chopped
    (without salt)
10 ml (2 t) fresh rosemary
10 ml (2 t) chopped fresh marjoram or oregano
48 fresh bay leaves
24 fresh lemon leaves
2 carrots, scraped and thinly sliced
1 large onion, halved lengthways,
    peeled and thinly sliced

SWEET POTATO SALSA
juice of 2 lemons
1 litre (4 cups) water
2 large sweet potatoes, peeled,
    sliced and the slices then cut into strips
salt and pepper
400 g (500 ml/2 cups) soft brown sugar
250 ml (1 cup) brown vinegar
250 ml (1 cup) muscadel
1 tin (410 g) apricots,
    puréed with syrup
50 ml (4 T) dark soy sauce
10 ml (2 t) ground ginger
10 ml (2 t) cayenne pepper
1 packet (100 g/250 ml/1 cup) walnuts,
    coarsely chopped

1. Rub half the juniper berries into the top of the meat. Pour a little olive oil over the meat and rub it in. Turn the meat over, rub the rest of the juniper berries in and rub in more oil. Place the meat in a large, shallow dish and pour ½ cup oil over. Cover with cling wrap and marinate for 48 hours in the refrigerator. Turn the meat 4 times during marinating and rub marinade in well by hand. Add more oil, if necessary.

2. TO COOK: Remove the meat from the refrigerator, pat dry and season well with salt and pepper. Mix the garlic, rosemary and marjoram and rub thoroughly into the meat. Oil the rack of a roasting pan with the oil remaining from the marinade. Arrange half the bay and lemon leaves on it. Place the meat on the leaves. Spread the carrots and onion out evenly over the meat. Sprinkle a little olive oil over. Season lightly with more salt and pepper. Arrange the remaining leaves on top.

3. Place the roasting pan in the centre of the oven preheated to 160 °C (325 °F). Roast for 15-20 minutes for each 500 g meat, plus an extra 20 minutes. The cooking time for a 3,5 kg leg will therefore be ± 2 hours.

4. SWEET POTATO SALSA: Mix the lemon juice and water in a saucepan. Add sweet potato strips. Season well with salt and lightly with pepper. Heat to boiling point, reduce the heat and simmer the strips for 2 minutes, until almost tender. Drain and set aside. Place the sugar, vinegar, muscadel, apricot purée, soy sauce, ginger and cayenne pepper in a large, shallow pan or saucepan and stir over low heat until the sugar has dissolved. Increase the heat and boil for 1 minute. Add the sweet potato strips and stir-fry until they are covered with sauce. Simmer, uncovered, until the sweet potatoes are just tender.

5. TO SERVE: Leave the meat to rest in the warming drawer for 20-30 minutes. Scratch off the topping and remove the meat from the bed of leaves. Place on a wooden board and cut into slices. Arrange the meat on a large, heated serving platter and spoon sweet potato salsa down the length of the meat on the platter, using a slotted spoon. Pour the remaining sauce into a sauce boat. Serve with broccoli or romanesco.

From funeral rice to tagliatelle

RICE HAS BEEN part of the South African diet since the days of Jan van Riebeeck. First it had to provide for the needs of the Malays, then it became part of the settlers' diet. Then the Indians came to Natal, and in the twentieth century we were exposed to so many influences that all methods of cooking rice and all kinds of rice became an irreplaceable part of our diet. Italian immigrants, in particular, were responsible for this. Don't be surprised if you're served a risotto as a first course in an Afrikaner's home, or taste it at black South Africans' parties. Rice travels far.

Risotto is an Italian rice dish, traditionally served as a starter. It is slightly mushy, creamy and the grains are slightly firm (al dente). Risotto is made from arborio rice. In the past, it was only imported for restaurants or cooks with fat purses. Fortunately, today it is available in ordinary supermarkets as Tisotto.

South Africa's oldest rice dish is *vendusierys* (auction rice) which was later known as *huweliksrys* (wedding rice) or *begrafnisrys* (funeral rice). It is simply yellow rice with raisins. When the first auction was held at the Cape, buyers from far afield travelled in their oxwagons, which were then drawn into laagers. Malay slaves had to make large pots of food, and afterwards the name *vendusierys* was bandied about. At a wedding feast it was renamed *huweliksrys*, but it was the large country gatherings for communion, at which auctions were also held, which kept the name *vendusierys* alive. Farmers' wives cooked less rice for wedding feasts, but a lot for a funeral. It was said, jokingly, that *huweliksrys* became *begrafnisrys* if a few tears fell into the rice.

The name fell into disuse during the first seven, unimaginative, decades of the twentieth century, but today it is back in fashion. The rice tradition of the East was kept alive on the Rand by Chinese miners and their families. Although a large number of

Spaniards worked in the fishing industry, it was the magazine food writers who not only established paella, but also made a number of different versions extremely popular.

Coconut rice and dahl rice were not really incorporated in the repertoires of white and black South Africans, but remained exclusively part of Indian and Malay dishes. Today, because so many people have become vegetarians, it is being cooked more and more often. 'Dahl' is the Indian word for lentils, and lentils and chickpeas are good accompaniments to duck and Muscovy duck. Curried dahl is a popular dish on a curry table. But beware: Samp and beans are just a short way behind.

HOW TO COOK RISOTTO

Unlike ordinary rice which is boiled in water, for risotto you need a liquid that is partly water or stock, or a combination of stock, wine and water. The liquid must be hot. Often, a very small quantity of leeks or onions are first fried in butter or oil, then the rice is stirred in until covered completely with the butter mixture. Then the hot liquid is added to the rice, a little at a time, as it simmers over moderate heat. Make sure that the rice has absorbed all the liquid each time, before adding the next quantity of liquid. How much liquid is needed? Recipes usually give an estimated quantity of liquid. Use as much of it as the rice needs to cook, without becoming too mushy. All kinds of flavourings may be added during cooking. Chopped fresh herbs, if called for in a recipe, are usually added at the end. Tomatoes, mushrooms or Italian *ragu* (cooked minced beef with cream, wine and a little tomato – better known as the meat sauce of lasagne or spaghetti bolognaise) may also be simmered as part of the risotto. Ground black pepper and Parmesan cheese, either grated or shaved, complete some risottos very appropriately.

BURIYANI

Pasta came to South Africa during the past century, when Italian miners and their families continued the traditions of their fatherland. Two families, called Fatti and Moni (who were not related), correctly forecast the need for spaghetti and macaroni and, independently of each other, established factories to manufacture pasta in Johannesburg. The success on the Rand led to their bringing their pasta to the south. In 1926 the two businesses amalgamated, and that is how Fatti's and Monis staked their claim – and held it – in our country. After the Second World War, more and more Italians – especially those with food training and experience in the restaurant industry – established themselves in South Africa. Literally thousands of Italian eateries opened their doors, even in the smallest rural towns. Their food was affordable, the atmosphere was informal, and the warm welcome they offered guests soon ensured that the whole of South Africa enjoyed the pasta revolution.

Funeral rice

(MAKES 8 SERVINGS)

1,5 litres (6 cups) water
400 g (500 ml/2 cups) rice
10 ml (2 t) salt
20 g (25 ml/2 T) yellow sugar
3 ml (½ t) saffron or 10 ml (2 t) turmeric
3 sticks cinnamon or cassia
8 cardamom seeds
15 ml (3 t) naartjie peel,
  cut into strips
50 g (50 ml/4 T) butter
75 g (125 ml/½ cup) sultanas, mixed with:
75 g (125 ml/½ cup) raisins or 150 g
  (250 ml/1 cup) seedless raisins

1. Heat the water to boiling point in a large saucepan. Meanwhile, rinse the rice, and place it in the boiling water. Stir in the salt, sugar and saffron, and add the sticks of cinnamon, cardamom seeds and naartjie peel. Cover, reduce the heat and then simmer for 20-30 minutes.
2. Remove the saucepan from the heat and pour off the water. Add the butter, sultanas and raisins and stir to blend. Spoon into a colander. Meanwhile, boil a kettleful of water and pour it into the saucepan in which the rice was cooked. Heat to boiling point. Place the colander of rice on top, cover and steam until the rice has swollen and the raisins are soft and plump.

VARIATION: COCONUT RICE

Stir in 250 ml (1 cup) coconut or toasted coconut along with the raisins.

Savoury rice

(MAKES 4 SERVINGS)

This accompaniment is today undoubtedly the most popular rice dish countrywide.

30 ml (6 t) oil
1 onion, halved lengthways, peeled,
  sliced and then chopped
2 celery stalks, threads removed,
  then sliced thinly
1 red sweet pepper, halved,
  seeds and membranes removed,
  cut into strips and then chopped
200 g (250 ml/1 cup) rice
750 ml (3 cups) hot chicken stock,
  made from 1 stock cube
5 ml (1 t) salt

1. Heat the oil in a saucepan with a tight-fitting lid. Add the onion and fry until softened and transparent, but not browned. Add the celery and sweet pepper and stir-fry for 1 minute. Add the rice and stir-fry for 2 minutes.
2. Add the stock and salt, heat to boiling point, cover and reduce the heat. Simmer for 20-25 minutes or until rice has absorbed all the liquid.

Chicken buriyani (Breyani)

(MAKES 24 SERVINGS)

This is another of the most popular recipes for entertaining in South Africa, and is just as much a part of the Cape food tradition as the 'table-cloth' over Table Mountain. The recipe may be halved. My friend, Cass Abrahams, is our best Malay cook. In her book, *The Culture and Cuisine of the Cape Malays*, she explains Malay dishes in detail. She says that breyani was traditionally served at the end of the Tamat ceremonies, when children symbolically celebrated their entrance into adult life. Today, everyone eats this delicious rice dish.

4 chickens of ± 1,5 kg each, rinsed and cut
  into portions

MARINADE

1 litre (4 x 250 ml/4 cups) sour milk
  or buttermilk
25 ml (2 T) turmeric
40 ml (8 t) salt
40 ml (8 t) finely chopped fresh ginger root
25 ml (2 T) finely chopped fresh garlic
2 tins (410 g each) Indian tomatoes
8 small red chillies, halved lengthways
  and seeded
250 ml (1 cup) fresh coriander leaves

RICE MIXTURE

1 packet (2,5 kg) Basmati rice
salt
375 g (375 ml/1½ cups) butter,
  melted and foam skimmed off
375 ml (1½ cups) oil
4 packets (500 g each) brown lentils,
  soaked overnight in water
50 ml (4 T) oil
8 onions, halved lengthways, peeled and sliced
50 ml (4 T) Garam masala (p. 100)
24 medium-sized potatoes, peeled, halved lengthways and each half halved again horizontally
4 sticks cinnamon
24 cardamom seeds, shelled

GARNISH

24 hard-boiled eggs, shelled and halved
extra fresh coriander leaves

1. Rinse the chicken portions well under cold running water, pat dry with kitchen paper and place in 2 large mixing bowls. Mix all the marinade ingredients, divide between the two bowls and pour over the chicken. Cover with cling wrap and marinate overnight in the refrigerator.
2. PREPARE THE RICE: Boil the rice in well-salted water until almost tender. (See directions on packet.) Rinse under cold running water and drain, a little at a time, in a colander. Place in a large saucepan and taste. Season lightly with salt and stir in 125 ml (125 g/½ cup) each butter and oil.
3. Drain the lentils, place in a large saucepan and cover with water. Season with 50 ml (4 T) salt and heat to boiling point. Reduce the heat and simmer until almost cooked. Drain, rinse under cold running water and drain again. Place in a pan and taste. Season lightly with salt.
4. Heat the oil in a large pan and add the onions. Stir-fry for 3 minutes and sprinkle the garam masala over. Continue to stir-fry, adding water, a little at a time, to avoid scorching the masala. Stop stir-frying as soon as the onions have softened but are not yet cooked.
5. Mix half the remaining butter with half the remaining oil and divide equally between

2 large baking pans. Place a quarter of the rice in each pan and level the surface. Do the same with the lentils. Remove the chicken from the marinade and reserve the marinade. Divide the chicken portions between the 2 pans. Spoon half the potatoes over the chicken in each pan. Add half the marinade to each pan. Divide remaining lentils equally between the 2 pans. Do the same with the rice. Divide onions between pans. Divide remaining butter and oil between pans. Add 2 cinnamon sticks to each pan and sprinkle cardamom seeds over. Sprinkle 250 ml (1 cup) cold water over each pan.

6. Cover with aluminium foil, shiny side in, and bake for 90 minutes in a preheated oven at 160 °C (325 °F). Do not disturb the pans during baking.

7. Remove from the oven and spoon into large serving dishes, or leave in the pans. Garnish with egg halves and coriander leaves. Serve with *dahi* (see below).

Risotto

(MAKES 6 SERVINGS AS A FIRST COURSE AND 4 SERVINGS AS AN ACCOMPANIMENT)

Buy a 1 kg pack Tisotto and make leek and wine risotto (see Variation) and pumpkin risotto as well (see p. 127). The first two use 400 g each, and the last the remaining 200 g. If you do not have a scale, divide the rice into five equal-sized portions and use two each for the first two recipes and the remaining rice for the last one.

1 litre (4 cups) chicken stock,
*   made from 2 stock cubes*
37,5 g (37,5 ml/3 T) butter
25 ml (2 T) oil
25 g pancetta or 3 rashers streaky bacon,
*   shredded*
1 small leek, rinsed and white parts finely
*   chopped, or 1 small onion,*
*   peeled and finely chopped*
400 g uncooked arborio rice (Tisotto)
3 ml (½ t) saffron or 10 ml (2 t) turmeric
salt, if necessary

TO SERVE
± 50 g (50 ml/4 T) butter
coarsely ground black pepper
finely grated Parmesan cheese

1. Heat the stock to boiling point in a saucepan. Reduce the heat and keep stock boiling hot.
2. Place the butter and oil in a large, heavy-bottomed saucepan and heat over moderately high heat. Add the bacon and leek and stir-fry for 2-3 minutes. Add all the rice and stir-fry for 1-2 minutes, until rice is coated all over with oil. Add ± 125 ml (½ cup) of the hot stock and stir to mix. Heat to boiling point, stirring constantly so that the rice does not stick to the base of the saucepan. Wait until the stock has been absorbed, then add extra stock, a little at a time. At this stage, 15 minutes' cooking time should have elapsed and there should still be some stock left.
3. Meanwhile, dissolve the saffron in 375 ml (1½ cups) boiling water. Add half the hot saffron liquid to the rice and boil until absorbed. Repeat with the other half. Boil rice until cooked, adding remaining stock as required. Taste. (The quantity of salt in the stock will give the dish a naturally salty flavour. If you used salted butter, the salt is already there. And remember that, if you are going to sprinkle Parmesan cheese over the risotto at the end, it will also add salt. Taking all this into account, you could – particularly if your family likes a fair amount of salt in their food – add an extra pinch of salt. Italians do not like a lot of salt.)
4. TO SERVE: Stir in the butter and grind a little pepper over. Serve and grind more pepper over each serving, if desired. Sprinkle liberally with Parmesan cheese.

VARIATION: LEEK AND WINE RISOTTO
Follow the recipe above, but use 2-3 leeks and replace the saffron liquid with dry white wine. Sprinkle snipped chives over at the end. Vegetarians can leave out the bacon.

Tomato rice

(MAKES 4 SERVINGS)

This recipe calls for cooked rice, and may be used as a stuffing for a whole fish or chicken. It makes a delicious accompaniment to fried chops or chicken.

50 ml (4 T) oil
2 leeks, rinsed and thinly sliced,
*   or 1 medium-sized onion, peeled and chopped*
2 plump garlic cloves, bruised,
*   peeled and crushed with:*
5 ml (1 t) salt
1 each red and green sweet pepper, halved,
*   seeds and membranes removed,*
*   cut into strips and then cubed*
1 tin (410 g) tomatoes, chopped
125 ml (½ cup) canned green olives,
*   stoned and coarsely chopped*
5 ml (1 t) chopped fresh oregano
500 ml (2 cups) cooked rice
15 ml (3 t) chopped fresh basil
freshly ground black pepper

Heat the oil in a saucepan, add the leeks and fry until softened. Stir in the garlic and sweet peppers and stir-fry for 3 minutes. Add the tomatoes and cook over fairly high heat until the mixture thickens. Add the remaining ingredients, turn off the heat, cover and leave to stand for 5 minutes. Stir and serve.

Dahi

(MAKES 24 SMALL SERVINGS)

1 carton (500 ml/2 cups) buttermilk
3 ml (½ t) salt
5 ml (1 t) finely chopped red chillies
*   (with or without seeds)*
5 ml (1 t) ground cumin
25 ml (2 T) finely chopped fresh coriander
*   leaves*
125 ml (½ cup) ice-cold water

Mix all the ingredients and refrigerate until the breyani is served. Double the recipe if more sauce is desired

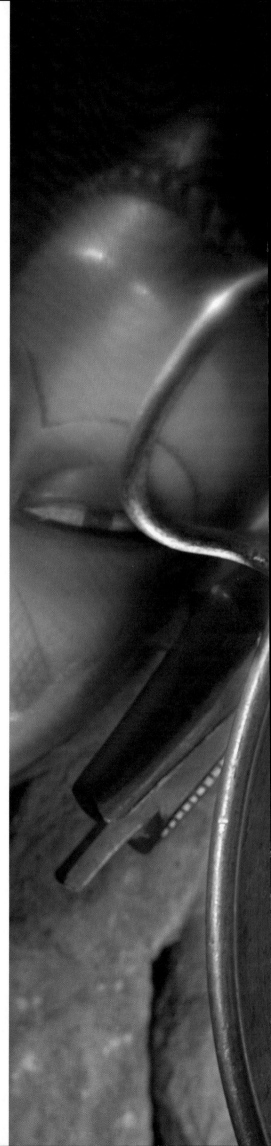

Paella

(MAKES 6-8 SERVINGS)

There are literally hundreds of versions of this Spanish rice dish in South Africa. The recipe that follows is closest to the standard recipe for the South African version, which should be seen as a special dish for entertaining. This recipe is used, more or less, by the Spanish fishing community, employed in the West Coast fishing industry.

15 ml (3 t) oil
2 plump garlic cloves, bruised,
    peeled and crushed with:
5 ml (1 t) salt
1 small onion, halved lengthways,
    peeled and finely chopped
1 each large red and yellow sweet peppers,
    halved, seeds and membranes removed,
    then cut into strips
6 chicken drumsticks
salt and freshly ground pepper
400 g pork, cut into strips
250 g cooked ham, cubed
4 English tomatoes, skinned,
    quartered and seeded
400 g (500 ml/2 cups) rice
hot, strong chicken stock
3 ml (½ t) turmeric, dissolved in:
125 ml (½ cup) boiling water
1 tin (410 g) red kidney beans,
    drained and rinsed under cold running water
1 tin (410 g) artichoke hearts,
    drained and cut into smaller pieces
250 g white fish (eg kabeljou),
    skinned and cubed
2 crayfish tails, flesh removed from shells and
    alimentary canals removed, then sliced,
    or 500 g monkfish, cubed
6-8 prawns
18-24 fresh mussels, scrubbed and well soaked
    in fresh water
100 g chorizo sausage, sliced
125 g calamari rings

GARNISH
chopped fresh dill and parsley

1. Place the oil in a large paella pan or an electric frying pan and heat over moderate heat. Add the garlic, onion and sweet peppers and stir-fry for 1 minute. Remove with a slotted spoon and set aside.
2. Fry the chicken until lightly browned all over. Remove and season with salt and pepper. Add extra oil to the pan if necessary, and fry pork until golden brown. Season with salt and pepper. Return the onion mixture and

chicken to the pan and add the ham, tomato and rice. Mix well. Add the turmeric, water and enough stock to the pan to just cover all the ingredients. Heat to boiling point, reduce the heat immediately, cover and simmer for 30 minutes.
3. Remove the lid and stir in the beans and artichokes. Cover and simmer for 5 minutes.
4. Remove the lid and add the fish, crayfish, prawns and mussels. Cover and simmer for 10 minutes. Meanwhile, heat the warming drawer until hot. Add the sausage and calamari and place the covered pan in the warming drawer for 30 minutes. Remove, taste and season lightly with salt and pepper if necessary. Stir and sprinkle dill and parsley over.

Samp and beans

The best samp and beans I have ever eaten was made by Miriam Moss, my housekeeper. She comes from Douglas, and says that they ate soured maize porridge for breakfast. It was served with ordinary milk. When *stywe pap* (maize meal porridge) was made, it was served with sour milk. For lunch, *roosterkoek* was eaten with fat, but at night there was samp and beans, served mainly with tripe or *konyana*, the meat of a newborn lamb that was first wind-dried and then cooked. It takes time to prepare good samp and beans.

750 g samp
10 litres (40 cups) water
1 packet (500 g) white kidney beans
salt and pepper
12,5-25 ml (1-2 T) vegetable or other fat

1. Rinse the samp twice under cold running water, place in a large bucket, cover with fresh water and soak for a few minutes. Remove shells or anything else floating on top.
2. Drain the samp, place in a large saucepan and cover with 10 litres of water. Heat to boiling point, reduce the heat immediately and cook for ± 4 hours.
3. Meanwhile, soak the beans in boiling water, rinse and add to the samp. Cook until everything is tender and cooked. Season with salt and pepper and stir in the fat.

VARIATION
The current trend is to stir about 25 ml (2 T) chilli beef stock powder into the cooked samp and beans.

SAMP AND BEANS

Pumpkin risotto

(MAKES 4 SERVINGS
AS AN ACCOMPANIMENT)

Do not serve this dish as a first course. It is delicious, because it contains honey, and goes well with roast chicken, duck, Muscovy duck, goose, pheasant, guineafowl and quail.

1 small onion, peeled and finely chopped
25 g (25 ml/2 T) butter
25 ml (2 T) oil
250 ml (1 cup) grated, uncooked pumpkin
750 ml (3 cups) hot vegetable stock
3 ml (½ t) turmeric
3 ml (½ t) ground ginger
200 g arborio rice (Tisotto)
50 ml (4 T) honey
salt, if needed

Fry the onion in butter and oil until softened, but not browned. Add pumpkin and 125 ml (½ cup) stock, heat to boiling point and stir until the pumpkin is tender. Sprinkle the turmeric and ginger over. Add all the rice and complete as in the basic recipe on p. 123. Add more water at the end if necessary.

Pearl wheat

(MAKES 4 SERVINGS)

Pearl wheat with potroast goat meat is one of the most typical dishes of the older generation of farmers. Stewed dried peaches, especially the whole ones, with the stone, were the only accompaniment. Vegetarians and yuppies eat pearl wheat or samp and beans to be politically correct!

200 g (250 ml/1 cup) pearl wheat
1 litre (4 cups) water
3 ml (½ t) salt
15 ml (3 t) butter
75 g (125 ml/½ cup) seedless raisins
(optional)

Place all the ingredients in a pressure cooker and cook for 15 minutes at 100 kPa, or simmer for 1-1½ hours in an ordinary saucepan.

HOME-MADE PASTA

Make your own pasta

Home-made pasta dough does not contain any salt. Salt hinders the development of the gluten and it takes longer for the pasta to become elastic. The granular texture of salt may cause the pasta to tear when it is rolled out very thinly. Boil the finished pasta in well-salted water.

240 g (500 ml/2 cups) white bread flour
2 extra-large eggs
2 extra-large egg yolks
12,5 ml (1 T) olive oil
boiling water

1. Place the flour, eggs and egg yolks in the bowl of a food processor. Drizzle the oil over, pulsing until the mixture resembles coarse breadcrumbs. Pour just enough boiling water through the funnel of the food processor, with the motor running, until the crumbs blend and just begin to form a dough around the blade. Remove from the bowl immediately and knead for 2-3 minutes until the dough is smooth. Wrap in a damp (*not wet*) cloth and set aside.
2. Roll a piece of the dough (about a fifth) at a time up to 50 times through a pasta machine set at its thickest, until it is *completely smooth* and feels like satin when you rub your finger over it. Work in small quantities of flour if it looks as if the dough will stick to the rollers, but *take care* not to add too much extra flour, otherwise the pasta will become hard and dry, and crack when it is rolled out thinner. Only once the pasta is as smooth as silk can the process be continued.
3. Cut into tagliatelle or fettuccine through the cutting rollers of the machine, or cut flat strips of pasta into sheets of lasagne or strips of pappardelle using a pastry wheel. Hang long strips of pasta to dry over a reed or any other long stick, which has been sprinkled with flour, or pack sheets of pasta on a wire rack to dry. Store dried pasta in an airtight container.

How to cook home-made pasta

Home-made pasta cooks much faster than commercial pasta. The cooking time for home-made pasta is 4-6 minutes, depending on how thick and how dry the pasta is before cooking. Pappardelle take slightly longer. Sheet pasta for lasagne should be cooked for only 1 minute, then removed and refreshed under cold running water. Pasta should, preferably, be completely dry before cooking. Wet pasta takes longer to cook. The cooking time also depends on the kind of pasta being prepared. Round pasta, like spaghetti, macaroni, screw noodles, rigatoni and penne, cannot be made successfully at home; flat pasta, like lasagne, pappardelle, tagliatelle, fettuccine and the folded kind (also made from sheets of flat pasta, with a filling), like ravioli, tortellini, pansotti and many more, can be made successfully at home. Wet home-made pasta can also be bought from Italian delicatessens. Dried home-made pasta, especially tagliatelle, in a variety of colours and flavours, has begun to appear on the speciality shelves of larger supermarkets over the past few years.

1. Heat a large saucepan of water (at least 5 litres/20 cups) to boiling point and add a handful (50-75 ml/4-6 T) salt. It is not necessary to add oil to the water.
2. Add the pasta and boil the home-made tagliatelle or fettuccine for about 4-6 minutes (see introductory paragraph) until tender but not mushy, and firm to the bite (al dente). For lasagne, spread sheets out on a large cloth, ready for packing.
3. Cover with oil mixture (see Hint).

HINT: *Always* make an oil mixture when cooking pasta. Spoon about 50 ml (4 T) each olive oil and butter into a small saucepan and season with freshly ground black pepper and nutmeg. Heat for 5 minutes over low heat, without browning the butter. Spoon the mixture over 500 g cooked, hot, drained pasta and shake well to mix, so that the pasta is covered with the oil mixture and absorbs it. This improves the taste a thousandfold and also prevents cooked pasta from sticking. The technique of using a peppered oil on pasta, which is then served with grated Parmesan cheese or shavings of Grana Pedana, is known as *con pepe*. This oil treatment of any cooked pasta, irrespective of the sauce with which it is to be served, is typically South African. Cook commercial pasta according to the packet instructions, and cover it with the oil mixture.

Macaroni cheese

(MAKES 6 LARGE
OR 8 ORDINARY SERVINGS)

PASTA
1 packet (500 g) macaroni,
    cooked as described on p. 127
50 ml (4 T) olive oil
50 g (50 ml/4 T) butter
5 ml (1 t) freshly ground black pepper
5 ml (1 t) grated nutmeg
5 ml (1 t) pinch of herbs or 24 basil leaves,
    washed, rolled up and cut into thin strips

SAUCE
100 g (100 ml/8 T) butter
60 g (125 ml/½ cup) cake flour
500 ml (2 cups) milk
250 ml (1 cup) cream or milk
salt, pepper and cayenne pepper to taste
5 ml (1 t) prepared English mustard
3 ml (½ t) turmeric
100 g (250 ml/1 cup) grated mature
    Cheddar cheese
4 extra-large eggs
margarine

OPTIONAL
1 packet (500 g) Vienna sausages,
    coarsely grated
50 g (125 ml/½ cup) blue cheese, grated

TO SERVE
2 large, ripe red tomatoes, skinned and sliced
100 g (250 ml/1 cup) grated Cheddar cheese
250 ml (1 cup) fresh white breadcrumbs
knobs of butter
paprika

1. Boil the pasta as described on p. 127, prepare the oil mixture in a large saucepan (as in
Hint on p. 127) and stir in the herbs. Drain
the pasta and stir in the oil mixture. Set aside.
2. SAUCE: Melt the butter over moderate
heat, add the flour and stir for 1 minute.
Remove from the heat and stir in the milk, a
little at a time. Beat well with a wire whisk.
Return to the heat and stir until the sauce is
hot. Add the cream and heat to boiling
point. Season with salt, pepper, cayenne
pepper, mustard and turmeric. Taste and
season with more salt if necessary. Add the
cheese and stir until it has melted. Remove
from the heat and beat in the eggs, one at a
time. Mix ⅔ of the sauce with the macaroni.
3. Grease a baking dish with margarine.
Spoon half the pasta mixture into the dish.
Sprinkle over the sausage and blue cheese (if
used) and spoon the remaining pasta on top.

Smooth the surface. If sausages and blue
cheese are not used, spoon all the pasta mixture into the dish and smooth the surface.
Spoon the rest of the sauce over and smooth
the surface.
4. TO SERVE: Arrange the tomato slices on
top. Mix the cheese and crumbs and sprinkle
over. Dot with butter. Bake for ± 30 minutes
in a preheated oven at 160 °C (325 °F).
Remove from the oven, sprinkle paprika over
and dot with more butter. Bake until set.
Serve with crusty bread and a green salad.

Lasagne verdi

(MAKES 6 LARGE OR
8 ORDINARY SERVINGS)

In classic Italian cuisine, you will not often
find onions and garlic in the same recipe.
This meat sauce, known as *ragu*, is a good
example. All kinds of lasagne are part of our
food repertoire, from runny sauces to too
much meat, to toppings of cottage cheese.
This recipe is closer to the Italian community's view of lasagne.

MEAT MIXTURE
1 small onion, halved lengthways,
    peeled and finely chopped
50 ml (4 T) olive oil
25 g (25 ml/2 T) butter
2 celery stalks, rinsed and threads removed,
    then thinly sliced
500 g lean beef mince, or ½ beef mince
    and ½ lean pork mince
2 large carrots, scraped and coarsely grated
25 ml (2 T) tomato concentrate
salt and freshly ground pepper
125 ml (½ cup) white wine
185 ml (¾ cup) meat stock
185 ml (¾ cup) cream
grated nutmeg
12 fresh basil leaves, washed,
    rolled up and cut into thin strips (optional)

OTHER INGREDIENTS
1 packet (500 g) green lasagne sheets
750 ml (3 cups) hot white sauce
80 g (200 ml/⅘ cup) grated cheese,
    preferably Parmesan cheese

1. MEAT SAUCE: Fry the onion in oil over
low heat until softened and transparent, but
not browned. Add the butter, celery and carrots and stir to blend. Cover with a sheet of
buttered waxed paper, close to the surface of
the vegetable mixture, reduce the heat, cover
and braise for 30 minutes.

2. Remove the lid and paper and stir the
meat, a little at a time, into the vegetable mixture, using a large, two-pronged fork to ensure
that the meat will be loose. Increase the heat
and stir-fry for 5 minutes until the mixture
begins to brown. Stir in the tomato concentrate and season with salt and pepper. Add the
wine, reduce the heat and simmer until all the
liquid has evaporated. Add the stock and simmer until almost all the liquid has been
absorbed. Stir in the cream and simmer until
the sauce is thick. Taste, season with more salt
and pepper if necessary, and grate nutmeg
over. Stir in the basil (if used) and set aside.
3. Boil the lasagne sheets (see How to cook
home-made pasta, p. 127).
4. Spoon the surface oiliness off the meat
mixture and use to grease the base of a baking dish. Cover the base of the dish with
lasagne sheets and spoon a thin layer of
white sauce over, then a layer of meat sauce,
then more pasta. Continue in this way until
all the meat sauce, pasta and white sauce
have been used, ending with a layer of white
sauce. Remember that the meat sauce layer
must be very thin. Do not pack the pasta
right to the edge of the dish, as it will dry out
during baking. Sprinkle cheese over and
bake for 20-30 minutes in a preheated oven
at 160 °C (325 °F). Allow to rest in the
warming drawer for 20 minutes. Cut into
blocks and serve with home-made crusty
bread and a mixed salad.

Spaghetti bolognaise

(MAKES 4-6 SERVINGS)

In its original form, this dish was made with
tagliatelle, but spaghetti has been popularised to such an extent through the
decades that today spaghetti bolognaise is
chiefly family fare.

meat sauce (see Lasagne above)
1 packet (500 g) spaghetti
finely grated Parmesan cheese

1. Make meat sauce (or *ragu alla bolognese*)
and keep warm.
2. Boil spaghetti (see How to cook home-
made pasta, p. 127) and treat with oil mixture (see Hint, p. 127).
3. Place the pasta in a heated serving dish
and spoon the meat sauce over. Finish with
Parmesan cheese and serve with extra finely
grated cheese.

SPAGHETTI BOLOGNAISE

Cannelloni

(Makes 6 servings)

12 cannelloni tubes, 12 sheets home-made pasta
or 12 pancakes

Filling
1 small onion, halved lengthways,
peeled and finely chopped
50 ml (4 T) olive oil
1 celery stalk, washed and threads removed,
then thinly sliced
1 carrot, scraped and thinly sliced
2 plump garlic cloves, bruised,
peeled and crushed with:
10 ml (2 t) salt
12 sprigs Italian flat-leaf parsley,
washed and leaves finely chopped
½ punnet (125 g) button mushrooms,
wiped clean and finely chopped
125 g ham, finely chopped
250 g beef mince
250 g minced chicken breasts or sausage meat
250 ml (1 cup) red wine
37,5 ml (3 T) tomato concentrate
250 ml (1 cup) beef stock
salt and freshly ground black pepper

Sauce
50 g (50 ml/4 T) butter
30 g (65 ml/¼ cup) cake flour
625 ml (2½ cups) milk
extra salt and black pepper
cayenne pepper and grated nutmeg to taste
1 ml (pinch) ground cloves
butter

Topping
65 ml (¼ cup) finely grated Parmesan cheese

1. Fry the onion in oil in a large frying pan until softened and transparent, but not browned. Add the celery, carrot, garlic, parsley, mushrooms and ham, cover and simmer for 5 minutes over low heat. Remove, allow to cool and purée in a food processor.
2. Place the mince, chicken, wine, tomato concentrate and stock in the pan in which the onion was fried and cook over moderate heat until all the liquid has evaporated. Stir in the puréed ham mixture, taste and season with salt and pepper. Allow to cool, then use to fill the cannelloni tubes.
3. Sauce: Melt the butter in a saucepan, stir in the flour and cook for 2-3 minutes. Remove from the heat and stir the milk in gradually. Beat well with a wire whisk and make sure that there are no lumps. Return to the heat and heat to boiling point, stirring

constantly. Season with salt, pepper, cayenne pepper, nutmeg and cloves.
4. Grease 6 cannelloni dishes lightly with butter and place a spoonful of sauce in each dish. Place 2 filled cannelloni tubes in each dish. Divide the remaining sauce among the dishes and spoon over the cannelloni. Sprinkle cheese over and bake for 25 minutes in a preheated oven at 180 °C (350 °F).

Variation
If pancakes are used, place the dish in the oven for ± 15 minutes to heat through, then serve.

Penne with sweet pepper sauce

(Makes 6 servings)

3 each red and yellow sweet peppers, baked
(see p. 146)
125 ml (½ cup) olive oil
1 large onion, preferably red, halved lengthways,
peeled and coarsely chopped
500 g ripe red tomatoes, skinned, seeded
and chopped (see Hint, p. 127),
or 1 tin (410 g) Italian tomatoes
salt and freshly ground pepper
12 fresh basil leaves, washed, rolled up
and cut into thin strips
5 ml (1 t) fresh oregano
1 packet (500 g) penne or rigatoni

Topping
grated Parmesan cheese
extra freshly ground black pepper

1. Cut sweet peppers into 5 mm (¼ in) strips and set aside. Pour oil in roasting pan (from sweet peppers) through a sieve and set aside.
2. Meanwhile, place the onion in a bowl of cold water and leave for 30 minutes.
3. Place reserved sweet pepper oil in a large frying pan and heat over moderate heat until hot. Drain the onion thoroughly, add to the pan and stir-fry for 3 minutes. Reduce the heat, cover and simmer for 15 minutes. Remove the lid, add the tomatoes, cover and simmer for a further ± 15 minutes or until the sauce begins to thicken. If the mixture is still very watery after 15 minutes, remove the lid and continue to simmer the mixture until it begins to thicken. Taste and season with salt and pepper. Stir in the basil, oregano and sweet peppers, cover the pan and simmer for 10 minutes.
4. Meanwhile, cook the penne (see How to cook home-made pasta, p. 127) and treat with oil mixture (see Hint, p. 127).

5. To serve: Spoon the hot sauce over hot penne and mix well. Cover and set aside for 2 minutes. Serve with Parmesan cheese and extra ground black pepper over each serving.

Screw noodles with pesto

(Makes 4-6 servings)

This is real yuppie food, and an example of hardly-any-effort cuisine, but using good ingredients: only the best, delicately flavoured olive oil, well-matured cheese, expensive nuts, and bunches of garden-fresh herbs blended to make pesto – perfect for the status of the young, up-and-coming professional generation. This pesto recipe is not the classic version, but it is indicative of changing times and the excitement of experimenting with new ideas on an old theme.

Pesto
375 ml (1½ cups) olive oil
1 packet (100 g/250 ml/1 cup) walnuts
25 ml (2 T) pine kernels
1 litre (4 cups) fresh basil leaves,
rinsed, patted dry and broken into pieces
50 ml (4 T) finely chopped blanched spinach
3 plump garlic cloves, bruised and peeled
100 g (250 ml/1 cup) finely grated
Parmesan cheese
salt and freshly ground black pepper

Pasta
1 packet (500 g) screw noodles, cooked as
described on p. 127, not given the oil
treatment, and cooking liquid reserved

Topping
extra grated Parmesan cheese

1. Place 125 ml (½ cup) of the olive oil in a food processor, add the nuts and pine kernels and purée until smooth. Add half the basil and pulse for 30 seconds. Repeat with remaining basil. Switch on the machine and add 125 ml (½ cup) of the oil in a thin stream. Add the spinach, garlic and cheese, season with salt and pepper and switch machine on again. Add the remaining oil in a thin stream, to make a smooth purée. Spoon into a bowl and set aside.
2. Add 25 ml (2 T) of the water in which the pasta was cooked to the basil purée and mix to blend. Immediately spoon basil mixture over the hot pasta and mix well, to ensure that pasta is completely covered with the purée. Heat through for 1 minute. Sprinkle extra grated Parmesan cheese over each serving and serve.

Spaghetti with tomato sauce (Spaghetti alla marinara)

(MAKES 4-6 SERVINGS)

A very simple tomato sauce is made for this dish. In its most original form, *alla marinara* means that sun-ripe tomatoes are added to a dish, such as pasta, along with olive oil and garlic. Because mussels and clams combine so well with these basic ingredients, many people mistakenly believe that these 'fruits of the sea' are part of *alla marinara*. When seafood is added, it is known as *alla vongole* (see Variation). Cheese is not, strictly speaking, sprinkled over the dish, of which this tomato sauce forms the base.

125 ml (½ cup) olive oil
2-3 plump garlic cloves, bruised,
*   peeled and coarsely chopped*
leaves of 8-12 Italian flat-leaf parsley sprigs,
*   washed, patted dry and coarsely chopped*
1 kg ripe red tomatoes, skinned, seeded,
*   coarsely chopped (see Hint, p. 27)*
*   and the juices reserved*
salt and freshly ground black pepper
1 packet (500 g) spaghetti

SERVE WITH (OPTIONAL)
50 ml (4 T) canned capers
25 ml (2 T) chopped stoned black olives
12,5 ml (1 T) finely chopped
*   fresh Italian parsley*

1. Heat the oil until hot in a large saucepan over moderate heat. Add the garlic and parsley and stir-fry for 1 minute. Add the tomatoes and reserved juices and heat to boiling point. Reduce the heat and simmer for 20 minutes. Stir from time to time. Spoon the tomato mixture into a food processor, purée and then rub through a sieve into a clean saucepan. Taste, season with salt and pepper and simmer for a further 5-10 minutes.

2. Boil the spaghetti (see How to cook home-made pasta, p. 127) and treat with oil mixture (see Hint, p. 127).

3. Spoon the hot sauce over the hot pasta and toss to blend. Spoon into a large heated serving dish and sprinkle the capers, olives and parsley over (if used). Serve the pasta immediately.

VARIATION:
SPAGHETTI ALLA VONGOLE

Add 1 kg cleaned, steamed mussels or clams to the tomato sauce and heat through. Spoon over the pasta, toss to mix and serve. There is also a second version of this dish, in which the oil mixture, as for the *alla marinara* version, is made. It is mixed with the pasta, along with the mussels, and is still *vongole*, but the *in bianco* version.

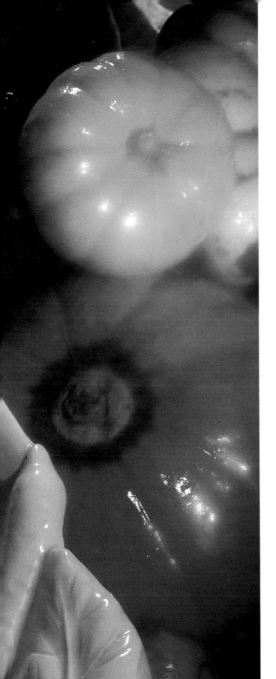

From the sweetness of cane: vegetables and dried fruit

IRONY SOMETIMES prevails – as in the case of the English who taught the Boers to appreciate sweet things, but did not really indulge in sweet things themselves. When Britain established the greatest commonwealth of all time, she also had to contend with an over-production of cane sugar. This was used, among other things, to make golden syrup and other syrups, which were exported to the colonies. With the establishment of our own sugar industry in Natal, even more syrup was marketed locally. This suited the white and Coloured Afrikaner communities to a T, as they had already developed a sweet tooth from Malay food. Golden syrup, in particular, supplemented jam, honey and sticky-sweet products like koesisters. No wonder, then, that certain kinds of vegetables soon became sweet too. Even half a squash had to get a knob of butter and a pinch of sugar. To the astonishment of European visitors, sweetened vegetables are today a characteristic of South African food – and rightfully so, as they are the logical accompaniment to certain dishes. Malay, Indian and Afrikaner cooks like it. The English community also learnt the method, but do not apply it daily. Sweetened vegetables are cooked in the townships, but the vast majority of black people traditionally cook without sugar. First the pumpkin is placed in the pot to cook briefly before the maize meal is added. Pumpkin pips are important to all population groups: fried or grilled, they are sprinkled over porridge, added to the dough of health loaves, or simply sprinkled over bread dough before baking, as part of the topping. Pumpkin bredie is much loved by all South Africans who enjoy their food.

PUMPKIN FRITTERS

Pumpkin is a member of the squash family, but is much larger and less watery. Most of them are round and flat. Some, like the boer pumpkin, grow very large and become extremely heavy – especially when they get enough water and are planted in fertile soil. There have even been boer pumpkins on display at agricultural shows that weighed more than the average man; in other words, more than 100 kg. Boer pumpkins keep well for a long time, even after cutting. The skin is usually white, and the flesh a bright orange.

Something which became very popular during the first half of the twentieth century was the early pumpkin (*vroeëpampoen*). These pumpkins are already ripe in December, and ready for the pot. Some grow very large, with a diameter of up to half a metre. Some are creamy white, others multi-coloured with green tufts, and others are grey-green. The flesh is similar to that of boer pumpkin, but slightly lighter. Vegetable marrows are long and usually have a green skin, but can also have a white skin. They are closer to a firm squash than a pumpkin, but are cooked like pumpkin. The flesh is white and watery. Today's baby marrows stem from the vegetable marrow.

Hubbard squash looks rather like a rugby ball, but is plumper around the middle and thinner at the ends. The skin is either green, or green with yellow and orange, and is full of bumps. The flesh is orange, dry and naturally sweet. It should be prepared with very little sugar. Baby pumpkins, with their frilly edges, were called *pasteipampoentjies* (pie pumpkins) because they reminded an earlier generation of a pastry crust. The flesh is almost like that of a ripe squash – watery – and they are traditionally prepared with bread cubes. A popular pumpkin is the longish, slightly crook-necked Ceylon pumpkin, which has an orange peel from which *meelpampoen* (pumpkin porridge) is cooked.

Butternut squash has just about taken the place of pumpkin over the past two decades.

They are cooked in lightly salted water and halved lengthways before the seeds are scraped out and the squash are served.

Chayote is almost a weed. If you plant one and allow it to climb along a wire fence, you will have a member of the pumpkin family for the pot throughout the year. They are cooked in all kinds of ways, but the basic cooking method is the same as for vegetable marrow. The round-fruited calabash marrow is treated like sweet potatoes.

Baked boer pumpkin, pumpkin fritters and *pampoenmoes* (pumpkin mash) were intended specifically for serving with the Sunday leg of lamb. Often they are supplemented further by sweet potatoes, glazed carrots and sweet, stewed dried fruit. Dried fruit is excellent with curried dishes. Sweetened vegetables lend themselves to the baking of desserts. Pumpkin fritters are sometimes served as dessert, while pumpkin and sweet potato puddings are examples of cooked vegetables being mixed with egg-rich custard and baked with a meringue topping. Rural folk often made pumpkin tart, which was replaced by the Tex-Mex pumpkin pie during the eighties.

Carrots were cooked with extra sugar, sometimes with orange juice and even, so I'm told, made excessively sweet with custard powder and peas.

Sweet potatoes are excellent with duck, Muscovy duck, pheasant, quail and guinea-fowl. These days, they are puréed and scooped into neat 'eggs' onto a plate alongside other purées. Or they are baked, and served, in the skin, as in the past. Choke potatoes no longer exist. They were also earlier called *teehouers* (tea caddies). In the days of great poverty during the first half of the century, they were often the only food for supper. The area stretching from Ladismith in the Cape to Knysna was once called Patattaland.

Dried fruit is typically South African. Because we have a lot of fruit which cannot all be exported, grapes, to give one example, are used to make *moskonfyt* (must jam) and raisins. Otherwise, fruit is canned or dried. Sun-dried whole peaches, complete with stone, are soaked, often in a sweet wine like muscadel or port, until they swell up, then boiled or stewed with lots of butter. Delicious, especially with chicken pie.

Soetpampoen (Sweetened pumpkin)

(MAKES 8 SERVINGS)

Each cook has his or her own way of making sweetened pumpkin and stewed sweet potatoes. The French, it is said, have more kinds of cheese than there are days in the year; this is also true of cooking methods for sweetened vegetables. A few of these are given in the variations.

250 g (250 ml / 1 cup) butter
1,5 kg boer pumpkin, peeled and cut into pieces
salt
200 g (250 ml / 1 cup) sugar
250 ml (1 cup) golden syrup
2 sticks cinnamon, broken

1. Grease a large baking pan or dish with a little butter. Place the pumpkin in it, in a single layer. Season with salt. Sprinkle with sugar and pour the golden syrup over. Dot with the rest of the butter and sprinkle the cinnamon pieces over. Cover with aluminium foil, shiny side in, and bake for 20-30 minutes in a preheated oven at 180 °C (350 °F).
2. Remove the aluminium foil. Increase the temperature to 200 °C (400 °F) and bake until the liquid begins to caramelise. Turn pumpkin pieces once only with a flat slice, egg slice or spatula, or they will break and not brown well. Take care that the sugar mixture does not burn.

VARIATIONS
● Old hands dry naartjie peels and store them in the sugar. A few dried naartjie peels are added with the cinnamon.
● Use honey instead of golden syrup.
● A friend assures me that oil (the same quantity as the butter above) – ordinary sunflower oil – gives pumpkin a better shine than butter. I prefer the taste of butter.
● Others swear by yellow sugar instead of white sugar.
● The baked pumpkin may be rubbed through a sieve. Place in a piping bag and pipe into cooked halved squash, from which the pips have been removed.
● Cooking does not have to take place in the oven – you could also use the method given below for sweet potatoes.

Pampoenmoes (Pumpkin mash)

(MAKES 6 SERVINGS)

Traditionally this is known as *pampoenmoes* or pumpkin mash, but it is actually stewed pumpkin with cubes of bread in it. Usually it is cooked in the oven along with a leg of mutton.

650 g peeled, thinly sliced boer
pumpkin, Ceylon pumpkin, Hubbard squash
or butternut squash
a few pieces cassia
2 slices white bread, buttered on both sides,
crusts discarded, then cubed
1 ml (pinch) salt
25 g (25 ml / 2 T) butter
25 ml (2 T) water
50 ml (4 T) or more yellow sugar

1. Place half the pumpkin in a well-greased baking dish. Arrange a few pieces of cassia on top, cover with bread cubes and then the rest of the pumpkin. Sprinkle salt over and place a few more pieces of cassia on top.
2. Dot with butter and sprinkle the water and sugar over. Cover and bake in a preheated oven at 160 °C (325 °F) until cooked. Remove the lid and brown lightly under the grill.

VARIATION: WITH 'PIE' PUMPKIN
Follow the recipe above, but cook it on top of the stove. First cube young 'pie' pumpkin or vegetable marrow. Add all the ingredients, except the bread, and heat until hot. Stir, cook until the sugar dissolves and then add the bread cubes. Simmer, uncovered.

Meelpampoen (Pumpkin porridge)

(MAKES 4 SERVINGS)

This dish is also known as *pampoenpap* or pumpkin porridge and was often, in the past, served as a breakfast dish instead of maize porridge. Today it is enjoyed with grilled pork chops or boerewors.

baked pumpkin (see Pampoenmoes, p. 134)
12,5 ml (1 T) cake flour
cinnamon sugar
1-2 spoonfuls butter

1. Remove the cassia from the cooked pumpkin and mash the pumpkin finely with a fork, or purée it in a food processor, to make 500 ml (2 cups) mash.
2. Place the mash, as well as any liquid that formed during baking, into a saucepan and sprinkle the flour over. Stir to blend and simmer over low heat. Sweeten with extra cinnamon sugar and stir in the butter. Stir often and continue simmering until the mixture recedes from the sides of the saucepan.

Pumpkin fritters

(MAKES 24-36 FRITTERS)

1 litre (4 cups) pumpkin mash
  (see Hint)
130 g (250 ml/1 cup) self-raising flour
salt to taste
10 ml (2 t) ground cinnamon
  or mixed spice
25 ml (2 T) orange concentrate (optional)
grated rind of 2 oranges
4-6 extra-large eggs

TOPPING
cinnamon sugar
lemon wedges

1. Preheat the oven to 180 °C (350 °F). Place pumpkin mash in a large mixing bowl.
2. Sift the flour, salt and cinnamon. Sift one third of the flour mixture over the pumpkin and fold it in. Beat together the orange concentrate (if used), rind and eggs (only 4 to begin with). Stir one third of the egg mixture into the pumpkin mixture. Repeat twice with the rest of the flour mixture and the egg mixture. If the mixture is too stiff –

it should be runny – add an extra egg, and, if necessary, another egg. The more egg the mixture contains, the higher the fritters will rise during baking.
3. Grease muffin pans lightly with margarine and line the base of the hollows with baking parchment. Grease the parchment. Deep muffin pans will make 24 fritters; shallow ones will make 36. Fill each hollow to about two-thirds full and bake for 20 minutes.
4. Remove from the oven and loosen around the edges with a sharp knife. Sprinkle cinnamon sugar into the base of a serving dish and arrange the fritters on top. Sprinkle sugar over again and repeat. Serve with lemon wedges.

HINT: Here is a new method for preparing an old favourite so that the result is not fatty. Slice boer pumpkin. Wrap in aluminium foil, shiny side in, place in a baking pan and bake in a preheated oven at 140 °C (275 °F) until the pumpkin is tender. Remove from the oven, remove the aluminium foil and remove the pumpkin flesh from the skin. Purée or rub through a sieve. If the pumpkin is watery, spoon it into a saucepan and simmer it over low heat, stirring constantly, until the mixture is thick.

Stewed sweet potatoes

(MAKES 6 SERVINGS)

125 g (125 ml/½ cup) butter
250 ml (1 cup) honey
100 g (125 ml/½ cup) sugar
25 ml (2 T) lemon juice
grated rind of 2 oranges and 2 lemons
250 ml (1 cup) water
1 kg sweet potatoes, peeled, cut into equal-sized
  pieces and placed in water to which lemon
  juice and ½ t salt have been added
naartjie rind
cassia or stick cinnamon, broken

1. Mix the butter, honey and sugar and stir over low heat until the sugar has dissolved. Add the juice and rind, increase the heat and stir-fry for 1 minute.
2. Remove the sweet potatoes from the lemon water and add to the honey mixture with the naartjie rind and cassia. Cover with the lid, reduce the heat and simmer for 10-15 minutes until crisp-tender.

3. Remove the lid and simmer the sweet potatoes until dry. *Do not* stir; leave them alone. Increase the heat slightly and allow sweet potatoes to caramelise. Carefully insert a flat slice underneath the sweet potatoes when they have formed a thin, golden-brown layer, and turn them over.

VARIATIONS
● For darker sweet potatoes: Replace honey with the same quantity of golden syrup, and use brown sugar instead of white.
●Add 12,5 ml (1 T) finely grated fresh ginger root with the grated rind.

Stewed dried fruit

1. Half-cover any kind of dried fruit, or a mixture, with boiling water and leave until plump. The fruit may also be covered with a sweet wine like muscadel or port and heated to boiling point. Remove from the stove and stir from time to time.
2. Place the saucepan on the stove, add a knob or two of butter, heat over low heat and simmer until cooked. Cloves and/or sticks of cinnamon may be cooked with the fruit, but do not use too much, as they will overpower the natural aroma of the fruit.

Spiced peaches

(MAKES 6 SERVINGS)

1 kg sun-dried peaches (preferably whole)
water
vinegar
200 g (250 ml/1 cup) sugar
stick of cinnamon
8 cloves
6 allspice berries
10 black peppercorns

1. Place the peaches in a saucepan and add enough water to cover them halfway. Measure the water, and add half the quantity of vinegar. Add the remaining ingredients and stir over low heat until the sugar has dissolved. Increase the heat and cook for 5 minutes. Switch off the stove and allow the peaches to cool. Test to determine whether peaches are cooked. Remove all the spices (as they will be too overpowering). Cook longer, if necessary.
2. Serve with venison, lamb or pork.

Vegetables, a new eating experience

IF THERE WERE any doubt about whether a geographic environment and a specific cultural landscape could change the diet of a country, nothing would illustrate it better in South Africa than the cooking and serving of vegetables: sweetened vegetables and almost-but-not-quite bredies made from vegetables for the Afrikaners, steamed or boiled vegetables for English-speaking South Africa, and virtually no vegetables for blacks. That was the picture until recently, and it is still partly true. New-wave cooking methods are now uniting tastes, and it is not unusual to have seven or more vegetables on the table at one meal.

Vegetables that are cooked for seconds or at the most a minute or two, and then glazed with butter, herb butter, or sugar and butter, are the order of the day. Add to this flavoursome, velvety purées, contrasted with crisply fried herbs from the deep-fryer, or chopped fresh herbs mixed with crushed garlic and lemon rind. Potatoes, rice or another source of starch completes the picture. Drizzle a special vegetable sauce here and there over the plate, and no one will be surprised at the increasing popularity of vegetables.

The potatoes, meat and rice generation is dying out and the new generation is creating a new African diet. Slimmer figures demand lighter meals; this has sparked the new emphasis on vegetables. These days, vegetables are even served as a course in their own right, before the main course. The combination depends on the main dish.

HOW TO REMOVE SAND FROM VEGETABLES

Sand is a problem with some vegetables:
● Scrub baby marrows with a small brush to remove any sand and rinse under cold running water. Soak for 30 seconds in salted water and rinse again.

● Make 4 cuts in the green part of a leek and rinse well under cold running water. Soak for 30 minutes in salty water and rinse again.

HOW TO PREVENT DISCOLORATION OF VEGETABLES

Some vegetables, including turnips and sweet potatoes, discolour after peeling, as a result of the loss of ascorbic acid. Place them immediately in water to which fresh lemon juice has been added.

GLAZED, COOKED VEGETABLES

1. Rinse vegetables thoroughly.
2. Heat a saucepan of water to boiling point. Add a handful of vegetables and blanch for a few seconds, rather than a few minutes. Remove the vegetables with a slotted spoon. (Do not blanch mangetout. Keep them raw and glaze directly in butter, water and sugar until cooked.)
3. Now glaze each kind of vegetable separately. Spoon a knob of butter and a spoonful of water into a saucepan and season with salt and pepper (see Hints). Spoon one kind of vegetable at a time into the saucepan and shake until the vegetables are glazed and brightly coloured.
4. Garnish vegetables (see Garnishing, p. 138) and serve immediately (see Hints).

HINTS

● Slice vegetables, cut into barrel shapes, or press out decorative patterns with special small cutters.
● Add 5 ml (1 t) sugar to the butter in which carrots, turnips, baby squash, yellow baby squash, parsnips, butternut slices, cucumber and mangetout are glazed. Broccoli, cauliflower, cabbage and Brussels sprouts do not need sugar, but do require grated nutmeg.
● Many people prefer not to cook until the last moment. Prepare the vegetables, allow to get cold and heat at 100% power in the microwave oven. Small carrots and harder vegetables take longer to heat up than the flatter, softer kinds, such as mangetout. Do not reheat hard and soft vegetables together.

A VARIETY OF VEGETABLES
FRESH FROM THE GARDEN

Vegetable purée

1. Boil vegetables in water or light stock until tender.
2. Purée in a food processor, with a little of the cooking liquid, or press through a sieve.
3. Spoon into a saucepan and stir over low heat until all the water in the purée has evaporated.
4. Season with salt, pepper and other flavourings that are appropriate for the purée. For a creamier texture, add a few spoonfuls of cream and a knob of butter. Stir over moderate heat until the mixture begins to cook dry and retains its shape. Use two spoons to place spoonfuls of purée on the plate, so that they look like eggs, and garnish (see Garnishing below).

GARNISHING

• Garnish each kind of vegetable with appropriate chopped fresh herbs (see recipes for specific vegetables).
• A new method is to choose a few kinds of vegetables for their colour, taste and affinity to one another, and then to serve them on a thin purée. For example, boil mangetout until tender and purée with a little cooking liquid, a spoonful of cream and a knob of butter. Season with salt, pepper and a pinch of sugar. Divide among plates. Place *pommes duchesses*, 3 mangetout, 1 each of cucumber, turnip and carrot shapes and 2 French beans, arranged crosswise, on top and drop a small spoonful of bamboo shoots mixed with chopped chives and fresh coriander leaves at the point where the beans cross. Doesn't that look good?
• Where appropriate, spoon Savoury butter (p. 46) or Vegetable sauce (below) over the vegetables.

Vegetable sauce

(MAKES 4 SERVINGS)

250 ml (1 cup) strong vegetable
  or mushroom stock
250 ml (1 cup) cream
salt and pepper
knob of butter
25 ml (2 T) Van der Hum

1. Reduce the stock to about 50 ml (4 T). Add half the cream and reduce again to 50 ml (4 T). Stir in rest of the cream and season lightly with salt and pepper.
2. Simmer the sauce over low heat until thick. Stir in the liqueur, and drizzle here and there on a heated plate on which the vegetables have been arranged.

Potatoes cooked in their jackets

1. Scrub large or small potatoes and rinse under cold running water.
2. Place the potatoes in a saucepan, cover with water and add salt to taste. Heat to boiling point, reduce the heat and simmer until cooked.

SEASONINGS FOR POTATOES

Salt, pepper, chopped chives, parsley, garlic and nutmeg.

Potato balls

1. Using a melon baller, scoop balls from large, peeled potatoes. (Use the hollowed-out parts to make mashed potatoes.)
2. Place the balls in a saucepan, cover with water and add salt to taste. Heat to boiling point, reduce the heat and simmer for 10 minutes. Switch off the heat and leave the balls until cooked. Drain. Season with salt, pepper and grated nutmeg. Add a lump of Maître d'hôtel butter (p. 46) or ordinary butter, chopped parsley and/or chives and/or crushed garlic. Shake over moderate heat and serve.

VARIATIONS

• Fry the potato balls in a mixture of butter and oil and season with salt, pepper, nutmeg, paprika or roasted sesame seeds.
• Heat a clove or two of bruised garlic with the butter.

Miriam's potatoes

(MAKES 4 SERVINGS)

4 large potatoes
oil
1 small onion, finely chopped
salt, pepper and grated nutmeg

1. Rinse the potatoes thoroughly under cold running water, peel and cube. Place in a saucepan, cover with cold water and season with salt. Boil for 5 minutes. Drain.
2. Pour a little oil in a frying pan and heat over high heat. Add the potato cubes and fry for 2 minutes. Reduce the heat and continue to fry, without stirring, until the potatoes have browned underneath. Shake the pan, turn the cubes and continue frying until all the cubes are golden brown.
3. Add the onion and stir with a spatula. Season lightly with salt, pepper and nutmeg. Serve with fried mutton chops or roast chicken.

Château potatoes

1. Peel small new potatoes and cut them into the shape of barrels.
2. Blanch and fry over low heat with chopped bacon rashers and butter until the potatoes are browned. Season with salt and pepper. Serve with Châteaubriand (p. 72).

Game chips

1. Peel Van der Plank potatoes, halve them lengthways and halve each half horizontally. Pour a little fat or oil in a roasting pan and place in a preheated oven until hot.
2. Arrange the potato slices, cut sides down, in the pan. Place the rack of the roasting pan holding a roasting cut – especially meat larded with bacon – on top. Roast for 40-50 minutes at 160 °C (325 °F). The fat dripping from the meat drops constantly on the potatoes during cooking.
3. Remove cooked potatoes with a spatula and drain on kitchen paper. Season lightly with salt. A few spoonfuls of strong meat stock, if available, can first be heated with the fat in the pan. Serve with venison.

Roast potatoes

1. Prepare as for Game chips, but halve the potatoes once only, scrape them with a fork and shake them in a bag containing cake flour seasoned with salt, pepper, turmeric and paprika. Remove the potatoes from the bag and shake off excess flour.
2. Place the potatoes, rounded sides down, in hot oil. Add more oil to the oil in the pan during roasting, if necessary. Turn potatoes after 20-25 minutes in the oven, so that the flat sides are down. Complete as above.

Rösti

(MAKES ABOUT 24 RÖSTI)

6 large potatoes, rinsed but not peeled
cold water
salt and pepper
grated nutmeg
125 g (125 ml / ½ cup) butter
extra butter

1. Place the potatoes in a saucepan and cover with water. Heat to boiling point and boil for 10 minutes. Remove from the heat and allow the potatoes to cool completely.

Drain. Refrigerate overnight. Pull off the skins and grate the potatoes coarsely into a large mixing bowl. Loosen slightly with a large fork. Season with salt and pepper and sprinkle with nutmeg to taste.

2. Melt the butter and sprinkle over. Use a large two-pronged fork to mix once, thoroughly.

3. Spoon the mixture into a greased muffin pan with 12 hollows. Press down lightly and dot each rösti with butter. Bake for 20-25 minutes in a preheated oven at 180 °C (350 °F) until browned and crisp. Cool slightly and remove carefully.

HINT: The rösti may also be pre-shaped into 12 larger circles. Remove the circles, place the rösti on a baking sheet lined with Bakewell paper, and fry – preferably in a small cast-iron pan, like pancakes.

Chips

(MAKES 4 SERVINGS)

The secret remains the same: serve the chips as soon as they are cooked.

4 large potatoes, peeled and well rinsed
sunflower oil
salt

1. Cut the potatoes into 12,5 mm (½ in) thick slices and cut each slice into strips 12,5 ml (½ in) wide to make chips. Place chips in fresh cold water.

2. Meanwhile, heat the oil to 180 °C (350 °F) in a deep, stainless steel saucepan (see Hint). Remove ¼ of the chips from the water and pat dry with a clean tea towel.

3. Place the chips in a frying basket, or place in the oil with a slotted spoon. Fry until almost cooked. Remove the frying basket from the oil, or remove the chips with a slotted spoon and place in a large bowl. Repeat with the rest of the chips.

4. Heat the oil to 190 °C (375 °F). Return all the chips to the oil and fry until they begin to brown. Spoon out onto kitchen paper or crumpled brown paper and absorb all the excess oil with an extra piece of paper. Season with salt and serve immediately.

HINT: If you do not have a thermometer to measure the temperature of the oil, you can use a small cube of (crustless) white bread. Let the bread sink down in the oil. If it rises to the surface after a few seconds and browns gradually, the oil is the right temperature; if it browns and darkens

quickly, the oil is too hot; and if it takes more than 5 seconds to rise to the top, the oil is too cold.

SEASONING VARIATIONS

● VINEGAR: The irresistibility of fish and chips must lie in the smell of old oil when you enter the fish and chips shop – and, of course, the chips, thick with salt and vinegar. It may not be everyone's choice, but it is part of our heritage.

● Sprinkle a mixture of cayenne pepper and paprika over the cooked chips. Decide on the proportion according to your own taste, but remember that the more cayenne pepper there is, the greater the bite!

● Sprinkle Aromat or Fondor over if you must, but your own mixture would be better: 10 ml (2 t) salt, 3-5 ml (½-1 t) freshly ground black pepper, 5 ml (1 t) pinch of herbs and a few shakes of cayenne pepper. Season hot chips immediately.

Mashed potatoes

(MAKES 4 SERVINGS)

4 large potatoes, peeled and cubed
salt
50 g (50 ml/4 T) butter
50 ml (4 T) milk or cream
white pepper
grated nutmeg
50 g (50 ml/4 T) butter (optional)

1. Boil potatoes in salted water until tender. Drain. Add the butter and cream and heat until the butter has melted and the mixture is warm. Remove from the heat.

2. Mash the potatoes until smooth with a potato masher. Taste and season with pepper and a little nutmeg. If you wish, beat more butter in for even creamier potatoes.

HINT: Some people believe that adding 3 ml (½ t) baking powder makes mashed potato lighter. I do not; if you want it to be fluffier, you can stir in a (separately whisked) egg white.

Potatoes Anna

(MAKES 6-8 SERVINGS)

Nothing is quite as delicious as roast rack of lamb served with this potato cake. Use a springform pan, if possible, and place it on a baking sheet to catch up any butter running

out during baking – as it may drip onto the base of the oven and burn. An ordinary cake pan will also work, but then you don't need the baking sheet. Choose potatoes of approximately the same size. For this recipe, it is important that the potatoes are not peeled beforehand; peel them one by one as you build up the layers of the cake. The potatoes should also under no circumstances be left in water, as this will remove the starch and the layers of the cake will then not adhere to one another. Peel one potato at a time and slice it thinly, or use a food processor fitted with the cutting blade. You may have to cut the potatoes slightly smaller so that they will fit in the feeder tube of the food processor.

750 g-1 kg equal-sized potatoes, rinsed
salt and pepper
grated nutmeg
100 g (100 ml/8 T) butter, melted

1. Grease the base and sides of a baking pan with a little of the butter. Slice 1 potato and arrange in a circle around the outer edge of the base of the pan, with the slices overlapping slightly. Repeat in ever-smaller circles, with the circles overlapping one another, until the base is covered. Season lightly with salt, pepper and nutmeg. Brush a little butter over. Repeat the potato layers, seasonings and butter until all the ingredients have been used and the pan is full.

2. Bake the 'cake' on the bottom rack in a preheated oven at 180 °C (350 °F) until cooked and browned on top.

3. Remove from the oven and flatten carefully with a potato masher so that the excess butter rises to the surface. You can pour off the butter, or leave it as it is. Keep the cake warm. When you are ready to serve, turn the potato cake out of the pan and invert it so that the browned side is on top. Slice like a cake and serve.

VARIATIONS

● Sprinkle a little finely grated Parmesan cheese between the layers and on top before the cake is baked. A little paprika may also be sprinkled over during the last 15 minutes of baking to ensure a good colour on top.

● Spoon over 125 ml (½ cup) chicken or beef stock before the cake is baked. Remember to place a springform pan on a baking sheet.

● Spoon 12,5-25 ml (1-2 T) cream on to each layer and spread it out with the back of a spoon. Top with cream.

● Sprinkle finely chopped, crisply fried bacon between the layers.

Creamed potatoes

(MAKES 6 SERVINGS)

4 large or 6 medium-sized potatoes,
peeled and placed in cold water
salt, pepper and grated nutmeg
250 ml (1 cup) white or béchamel sauce
or cream
5 ml (1 t) grated onion
butter

1. Remove 1 potato from the water and slice it thinly. Arrange a layer of slices in the base of a greased, medium-sized dish and season lightly with salt, pepper and nutmeg. Pour a thin layer of white sauce over the potato. Sprinkle onion over. Repeat until all the potatoes have been used. Pour the rest of the white sauce over and dot with butter.
2. Cover with aluminium foil, shiny side in, and bake for ± 1 hour in a preheated oven at 180 °C (350 °F).

VARIATIONS
● Sprinkle 1-2 crushed garlic cloves or 25 ml (2 T) snipped chives or spring onions between potato layers.
● Remove the aluminium foil after 45 minutes' baking and sprinkle 50 ml (4 T) finely grated Parmesan cheese and 5 ml (1 t) paprika over. Bake for 15 minutes.

Potato purée

(MAKES 6-8 SERVINGS)

1 kg potatoes, peeled and halved
50 g (50 ml/4 T) cold butter, cubed
250 ml (1 cup) milk
50 ml (4 T) thick cream
salt, pepper and grated nutmeg

1. Boil the potatoes in well-salted water until they are tender.
2. Pour off the water and mash the potatoes with a potato masher. If desired, purée the potatoes, a little at a time, in a food processor and return to the saucepan. Add the butter and beat with a wooden spoon until melted. Add the milk and cream and mix. Taste and season with salt, pepper and nutmeg to taste. Serve with fried sausage or baked liver.

VARIATIONS
● PEA AND POTATO PURÉE: Cook 250 g thawed frozen peas in 250 ml (1 cup) strong meat stock. Purée, rub through a sieve and stir into 500 g potato purée. Serve with poached fish.
● HERB AND POTATO PURÉE: Stir 15 ml (3 t) snipped chives, 15 ml (3 t) finely chopped fresh parsley, and 10 ml (2 t) finely chopped fresh thyme leaves into 500 g potato purée. Serve with fried mutton chops.
● CARROT AND POTATO PURÉE: Cook 350 g scraped and thinly sliced carrots in 250 ml (1 cup) strong chicken stock until tender. Purée in a food processor, rub through a sieve and stir into Potato purée (this page). Taste and season with pepper if necessary. Serve with roast duck, quail or pheasant.
● Stir 1 medium-sized onion, peeled, thinly sliced and cooked until tender, into complementary vegetables before puréeing.
● For a richer flavour, grated mature Cheddar, Parmesan or Gruyère cheese can be stirred in.
● POTATO PURÉE WITH OLIVE OIL: Use 150 ml (⅗ cup) olive oil instead of the butter and milk. Garlic, baked and the soft insides pressed out, may also be stirred in. Serve with roast beef.

Baked potatoes

1. Scrub large potatoes, but do not pat dry – a little water must cling to them to form steam during cooking.
2. Cut a cross, about 12,5 mm (½ in) deep in the flattest side of each potato. Sprinkle a few grains of coarse salt over, wrap each potato separately in aluminium foil, shiny side in, and place in a baking pan. Bake for 40-60 minutes in a preheated oven at 180 °C (350 °F). Remove from the oven and test for doneness. If cooked, remove from the foil and press the potato so that it will 'blossom' upwards. Serve at a braai with sour cream and chopped chives.

Endive

1. Blanch the bitter leaves twice in fresh, cold water heated to boiling point. Refresh the leaves in ice-cold water, pat dry and cut into strips.
2. Stir-fry in a little melted butter and season with salt, pepper and grated nutmeg.

Artichokes

There are two kinds of artichoke: the globe artichoke and the Jerusalem (or root) artichoke. When preparing globe artichokes, have sharp scissors and half a lemon handy.

globe artichokes
1½ lemons
salt
whole peppercorns
2-3 bay leaves

1. Cut the stalk level and immediately rub with ½ lemon. Now cut off the tip of each prickly leaf with scissors and rub each leaf with lemon.
2. Add the seasonings and the whole lemon – thinly sliced, with the skin – to water in a large saucepan and heat to boiling point. Add all the artichokes at the same time, heat to boiling point again, cover, reduce the heat to moderate and simmer for 20-30 minutes. Switch off the heat.
3. Remove 1 artichoke with a slotted spoon and test it by pulling off a bottom leaf and pressing the thick part between your thumb and forefinger. If the flesh slips out easily, the artichoke is ready. If it is not ready, leave the artichokes in hot water a little longer. Remove and drain, upside down. Enclose the artichokes, one at a time, in your palm and press lightly to remove any remaining water. Place 1 artichoke per person on a heated plate and serve.

HOW DOES ONE EAT ARTICHOKES? Pull off the leaves, one at a time, with one hand, dip the thick, fleshy part in melted butter, Hollandaise sauce (p. 53) or Vinaigrette (p. 154) and suck out the flesh. Continue in this way until you reach the fluffy middle part. Remove it carefully from below. Spoon a little melted butter or sauce over the base – it is the best part of the artichoke – and eat it with a first-course knife and fork.

Jerusalem artichokes

Jerusalem artichokes
vinegar water
salt and pepper
butter
lemon juice

1. Peel the artichokes and immediately place them in a weak solution of vinegar and water. Boil water in a saucepan and add salt. Add the artichokes, heat to boiling point and boil rapidly over high heat until tender.
2. Drain and glaze with a knob of butter, salt, pepper, and a few drops of lemon juice.

VARIATIONS
• A popular way of serving Jerusalem artichokes in the twenties was to fry a half-ripe banana (sliced) in lemon butter, add it to cooked artichoke slices and garnish with finely chopped parsley and chives.
• Mix cooked artichoke slices with thick béchamel sauce. Purée, mix half and half with mashed potatoes, pipe rosettes and bake.
• Deep-fry cooked artichoke slices in fat, like chips, drain and sprinkle a little finely grated Parmesan cheese over.

Asparagus

In the past, asparagus spears were first peeled with a vegetable peeler. These days, this is only necessary if they are very thick. Very thin asparagus spears generally do not have much flavour.

asparagus, more or less the same thickness
salt and pepper
butter

1. Cut off the bottom 25 mm (1 in) or so from asparagus spears and place, stem end down, in an empty 410 g tin. Fill the tin halfway with well-salted water. Place tin in a saucepan and fill the saucepan with enough boiling water to come halfway up the sides of the tin. Cover, heat and steam for a few minutes. Take care not to cook them for too long.
2. Turn out and drain. Season with salt and pepper and glaze with a knob of butter. Serve with Hollandaise sauce (p. 53) or maltaise sauce (Hollandaise into which 10 ml/ 2 t finely grated orange peel and 5 ml/1 t lemon peel have been stirred).

HINT: Asparagus tips make a pretty garnish for salads or vegetables. Spears can be cut diagonally as part of mixed vegetables.

Avocado purée

This is one of the "new vegetables".

1 small onion, peeled and finely chopped
butter and oil
10 ml (2 t) Garam masala (p. 100)
2 avocados
salt, black pepper and cayenne pepper
lemon juice
pinch of shredded red chilli

1. Fry the onion in the butter and oil until softened. Season with garam masala and fry for 1 minute more.
2. Add the avocado flesh and season with salt, pepper, cayenne pepper, lemon juice and chilli. Stir-fry for 1 minute, spoon into hollowed-out yellow baby squash and serve.

Beetroot

1. Cut off the beetroot leaves 12,5-25 mm (½-1 in) from the top of the bulb. Do the same with the roots. Rinse quickly, but do not pat dry. Wrap beetroot, one at a time, in aluminium foil, shiny side in. Place the beetroot in a baking pan and bake for 45-60 minutes in a preheated oven at 120-140 °C (250-275 °F), or until tender.
2. Remove the beetroot from the oven and allow to cool for 10 minutes. Remove the aluminium foil and pull off the beetroot skins. Cut off the tops and halve the beetroot lengthways.
3. Serve with horseradish butter or yoghurt with chopped, fresh herbs, or make a purée (see Vegetable purée, p. 138).

Cauliflower

cauliflower
butter
salt and pepper
grated nutmeg

1. Break off the florets and rinse thoroughly under cold running water. Soak for 30 minutes in salted water. Drain, rinse and cook. Pack the florets, stem side down, in a saucepan with a little water. Add a knob of butter to the water and season lightly with salt and pepper. Dot the cauliflower with butter and season with salt, pepper and nutmeg.
2. Cover and steam for a few minutes. Remove with a slotted spoon and reduce the liquid in the saucepan until thick. Return the cauliflower to the saucepan and shake for a minute over moderate heat. Serve.

VARIATIONS
• Place the cauliflower in a greased dish and cover with well-seasoned white sauce, lightly enriched with cream. Sprinkle with a mixture of freshly grated cheese and fresh crumbs and brown under a heated grill.
• A very popular method is to cover cooked cauliflower with fresh white breadcrumbs fried in butter, then mixed with the finely chopped whites of 2 hard-boiled eggs and 12,5 ml (1 T) finely chopped parsley. Rub the egg yolks through a sieve over the cauliflower.
• Use broccoli or Romanesco instead of the cauliflower. To prepare, cover it with cold water in a mixing bowl. Add a little salt and leave it to stand for 10 minutes. Pour off the water through a colander and rinse.

Green beans

• Young French beans are at their best blanched and served with herb butter.
• Stir chopped, fresh savory and 5 ml (1 t) tomato paste into butter. Sprinkle lightly roasted almond flakes over afterwards.
• Older green beans should be sliced and cooked in the old-fashioned way. Add a sliced onion to the green beans, as well as a large peeled and cubed potato. For extra flavour, add a seeded and finely chopped chilli. Season beans well with salt and pepper and boil until tender. Mash with a potato masher. Improve the appearance by spooning a tomato sambal on top of the bean mixture.
• BROAD BEANS: Remove the beans from the pods and shake them quickly with a spoonful or two of water, a knob of butter and salt and pepper over high heat, until the liquid has evaporated. Wonderful with fish.

Brussels sprouts

Brussels sprouts
5 ml (1 t) salt
juice of 1 lemon
knob of butter
salt, pepper and grated nutmeg

1. Trim stems neatly underneath. Place in a mixing bowl, cover with water and add salt and lemon juice. Leave to stand for 30 minutes, drain and place in a saucepan. Just cover with fresh water and boil over high heat until tender but not mushy.
2. Drain and add a knob of butter. Sprinkle nutmeg over and season with salt and pepper. Shake and serve with red meat, preferably pork or Kassler ribs.

Fried brinjal slices

(MAKES 4 SERVINGS)

Brinjals are sometimes peeled, sometimes not. If colour is important to the presentation, as in a marinated salad, it would be preferable to retain the skin. When the brinjals form part of a dish, they should be peeled.

2 brinjals, each 250 g
lemon juice
salt

BATTER
120 g (250 ml/1 cup) cake flour
3 ml (½ t) salt
1 ml (pinch) each turmeric and cayenne pepper
2 egg yolks, beaten
15 ml (3 t) oil
125 ml (½ cup) milk
1 egg white
oil for frying

1. Prepare brinjals (see box, this page), but first drip lemon juice over and sprinkle with salt.
2. IN THE MEANTIME, PREPARE THE BATTER: Sift flour, salt, turmeric and cayenne pepper. Make a well in the centre. Using a wooden spoon, beat egg yolks and oil. Spoon into well in the flour mixture. Work some of the flour into the egg mixture. Stir milk in and beat until smooth. Cover and set aside for 30 minutes.
3. Beat egg white with a pinch of salt until stiff. Fold into batter. Heat oil in a pan over medium heat until hot. Dip 3 brinjal slices at a time into batter, remove with a slotted spoon, allow excess batter to drip off and fry 3 slices at a time in hot oil until done. Drain on crumpled paper towels and arrange on a warm serving plate. Excellent served with lamb.

VARIATIONS
● Sprinkle a handful of ground almonds, mixed with Parmesan cheese, over the top.
● Brinjals may be served as a starter or as a vegetarian dish on a pool of fresh tomato sauce. Thin the tomato sauce with a little tomato juice. Use oven-baked whole garlic to complete the dish.

Peas

1. Shell peas, cover with lightly salted water to which sugar has been added, and boil over a high heat for 3 minutes. Remove saucepan from heat and set aside for 5 minutes.
2. Drain and stir in a knob or two of butter.

HOW TO PREPARE BRINJALS
Cut the brinjals into 12,5 mm (½ in) thick slices and arrange them in a single layer on a flat surface. Sprinkle salt over and leave for 30 minutes, or until the brinjals begin to draw water. Rinse thoroughly under cold running water. Pat dry lightly. Take care not to add too much salt afterwards. Some of the salt will have been absorbed by the brinjals, even though you have rinsed them.

VARIATIONS
Sugar snap peas are cooked in a little water, salt, pepper and sugar, while mangetout are blanched in slightly more water. Drain and glaze with a few drops of olive oil and a little sugar.

Baked garlic

whole garlic bulbs
butter or olive oil

1. Skin the garlic bulbs. The cloves should remain intact. Spread butter over squares of aluminium foil, shiny side to the inside, and wrap garlic bulbs separately in foil. Place in an oven pan and bake for it 1½-2 hours at 120 °C (250 °F) until soft.
2. Remove from foil and halve widthways. Serve half a bulb per person. Garlic is good with stewed dishes such as chicken in red wine, or for adventurous people, with Bone soup (p. 30) or Snoek-head soup (p. 32).

VARIATIONS
● Press the sweet garlic paste out and stir into potato or carrot purée, or serve with Fried brinjal slices (on this page).
● Garlic paste tastes great on oven-baked mushroom slices, especially when used as a topping for fillet steak.
● Garlic paste is a delicious flavouring for braaied meat, especially Butterflied leg of mutton (p. 68).
● Garlic paste may be mixed with butter, parsley, freshly ground black pepper and salt and spread on bread.

Kohlrabi

Kohlrabi has numerous common names among country folk, including *raapkool*, *knolkool* and *kool-raap-bo-die-grond*. Bulbs should

---

be young, and smaller than a cricket ball. They are greatly underrated as a salad, finely grated, and suitable as an accompaniment to virtually any dish. At the beginning of the twentieth century, kohlrabi soup was very popular (see Variations).

kohlrabi bulbs, peeled and sliced
salt
12,5 ml (1 T) butter
finely chopped fresh parsley

1. Cover the kohlrabi with water, add salt and boil for 20-25 minutes, until tender.
2. Drain and add a large knob of butter and the parsley.

VARIATIONS
● Cover with a cheese sauce and brown quickly under the grill.
● Use kohlrabi in coleslaw, instead of cabbage.
● KOHLRABI SOUP: Mash the cooked bulbs and stir in milk and cream to make a thick purée. Season with salt, pepper, grated nutmeg and a pinch of cayenne pepper. Spoon the thick creamed soup into soup plates and garnish with coarsely chopped hard-boiled eggs mixed with finely chopped fresh parsley, chives and finely grated cheese.

Cucumber

English cucumber, washed well
12,5 ml (1 T) water
butter
salt and pepper
5 ml (1 t) sugar
finely chopped fresh sage, pineapple sage or dill

1. Halve the cucumber lengthways, scrape out the seeds with a teaspoon and slice the cucumber. Boil in water with a large knob of butter, salt, pepper and sugar until the liquid has evaporated and the cucumber is beautifully green.
2. Season with sage.

VARIATIONS
● Mix cooked cucumber with sliced carrot, cooked the same way. A few spoonfuls of petits pois can also be stirred in.
● Add maize kernels to the cucumber.
● Make an interesting mixed vegetable dish by adding, preferably, young French beans.

ASPARAGUS

Cabbage

cabbage, quartered and centre stalk removed
salt, pepper and grated nutmeg
butter

1. Soak the cabbage in lightly salted water for 30 minutes. Drain. Cut into eighths, place in a saucepan, add a little water and a few knobs of butter.
2. Cover and boil until tender and cooked. Season with salt, pepper and nutmeg.

VARIATIONS

• Shred the cabbage, spoon into a saucepan, cover with water and heat to boiling point. Boil for 1 minute, drain and return to the saucepan. Season with salt, pepper, caraway seed and a pinch of ground cloves. Add a knob or two of butter and 125 ml (½ cup) water. Cover and boil until done. Season with freshly grated nutmeg and, if necessary, with salt and pepper.

• Fry onion slices in butter and oil until softened and transparent but not browned. Streaky bacon may also be fried with the onion. Add the cabbage, as well as 250 ml (1 cup) water and 2 large peeled and cubed potatoes. Cover and cook until liquid has evaporated and cabbage is cooked. Stir in an extra knob of butter. Season with salt, pepper and grated nutmeg. Stock may be used instead of water.

Calabash marrows

1. Peel and seed the marrows and cut them into slices or cubes. Cook the marrows on top of the stove like sweet potatoes (chapter 14). Do not touch, or stir, the vegetables during cooking; they will have a clear and syrupy glaze if you leave them alone.
2. Season afterwards with a pinch of ground cinnamon. Serve with duck, pheasant, Muscovy duck, turkey or leg of mutton.

Corn on the cob

There are many kinds of maize, or corn on the cob, and I don't mean the baby cobs available today. You have a choice of young or older corn on the cob. When corn is very young with soft kernels, it is best first to remove the husks and the silks, or they will be overcooked and very difficult to remove from the cooked cobs. Older corn on the cob, with thicker silks, may be cooked without removing the leaves.

1. Heat a large saucepan of water to boiling point and season well with salt. Place corn in the saucepan and boil for 20-40 minutes, depending on how hard the kernels are.
2. Remove with tongs and pull off any leaves. Serve hot with butter or savoury butter – delicious as a braai accompaniment! The kernels may also be cut off and served as a vegetable.

Sweetcorn fritters

(MAKES 12 FRITTERS)

120 g (250 ml/1 cup) cake flour
3 ml (½ t) bicarbonate of soda
1-2 ml (¼ t) cream of tartar
1-2 ml (¾ t) salt
2 eggs, separated
100 ml (8 T) milk
25 ml (2 T) butter, melted
3 ml (½ t) lemon juice
10 ml (2 t) sugar (optional)
corn on the cob kernels to make 250 ml (1 cup)
    (see Corn on the cob, above), or 1 tin
    (325 g) whole-kernel corn (the kind
    canned with only a little liquid),
    drained and the liquid reserved
oil

1. Sift the flour, bicarbonate of soda, cream of tartar and salt.
2. Beat egg yolks, milk, butter, lemon juice, sugar (if used) and canning liquid and stir into flour mixture. (If fresh corn kernels are used, add 25 ml/2 T water.) Stir in kernels, cover and set aside for 30 minutes.
3. Whisk egg whites with a pinch of salt until stiff peaks form, and fold into sweetcorn mixture. Heat a heavy-bottomed frying pan over moderate heat and pour a thin layer of oil into it. Drop spoonfuls of batter, 2-3 at a time, into the oil and fry first on one side and then on the other until golden brown. Drain on kitchen paper, keep warm and serve with Chicken Maryland (p. 110) or any other chicken dish.

HINT: 250 ml (1 cup) self-raising flour may be used instead of the cake flour, bicarbonate of soda and cream of tartar.

Ratatouille

(MAKES 4-6 SERVINGS)

50 ml (4 T) olive oil
3 medium-sized onions, halved lengthways,
    peeled and sliced
350 g unpeeled brinjal slices, prepared (see p. 142)

freshly ground black pepper
1 each green and red sweet peppers, halved,
    seeds and membranes removed,
    then cut lengthways into thin strips
3 plump garlic cloves, bruised,
    peeled and crushed with:
5 ml (1 t) salt
350 g young baby marrows, scrubbed,
    topped and tailed and halved lengthways
350 g ripe red tomatoes, skinned,
    seeded and coarsely chopped
    (see Hint, p. 22)
15 ml (3 t) finely chopped fresh parsley
25 ml (2 T) snipped chives

GARNISH
12 fresh basil leaves, washed, rolled up
    and cut into thin strips

1. Heat the oil in a saucepan, add the onions and stir-fry until softened and transparent but not browned. Cover the onions with the brinjal slices and season each layer lightly with pepper. Spoon the sweet pepper strips on top of the brinjal slices. Dot with garlic, cover and simmer for 15-20 minutes over moderate heat.
2. Add the baby marrows, tomatoes, parsley and chives. Cover and simmer for 5 minutes over moderate heat. Remove the lid and simmer until most of the liquid has evaporated. Spoon into a serving dish and sprinkle basil and chives over.

VARIATIONS

• Add a handful of stoned black olives with the tomatoes.

• Some cooks like to add 1 celery stalk, rinsed and the threads removed, then cut into 25 mm (1 in) lengths, to the saucepan after frying the onions.

Okra

(MAKES 4 SERVINGS)

1 medium-sized onion,
    halved lengthways,
    peeled and finely chopped
25 ml (2 T) oil
500 g okra, stem end cut off,
    halved lengthways and again widthways
5 ml (1 t) ground coriander
3 ml (½ t) peri-peri powder
5 ml (1 t) curry powder
5 ml (1 t) lemon juice
1 ripe red tomato, skinned, seeded
    and coarsely chopped (see Hint, p. 27)
salt

1. Fry the onion in the oil until softened and transparent. Add the okra and stir to blend. Add the rest of the ingredients.

2. Cover and cook for 20 minutes over moderate heat, or until the okra is tender. Add a little water if necessary. Taste and season with a little extra salt if desired.

Pumpkin

Although traditionally a sweetened vegetable in South Africa, it can also be prepared in other ways.

boer pumpkin or butternut squash,
  cut into flat slices or cut into
  decorative shapes using small cutters
mango or apricot juice
salt and pepper
butter

1. Blanch the pumpkin for 2 minutes in boiling water and refresh in ice-cold water.

2. Pour enough mango juice into a saucepan to cover the base. Season with salt and pepper and add a knob of butter, but no sugar. Add the pumpkin, cover and simmer for 5 minutes. Allow to cool so that the pumpkin can absorb the liquid and be tender but not mushy.

Leeks

Many South Africans got to know leeks through savoury tarts. In the sixties, they were boiled until very tender, but in the new cuisine they are steamed.

leeks, cleaned (see How to remove sand from
  vegetables, p. 137)
butter
salt and pepper

1. Cook leeks in lightly salted water over low heat until tender. Drain well.

2. Shake in a little melted butter, season lightly with salt and pepper and serve with leg of mutton.

VARIATIONS

• Sometimes, a little well-seasoned white sauce is poured over part of the leeks.

• NEW VARIATION: Cut cleaned leeks diagonally into slices, soak in salted water and drain. Place leeks and a large knob of butter in a saucepan, cover with buttered paper and braise over low heat until tender. Add snipped chives and 1 crushed garlic clove,

shake and spoon into the centre of a plate. Serve with fried lamb chops (with frenched bones) or grilled line fish on top. Surround chops – and fish – with a meat sauce.

Turnips

1. Peel and place immediately in water to which vinegar or lemon juice has been added, to prevent discoloration. Drain.

2. Shake and fry with butter, salt, pepper and a little water in a saucepan. They can also be covered with a sheet of buttered paper, placed directly on the turnips. Place the lid on the saucepan and cook over moderate heat until done.

VARIATION

Make a purée and place a spoonful on a plate. Arrange broccoli on top and cover with Hollandaise sauce (p. 53).

Red cabbage

(MAKES 6 SERVINGS)

1 red cabbage, cut into eighths,
  hard core removed and discarded,
  then cut into thin strips
salted water
10 ml (2 t) oil or duck fat
2 cloves
2 bay leaves
1 small red chilli, halved lengthways,
  seeded and shredded
1 large onion, halved lengthways,
  peeled and finely chopped
1 plump garlic clove, bruised,
  peeled and crushed with:
5 ml (1 t) salt
10 ml (2 t) sugar
4 Granny Smith apples, peeled,
  cored and sliced
freshly ground black pepper
  and grated nutmeg
375 ml (1½ cups) red wine
grated rind and juice of 1 lemon
25 g (25 ml/2 T) butter or duck fat
15 ml (3 t) finely chopped parsley

1. Cover the cabbage with salted water and soak for 20 minutes. Drain well.

2. Place the oil, cloves, bay leaves and chilli in a saucepan and stir-fry for 1 minute over high heat. Reduce the heat, add the onion and stir-fry for 1 minute. Add the garlic and sugar and stir-fry for 1 minute. Stir in the apple slices, spoon the cabbage on top, sea-

son with pepper and nutmeg and stir to blend. Add wine and heat to boiling point. Reduce the heat, cover and cook until tender and the liquid has evaporated.

3. Add the lemon rind, juice, butter and parsley. Taste and season with more salt, pepper and nutmeg. Serve with roast duck or any pork dish.

Fried button mushrooms

1 punnet (250 g) button mushrooms,
  wiped clean
30 g (30 ml/2 large T) butter
10 ml (2 t) oil
30 ml (2 large T) chopped chives
salt and pepper

1. Place the mushrooms in a saucepan, cover with water, heat to boiling point and drain in a colander.

2. Heat the butter and oil until boiling hot. Add the mushrooms and shake the saucepan for 4-5 minutes. Remove from the heat and add the chopped chives. Season with salt and pepper. Stir to blend. Excellent with fried lamb chops or steak.

Creamed mushrooms

(MAKES 6 SERVINGS)

1 small onion, halved, peeled
  and finely chopped
1 garlic clove, bruised, peeled
  and crushed with:
5 ml (1 t) salt
4 rashers rindless bacon, shredded
50 g (50 ml/4 T) butter
2 punnets (500 g) button mushrooms,
  wiped clean and sliced
salt, pepper, grated nutmeg,
  mustard powder and cayenne pepper
250 ml (1 cup) thick cream
25 ml (2 T) finely chopped
  fresh parsley

1. Place the onion, garlic, bacon and butter in a saucepan. Stir over low heat until the onion has softened. Add the mushrooms, stir to blend and simmer until the liquid has evaporated.

2. Season with salt, pepper, nutmeg, mustard and cayenne pepper. Add the cream, stir to blend and reduce by half. Sprinkle the parsley over and serve with grilled fish, poultry or meat. Excellent stirred into any cooked pasta.

Celery

celery stalks, washed and threads removed
butter
1-2 ml (1-2 pinches) sugar
salt and pepper

1. Cut celery into 25 mm (1 in) long diagonal slices and, if desired, cut into strips. Place in a saucepan and add just enough water to cover.
2. Cook over high heat until all the water has evaporated.
3. Stir in a knob of butter, sugar, salt and pepper to taste and shake until the strips are glazed. Serve as part of mixed vegetables.

VARIATIONS

● Cut rinsed celery stalks (threads removed) into 25 mm (1 in) thick slices, cut each into 3 strips and place in a saucepan. Add finely grated rind and juice of 3 oranges and 25 g (25 ml/2 T) butter. Cook until the liquid has almost evaporated, season with a pinch of salt and lots of freshly ground black pepper. Stir in ½ packet (50 g/125 ml/½ cup) coarsely chopped walnuts.
● CELERIAC: Press each one to make sure that they are not spongy in texture. Peel thickly and cover immediately with water to which lemon juice or vinegar has been added. Cook in the same water, but add a pinch of salt. Purée or slice and fry like Brinjal slices (p. 142).
● The old-fashioned way is to serve celeriac slices hot, in *slaphakskeentjie* sauce (see p. 150). Ideal with duck or pork.

Chicory

In the past, the dried root was ground and used as an addition to coffee. The silvery leaves with their green-tinted edges are often – wrongly – used just as they are in salads. They should preferably be blanched twice and each time refreshed in ice-cold water before use.

8 whole chicory heads
50 g (50 ml/4 T) butter
25 ml (2 T) fresh lemon juice
50 ml (4 T) water
8 slices ham
125 ml (½ cup) thick béchamel sauce
50 g (125 ml/½ cup) finely grated
*   Gruyère cheese*

1. Arrange the chicory heads next to one another in a saucepan. Dot with butter. Pour the lemon juice and water over. Cover and cook until the liquid has evaporated and the chicory is tender.
2. Squeeze each chicory head to remove the water. Wrap each in a slice of ham and arrange next to one another in a single layer in a greased baking dish. Spread béchamel sauce over and sprinkle cheese on top. Bake for 10-12 minutes in a preheated oven at 200 °C (400 °F). Serve as a first course or entrée, or 1 chicory per person as an accompaniment to fried chicken.

Chayote

1. Peel chayotes and slice or cube. Cook in a little water seasoned with salt, pepper and sugar. Adding a knob of butter makes this vegetable even tastier.
2. Fry onions and stir in a little garlic and chopped, skinned tomatoes. Add to chayote.

VARIATIONS

● Another method is to cook chayote as earlier generations cooked *vroeëpampoen* (early pumpkin): cube and stew with plenty of sugar and butter, a little fresh orange juice, cinnamon sticks and bread cubes.
● Yet another method is to cook chayote like cabbage and season it with nutmeg.
● Chayote may also be boiled in lightly salted water. Drain and purée. Return to the saucepan and add a little cream. Season with salt, pepper and sugar and stir-fry until all the liquid has evaporated. Spoon into halved, seeded and cooked gem squash.

Scorzonera

Scorzonera, also known as black salsify, *oesterplant* or *hawerwortel*, looks like a parsnip and has a thick white or black skin. There is a hint of oyster in the flavour.

1. Scrub the roots thoroughly and cook for ± 40 minutes in salted water until tender. Drain and pull off the skins.
2. Serve with Hollandaise sauce (p. 53) or fry, shaking constantly, in nut butter to which a little lemon juice has been added.

Gem squash

Gem squash are surely among the best-loved vegetables in this country. Leave them whole or halve them horizontally and boil them in salted water. Spoon out the seeds and serve them just as they are, or dot with a little butter.

VARIATIONS

● During the middle decades of this century, gem squash were often filled with minted peas. In true sweetened vegetable tradition, a little cinnamon sugar or nutmeg sugar was also sprinkled over.
● Today, small, young squash are halved horizontally and the skins scored to make a striped pattern before steaming for 2-3 minutes in a little water, a knob of butter, salt, pepper and sugar. Serve, pips and all.
● Cook baby marrows in the same way as young squash (see also How to remove sand from vegetables, p. 137).

Roasted sweet peppers

1. Preheat the grill in the oven. Grease the rack lightly with oil. Pack the halved peppers, skin side up, in a baking pan and spread the oil over. Place the pan about 30 cm (12 in) from the preheated grill and roast for 3 minutes.
2. Remove the pan, spoon more oil over the peppers and return to the oven. Repeat a few times until the peppers become tender and the skin blackens and blisters. Remove the pan and turn the peppers with tongs so that the skin side is covered in oil. Allow to cool. Pull off the skin and remove the core and seeds. Mix with fried brown mushrooms, for example, or serve with mixed vegetables.

Spinach

1. Rinse spinach very well and soak in a large bowl of lightly salted water. Drain and rinse again.
2. Cut out and discard the white ribs and stack 6 leaves on top of one another. Roll up tightly and cut into strips. Place in a large saucepan in which a knob of butter and a little oil have been melted. Stir-fry until spinach is just wilted. Season with salt, pepper and grated nutmeg. Stir in a little crushed garlic, if desired, and serve with virtually any fish or meat dish. A spoonful of Hollandaise sauce (p. 53) or Parmesan shavings may be placed on top.

VARIATION: CREAMED SPINACH

Cook the spinach until tender. Drain and add 1-2 spoonfuls of white sauce, cheese sauce or cream. Purée in a food processor, return to the saucepan and stir in crushed garlic. Taste and season with salt, pepper and grated nutmeg.

Stuffed tomatoes

(MAKES 6 SERVINGS)

3 tomatoes, halved
salt
1 plump garlic clove, bruised,
   peeled and chopped
25 ml (2 T) shredded spring onions
25 ml (2 T) shredded basil leaves
   or chopped parsley
5 ml (1 t) fresh or 3 ml (½ t) dried thyme
   leaves
65 ml (¼ cup) dried, crushed white
   breadcrumbs
freshly ground black pepper
65 ml (¼ cup) finely grated mature Cheddar
   cheese or Parmesan cheese
25 ml (2 T) olive oil

1. Scoop out the insides of the tomatoes with a teaspoon and place in a mixing bowl. Season tomato shells inside with salt and turn upside down on a wire rack.
2. Using scissors, cut tomato insides into smaller pieces. Add garlic, spring onions, basil, thyme and crumbs, taste and season with pepper. Add half the cheese and mix lightly with a large two-pronged fork.
3. Spoon 50 ml (4 T) water into a greased baking dish. Place the tomatoes, hollowed-out sides up, in the dish. The tomatoes should not touch one another. Season with more pepper. Divide the stuffing among the tomatoes, but do not pack it in tightly. Divide the oil among the tomatoes and pour over the stuffing. Sprinkle the remaining cheese over the tomatoes. Bake for 10 minutes in a preheated oven at 200 °C (400 °F). Serve with lamb.

Braised onions

Braised onions, fried liver and mashed potatoes are a South African favourite.

25 ml (2 T) butter
25 ml (2 T) oil
4 onions, halved lengthways, peeled and sliced
salt, pepper and sugar

Place the butter and oil in a saucepan, place the onions on top and season with salt, pepper and sugar. Cover and simmer over moderate heat until the onions have browned.

Braised baby onions

(MAKES 6-12 SERVINGS)

24 small onions
boiling water
125 ml (½ cup) chicken stock
50 ml (4 T) dry white wine
30 g (30 ml/2 large T) butter
salt and freshly ground pepper

TIE TOGETHER
2 sprigs parsley
1 sprig thyme
1 bay leaf

1. Cover onions with boiling water, leave to stand for 10 minutes and spoon them out. The skins will come off more easily. Cut off the brown tops neatly with scissors and cut off the root ends.
2. Place all the ingredients in a large, flat-bottomed frying pan, cover and simmer for 50 minutes over very low heat. Shake the pan from time to time. Remove the onions with a slotted spoon. Remove the sprigs of herbs and reduce the liquid until almost syrupy. Return the onions to the pan and shake the pan to cover the onions all over with the glaze.

Honeyed baby onions

(MAKES 6-12 SERVINGS

This dish may be made up to two days in advance and stored in the refrigerator.

24 small onions, peeled as described above
500 ml (2 cups) weak chicken stock
125 ml (½ cup) honey
10 ml (2 t) mustard powder
5 ml (1 t) turmeric
25 ml (2 T) oil
12,5 ml (1 T) lemon juice

GARNISH
fresh coriander leaves

1. Place the onions in a saucepan and add the stock. Simmer until almost cooked. Remove the onions with a slotted spoon.
2. Add the honey, mustard, turmeric, oil and lemon juice and reduce over high heat until the sauce just begins to become syrupy. Return the onions to the saucepan. Reduce the heat and shake the saucepan until the onions are glazed. Serve cold or hot, garnished with coriander leaves. Excellent with ham, pickled tongue or any pork dish.

Fennel

Fennel is perhaps one of the most underrated vegetables in South Africa.

fennel bulbs
butter
salt and pepper
sugar
finely chopped fresh dill

1. Rinse the bulbs well under cold running water and soak for 30 minutes in salted water. Drain and spoon into a saucepan. Cover with water and cook until tender.
2. Drain, halve and return to the saucepan. Add the butter and season with salt, pepper, a pinch of sugar and finely chopped dill. Serve with seafood.

VARIATION
Fennel may also first be grated coarsely, cooked and drained. Mix with a spoonful of mascarpone, thick cream or crème fraîche. Use as a bed for steamed, baked or grilled fish.

Parsnips

1. Peel parsnips, cover with lots of water and cook until tender.
2. Drain the parsnips, halve lengthways and return to the saucepan. Add the butter and 10 ml (2 t) sugar. Fry, shaking the pan, over moderate heat until the parsnips are glazed. Season with a pinch of cayenne pepper and salt if necessary. Serve with any poultry or as part of mixed vegetables.

Carrots

Cook as for parsnips. Scraped and sliced carrots, cooked with chopped onions and potato cubes, are part of our heritage.

CHAPTER 16

Salads and sambals

DURING THE FIRST six decades of the twentieth century, salad was served as an accompaniment to meat dishes, instead of being a course on its own. In Malay cooking, salads in the form of sambals were eaten with meat. The 'boerekos' eating pattern emphasised *sousbone* (bean salad), *slaphakskeentjies* (onion salad), chopped cucumber salad, tomato and onion salad and beetroot salad as part of the main dish, but there was no salad on the tables of black South Africans. Potato salad was the premier mayonnaise salad of the time, and still is – but infinitely better. Various groups of immigrants helped to make salad more acceptable to the local inhabitants. Dutch immigrants of the fifties, for example, introduced chicory as a vegetable, but also as a salad.

Insalata, Italian for salad, was served to South Africans in any number of ways by the Italians. *Di funghi crudi* are mushrooms that are thinly sliced, mixed with thin slices of spring onion and moistened with lemon juice and olive oil. The almost too well-known Cape tomato sambal was enriched with basil and garlic.

A salad that was very popular at the beginning of the century but that has now vanished completely is the British salamagundy (see box), enjoyed in England, particularly during the seventeenth and eighteenth centuries. Modern cooks would do well to reintroduce it.

Moulded salads that are set in aspic or jelly – especially a combination of beetroot and peas, tomato and celery, or cucumber and egg – were extremely popular up to the eighties, when they lost popularity with the arrival of the salad leaf selection and the impact of the Midi, the region of the noonday sun.

The salad we call Greek salad is worth preparing (see box).

In the first half of the century, the most elegant salad was undoubtedly Caesar salad which, with fried steak, was a lunch enjoyed by most businessmen (see box).

GREEN SALAD

> ### GREEK SALAD
> Mix torn, rinsed and dried lettuce leaves with tomato quarters, halved thin slices of English cucumber, onion rings, green sweet pepper strips, radish slices, artichoke hearts, black olives and cubes of feta cheese, and add fresh oregano or thyme. Moisten with a Vinaigrette (p. 154) containing a generous quantity of garlic and lemon juice.

Caesar salad made way for salad Niçoise, that evergreen creation from the south of France. Four-bean salad took over from the salad of Nice because it was easier for South Africans to obtain all kinds of dried beans. Fried livers, especially chicken livers cooked the Portuguese way, also found their way to the salad bowl, but the ordinary hostess often flung together vegetables, salad leaves and fruit and served it as a mixed salad.

Salad became more popular from the mid-seventies onwards, and literally thousands of recipes were published. Salsas joined sambals, and today, with the great variety produced by small-scale farmers, every South African cook can whip up her own salad creation.

> ### SALAMAGUNDY
> Arrange rinsed, dried and torn salad leaves around the rim of a very large, flat, round salad bowl. Choose a mixture of curly-leaved, oak-leaved and butter lettuce, with a few pieces of red lettuce for dotting here and there. Moisten with salad dressing. Arrange thinly sliced, cooked chicken breasts moistened with herb mayonnaise in a circle next to the salad leaves. Follow, as you work inwards, with cooked tongue (moisten each slice with mustard mayonnaise), halved hard-boiled eggs with an asparagus filling, baked, sliced beetroot with a rollmop on each slice, dill pickles, olives, orange segments, seeded and quartered tomatoes and fresh basil as garnish.

Slaphakskeentjies (Onion salad)

(MAKES 8 SERVINGS)

1 kg small or pickling onions
5 ml (1 t) turmeric
salt and pepper

SOUR SAUCE
3 extra-large egg yolks
1 extra-large egg
65 ml (¼ cup) sugar
3-5 ml (½-1 t) salt
25 ml (2 T) strong mustard powder
65 ml (¼ cup) vinegar (preferably wine vinegar)
125 ml (½ cup) water
1-2 ml (1-2 pinches) cayenne pepper
2 fresh bay leaves

GARNISH
bean sprouts

1. Place the onions in a mixing bowl, cover with boiling water and leave for 15 minutes. (This will make it easy to peel them, and your eyes won't water.) Meanwhile, heat water to boiling point in a large saucepan. Add the turmeric and season well with salt and lightly with pepper. Add the peeled onions to the boiling water, cover and heat to boiling point. Boil for 1 minute, remove saucepan of onions from the heat and set aside. Check the saucepan from time to time to see if the onions are tender. *Do not* boil the onions until they are tender – the centres will come out during cooking and the salad will look limp and tired.

2. Meanwhile, begin making the sour sauce: Place the egg yolks, egg and sugar in a glass mixing bowl and beat for 30 seconds. Add the salt and mustard and beat together. Place the mixing bowl over steam and beat with a wire whisk until the egg mixture is light, thick and foamy. Mix the vinegar and water and heat until hot but not boiling. Add the vinegar mixture to the egg yolk mixture, a little at a time, beating constantly with a wire whisk. The mixture will thicken, become light yellow, and treble in volume. Taste and season with cayenne pepper and extra salt to taste. Add the bay leaves. By this time the onions should be cooked.

3. Drain the onions in a colander and place them in a glass dish. Spoon the sour sauce over and mix lightly.

4. TO SERVE: Served hot, it is particularly tasty with cooked, pickled tongue. Spoon into an attractive serving dish and garnish with little heaps of bean sprouts if desired.

Served cold, it is a delicious salad with ham, other cold meats or braaied meat. Refrigerate the onions in the sauce overnight, then spoon into an attractive salad bowl and garnish with bean sprouts if desired.

Beetroot and onion salad

(MAKES 4 SERVINGS)

In the past, beetroot was boiled in water. Today, whole beetroot are baked.

4 beetroot, baked (see p. 141) and sliced
1 small onion, peeled, sliced and separated into rings
sambal dressing (see p. 157)

Arrange the beetroot slices, slightly overlapping, on a flat salad plate. Arrange the onion rings on top and sprinkle the dressing over. Cover with cling wrap, marinate for 1 hour in the refrigerator and serve.

Sousbone (Bean salad)

(MAKES 6 SERVINGS)

500 ml (2 cups) sugar beans
* or other dried beans*
water
25 ml (2 T) cornflour
25 ml (2 T) sugar
25 ml (2 T) vinegar
5 ml (1 t) salt
pepper to taste

EXTRAS (OPTIONAL)
1 red chilli, chopped (seeds and all)
2 bay or lemon leaves
1 ml (pinch) ground cloves

1. Pick the beans over and rinse well. Cover with tap water and soak overnight.

2. Drain the beans. Heat fresh water to boiling point in a saucepan. Add the beans and cook for ± 2 hours over moderate heat, until tender. Add more water, if necessary.

3. Mix the cornflour, sugar, vinegar and salt to a smooth paste. Add a spoonful of the hot cooking liquor to the cornflour mixture and mix. Add the cornflour mixture to the saucepan and stir constantly until the mixture begins to thicken slightly. Reduce the heat and simmer the mixture for 15 minutes. Taste and season with more salt and pepper to taste. Add the chilli, leaves and cloves (if used) for extra flavour.

CAESAR SALAD
Fry white bread cubes in olive oil and drain on paper towels. Wipe a salad bowl with crushed garlic and fill it with torn lettuce leaves. Then add a salad dressing flavoured with Worcestershire sauce. Sprinkle the bread cubes over, as well as chopped anchovy fillets and a coddled (lightly cooked) egg. Finally, sprinkle Parmesan cheese over and toss the entire salad before serving.

Hint: These days, sousbone are garnished with poached fresh green asparagus, marinated in Vinaigrette (p. 154) for a minute.

Copper penny salad

(MAKES 8 SERVINGS)

In 1981, a recipe for copper penny salad appeared in the *Huisgenoot* and was a hit countrywide. The following recipe is a variation of the *Huisgenoot* version and comes from the American west coast.

1 kg large carrots, scraped and sliced
2 onions, halved lengthways, peeled and sliced
50 ml (4 T) tomato concentrate
250 ml (1 cup) water
200 ml (⅘ cup) white wine vinegar
125 ml (½ cup) oil, preferably olive oil
200 g (250 ml / 1 cup) sugar
1 whole red chilli
15 ml (3 t) Worcestershire sauce
10 ml (2 t) whole-grain mustard
3 fresh lemon or bay leaves (optional)
2 red sweet peppers, baked (see p. 146)
* and cut into strips*
salt and freshly ground pepper

1. Cover the carrots with water and parboil them. Drain.

2. Place the onions in a saucepan, add the tomato concentrate, water, vinegar and oil, sugar, chilli, Worcestershire sauce, mustard and leaves. Heat to boiling point, boil for about 3 minutes and remove from the heat. Stir in the carrots and sweet pepper strips, taste and season with salt and pepper. Spoon into a suitable container and allow to cool completely. Cover with cling wrap and marinate for at least 2 days in the refrigerator.

SOUSBONE (BEAN SALAD)

Curried beans

(MAKES 12-16 SERVINGS)

1 kg green beans, topped and tailed
    and threads removed, then shredded
2 large onions, halved lengthways,
    peeled and sliced
500 ml (2 cups) water
15 ml (3 t) salt
15 ml (3 t) cornflour
10-15 ml (2-3 t) hot curry powder
3 ml (½ t) turmeric
250 ml (1 cup) white vinegar
200 g (250 ml/1 cup) sugar
1 whole red chilli

1. Place the beans, onions, water and salt in a saucepan, heat to boiling point and boil for 5 minutes.
2. Mix the cornflour, curry powder and turmeric to a smooth paste with the vinegar. Remove the saucepan from the heat and stir in the curry paste, sugar and chilli. Stir until the sugar has dissolved. Return to the heat and stir until the sauce begins to thicken and the beans are cooked. Place in hot, sterilised jars and seal.

Curried peaches

(MAKES 6 SERVINGS)

1 tin (825 g) peaches, drained
2 Golden Delicious apples,
    cored and thinly sliced
2 onions, halved lengthways,
    peeled and finely chopped
10 ml (2 t) mixed spice
2 cloves
5 ml (1 t) turmeric
15 ml (3 t) curry powder
200 g (250 ml/1 cup) sugar
125 ml (½ cup) vinegar
25 ml (2 T) cornflour

1. Place all the ingredients, except the cornflour, in a saucepan and heat to boiling point. Reduce the heat and then simmer for 15 minutes.
2. Mix the cornflour until runny with a little water. Remove the peaches from the heat and stir in the cornflour mixture. Return to the heat and stir until the mixture reaches boiling point. Reduce the heat and simmer until the sauce clears. Remove from the heat and place in a draughty spot until cold. Spoon into an attractive salad bowl, cover with cling wrap and refrigerate until ice cold. Serve with potroasted red meat.

Rice salad

(MAKES 12 SERVINGS)

RICE
400 g (500 ml/2 cups) uncooked rice
1,25 litres (5 x 250 ml/5 cups) cold water
10 ml (2 t) vegetable or chicken stock powder
10 ml (2 t) salt
5 ml (1 t) turmeric

SALAD
12 pickled gherkins, halved lengthways
250 ml (1 cup) petits pois
2 celery stalks, washed and threads removed,
    then thinly sliced
24 black olives, stoned
12 radishes, rinsed and thinly sliced
1 green sweet pepper, halved,
    seeds and membranes removed,
    then cut into thin strips
1 small onion, preferably red,
    halved lengthways, peeled
    and finely chopped
25 ml (2 T) finely chopped chives

DRESSING
250 ml (1 cup) thick mayonnaise
125 ml (½ cup) orange juice
25 ml (2 T) strong prepared mustard
salt, pepper and cayenne pepper to taste

GARNISH
3 hard-boiled eggs, whites and yolks
    rubbed separately through a sieve
3 hard-boiled eggs, sliced horizontally
12-24 cherry tomatoes, halved
watercress or other small salad leaves

1. RICE: Place the rice, water, stock powder, salt and turmeric in a saucepan with a tight-fitting lid. Heat to boiling point, reduce the heat immediately and simmer over low heat until rice is cooked and liquid absorbed. Remove from heat and cool completely.
2. SALAD: Mix the gherkins, petit pois, celery, olives, radishes, sweet pepper strips, onion and chopped chives.
3. DRESSING: Mix the mayonnaise, orange juice and mustard. Taste and season with salt, pepper and cayenne pepper – the dressing should have a bite. Mix half the rice with half the dressing and spoon into a glass dish. Mix the rest of the rice with the salad ingredients, add the rest of the dressing and mix lightly with a large two-pronged fork. Spoon into the salad bowl, cover with cling wrap and refrigerate until needed – the salad could even be left to marinate overnight in the refrigerator.

4. GARNISH: Remove the salad from the refrigerator, remove cling wrap and sprinkle sieved egg over. Garnish with egg slices and tomatoes and finish with watercress.

Potato salad

(MAKES 6 SERVINGS)

8 medium-sized potatoes, rinsed
salt
50 ml (4 T) olive oil
ground black pepper
grated nutmeg
1 garlic clove, bruised,
    peeled and finely chopped
1 small onion, peeled and finely chopped
8 gherkins, finely chopped
250 g cooked ham, diced (optional)

SALAD DRESSING
250 ml (1 cup) mayonnaise
125 ml (½ cup) cream or sour cream
salt and freshly ground pepper
12,5 ml (1 T) prepared mustard
25 ml (2 T) whole-grain mustard (optional)
25 ml (2 T) chopped fresh parsley
10 ml (2 t) chopped chives

GARNISH
4 extra-large hard-boiled eggs, quartered
paprika

1. Boil the potatoes, skins and all, in salted water until tender but not too soft. The skin should not burst. Remove the potatoes from the water, then pull off the skins and slice the potatoes.
2. Meanwhile, mix the oil, pepper and nutmeg and heat until hot. Sprinkle over the potatoes and set aside to cool.
3. Rub the inside of a salad bowl with finely chopped garlic. Place the onion, gherkins and ham on top of the cold potato slices and mix lightly.
4. SALAD DRESSING: Mix the mayonnaise and cream and season with salt, pepper, mustard, parsley and chives. Taste and season with more salt and pepper if necessary. Place half the potato slices in the salad bowl and spoon half the salad dressing over. Repeat with the rest of the potato slices and dressing. Cover with cling wrap and refrigerate for at least 6 hours for the salad to get cold and the flavours to develop.
5. GARNISH: Remove the salad from the refrigerator just before serving and remove the cling wrap. Garnish with egg quarters and sprinkle paprika over.

Coleslaw

(MAKES 8 SERVINGS)

1 large cabbage
1 large onion, halved lengthways,
    peeled and finely chopped
1 each red and green sweet peppers,
    halved, seeds and membranes
    removed, cut first into strips
    and then cubed
5-10 ml (1-2 t) lemon juice

SALAD DRESSING
125 ml (½ cup) mayonnaise
125 ml (½ cup) thick cream
65 ml (¼ cup) sour cream
15 ml (3 t) prepared mustard
30 ml (6 t) lemon juice
15 ml (3 t) sugar
3-5 ml (½-1 t) salt
freshly ground pepper to taste
cayenne pepper or Tabasco sauce (optional)
50 ml (4 T) horseradish cream (optional)
12,5 ml (1 T) caraway seeds (optional)

1. Remove outer leaves from the cabbage. Halve the cabbage lengthways, rinse well and cut out the thick stem. Place 1 cabbage half, flat side down, on a wooden board and cut into paper-thin strips with a vegetable knife. Repeat with other half. Arrange half the cabbage in a deep glass dish. Sprinkle the onion, sweet peppers and lemon juice over. Place the remaining cabbage on top and mix. Set aside.

2. SALAD DRESSING: Beat the mayonnaise, cream and sour cream. Add the mustard, lemon juice and sugar and season with salt and pepper. Beat to mix, taste and season with more salt and pepper if necessary. If you like a bit of a bite, add cayenne pepper or Tabasco sauce. Stir in the horseradish cream and caraway seeds (if used) and spoon over the salad. Mix the salad well with 2 large spoons or forks. Cover with cling wrap and refrigerate the salad for at least 2 hours to allow it to cool and the flavours to develop before serving.

VARIATIONS

● Use a combination of red and ordinary cabbage. Spinach leaves, ribs removed and the leaves rinsed thoroughly, may also be used. Roll up the leaves and cut them into thin strips. Use chopped, crisply fried bacon instead of the sweet peppers. Use lightly roasted sesame seeds and/or chopped walnuts or pecan nuts instead of the caraway seeds.

● Use 2-3 scraped and coarsely grated carrots instead of the sweet peppers. Add 1 celery stalk, washed and threads removed, then cut into thin slices. A small tin (410 g) of pineapple and a handful of raisins or sultanas may also be added.

● If you prefer a less-rich salad dressing, use Bulgarian yoghurt instead of cream and sour cream. The mayonnaise remains part of the salad, as low-oil mayonnaise may be used.

Marinated vegetables

(MAKES 6-8 SERVINGS)

It was in the early eighties that South Africans discovered herbed, marinated vegetables – baked or grilled – especially those from the Midi. They then quickly became fashionable, and today they are served with braaied meat and – since the nineties, when European breads were introduced here – with bread, marinated cheeses like mozzarella; with tomato and mozzarella; with stoned and stuffed green and black olives; or with anchoïade, tapenade, taramasalata, tahini and dolmades, with lots of olive oil drizzled over them.

2 each red, yellow and green sweet peppers,
    baked (see p. 146)
2 brinjals, prepared as described on p. 142
    and cut into 6 mm (¼ in) thick slices
125 ml (½ cup) olive oil
salt and pepper
freshly ground black pepper
6 garlic cloves, bruised, peeled and finely
    chopped
10 ml (2 t) chopped fresh oregano
12 baby marrows, rinsed thoroughly
    and sliced or halved lengthways
1 punnet (250 g) brown mushrooms,
    skins peeled off, then sliced horizontally
25 ml (2 T) sunflower oil
12,5 ml (1 T) lemon juice
3 ml (½ t) mustard powder
extra salt and pepper
12,5 ml (1 T) wine vinegar
2 garlic cloves, bruised, peeled and
    coarsely chopped
1 sprig thyme
24 young green beans, blanched
6-8 oven-dried tomatoes (see p. 154)

GARNISH
fresh basil leaves
12-16 sprigs fresh parsley, deep-fried in oil
12-16 stoned black olives

1. Place the sweet peppers in a shallow container and pour the olive oil remaining in the baking pan over them, through a sieve. Allow to cool completely, then cover and refrigerate.

2. Arrange brinjal slices in a single layer in a baking pan brushed with 25 ml (2 T) of the olive oil. Season with pepper and sprinkle the garlic over. Drizzle with 50 ml (4 T) of the oil and bake for 3-5 minutes in a pre-heated oven at 200 °C (400 °F). Brush 25 ml (2 T) of the olive oil over the brinjals and bake for 10 minutes. Brush the remaining oil over, sprinkle the oregano over and bake until the brinjals are cooked. Remove the pan from the oven, transfer the brinjals to a shallow container with a spatula and leave until cold. Do not wash the pan.

3. Draw the baby marrows through the pan juices from the brinjals to coat them, then place in the oven until beginning to become tender. Remove. Do not wash the pan.

4. Arrange the mushrooms in the baking pan. Mix the oil, lemon juice and mustard and use to brush the mushrooms. Season with salt and pepper. Place in the oven for 3-5 minutes. Remove from the oven and allow to cool completely in the pan.

5. Pour off the oil from the sweet peppers to make 50 ml (4 T) – add more oil, if necessary. Beat in the vinegar and season with salt and pepper. Stir in the garlic and the thyme. Add the hot green beans to the salad dressing.

6. TO SERVE: Arrange the sweet peppers, brinjal slices, mushrooms and baby marrows on a large salad platter. Place bundles of green-beans and tomatoes in between them. Garnish with the basil, parsley and olives. Pour over any remaining liquid from the sweet peppers, brinjals, baby marrows or green beans, and serve.

VARIATIONS

● Garnish the salad with anchovy fillets.
● Add hard-boiled eggs, halved and then quarted lengthways.
● Insert various fresh, young salad leaves here and there.
● Sprinkle chopped chives over.
● Serve the entire salad with fresh, uncooked cubes of tuna, quickly fried in a heated, ridged, cast-iron frying pan.

Green salad

Green salad includes everything young, green and fresh from the garden: various salad leaves (but no bronze varieties), vegetables, fruit and herbs, all crisp, rinsed and dried in a salad spinner. Everything is placed in a salad bowl or arranged on an attractive salad platter and moistened, just before serving, with vinaigrette (see below). Do not use too much dressing; the salad should not be swimming in dressing.

- LEAVES: Lolla Bionda, green oak-leaved lettuce, butter lettuce or ordinary lettuce, all broken into smaller pieces (never cut).
- VEGETABLES: Young baby marrows, mangetout, young French beans, asparagus, all blanched and immediately dipped in vinaigrette (see p. 154).
- ALSO: Cucumber slices; celery stalks, rinsed and threads removed, then thinly sliced, as well as the young leaves; avocado slices, dipped in vinaigrette.
- FRUIT: Kiwi fruit, peeled and sliced; pitted green grapes; green melon (cantaloupe), peeled and cubed or scooped out into balls with a melon baller.
- HERBS: Watercress sprigs; coriander leaves; basil leaves, rinsed, rolled up and cut into thin strips.

Vinaigrette (with herbs)

(MAKES 750 ML/3 CUPS)

Personal preferences play an important role in the preparation of vinaigrette.

550 ml (2 cups plus 4 T) oil
137,5 ml (11 T) wine vinegar
5 ml (1 t) sugar
10 ml (2 t) salt
3-5 ml (½-1 t) freshly ground pepper
3 ml (½ t) mustard powder
1-2 ml (1-2 pinches) cayenne pepper
2 plump garlic cloves, bruised and peeled
1 sprig fresh thyme and/or tarragon
  and/or a few fresh basil leaves

Place all the ingredients in a screw-topped bottle, seal and shake well. Taste and adjust seasoning. Add a little lemon juice to taste for a slightly more sour flavour.

Pasta salad for diabetics

(MAKES 4 SERVINGS)

I dedicate this dish to my friend, EWS Hammond, who is a diabetic. Edward was the first South African poet to dedicate a poem to me; others, like Petra Müller, followed.

200 g (375 ml/1½ cups) shell noodles
15 ml (3 t) olive oil
3 ml (½ t) freshly ground black pepper
10 ml (2 t) sesame seeds
1 celery stalk, rinsed and threads removed,
  then sliced
4 spring onions, rinsed and roots cut off,
  then shredded
1 red sweet pepper, baked (see p. 146)
  and cut into strips
4 each yellow and red cherry tomatoes, halved
8 whole, stoned dates, coarsely chopped
grated rind and juice of 2 oranges
12,5 ml (1 T) finely chopped fresh parsley

1. Heat a saucepan of water to boiling point and add the noodles, a few at a time. Heat the oil, pepper and sesame seeds in a second saucepan. Boil the noodles until done, drain and spoon into the saucepan of hot oil. Remove from the heat, mix well and spoon out the noodles to cool completely.
2. Add the celery, spring onions, sweet pepper, tomatoes, dates, orange rind and juice. Mix into a salad dish and sprinkle the parsley over.

Spinach and bacon salad

(MAKES 6 SERVINGS)

1 packet (500 g) fresh spinach leaves,
  washed and ribs removed, leaves patted dry
  and broken into smaller pieces
freshly grated nutmeg
1 orange, thickly peeled and segments removed
50 g (125 ml/½ cup) walnuts,
  coarsely chopped
1 packet (250 g) rindless streaky bacon,
  shredded
2 plump garlic cloves, bruised,
  peeled and crushed with:
5 ml (1 t) salt
125 ml (½ cup) olive oil
1 red chilli, halved lengthways,
  seeded and cut into strips
2 slices white bread, lightly toasted
  and crusts removed, then cubed
grated rind and juice of 1 large lemon
freshly ground black pepper
3 ml (½ t) prepared English mustard

1. Place the spinach in a salad bowl and grate the nutmeg over. Sprinkle orange segments and walnuts over.
2. Fry the bacon in a frying pan over low heat until crisp. Spoon the hot bacon over the spinach.
3. Place the garlic in the same pan in which the bacon was fried, add a little olive oil and fry for 1 minute. Add bread cubes and fry until hot and the oil has been absorbed – ± 1 minute. Add to the spinach. Pour the rest of the oil into the pan and remove from the heat. Add the lemon juice and rind, season with pepper and stir in the mustard. Spoon over the salad, mix and serve.

Oven-dried tomatoes

It is more hygienic to dry tomatoes in the oven, rather than in the sun, and they also taste much better.

ripe tomatoes, halved horizontally
olive oil
5 ml (1 t) sugar
salt, pepper, chopped basil and thyme or oregano
olive oil

1. Scoop out the seeds and pulp from the tomatoes into a large saucepan, so that only the skins and their flesh remain. Pack the tomato shells on an oiled wire rack placed over a baking pan and bake for 2 hours in a preheated oven at 100 °C (200 °F).
2. Meanwhile, heat the tomato pulp and seeds to boiling point over moderate heat and simmer for 30 minutes. Pour through a sieve and discard the seeds. Place the tomato pulp in a large, clean saucepan, heat to boiling point, reduce the heat and simmer until the mixture is thick. Stir in the sugar and continue cooking, stirring, until the mixture is toffee-like. Remove from the heat and season with salt, pepper, basil and thyme.
3. Remove the tomato shells from the oven and divide the 'toffee' mixture among them. Spread the mixture out in each shell, using the back of a teaspoon, and return to the oven. Dry for a further 3-4 hours.
4. Place the tomatoes in a sterilised jar and add enough olive oil to cover them. Extra fresh basil may also be added to the jar. Seal and store in the refrigerator.

PEACH CHUTNEY

Peach chutney

(MAKES 2 LARGE JARS)

It seems that whenever South African emigrants are homesick, the thing they long for most is Mrs Balls chutney.

1,5 kg ripe cling peaches,
    removed from the stone
1 large onion, halved lengthways,
    peeled and chopped
2 plump garlic cloves, bruised and peeled
1 packet (500 g) seedless raisins
400 g (500 ml/2 cups) sugar
10 ml (2 t) salt
10 ml (2 t) ground ginger
5 ml (1 t) English mustard powder
cayenne pepper to taste
1 litre (4 cups) vinegar

1. Pulse peaches, onion and garlic in a food processor until roughly chopped.
2. Spoon peach mixture into an enamel or stainless steel saucepan and add the rest of the ingredients. Stir over low heat until sugar has dissolved and boil slowly until the mixture is very soft and thick. Stir through every now and then.
3. Spoon into sterilised jars and seal immediately.

VARIATIONS

• Substitute peaches with apricots. Cut apricots to the stone, turn in opposite directions to halve them and remove stones.
• Chop 500 g sour apples, peeled, cored and seeded, together with peaches.
• For extra flavour, add 15 ml (3 t) roasted, ground coriander seed (see p. 60) and 5 ml (1 t) ground cinnamon.
• For extra bite, 1-2 red chillies, seeds and all, can be chopped with the peaches.

Raïta

(MAKES 4-6 SERVINGS)

250 ml (1 cup) unflavoured yoghurt
1 English cucumber, grated and drained
12,5 ml (1 T) chopped fresh mint leaves
25 ml (2 T) chopped fresh coriander leaves
3 ml (½ t) salt
5 ml (1 t) sugar
freshly ground pepper and cayenne pepper
    to taste

Mix all the ingredients and refrigerate until just before needed.

Sweetcorn and sweet pepper salsa

(MAKES 4 SERVINGS)

1 onion, halved lengthways, peeled and sliced
25 ml (2 T) oil
2 garlic cloves, bruised, peeled and crushed
1 red sweet pepper, halved,
    seeds and membranes removed,
    cut into thick strips and then cubed
3 large, ripe tomatoes, quartered,
    seeds removed, cut into thick strips
    and then cubed
1 tin (200 ml) tomato juice
1 tin (340 g) sweetcorn kernels, drained
salt and freshly ground black pepper
12 fresh basil leaves, rinsed,
    rolled up and cut into strips
1 bunch spring onions, thinly sliced

Fry the onion in oil over moderate heat until almost soft. Stir in the garlic and stir-fry for 1 minute. Add sweet peppers and stir-fry for 2-3 minutes. Turn up heat, add tomatoes and tomato juice and cook for 3 minutes. Add sweetcorn kernels and heat through. Taste and season with salt, pepper and basil. Set aside for 1 minute and serve with chicken, pork or veal dishes.

Quince sambal

(MAKES 4 SERVINGS)

Quince sambal is delicious with any curry, but even better with fish dishes. Try it next time you make fish cakes.

1 ripe quince, peeled and coarsely grated –
    take care not to grate the seeds
salt
2 carrots, scraped and finely grated
50 ml (4 T) brown vinegar
25 ml (2 T) soft brown sugar
1 chilli, seeded and chopped,
    or 5 ml (1 t) finely grated fresh ginger root
fresh coriander leaves (optional)

1. Place the quince in a large glass or ceramic dish, sprinkle lightly with salt and set aside for 30 minutes. Press out and discard all liquid from the quince. Add the carrots to the quince.
2. Mix the vinegar and sugar and stir until the sugar has dissolved. Add the chilli or ginger (or both, if you like a fiery flavour) and pour over the quince mixture. Stir to blend. Spoon into a container and refrigerate. It will keep well for up to a week. Chop the coriander leaves just before the sambal is to be served, and stir them into the sambal.

Tomato and chilli sambal

(MAKES 4 SERVINGS)

2 ripe red tomatoes, quartered,
*   seeded and chopped*
1 red onion, halved lengthways,
*   peeled and finely chopped*
2 red chillies, halved, seeded
*   and finely chopped*

1. Mix all the ingredients, spoon into a suitable container, cover with cling wrap and refrigerate until just before needed.
2. Moisten with Sambal dressing (see p. 157) and serve. Do not prepare too long in advance, as the tomatoes will draw water and the sambal will be limp.

Cucumber and coriander sambal

(MAKES 4 SERVINGS)

1 English cucumber, halved (unpeeled)
*   lengthways, seeded and chopped*
1 small onion, peeled and finely chopped
25 ml (2 T) finely chopped fresh
*   coriander leaves*

Mix all the ingredients and complete as for Tomato and chilli sambal.

Sour fig and pineapple sambal

(MAKES 4 SERVINGS)

24 sour figs
125 ml (½ cup) strong, hot rooibos tea
1 small pineapple, peeled, cored and chopped
1 small onion, peeled and chopped
5 ml (1 t) finely grated ginger root

1. Soak the sour figs overnight in the tea. Drain, remove all messy bits, and chop finely.
2. Mix the figs with the pineapple and onion and moisten with Sambal dressing (see p. 157). Add the ginger. Spoon into a suitable container, cover with cling wrap and marinate for 1 hour in the refrigerator.

Sambal dressing

(MAKES 25 ML (2 T))

25 ml (2 T) wine vinegar
salt and freshly ground white pepper
5 ml (1 t) sugar
1 ml (pinch) cayenne pepper (optional)

Mix all the ingredients and stir until the sugar has dissolved. Set aside until needed.

Date sambal

(MAKES 6 SERVINGS)

Marvellous with any mutton dish.

1 slab (250 g) stoned dates, coarsely chopped
25 ml (2 T) wine vinegar
1 large onion, halved lengthways,
*   peeled and very thinly sliced*
coarse salt
castor sugar

1. Place the dates in a mixing bowl and mix with the vinegar. Cover the mixture and set aside for 24 hours.
2. Spoon a layer of onions into a shallow dish and cover with coarse salt. Repeat twice. Cover with cling wrap and set aside for 24 hours. Rinse well under cold running water and mix with the dates. Taste and season with a little castor sugar, if necessary.

Are vegetarians on the right track?

VEGETARIANS PROBABLY follow a more healthy diet than other people in certain respects, because their diet contains fewer chemicals and preservatives, which are present in processed foods in particular. They are also inclined to aim for a higher general level of fitness. Because of their high fibre intake, there is a smaller incidence of breast and stomach cancer among vegetarians. The greatest single disadvantage of vegetarianism, however, is an unbalanced diet. Many vegetarians eat only vegetables, fruit and nuts – and then in the wrong combinations. Vegetarians should, therefore, be intelligent thinkers and take a great interest in food, or they may be treading on a path strewn with thorns which can only be to their disadvantage.

A healthy, energy-giving diet provides the body with proteins for growth, to renew and maintain it. Carbohydrates and fats provide energy, and fat is a medium through which fat-soluble vitamins like A, D, E and K can be absorbed. Although the body needs few vitamins and minerals, they are extremely important for the proper functioning and regulating of bodily functions.

The greatest objection is not to vegetarianism itself, but to vegetarians who have only fragmentary knowledge of what a complete diet should consist of, particularly when it comes to protein. This is particularly important as far as children are concerned. Parents who embrace vegetarianism should not put their children on a vegetarian

SOYA BEANS, SPROUTS, NUTS AND SEEDS ARE IMPORTANT INGREDIENTS IN VEGETARIANISM. ON THE TRAY ARE BRINJAL LASAGNE (P. 161) AND SPICED SPROUT SALAD (P. 161), WHICH ARE PERFECT FOR 'PERVEGIES'. TOP RIGHT IS APRICOT AND NUT DESSERT (P. 161), BOTTOM RIGHT IS BAKED GARLIC AND BOTTOM LEFT BROCCOLI PURÉE (SEE CHAPTER 15) AND MANGETOUTS

diet before they are about 18 years old; they should also allow them to choose for themselves, for moral reasons.

A complete diet

Stir a little brewer's yeast into dishes. It is valuable because of the quantity of protein it contains: 100 g brewer's yeast is equivalent to 100 g of red meat. Protein intake may be further supplemented by pulses which have been soaked for 2-3 days in fresh water in a warm place, so that they begin to sprout. In this way, large quantities of vitamins B and C are made. Vegetable protein is also available canned or dried. The meat in all the curry dishes in this book may, therefore, be replaced by a dried product.

Adult bodies need 22 amino acid proteins, and children need an additional one. Eight of these acids, which are known as essential amino acids, cannot be manufactured by the body and should therefore be included in the diet. More important is that all eight must be eaten at the same time *and* in the right proportion for the body to put them to the best use.

Vegetarians should have five meals per day: breakfast and the other largish meal of the day should provide 50 per cent of the protein needs, and the other three, smaller meals the remaining 50 per cent.

Protein

The best complete, non-meat protein is soya. Dried pulses like lentils and peas are incomplete protein sources. Most food protein contains all eight acids, although sometimes in small quantities. These small quantities are nevertheless essential, as the acids affect the body's ability to use the remaining amino acids.

Vegetarians should, therefore, preferably include the following in one meal: a dairy product with a grain; a dried pulse, preferably soya; vegetables; nuts and seeds *or* a flour product with a dried pulse, preferably soya; and vegetables and dairy *or* vegetables with

grains, dairy, nuts and seeds. (There is a menu on p. 160-161 which non-vegetarians may use as a guide when entertaining ovo-vegetarians.)

One of the greatest mistakes that vegetarians make is that they do not always include sources of iron together with sources of vitamin C. The body is better able to absorb iron when it is eaten with something rich in vitamin C, such as citrus, guavas and sweet peppers.

Children who are raised as vegetarians need more than the usual daily requirement of nutrients. They should play outside often, so that sunshine can provide their vitamin D requirements. If the body does not receive sufficient vitamin B12, the bone will degenerate; a serious and irreparable condition. All other vitamins, minerals and nutrients are richly represented in a balanced vegetarian diet.

Carbohydrates

If vegetarians were to include sufficient carbohydrates in the form of grain products, pulses, root vegetables and nuts in their diet at one time, it would almost be a balanced diet. Adding enough fresh fruit, honey and milk would make it sufficient.

High-protein breakfast cereal

(MAKES 8 SERVINGS)

180 g (500 ml/2 cups) rolled oatmeal
100 g (250 ml/1 cup) soya flour
30 ml (6 t) bran
45 ml (9 t) wheatgerm
50 g (60 ml/4 large T) brown sugar
100 ml (8 T) vegetable oil
25 g (50 ml/4 T) roasted sesame seeds
25 g (50 ml/4 T) roasted sunflower seeds
100 g (175 ml/⅔ cup) raisins or sultanas

1. Preheat the oven to 160 °C (325 °F). Mix the oatmeal, soya flour, bran, wheatgerm, sugar and oil. Grease a shallow baking pan and bake the mixture for 40 minutes. Stir from time to time.
2. Remove from the oven, add the seeds and raisins and mix. Allow to cool completely, then spoon into airtight containers and store in the refrigerator.

VARIATIONS
● VEGAN: Serve with soya milk and nuts.
● LACTO-VEGETARIAN: Serve with nuts and yoghurt or full-cream milk.

High-energy breakfast cereal

(MAKES 8 SERVINGS)

450 g (5 x 250 ml/5 cups) one-minute oatmeal
50 g (85 ml/⅓ cup) dried apricots, chopped
50 g (85 ml/⅓ cup) stoned dates, chopped
100 g (250 ml/1 cup) sunflower seeds
1 packet (100 g/250 ml/1 cup) mixed nuts, chopped
50 g (85 ml/⅓ cup) raisins

Mix all the ingredients.

VARIATIONS
● VEGAN: Serve with soya milk and bananas.
● OVO-VEGETARIAN: Serve with honey, full-cream milk and bananas.

Soya croquettes

(MAKES 4 SERVINGS)

500 g cooked soya beans, chopped
2 onions, halved lengthways, peeled and finely chopped
1 carrot, peeled and finely grated
25 ml (2 T) chopped fresh parsley
65 g (125 ml/½ cup) whole-wheat flour
5 ml (1 t) aniseed
salt and pepper
2 eggs, beaten
cake flour
oil

TOPPING
Parmesan cheese

1. Mix the soya beans, onions, carrot, parsley, flour and aniseed. Season well with salt and pepper. Add the eggs and mix to make a stiff mixture.
2. Wet your hands with water and shape 8 croquettes. Roll the croquettes in flour, shake off excess flour, then place on a baking sheet lined with a paper towel. Allow to rest in the refrigerator for 20-30 minutes.
3. Heat the oil in a frying pan or deep-fryer and fry the croquettes slowly in shallow oil until golden all over, or for 3 minutes in a deep-fryer. Drain on paper towels. Sprinkle cheese over and serve.

Vegan salad

baked sweet peppers (see p. 146), cut into strips
cooked lentils
cooked chickpeas
yeast bread, cubed and fried in oil and garlic
chopped parsley
chopped chives and spring onions
salt and pepper
salad dressing
blanched red cabbage strips

Mix the sweet pepper strips, lentils, chickpeas, bread cubes, parsley, chives and spring onions. Season to taste and moisten with salad dressing. Spoon into salad bowls and sprinkle red cabbage over.

VARIATIONS
● Use lentil rice instead of lentils.
● Spoon the salad into baked potatoes that have been hollowed-out.

A MENU FOR OVO-VEGETARIANS
Broccoli fondue

(MAKES 8 SERVINGS)

2 whole broccoli heads, broken into florets
water
salt and pepper
grated nutmeg
125 ml (½ cup) well-seasoned white sauce, made with soya milk
25 ml (2 T) horseradish cream
62,5 ml (¼ cup) cream
24 mangetout, blanched

1. Set 8 broccoli florets aside and chop the small and large stems finely. Place the broccoli in a mixing bowl and cover with cold water. Add a little salt and set aside for 10 minutes. Pour water off through a colander, rinse the broccoli and place in a saucepan. Arrange the whole florets, stems down, on top of the finely chopped broccoli and season with salt, pepper and nutmeg. Add 1 cup (250 ml) water, cover and heat to boiling point. Reduce the heat slowly to very low and simmer until tender. Set aside for 15 minutes.
2. Set 8 florets aside. Purée the remaining broccoli with the white sauce, horseradish cream and cream. Return to the saucepan and heat over low heat. Taste and season. Spoon into dishes. Garnish with broccoli florets and mangetout.

Spiced sprout salad

(MAKES 8 SERVINGS)

selection of salad leaves, rinsed thoroughly,
    patted dry and broken into pieces
24 cherry tomatoes, halved
2 celery stalks, rinsed and threads removed,
    then chopped
2 carrots, scraped, parboiled and
    cut into strips
24 yound French beans, blanched
250 ml (1 cup) mixed sprouts,
    preferably soya and bamboo

DRESSING
50 ml (4 T) lemon juice
75 ml (6 T) olive oil
salt and pepper
1 ml (pinch) sugar
5 ml (1 t) curry powder
75 ml (6 T) yoghurt

GARNISH
6 spring onions, chopped and sprinkled over
    salad or placed, whole, on top

1. Arrange the salad leaves on individual plates
or in a large salad bowl. Sprinkle the tomatoes,
celery, carrots, green beans and sprouts over.
2. MAKE THE DRESSING: Beat all the
ingredients together and serve separately.
Garnish the salad with spring onions.

Apricot and nut dessert

(MAKES 8 SERVINGS)

300 g (500 ml/2 cups) dried apricots
rooibos or honey tea
25 ml (2 T) sugar
1 stick cinnamon
1 carton (350 g/350 ml) natural,
    low-fat yoghurt
3 egg whites
45 ml (3 large T) soft brown sugar
24 hazelnuts, roasted and skins rubbed off
1 packet (100 g/250 ml/1 cup)
    almond slivers

1. Place the apricots in a mixing bowl and
pour over enough tea to cover. Sprinkle the
sugar over. Cover and refrigerate overnight.

2. Place the contents of the mixing bowl in
a saucepan, heat to boiling point, reduce
heat and add the stick of cinnamon. Simmer
until fruit is tender. Remove the cinnamon
and drain. Purée the apricots and rub them
through a sieve. Allow to cool completely
and stir in the yoghurt. Meanwhile, whisk
the egg whites until stiff, adding the brown
sugar gradually. Whisk until the sugar has
dissolved (it takes quite a while). Add ⅓ of
the egg white mixture to the purée and mix.
Add the apricot mixture to the rest of the
egg white mixture and fold in carefully.
Spoon into 8 glasses and place in the refrigerator. Decorate each glass with 3 hazelnuts
and finish with almond slivers.

Brinjal lasagne

(MAKES 8 SERVINGS)

2 brinjals
salt
50 ml (4 T) olive or other oil
1 onion, halved lengthways, peeled,
    sliced and finely chopped
1 punnet (250 g) button mushrooms,
    wiped and sliced
1 tin (410 g) chopped tomatoes
125 ml (½ cup) tomato purée
75 g (125 ml/½ cup) soya beans, soaked
    overnight and cooked until tender
    in salted water
5 ml (1 t) each dried basil and oregano
5 ml (1 t) brown sugar
salt and freshly ground black pepper
250 g whole-wheat or ordinary lasagne
500 g ricotta or cottage cheese
2 eggs
200 g mozzarella cheese, coarsely grated
50 g (125 ml/½ cup) finely grated
    Parmesan cheese
handful of cashew nuts
25 ml (2 T) sesame seeds

1. Prepare brinjals as described on p. 142,
pat dry and chop coarsely.
2. Heat the oil in a large frying pan, add the
onion and fry until softened and transparent.
Add the brinjals and mushrooms, increase
the heat and fry for a further 5 minutes until
all the liquid has evaporated. Add the tomatoes, purée, soya beans, basil, oregano and
sugar, season lightly with salt and well with
pepper, reduce the heat and simmer for

about 30 minutes until the mixture is fairly
thick. Taste and season with more salt and
pepper if necessary.
3. Meanwhile, heat water to boiling point in
a large saucepan. Add a handful of salt.
Place the lasagne sheets, a few at a time, in
the water and cook for 3 minutes. Remove
and place in a dish of ice-cold water. Bring
water to boil again and cook next batch of
lasagne sheets. Repeat until all the pasta has
been cooked and placed in ice-cold water.
Drain the sheets and spread them out on
clean tea towels.
4. Beat the ricotta and eggs together well
until is smooth. Preheat the oven to 180 °C
(350 °F). Grease a baking dish lightly with a
little margarine. Spoon ⅓ of the brinjal sauce
into the dish and level the surface. Cover with
a single layer of lasagne sheets (⅓ of sheets),
followed by ⅓ of egg mixture and then ⅓ of
mozzarella. Repeat twice with remaining
brinjal sauce, pasta, egg mixture and mozzarella. Sprinkle Parmesan cheese, nuts and
sesame seed over. Bake for 25-30 minutes, or
until the cheese has melted and turned gold-
en brown. Serve immediately.

Crunchy-topped bananas

(MAKES 4 SERVINGS)

4 very ripe bananas, peeled
    and halved lengthways
4 oranges, thickly peeled and
    segments removed
2 red apples, rinsed, cored and sliced (unpeeled)
25 ml (2 T) lemon juice
15 g (50 ml/4 T) roasted coconut
20 g (50 ml/4 T) blanched almonds, roasted
20 g (50 ml/4 T) rolled oatmeal, roasted
3 ml (½ t) mixed spice
40 ml (8 t) oil
25 ml (2 T) smooth apricot jam
25 ml (2 T) soft brown sugar

1. Arrange the bananas, orange segments
and apples in dessert bowls. Sprinkle the
lemon juice over. Mix the coconut, almonds,
oatmeal and mixed spice.
2. Heat oil, apricot jam and sugar over low
heat and stir until sugar has dissolved.
Increase the heat and add coconut mixture.
Stir for 1 minute and spoon mixture over
fruit. Serve immediately.

Desserts

DESSERT, popularly known as pudding, suits all South African tastes, from sweet tooth to curmudgeon. During the first half of the twentieth century, small-town, Afrikaans-speaking ladies and their English-speaking city counterparts developed a dessert culture unequalled in any other part of the world.

Kotie van der Spuy, the *grande dame* of sugar cookery in South Africa, writes in her book about desserts and sweets that no meal is complete without a dessert: 'If there is no dessert, give me a spoonful of jam, as long as I can have just a little sweetness before the black coffee.' This sums up, very effectively, white South Africans' love of sweet things. Rural blacks are not really dessert eaters and content themselves mainly with canned fruit, except for the Zulus who have developed a great love for English trifle.

Before the flood of cookery books available from the sixties onwards, especially during the period before the urbanisation first of whites, then the coloured and black communities, most cooks had to rely on old favourites like *doekpoeding* (Cloutie dumpling, suet pudding or *waterbul*), honeycomb sponge (honeycomb sponge trifle, also known as Chippolata) and snow pudding for that extra-special occasion. Interestingly enough, egg whites had to be whisked stiffly with two forks or two flat pieces of bamboo, in a bowl. Everyday desserts were pumpkin fritters, *souskluitjies* (cinnamon dumplings) and rice dumplings, baked rice pudding or, on a rainy day, pancakes liberally sprinkled with cinnamon sugar, not to mention packet jelly.

At the beginning of the century, ice cream was restricted to posh hotels; later it became common, only to become Americanised in the fifties with Milky Lanes and banana splits. Sorbet, with the exception of lemon sorbet, has not really made an impact in this country. This was followed by baked Alaska (*omelette norvégienne*), which was carried, flaming, to the table. Ostentation was the result of this dessert; one Cape newspaper recorded an event at which the hostess placed a small canary

SNOW PUDDING

in half an egg shell on top of the Alaska and enclosed it with spun sugar. With the first incision into the Alaska, the little bird flew, with great aplomb, past the astounded guests.

Meringues and meringue shapes, especially nests and cases with fillings, reached their peak in the second half of the century with Pavlova – particularly in the seventies, when kiwi fruit became available. In the sixties, *île flottante* (floating island), consisting of poached meringue with nuts, became high fashion for government receptions.

Blancmange, with its ugly Afrikaans name of *mielieblomvorm* (cornflour mould), was the predecessor of jelly. My mother told me that they always steeped large peach leaves in the milk; those leaves that cluster on young shoots at the base of the tree. Wine jelly dates from the earliest days at the Cape, and enjoyed a revival in the sixties. Wine, especially sweet wine, was set first with seaweed (agar agar) and later with gelatine. Port jelly, in particular, became a regional speciality in Stellenbosch. Packet jelly, especially the reds and greens, was the order of the day: sometimes it was set with canned fruit or even cake crumbs, sometimes it had a layer of smooth cottage cheese on top and sometimes it was whisked with evaporated milk to make a snow. The *Huisgenoot* featured a winning recipe in which ginger biscuits, moistened with brandy, were set in jelly along with soaked dried fruit. Then there was jelly sponge, in which a packet of jelly powder and 45 ml (9 t) sugar were dissolved in a cup of boiling water before beating in 10 ice cubes, one at a time, then beating again for a short while.

Baked custard has stood the test of time, in spite of being served for a decade in a richer form as *crème de la crème* before reaching a climax as *crème brûlée*. The most traditional dessert sauce is custard, thick or thin, hot or cold. First it was made with eggs, then custard powder took over, then came custard in a commercial packaging … only to return, in the last decade, to the eggs, sugar, vanilla and milk of the past. Banana slices, covered with runny egg custard, sometimes with caramel condensed milk added, were baked in the oven. Sometimes this dessert had a coconut or soft meringue topping. Rhubarb and poached quinces were also baked this way. Custard-rich trifle was adopted from the

British by the Afrikaner community, who called it *koekstruif*. *Melktert* (milk tart) was a fashionable dessert at the beginning of the century, as it is once again, particularly if accompanied by a small serving of fruit preserve, whole or in chunks. Baked buttermilk pudding and set yoghurt in ice cream – as well as other cold moulded desserts often linked to the health brigade – illustrate how times have changed, from earlier ages to today. Strawberries with clotted cream (Devonshire cream) are as much at home here as they are at Wimbledon. Clotted cream gains another dimension heated with honey. Cheesecake, in its European baked form or in its American set guise, was the forerunner of tiramisu. Made from mascarpone, this is the dessert that set the pace for the nineties.

Fruit cream, known as a fool, was served in many households, while other cold desserts like mousses, soufflés, charlottes and Bavarian cream were only made from time to time – with the exception of chocolate mousse.

We live in a country renowned for its fruit. In one form or another, fruit has been a popular dessert since the first tree was planted at the Cape. We know that Simon van der Stel served cold watermelon slices at the end of a meal. Cold watermelon? The watermelons were picked very early in the morning, wrapped in damp hessian and left in a cool place, in a draught, and watered at regular intervals. Fruit salad became summer food and, with the passing of time, a hotch-potch of just about everything. Fortunately, sense prevailed in the late eighties, and today fruit is combined expertly and, most of the time, also macerated. Fruit sauces were spooned over ice cream; today we make a coulis from from a variety of fruits.

As the twentieth century marched on, the focus shifted from steamed puddings like speckled hen (currant pudding) or *Jonkmanspoeding* to baked puddings. Just about the only steamed pudding still around today is Christmas pudding. SJA de Villiers of *Cook and Enjoy* fame recreated canary pudding as a baked pudding known as 'Japie se gunsteling' (Japie's favourite). Similarly, baked puddings like rice, macaroni, and bread pudding were made with custard and meringue. Bread pudding was upgraded to queen of puddings, while roly-poly, sago pudding, apple pudding, potato pudding, sweet potato pudding and coconut pudding were fond favourites. Crumbles, of which apple is the best known, were served with hot custard. Brown puddings like vinegar pudding, *malvapoeding* and brandy pudding became international hits in their South African guise.

Sweet tarts served as dessert arrived, disappeared … and re-appeared. Melktert remains the most popular, but a wide variety of others, including ginger, Post Toastie and Van der Hum tarts, were served with afternoon tea or coffee, and as dessert in the evening together with custard or another sauce.

Pudding without a sauce is like a day without sun. The best-known sauces are wine, brandy (known as 'hardehoutsous'), caramel, ginger, lemon, nutmeg and chocolate.

Because space is limited, I have had to leave out ice cream, Bavarian custard desserts and fruit salad. Those who would like to find out more about them, should consult my book *Desserts*.

Snow pudding

(MAKES 8 SERVINGS)

This pudding is an old favourite, and can be set in a large oiled mould, in cups, or in dariole or other decorative moulds. Remember to oil small moulds too.

30 g (45 ml/3 large T) gelatine
375 ml (1½ cups) water
600 g (750 ml/3 cups) sugar
finely grated rind of 6 lemons,
  and enough juice to make 375 ml
  (1½ cups) (make up the quantity with
  water if necessary)
1 ml (pinch) tartaric acid
6 extra-large egg whites
1 ml (pinch) salt
cream (optional)

1. Sprinkle gelatine over 125 ml (½ cup) water and leave to sponge. Clarify in the microwave for 45 seconds at 100% power, or over steam on a stove. Mix the remaining 250 ml (1 cup) of water with the sugar in a deep saucepan and stir over low heat until sugar has dissolved. Increase the heat and boil for 3 minutes. Remove from the heat, add hot gelatine and stir until the mixture clarifies. Add the lemon rind, juice, and tartaric acid. Place over a dish of ice cubes and ice-cold water until the mixture begins to set.
2. Whisk the egg whites and salt until stiff and beat in the jelly, a spoonful at a time. Spoon into an oiled mould, cover with cling wrap and refrigerate overnight until set.
3. TO SERVE: Turn out the pudding and surround it with custard. Decorate the pudding with cream rosettes and other decorations, if you wish. Doing so is rather old-fashioned today – the simpler and more rustic, the better.

VARIATION: INDIVIDUAL SERVINGS
Set the pudding in 8 small moulds. Turn out in the centre of 8 large, cold plates and surround with custard. Garnish each with a variety of fresh fruit, such as watermelon and spanspek balls (in summer), mango and/or kiwi slices, pitted grapes (late summer), orange segments and guava strips (winter), or strawberries and more strawberries (spring). Brandy snaps (see p. 168) and candied rose leaves give this dessert a unique finish.

Trifle

The great French chefs did not really admire British cooking, but there was one exception: egg custard or *créme anglaise*. Custard was essential given all the hundreds of baked British puddings. The greatest dessert triumph, and undoubtedly the most popular pudding in the country, is English trifle which consists, basically, of cake and custard. This pudding came to South Africa during the last years of Queen Victoria's reign and was so popular that it was given pride of place at Sunday meals. At the end of the twentieth century, trifle is still the most popular, creative dessert, but vanilla ice cream with chocolate sauce is only a short step behind.

The original pudding required two sponge cake layers. The layers were sandwiched together with strawberry, cherry or any other red jam before being cut into slices. With the arrival of Davis gelatine in South Africa, instant jellies were adopted with gusto. In poorer households, in particular, chopped set jelly quickly made its way to the trifle dish, where it alternated with the layers of sponge cake and custard. In the nineteenth century and at the beginning of the twentieth century, trifle was moistened with sweet wine, better known as *nagmaalwyn* (communion wine) or jerepigo. Since the forties, sweet wine has given way to Old Brown Sherry. From the economic boom of the late sixties onwards, wealthy cooks increasingly used liqueur to sprinkle over the cake and to flavour the cream that topped the trifle. I think it's a shame, even if I am sometimes guilty of doing so myself!

FRUIT SALAD

Basic trifle

(MAKES 6-8 SERVINGS)

2 sponge cake layers, 1 long trifle sponge
   or 1 swiss roll
125 ml (½ cup) red jam (read p. 164),
   slightly melted
60 ml (4 large T) brown sherry
18 nut meringues
500 ml (2 cups) egg custard (see Hint)
25 g (65 ml/¼ cup) almond flakes, lightly roasted

TOPPING
250 ml (1 cup) cream, whipped to soft peaks

1. Halve each cake layer horizontally and spread jam over 2 layers. Place other 2 layers on top. Slice the cake, like bread. Pack the slices of 1 cake onto the base of a large, attractive glass dish. Sprinkle 12,5 ml (1 T) sherry over.
2. Break the meringues and sprinkle over. Sprinkle again with 12,5 ml (1 T) sherry. Spoon half the lukewarm custard over. Sprinkle almonds over. Arrange remaining sliced cake on top and sprinkle the rest of the sherry over. Spoon the rest of the custard over. Cover with cling wrap and refrigerate.
3. Spread the cream evenly on top and serve.

HINT: Make the egg custard, but beat 25 ml (2 T) custard powder and the egg yolks until the custard mixture is hot. Add milk and stir until the custard is nice and thick. Flavour with vanilla once cooled.

SOUTH AFRICAN VARIATIONS

● WITH GLACÉ FRUIT: During the first six decades of the twentieth century, when housewives often canned fruit and made preserves themselves, green fig preserve, in particular, was halved and packed on top of the first sponge cake layer. The topping was covered with cream, on which 6 cream rosettes were piped and each rosette was crowned with half a green fig. In many households, washed and dried glacé cherry halves were placed on cream rosettes and finished with 2 pieces of angelica, cut to look like leaves. Coarsely chopped or whole citron preserve, watermelon preserve and other glacé fruit were also used.
● WITH FRESH OR CANNED FRUIT: Banana slices covered with lemon juice and grated lemon peel, mango slices, fresh pineapple slices sprinkled with rum, or canned fruit – especially well-drained fruit cocktail – remain popular choices. Berries are not used in the trifle itself, but as decoration.

TRIFLE

● JELLY TRIFLE: Prepare one packet of red and one packet of green jelly according to packet instructions and leave them to set in separate containers. Chop coarsely and set a small quantity aside. Use 3 cake layers, so that 1 layer of jelly chunks can be spooned between the bottom 2 layers of cake, and the second colour can be spooned between the centre and top cake layers. Spoon cold custard over the jelly from time to time.

Chippolata

(MAKES 36 SERVINGS)

This recipe is ideal for a dessert buffet. The size of the dessert is determined by the size of your largest tray. Chippolata is really a trifle, and the custard is set with gelatine.

CUSTARD
25 ml (2 T) gelatine
75 ml (6 T) water
750 ml (3 cups) milk
60 g (75 ml/6 T) sugar
6 egg yolks

TRIFLE
1 large, square sponge cake,
   halved horizontally
500 g whole citron preserve, chopped
250 ml (1 cup) syrup from citron preserve
50 ml (4 T) brown sherry
1 large tin (875 g) peach slices, drained
1 packet (100 g/250 ml/1 cup) walnuts, chopped
500 ml (2 cups) cream

JELLY
1 packet (80 g) each green
   and red jelly
500 ml (2 cups) boiling water

TOPPING
36 small meringues
36 maraschino cherries, with stalks

1. CUSTARD: Sprinkle the gelatine over the water in a small mixing bowl and leave to sponge. Place the milk and sugar in a saucepan and stir over low heat until the sugar has dissolved. Beat the egg yolks with a wooden spoon and stir in some of the lukewarm milk. Add the egg mixture to the rest of the milk and stir with a wooden spoon until the custard begins to thicken and is almost boiling. Remove from heat and stir in the sponged gelatine. Place the custard over a saucepan of boiling water without heating the saucepan – it is used simply to keep the custard warm.

2. TRIFLE: Place 2 cake layers, side by side, on a large tray. Spread the preserve equally over the cake layers. Mix the syrup and the sherry and sprinkle over. Spread a thin layer of warm egg custard on top and leave to set. Remove the dish containing the rest of the egg custard from the heat, allow to cool completely and refrigerate until set. Spoon the egg custard into a piping bag and pipe over the cake layers. Arrange the peaches on top and sprinkle the walnuts over. Whip the cream until stiff and spread over the top and sides of the cake. Place in the refrigerator.
3. JELLY: Make jellies separately, using 250 ml (1 cup) boiling water for each. Allow to cool completely, then refrigerate until set. Chop finely and arrange spoonfuls of green and red jelly alternately around cake on tray. Arrange meringues and cherries on the cream layer.

Créme anglaise (Egg custard)

(MAKES 500-625 ML/2-2½ CUPS)

5 extra-large egg yolks
100 g (125 ml/½ cup) sugar
400-500 ml (1⅗-2 cups) milk
   (depending on how thick the custard is)
5-10 ml (1-2 t) vanilla essence

1. Place a heavy-bottomed saucepan on a baking pan. Surround the saucepan with ice cubes and ice-cold water and place 2 ice cubes in it. This will cool the hot custard so that it does not continue to cook and then curdle.
2. Beat the egg yolks and sugar in a mixing bowl over steam until thick and light yellow in colour. Dip your finger in the mixture to check whether it is warm. Continue beating if it is not. Heat the milk to boiling point, pour through a sieve and stir a little of it into the egg yolk mixture with a wooden spoon. Repeat with a little more milk. Reheat the rest of the milk to boiling point and add it all to the egg yolk mixture. Stir the mixture with a wooden spoon until it thickens. Pour through a sieve into the saucepan standing in ice-cold water. Stir until the custard begins to cool, add the essence and stir until completely cold. Cover with cling wrap, right on the surface of the custard, and refrigerate.

VARIATIONS
● BRANDY CUSTARD: Add 50 ml (4 T) brandy to the custard.
● The custard may also be flavoured with whisky, Van der Hum or Kalahari Thirstland.

Lemon soufflé

(MAKES 6 SERVINGS)

Lemon and granadilla soufflés, beautifully risen above the edge of a soufflé dish, were South Africa's answer to Europe's *Soufflé glacé au Grand Marnier* – which sounds impressive, but is nothing more than egg custard enriched with cream, flavoured with Grand Marnier liqueur and set with gelatine before freezing. A cold soufflé is much easier and more convenient to make than a hot one.

grated rind and juice of 2 large lemons
grated rind and juice of 1 orange
6 extra-large eggs, separated
105 g (125 ml/½ cup) castor sugar
30 ml (6 t) gelatine
500 ml (2 cups) cream
1 ml (pinch) salt

TOPPING
125 ml (½ cup) Chantilly cream (p. 181)
thin strips of pamplemousse or citron preserve,
  whole or chunks

1. Tie a doubled sheet of waxed paper around the outside of a ± 1 litre (4 cups) soufflé dish. Grease the inside of the paper with oil.
2. Beat the lemon and orange rind, egg yolks and ¾ of the castor sugar in a mixing bowl until light, creamy and thick.
3. Measure 100 ml (8 T) lemon juice in a measuring jug (make up the quantity with orange juice, if necessary). Sprinkle the gelatine over and leave to sponge. Clarify in the microwave at 100% power for 50 seconds, or over steam on the stove. Allow to cool, then stir into the egg yolk mixture. Place the mixing bowl over a larger mixing bowl or pan of ice cubes and ice-cold water. Whip the cream until soft peaks form and fold into the egg yolk mixture. Remove the mixing bowl from the ice.
4. Whisk the egg whites and salt until stiff peaks form, then gradually beat in the remaining castor sugar. Fold ⅓ of the egg white mixture into the egg yolk mixture. Then fold the egg yolk mixture into the egg white mixture and spoon into the prepared soufflé dish. Refrigerate for at least 4 hours. Remove, pull off the paper and decorate with cream rosettes and strips of preserve.

VARIATION: GRANADILLA SOUFFLÉ
Use 16 large granadillas instead of the lemons and orange. Halve the granadillas and press out the seeds and juice into a sieve placed over a saucepan. Measure off 150 ml (⅗ cup) liquid. Add 50 ml (4 T) sugar and stir over low heat until the sugar has dissolved. Increase the heat and boil for 1 minute. Cool and complete as described above. Decorate with extra granadilla halves.

Brandy snaps with brandy cream

(MAKES ± 24)

This delicacy may also be filled with stiffly whipped, unflavoured cream. The cream may be flavoured with liqueur, like Van der Hum or Kalahari Thirstland.

SNAPS
125 g (125 ml/½ cup) butter
125 g (315 ml/1¼ cups) soft brown sugar
125 g (125 ml/½ cup) golden syrup
80 g (185 ml/¾ cup) cake flour
5 ml (1 t) ground ginger
5 ml (1 t) lemon juice
12,5 ml (1 T) brandy

BRANDY CREAM
500 ml (2 cups) cream
50 ml (4 T) castor sugar
37,5 ml (3 T) brandy
10 ml (2 t) vanilla essence

1. SNAPS: Preheat the oven to 160 °C (325 °F). Place the butter, sugar and syrup in a small saucepan and stir over low heat until the sugar has dissolved. Remove from the heat and allow to cool slightly.
2. Sift the flour and ginger 3 times, then sift over the cooled butter mixture. Add the lemon juice and brandy and mix well. Drop teaspoonfuls of mixture 100 mm (4 in) apart on lightly greased baking sheets. Bake for 6-8 minutes. Don't try to bake all the snaps at once – bake 2 at a time if you are inexperienced, and 4 if you are more experienced. Remove from the oven and cool slightly. Loosen with a spatula and roll up over the lightly oiled handles of wooden spoons. (Snaps to be used to decorate desserts are folded like tiles on a lightly oiled rolling pin.) Allow to cool completely and harden, then pull carefully off the handles. Store in an airtight container.
3. Prepare the brandy cream only once the snaps are to be served, otherwise the snaps will become soft. The cream must be ice-cold. Place in a mixing bowl or the bowl of an electric mixer and beat until soft peaks form. Add the castor sugar, brandy and vanilla and beat until stiff peaks form. Spoon into a piping bag fitted with a star nozzle and pipe into both ends of the snaps. Place on an attractive plate with a doiley on it.

Moulded cream

(MAKES 6-8 SERVINGS)

Better known as *panna cotta*, this simple moulded cream is another hit. Surround it with a Coulis (p. 171) of fresh fruit and decorate with macerated fresh fruit.

17,5 ml (3½ t) gelatine
85 ml (⅓ cup) milk
750 ml (3 cups) cream
150 g (185 ml/¾ cup) sugar
15 g (15 ml/3 t) vanilla essence

1. Sprinkle the gelatine over the milk and leave to sponge. Clarify in the microwave at 100% power for 40 seconds, or over steam on the stove.
2. Place 500 ml (2 cups) of the cream in a saucepan and add the sugar. Stir over low heat until the sugar has dissolved. The mixture should not boil. Remove from the heat and stir in the hot gelatine. Place over ice cubes and ice-cold water.
3. Whip the rest of the cream with the vanilla until stiff peaks form and fold into the cream base as soon as it is cold and about to set. Spoon into 6-8 ramekins, a decorative mould or a soufflé dish, the base lined with Bakewell paper and then oiled. Cover with cling wrap and refrigerate until set. Turn out and arrange in the centre of a dessert plate. Decorate with a sauce and fruit.

Wine jelly

(MAKES 6 SERVINGS)

1 bottle (750 ml/3 cups) dry white wine
1 clove
small stick cinnamon
¼ star anise
100 g (125 ml/½ cup) sugar
25 ml (2 T) gelatine
75 ml (6 T) water

1. Heat the wine and spices over very low heat and leave to infuse for at least 30 minutes. Remove the spice, add the sugar to the wine and stir over low heat until the sugar has dissolved. Increase the heat and boil for 3 minutes. Remove from the heat.

2. Sprinkle the gelatine over the water and leave to sponge. Clarify in the microwave at 100% power for 50-60 seconds, or over steam on the stove. Skim off the foam and stir into the hot wine. Place over ice cubes and ice-cold water until just about to set.

3. Spoon into 6 wine glasses, cover with cling wrap and refrigerate until set. Serve with poached fresh figs and a spoonful of cold mascarpone.

VARIATIONS

● Use port or muscadel instead of dry white wine and omit the sugar.

● Reduce the quantity of dry wine to 500 ml (2 cups) and omit the sugar. Heat the wine and spices as described above, remove the spices and stir in port wine jelly powder. This will make 4 servings.

Everyman's pudding (Bazaar pudding)

(MAKES 8 SERVINGS)

2 packets (80 g each) strawberry jelly
500 ml (2 cups) boiling water
1 tin (397 g) condensed milk
1 tin (410 g) evaporated milk, chilled

TOPPING
fresh strawberries, rinsed thoroughly
  and leaves removed
icing sugar
a few drops vinegar
a few drops appropriate liqueur (optional)
250 ml (1 cup) cream
25 ml (2 T) castor sugar
10 ml (2 t) vanilla essence

1. Dissolve the jelly in boiling water and stir in the condensed milk. Allow to cool, then refrigerate until cold.

2. Whip the evaporated milk until stiff, then gradually beat in the almost-set jelly. Spoon into a dessert bowl, cover with cling wrap and refrigerate until set.

3. TOPPING: Arrange the strawberries in a single layer in a container and sift the icing sugar over. Sprinkle the vinegar and liqueur (if used) over. Cover and refrigerate until the pudding has set.

4. Whip the cream until almost stiff and add the castor sugar and vanilla. Beat until stiff. Spoon into a piping bag fitted with a rose nozzle and pipe rosettes on top of the set pudding. Arrange the strawberries on top and serve.

VARIATIONS

● Use 500 ml (2 cups) cream instead of the evaporated milk. Whip the cream until stiff peaks form, then fold carefully into the jelly mixture before it sets.

● Use orange, lemon or lime jelly instead of strawberry jelly and decorate with macerated orange slices.

● Use pineapple jelly and stir 1 tin (410 g) drained, crushed pineapple into the melted jelly. Decorate with fresh pineapple slices and strawberries, or with halved pineapple rings and glacé cherries.

● Use green plum or lime jelly. Place 2 tins (115 g each) granadilla pulp in a mixing bowl and sprinkle the jelly powder over. Pour boiling water over and stir until the jelly has dissolved. Pour through a sieve and return ¼ of pips to the jelly. Discard the remaining pips. Complete as described above.

● Peach, apricot, raspberry or cherry jelly can also be used. Decorate with appropriate fruit.

Rhubarb fool

(MAKES 4 SERVINGS)

In the language of food, a fool is completely different from those idiots who write on walls and glasses. It is a centuries-old English dessert made from fresh or canned fruit, and decorated with the same fruit. Gooseberries, sliced quinces, guavas (pips removed) or other fruit may be used instead of the rhubarb.

125 ml (½ cup) water
100 g (125 ml/½ cup) sugar
500 ml (2 cups) cleaned, chopped rhubarb
5 ml (1 t) ground ginger (optional)
375 ml (1½ cups) cream

1. Place the water and sugar in a saucepan and stir over low heat until the sugar has dissolved. Increase the heat and boil for 3 minutes. Spoon the rhubarb into the syrup and sprinkle the ginger over (if used). Cover, reduce the heat and simmer for ± 20 minutes until the rhubarb is tender. Mash, rub through a sieve and leave to cool completely. Refrigerate until ice-cold.

2. Beat the cream stiffly and fold ⅓ into the rhubarb mixture. Add the rhubarb mixture to the rest of the cream and fold in, using the figure 8 method. Spoon into 8 tall glasses, cover with cling wrap and refrigerate. Serve just as it is, on a small, doiley-lined plate, with a long-handled spoon.

VARIATION

Add 4 very ripe bananas, puréed with 25 ml (2 T) lemon juice, to the cooked rhubarb. Add the grated rind of 2 lemons and mix. Refrigerate until ice-cold. Use 500 ml (2 cups) cream. Fill glasses, sprinkle 12,5 ml (1 T) soft brown sugar over and cover with cling wrap. Refrigerate overnight until the sugar has melted. (Makes 8 servings).

Chocolate mousse

(MAKES 8-12 SERVINGS)

2 large slabs (400 g) dark chocolate,
*   broken into squares*
325 g (325 ml/1 cup plus 6 T) unsalted
*   butter, cubed and chilled until ice-cold*
10 ml (2 t) fine instant coffee powder
8 jumbo eggs
50-75 ml (4-6 T) rum or
*   Kalahari Thirstland*
1 ml (pinch) salt
250 ml (1 cup) cream (optional)
25 ml (2 T) brandy, rum or
*   Kalahari Thirstland (optional)*

1. Place the chocolate in a glass mixing bowl and place over a saucepan of barely simmering water. Leave for 5 minutes. Stir with a wooden spoon until the chocolate melts and is smooth and shiny. Remove a few cubes of butter at a time from the refrigerator and stir into the chocolate. Do not add the next batch before the first has dissolved completely – or the mixture will lose its shine and be more and more difficult to stir. Continue stirring in the ice-cold butter. Stir in the coffee powder. When all the butter has been added, the mixture will be like thin cream. Remove from the heat.

2. Spoon the mixture into the bowl of a food processor and switch on the machine. Break and separate the eggs, one at a time. Keep the egg yolk in the half shell and drop it down the feeder tube of the processor, into the chocolate mixture, with the motor running. Add all the egg yolks in this way. Place the egg whites in a mixing bowl that has been wiped out with a vinegar-soaked cloth. Keep the motor running until the chocolate mixture is thick and very shiny. Pulse in the rum. Spoon the chocolate mixture into a clean mixing bowl.

3. Whisk the egg whites and salt until stiff peaks just start to form. Add ⅓ of the egg whites to the chocolate mixture and stir in. Add the chocolate mixture to the rest of the egg whites and fold in, using the figure 8 method. Spoon into an attractive glass pudding dish, individual pudding dishes or long-stemmed glasses and refrigerate until set.

4. OPTIONAL: The cream and brandy can be whipped together until stiff and folded into the chocolate mixture after the egg whites have been folded in. Complete as described above and refrigerate until set.

5. TOPPING: In the Basque region between Spain and France, the mousse was traditionally set in small chocolate mousse pots and served in the pots, on a doiley-lined small plate. The mousse was decorated with a cream rosette and a crystallised violet. Here, the mousse is still served with a cream rosette, and glacé cherries. These days, we decorate it with chocolate leaves.

Baked custard

(MAKES 8-10 SERVINGS)

South Africans are fond of serving sauce with a pudding. For this reason, extra sugar is melted to make more sauce, which is served separately with the baked custard.

CARAMEL
600 g (750 ml/3 cups) sugar
250 ml (1 cup) boiling water
10 ml (2 t) vanilla essence
25 ml (2 T) brandy

CUSTARD
750 ml (3 cups) milk
8 extra-large egg yolks
6 extra-large eggs
10 ml (2 t) vanilla essence
2-3 drops almond essence
50 ml (4 T) Van der Hum,
*   brandy or rum*

TO SERVE
orange segments, cut from the membranes
*   and macerated in brandy*

1. CARAMEL: Melt the sugar in a large, dry pan over *moderate* heat, stirring constantly with a large, two-pronged fork. The sugar will first become hot, then begin to melt from below and turn light brown here and there. *Stir constantly.* Remove the pan from the heat as soon as most of the sugar has melted. Continue stirring until the sugar has dissolved *completely*. If the sugar mixture is too hot, it will go very dark and have a bitter taste. Some people like it this way. Make sure that the sugar has dissolved completely. Spoon ⅓ of the caramel into a loaf pan ± 100 x 200 x 62,5 mm (4 x 8 x 2½ in) and tilt the pan to ensure that the base is covered with caramel. Set aside to harden. Grease the sides of the pan – which are not covered with caramel – lightly with oil.

2. Place the pan containing the rest of the caramel back over moderate heat and add boiling water, a little at a time, stirring constantly. The caramel syrup must dissolve in the water. Remove the pan from the heat as soon as the caramel syrup has dissolved completely and set aside to cool completely. Add the vanilla and brandy and spoon into a sauce boat. Cover and refrigerate (this sauce will be used later).

3. CUSTARD: Mix the milk and sugar in a saucepan and stir over low heat until the sugar has dissolved. Remove from the heat and allow to cool. Meanwhile, beat the egg yolks, eggs, essences and liqueur. Beat in the cooled milk mixture and skim off the foam that forms on top. Pour the mixture through a sieve into the prepared loaf pan. Preheat the oven to 160 °C (325 °F). Place the loaf pan in a baking pan and pour enough boiling water into the baking pan to come halfway up the sides of the loaf pan. Bake for 5 minutes. Reduce the temperature to 120 °C (250 °F) and bake for a further 60-70 minutes until the custard is just firm in the centre when you press your palm *lightly* onto the surface. Remove from the oven and allow to cool in the pan of water. Remove from the water and cool completely. Cover with cling wrap and refrigerate for at least 6 hours.

4. TO SERVE: Turn the baked custard out onto a flat plate. Slice, place a slice on each plate and surround with orange segments. Pour some of the extra sauce over and serve.

Tirami-sú

(MAKES 8 SERVINGS)

Italian desserts, apart from ice cream – especially cassata and *zuppa inglese* – did not gain popularity in South Africa. The exception is tirami-sú. Like cassata, the name has two meanings, which should not be confused: there is a dessert version and a teatime cake version.

10 ml (2 t) gelatine
500 ml (2 cups) strong coffee, cooled
24 sponge fingers
6 extra-large eggs, separated
100 ml (8 T) castor sugar
2 tubs (250 g each) mascarpone
1 ml (pinch) salt
200 g dark chocolate, coarsely grated

1. Sprinkle the gelatine over 50 ml (4 T) water in a cup. Microwave on 100% power for 20-30 seconds or place the cup in a saucepan of hot water and melt it over moderate heat. Stir and skim off the foam. Remove the cup from the saucepan of hot water. Allow gelatine to cool completely.

2. Pour the coffee into a shallow container, dip 12 sponge fingers in it, one at a time, and arrange them side by side in a rectangular or square dish.

3. Beat the egg yolks thoroughly, then beat the castor sugar in gradually. Continue beating until the sugar has dissolved and the egg mixture reaches the ribbon stage – until it is very stiff and not at all runny. Carefully stir in the mascarpone. Stir in the cold gelatine. Whisk the egg whites with a pinch of salt until stiff peaks form but the mixture is not dry. Fold ⅓ of the egg whites into the egg yolk mixture, using the figure 8 method. Add the egg yolk mixture to the egg whites and fold in. Spoon half the mixture over the sponge fingers in the dish and sprinkle half the chocolate over.

4. Dip the remaining 12 sponge fingers into the coffee and arrange in the dish. Spoon the remaining mascarpone mixture over and sprinkle the rest of the chocolate on top. Cover with cling wrap and refrigerate until set. Cut into 8 blocks and serve on a flat plate, without any decoration.

VARIATION

Use all the chocolate on the centre layer and sift cocoa, mixed with a little ground cinnamon, over the top.

Chocolate sauce

(MAKES 250 ML/1 CUP)

This delectable recipe may be served hot or cold. And in addition, the base can be refrigerated for weeks.

BASE
125 ml (½ cup) cream
10 ml (2 t) fine instant coffee powder
1 large slab (200 g) dark chocolate, broken into squares
1 large (100 g) Bar One, thinly sliced
1 ml (pinch) salt

TO SERVE
milk or cream
25 ml (2 T) liqueur (Van der Hum, Kalahari Thirstland, ginger, coffee, apricot or any citrus liqueur) or brandy, rum or whisky

1. Heat the cream to boiling point and stir in the coffee powder. Remove from the heat, add the chocolate, Bar One and salt. Cover and set aside for 3 minutes. Beat until smooth. The mixture is very thick.

2. HOT SAUCE: Heat the chocolate cream over moderate heat and stir in just enough milk to make a runny, fairly thick sauce. Stir in the liqueur. Pour over vanilla ice cream and sprinkle chopped nuts over.

3. COLD SAUCE: Thin the chocolate cream with liqueur and stir in enough cream to make a thick, but still runny, sauce.

Coulis (Fruit sauce)

A coulis is used mainly as a garnish for ready-made ice cream. Follow one of two basic methods: cooked sauces and raw or uncooked sauces.

COOKED SAUCES

The easiest method is to purée canned fruit, thin it with a little of the canning liquid and rub it through a sieve. Fruit that you have poached in sugar syrup yourself may also, of course, be used. The poaching liquid for fruit is usually prepared in the proportion of one part sugar to one part water. Spoon into a saucepan, stir over low heat until the sugar has dissolved then increase the heat, boil for 3 minutes and spoon fruit to be poached into the boiling syrup. Simmer until fruit is soft. Increase the quantity of sugar for sour fruit like plums or apricots.

UNCOOKED SAUCES

Fresh fruit, peeled and – if necessary – stoned, is placed in a container and then sprinkled with castor sugar. Use less sugar for sweet fruit and more for sour fruit. If berries are used, sprinkle a little liqueur over, especially Maraschino or Kirsch, and cover with cling wrap. Macerate for 2-12 hours in the refrigerator. Purée fruit and rub through a sieve. Thin purée to the desired thickness with sugar syrup, wine, water, liqueur or fruit juice, or a combination.

Rose sauce

(MAKES 1 LITRE/4 CUPS)

This sauce may be poured, just as it is, over vanilla ice cream served with fresh strawberries; alternatively, boil strawberries and pureé with the sauce, then rub through a sieve and serve as a cooked fruit sauce. See Coulis above for making the uncooked version. This sauce is also excellent with snow pudding (p. 164).

2 large, red beetroot, rinsed, peeled and coarsely grated
1 litre (4 cups) water
thinly pared rind of 2 lemons
800 g (4 x 250 ml/4 cups) sugar
10 ml (2 t) or more rose essence (not rose water)

1. Place the beetroot, water and rind in a saucepan, heat to boiling point, reduce the heat and simmer for 30 minutes. Strain through a gauze or muslin cloth.

2. Add the sugar to the beetroot water and stir over low heat until the sugar has dissolved. Boil to a fairly thick syrup and remove from the heat. Halve the lemons (from which the rind was pared) and squeeze out the juice. Stir the juice and rose essence into the syrup. Pour through a funnel into a bottle. Cover and refrigerate.

Steamed pudding

(MAKES 12-16 SERVINGS)

400 g (500 ml/2 cups) sugar
375 g suet (see Hint) or 250 g (250 ml/1 cup) butter
5 eggs
600 g (5 x 250 ml/5 cups) cake flour, sifted
500 g (2 cups) crumbs, made from day-old bread
25 ml (2 T) mixed spice
1 ml (pinch) salt
450 g (750 ml/3 cups) raisins
2 packets (500 g) dates, chopped
50 ml (4 T) smooth apricot jam
30 ml (6 t) vinegar
12,5 ml (1 T) bicarbonate of soda

1. Cream the sugar and butter and add the eggs one at a time. Sift the flour over and sprinkle the crumbs, spice and salt over and mix to blend with a large spoon.

2. Mix the raisins, dates, jam and vinegar and stir in. Dissolve the bicarbonate of soda in a little water and stir in.

3. Sift a small teaspoonful of flour over a pudding cloth and spoon the dough onto it. Gather the mixture up tightly in the cloth and tie the cloth just above your hand. If the pudding is tied too tightly, it will not have room to rise. Place on an inverted plate in a saucepan of boiling water. Cover and steam for 2½-3 hours. The pudding may also be steamed in a pudding mould or tin. Serve with Brandy sauce (p. 178).

HINT: It is better to use suet if the pudding is to be steamed in a cloth. Mix the suet and sugar and beat in the eggs one at a time, so that the sugar dissolves.

Old-fashioned cinnamon dumplings

(MAKES 8-10 SERVINGS)

This recipe comes from the handwritten cookery book of Mrs Hybie Kolver of Boshof in the Free State.

240 g (500 ml/2 cups) cake flour
10 ml (2 t) baking powder
3 ml (½ t) salt
125 g (125 ml/½ cup) butter
4 extra-large eggs
30 ml (2 large T) sugar

TO SERVE
200 g (250 ml/1 cup) sugar
25 ml (2 T) mixed spice
1 ml (pinch) salt
100 ml (8 T) brandy
250 g (250 ml/1 cup) butter
stick cinnamon

1. Sift the flour, baking powder and salt. Rub in the butter with your fingertips or cut butter into small cubes and place it in a food processor with flour mixture. Pulse until mixture resembles coarse crumbs.
2. Beat eggs and sugar until light and sugar has dissolved completely. Cut egg mixture into flour mixture with a spatula, until just mixed. *Do not* mix too much, and do not mix again after it has been mixed once. The mixture should not be too slack or too stiff – it should be like a drop scone mixture: not runny, but not so stiff that it can be rolled out. In dry areas, it could be necessary to add 1-2 t ice-cold water to achieve the desired results.
3. Mix sugar and spices and set aside.
4. Fill a large saucepan with a tight-fitting lid and as wide as possible a diameter (the shallower and wider, the better) to about 50 mm (2 in) deep with cold water. Add the salt, stir and heat to boiling point. Dip a pudding spoon in boiling water, shape a dumpling and place it in the water. Repeat and shape 4 dumplings – at the most 6 – at a time. Cover and steam for 10 minutes over moderately low heat. Spoon out with a slotted spoon and place in a greased baking dish. Sprinkle some of the spiced sugar over, then some of the brandy. Cover and keep warm. Add more boiling water and repeat with next batch, until all the mixture has been used.
5. Prepare the sauce once the dumplings have been steamed: Using the saucepan in which the dumplings were steamed, stir the butter into the water remaining in the saucepan and heat to boiling point. Skim off any foam. Add the remaining spiced sugar and brandy and stir until the sugar has dissolved.
6. Pour hot sauce through a sieve over hot dumplings and serve immediately with stick cinnamon and, if desired, lemon wedges.

Buttermilk pudding

(MAKES 4-6 SERVINGS)

3 eggs
200 g (250 ml/1 cup) sugar
25 ml (2 T) melted butter, without foam
120 g (250 ml/1 cup) cake flour
5 ml (1 t) baking powder
3 ml (½ t) salt
750 ml (3 cups) buttermilk
500 ml (2 cups) milk

TO SERVE
grated nutmeg

SAUCE
500 ml (2 cups) cream
125 ml (½ cup) honey

1. Beat the eggs and sugar until light and creamy. Add the butter and beat very well.
2. Sift the flour, baking powder and salt and stir into the egg mixture, alternately with the buttermilk and milk.
3. Spoon into a greased baking dish and bake for 1½-2 hours at 160 °C (325 °F), until set. Remove from the oven and grate nutmeg over.
4. SAUCE: Heat the cream and honey in a saucepan until just under boiling point. Serve in a sauce boat. If desired, the pudding can be served with *moskonfyt* (must jam) or honey, instead of the honey cream sauce.

Easy sago pudding

(MAKES 4 SERVINGS)

500 ml (2 cups) milk
50 g (85 ml/⅓ cup) sago
15 g (15 ml/3 t) butter
62,5 ml (¼ cup) sugar
3 ml (½ t) mixed spice
15 ml (3 t) finely grated lemon rind
2 eggs, separated
1 ml (pinch) salt

1. Place the milk in a large saucepan and heat to just under boiling point. Remove from the heat and add the sago. Leave overnight.
2. Heat the saucepan of milk and sago over moderate heat and stir until the sago boils and is transparent. Add a little water, if necessary, but make sure that the sago has swollen completely and no white pieces are visible.
3. Preheat oven to 180 °C (350 °F). Grease a 2 litre (8 cup) baking dish with butter. Reduce heat of plate on which sago was cooked to low and stir in sugar, spice and rind. Stir for 3 minutes until sugar has dissolved completely. Remove from heat and stir in egg yolks, one at a time. Whisk egg whites with salt until stiff peaks just form and fold into sago mixture. Spoon into the baking dish and bake for 30-35 minutes. Serve with poached fresh or dried fruit and stiffly whipped cream.

Vinegar pudding

(MAKES 6 SERVINGS)

SYRUP
750 ml (3 cups) boiling water
400 g (500 ml/2 cups) sugar
250 ml (1 cup) vinegar

BATTER
150 g (185 ml/¾ cup) sugar
250 g (250 ml/1 cup) butter
1 egg
10 ml (2 t) bicarbonate of soda
500 ml (2 cups) milk
360 g (750 ml/3 cups) cake flour, sifted
5 ml (1 t) ground ginger
50 ml (4 T) smooth apricot jam
½ packet (125 g) dates, chopped,
*   or 150 g (250 ml/1 cup) raisins*

1. SYRUP: Mix the water and sugar and stir over low heat until the sugar has dissolved. Add the vinegar and keep warm. If the pudding is to be baked, the vinegar must be added to the sugar syrup and simmered for 3 minutes to cook the vinegar. Keep warm.
2. BATTER: Cream the sugar, butter and egg.
3. Dissolve the bicarbonate of soda in the milk. Sift the flour and ginger and stir into the creamed mixture alternately with the milk mixture. Stir in the jam and dates. Spoon the mixture into the saucepan of boiling syrup, cover and simmer for 2 hours. The pudding may also be baked in a large tube pan at 180 °C (350 °F) for 35-40 minutes: turn out the hot pudding onto a wire rack over a tray or pan and spoon half the boiling syrup over slowly. Return the pudding to the oven for 5 minutes and place on a serving plate. Spoon the rest of the sauce over slowly. Serve hot with custard.

OLD-FASHIONED CINNAMOM DUMPLINGS

Christmas pudding

(MAKES 10-12 SERVINGS)

It is essential to take note of a few points before you proceed with this recipe. It is an example of the importance of taking your time for preparation. The pudding has to be steamed for 8 hours so that the batter will develop a deep, dark brown colour, and for 5 hours when reheated so that the flavours can blend again and develop. Keep your eye on the water level, and add more regularly. *Do not* add cold water – the fall in temperature will result in a doughy texture. In England, suet was traditionally used, but South African tastes prefer butter, which improves the flavour of the pudding.

Do not flambé pudding without noting this warning: protect your hand with a cloth when igniting the pudding. And lastly, sherry or port sauce may be served with the pudding instead of brandy butter.

BATTER
½ packet (50 g / 125 ml / ½ cup) each
*   blanched almonds, walnuts and*
*   Brazil nuts, coarsely chopped*
1 large carrot, scraped and coarsely grated
75 g (125 ml / ½ cup) pitted, shredded prunes
350 g (580 ml / 2⅓ cups) fruit cake mix
*   or a mixture of seedless raisins,*
*   sultanas and currants*
25 g (25 ml / 2 T) shredded mixed citrus peel
125 g (125 ml / ½ cup) butter
grated rind and juice of 1 lemon
grated rind of 2 oranges
120 g (150 ml / ⅗ cup) soft brown sugar
2 extra-large eggs, beaten
50 g (250 ml / 1 cup) fresh brown breadcrumbs
130 g (250 ml / 1 cup) whole-wheat flour
60 g (125 ml / ½ cup) cake flour, sifted
15 ml (3 t) mixed spice
5 ml (1 t) ground cinnamon
200 ml (⅘ cup) stout
25 ml (2 T) brandy
37,5 ml (3 T) molasses

BRANDY BUTTER
125 g (125 ml / ½ cup) unsalted butter
130 g (250 ml / 1 cup) icing sugar, sifted
¼ packet (25 g / 65 ml / ¼ cup) ground
*   almonds*
50 ml (4 T) thick cream
50 ml (4 T) brandy

TO SERVE
fresh holly leaves
10-12 well-scrubbed coins
brandy for flambé

TRADITIONS
Christmas pudding is traditionally mixed in the presence of the entire family, with each family member giving it one stir to bring good luck. There is a tradition in the eating too: make a wish with the first mouthful. If you find a coin in your serving, you will have a prosperous year. Naturally, the cook inserts sparkling clean coins in strategic places in the pudding so that each person can find one.

---

1. BATTER: Mix the nuts, carrot, prunes, fruit cake mix and citrus peel.
2. Beat the butter and stir in the juice and rind. Gradually beat in the sugar, then the eggs, a little at a time. Spoon on top of the fruit mixture, without mixing. Sprinkle the crumbs and whole-wheat flour over. Sift the cake flour, spice and cinnamon and sift over the whole-wheat flour. Mix the stout, brandy and molasses and spoon over the flour mixture. Use a large, strong wooden spoon to mix. Cover the mixture with waxed paper and then with cling wrap and refrigerate overnight.
3. Remove mixture from the refrigerator and beat well.
4. Prepare a muslin cloth (see also Hint): Fold a piece of muslin, half a metre by a metre, to make a double square. Sift half a cup of cake flour generously over the cloth. Spoon the batter into the centre of the cloth, on the flour, and pat it until smooth and slightly rounded. Hold the 4 points of the cloth together and tie cloth as for the Cloutie dumpling on p. 171. Insert a stick through the knot and suspend the cloth over a large saucepan so that it hangs free. Pour enough boiling water into the saucepan to just touch the edge of the cloth. It makes no difference if it is slightly immersed – but no more than 10 mm (⅖ in) – in the water. Cover the saucepan with aluminium foil. Steam for 8 hours, frequently adding more boiling water.
5. Remove the pudding and hold it up in the air. Pour the water from the saucepan, return the pudding to the saucepan and allow to cool for 30 minutes. Shape with your hands into a neat, round ball. Leave it hanging until completely cooled. Remove the cloth and tie the pudding in a clean muslin cloth, lightly sprinkled with flour. Refrigerate for 1 month.
6. BRANDY BUTTER: Beat the butter until softened and stir the icing sugar in gradually. Stir in the almonds, then the cream, a little

at a time. Beat in the brandy, a teaspoonful at a time – if everything is added at once, it will separate.
7. TO SERVE: Spoon the brandy butter into a piping bag with a plain nozzle and pipe rosettes onto a sheet of waxed paper on a baking sheet. Freeze. Reheat the pudding for 5 hours and turn out onto a serving plate. Arrange butter rosettes around the pudding. Decorate with holly leaves. Insert the coins and pour slightly heated brandy over. Ignite and serve, flaming.

HINT: The mixture is enough for 1 large pudding or 10 small ones. When steaming a large pudding, a single layer of muslin is folded in two; for small puddings, a double layer of muslin is folded in two. Small puddings are steamed for 6 hours and reheated for 3 hours. Remember to have a cloth of the same size ready after steaming the pudding(s). The batter may also be steamed in a metal pudding mould with a lid, or a porcelain pudding mould – each with a volume of 1,5 litres (6 cups) – or in a mixing bowl. The latter must be covered with buttered waxed paper before sealing it with aluminium foil.

Baked sago and raisin pudding

(MAKES 8 SERVINGS)

50 ml (4 T) sago
250 ml (1 cup) milk
25 ml (2 T) butter
150 g (185 ml / ¾ cup) sugar
2 eggs, lightly beaten
25 ml (2 T) smooth apricot jam
500 ml (2 cups) fresh breadcrumbs
125 ml (½ cup) seedless raisins or dates
8 ml (1½ t) bicarbonate of soda
12,5 ml (1 T) milk
1 ml (pinch) salt

SAUCE
250 ml (1 cup) cream
25 ml (2 T) honey
10 ml (2 t) vanilla

1. Soak the sago overnight in the milk.
2. Place sago in a saucepan and add 125 ml (½ cup) water. Boil over moderate heat until the sago has swollen up and is cooked.
3. Beat butter and sugar into the sago. Stir until the sugar has dissolved. Stir in the eggs and then the jam. Spoon crumbs on top of the mixture, then the raisins. Mix the bicarbonate of soda with the milk and and spoon over, with

the salt. Stir, spoon into a greased baking dish and bake for 40-45 minutes at 180 °C (350 °F).

4. Make the sauce 5 minutes before the pudding is cooked: Spoon the cream and honey into a small saucepan and heat to boiling point. Remove from heat and stir in the vanilla.

5. Prick the pudding with a fork and pour the hot cream mixture over. Serve with Rose sauce (p. 171).

Cape brandy pudding

(MAKES 10-12 SERVINGS)

BATTER
1 packet (250 g) stoned dates, chopped
250 ml (1 cup) boiling water
5 ml (1 t) bicarbonate of soda
125 g (125 ml/½ cup) butter,
*   at room temperature*
200 g (250 ml/1 cup) soft brown sugar
2 extra-large eggs
240 g (500 ml/2 cups) cake flour, sifted
5 ml (1 t) baking powder
3 ml (½ t) salt
5 ml (1 t) ground cinnamon
3 ml (½ t) ground ginger
1 ml (pinch) grated nutmeg
1 packet (100 g/250 ml/1 cup) walnuts,
*   chopped*
grated rind of 2 oranges

SYRUP
250 g (315 ml/1¼ cups) soft brown sugar
15 g (15 ml/3 t) butter
185 ml (¾ cup) water
1 stick cinnamon
10 ml (2 t) vanilla essence
1 ml (pinch) salt
125 ml (½ cup) brandy

1. IN ADVANCE: Preheat the oven to 180 °C (350 °F). Grease a 250 mm (10 in) diameter pie dish lightly with melted butter or margarine. Place a spoonful of flour in it and shake to coat base and sides. Invert dish and tip lightly to shake off excess flour.

2. Heat the dates and boiling water to boiling point in a saucepan. Remove from the heat, stir in the bicarbonate of soda, allow to foam and set aside.

3. Beat the butter and add the sugar gradually until half the sugar has been added. Beat the eggs until foamy and add, a little at a time. Beat in about half the eggs, followed by the rest of the sugar and eggs. Make sure that the sugar has dissolved.

4. Sift the flour, baking powder, salt, cinnamon, ginger and nutmeg 3 times. Fold the flour mixture into the egg mixture and spoon in the date mixture, nuts and rind. Mix well. Spoon into the pie dish and hollow the centre slightly. Bake for 30-40 minutes.

5. MAKE THE SYRUP: Mix the sugar, butter and water and stir over low heat until the sugar has dissolved. Increase the heat, boil for 1 minute, add the stick of cinnamon and remove from the heat. Set aside for a few minutes before the pudding has finished baking.

6. Remove the cinnamon from the syrup and reheat the syrup to boiling point. Add the vanilla, salt and brandy to the boiling syrup and remove immediately from the heat. Remove the cooked pudding from the oven and prick it. Pour the hot syrup over immediately, but slowly. Serve hot or cold with egg custard and/or slightly sweetened whipped cream and/or vanilla ice cream.

VARIATIONS
● Use 10 ml (2 t) mixed spice instead of the ground cinnamon, ginger and nutmeg.
● Replace the nuts with any other available nuts, except peanuts.
● Soak ½ packet (125 g) mixed, grated citrus peel overnight in 50 ml (4 T) brandy or Van der Hum. Omit the grated orange rind and stir peel mixture into the batter with the date mixture.

Baked glacé fruit pudding

(MAKES 8 SERVINGS)

The popularity of this kind of pudding reached a peak in the first half of the century, when it was common to make preserves, either whole or chunks. Today, people prefer buying the glacé fruit.

125 g (125 ml/½ cup) butter
105 g (125 ml/½ cup) castor sugar
2 eggs, lightly beaten
130 g (250 ml/1 cup) self-raising flour
1 ml (pinch) salt
60 g glacé fruit, chopped
30 ml (6 t) appropriate liqueur

TO SERVE
icing sugar

1. IN ADVANCE: Grease a Gugelhopf 750 ml (3 cups) tube pan lightly with margarine. Add in a spoonful of flour and shake to coat

sides and tube. Invert and tap lightly to shake off excess flour. Preheat the oven to 180 °C (350 °F).

2. Beat the butter until soft and add the castor sugar gradually. Beat until light and fluffy. Gradually beat in the eggs. Sift the flour and salt and sift over the butter mixture. Fold in with a large metal spoon.

3. Stir in the fruit mixture and liquer. Spoon into the pan and bake for 40 minutes. Test with a skewer. Turn out and sift icing sugar over. Serve hot with hot custard, Brandy custard (p. 167) or Rose sauce (p. 171).

VARIATIONS
Choose one of the following combinations:
● glacé cherries and angelica with cherry liqueur
● watermelon preserve with brandy
● green fig preserve with maraschino
● glacé pineapple and ginger preserve with rum
● glacé apricots and ginger preserve with ginger liqueur or rum
● pamplemousse or citron preserve, mixed with 10 ml (2 t) grated orange or lemon peel, with Van der Hum or Kalahari Thirstland (*Do not* use glacé orange segments.)

Velvet dumplings

(MAKES 6-8 SERVINGS)

This pudding falls somewhere between a *melktert* (milk tart) filling and a dumpling – making us remember the past with nostalgia, but nevertheless with a modern stamp on it.

1 stick cinnamon or a small piece
   (12 mm/½ in) peeled, fresh ginger root
1 piece dried naartjie peel
1 litre (4 cups) milk
45 ml (3 large T) cornflour
30 ml (2 large T) custard powder
30 ml (2 large T) cake flour
1 ml (pinch) salt
2 extra-large eggs, separated
1 ml (a few drops) almond essence

SAUCE
250 g (250 ml/1 cup) butter,
   melted and foam skimmed off

TO SERVE
100 g (125 ml/½ cup) castor sugar
10 ml (2 t) ground cinnamon or mixed spice
50 ml (4 T) Van der Hum and/or brandy

1. Heat the stick of cinnamon, peel and milk for 30 minutes in a small saucepan over low heat. Remove from heat and cool completely. Remove and discard the cinnamon and peel.
2. Mix cornflour, custard powder, flour and salt. Mix to a paste with a little of the flavoured milk. Add more milk and beat until smooth, runny and lump free. Heat the remaining milk until hot in a saucepan. Stir in the flour mixture. Continue stirring until mixture reaches boiling point and forms a thick 'porridge'. Take care that it does not burn. Remove from heat and immediately beat in egg yolks, one at a time. Cover with greased waxed paper, directly on the surface of the mixture, so that a skin does not form on top.
3. Whisk the egg whites, an extra pinch of salt and the essence until the mixture forms soft peaks. Fold the egg white mixture into the 'porridge' mixture. Spoon half the butter into a greased baking dish. Drop large spoonfuls of the 'porridge' mixture into the dish. Spoon the rest of the butter over the dumplings.
4. TO SERVE: Mix castor sugar and spices and sprinkle over dumplings. Place in a preheated oven at 120 °C (250 °F) for a few minutes until sugar has melted. The dessert may also be kept warm in the warming drawer. Sprinkle with Van der Hum and serve.

VELVET DUMPLINGS

Rice dumplings

(MAKES 6-8 SERVINGS)

DUMPLINGS
185 ml (¾ cup) Bonnet jasmine rice
500 ml (2 cups) water
75 g (125 ml/½ cup) currants
100 g (200 ml/⅘ cup) cake flour, sifted
1 ml (pinch) salt
8 ml (1½ t) baking powder
2 extra-large eggs
10 ml (2 t) vanilla essence
75 g (75 ml/6 T) butter, melted
milk, if needed

TO POACH
3 pieces cassia or 1 stick cinnamon

TO SERVE
cinnamon sugar

APRICOT AND CINNAMON SAUCE
250 ml (1 cup) apricot juice
25 ml (2 T) lemon juice
50 ml (4 T) smooth apricot jam
5 ml (1 t) ground ginger
10 ml (2 t) ground cinnamon
10 ml (2 t) cornflour
65 ml (¼ cup) liquid in which dumplings
   were cooked, cooled

1. Boil the rice in water in a saucepan with a tight-fitting lid over low heat until almost cooked and the water has almost all been absorbed. Add the currants and boil until the rice is cooked and the currants are plump. Remove from the heat and allow to cool.
2. Sift flour, salt and baking powder into a mixing bowl and make a well in the centre. Spoon rice mixture into the well and mix with a large, two-pronged fork. Beat eggs and vanilla essence and beat in half the butter. Mix egg and rice mixture and add a little milk, if necessary, to make a soft, creamy mixture that is not too runny. Set aside for 10 minutes.
3. TO POACH: Pour water to 75 mm (3 in) deep in a large pan or saucepan with a tight-fitting lid. Add the cassia and heat to boiling point. Dip a spoon in the hot liquid and drop spoonfuls of mixture into the boiling water. Cover, reduce the heat and simmer for 10 minutes. Cooked dumplings will rise to the surface.
4. Remove the dumplings with a slotted spoon and transfer to a heated serving dish. Sprinkle cinnamon sugar generously over the dumplings and spoon the rest of the butter over. (Spoon over more melted butter, if desired.)
5. MEANWHILE, MAKE THE SAUCE: Heat juices, jam, ginger and cinnamon in a small saucepan to just under boiling point. Mix cornflour with water in which dumplings were cooked and stir until smooth. Remove juice mixture from the heat and stir in the cornflour mixture. Return to moderate heat and stir constantly until the mixture reaches boiling point, thickens and clarifies. Spoon the sauce over the dumplings.

Bread and butter pudding

(MAKES 6 SERVINGS)

Bread pudding has a long history. The first recorded recipe comes from the writings of Aspicius, in the Roman era, when it was made from milk, eggs, honey and breadcrumbs. Old German cookbooks call for pumpernickel, and the French use baguettes sliced diagonally and baked with cream and eggs. Mrs Beeton's recipe is the one that caught on here.

4-6 thin slices white bread, crusts removed,
   buttered on both sides and cut into triangles
butter
3 ml (½ t) freshly grated nutmeg
3 ml (½ t) ground cinnamon
50 g (85 ml/⅓ cup) sultanas or currants
400 ml (1⅗ cup) milk
2 large eggs
25 g (30 ml/6 t) sugar

1. Arrange the bread, triangles slightly overlapping and points facing upwards, in a baking dish greased with butter. Season with nutmeg and cinnamon and sprinkle the sultanas over.
2. Heat the milk until hot but *not* boiling. Beat the eggs and sugar in a mixing bowl and season with nutmeg and cinnamon if desired. Stir the hot milk into the egg mixture, pour it over the bread and allow it to stand for 10 minutes. (Leaving it to stand is the secret of bread pudding. The bread swells up, expands and absorbs liquid.) Bake for 30 minutes in a preheated oven at 180 °C (350 °F).

APPLE VARIATION
Cube the buttered bread. Peel 6 apples, core each and cut into 8 slices. Cover the apple slices with lemon juice. Arrange the bread and apples in a greased baking dish. Sprinkle over 150 g (250 ml/1 cup) fruit cake mix, soaked in 75 ml (6 T) brandy. Double the quantity of custard mixture (above), spoon over and allow to stand for 30 minutes. Mix 75 ml (6 T) castor sugar with 10 ml (2 t) ground cinnamon and sprinkle over. Bake as above. The apples may also be fried in butter until golden brown and then flambéd with brandy before adding .

Pancakes

(MAKES 48-60 PANCAKES)

This recipe may be halved successfully.

500 g (4 x 250 ml / 4 cups) cake
*   flour, sifted*
5 ml (1 t) baking powder
10 ml (2 t) salt
12,5 ml (1 T) castor sugar
8 extra-large eggs
1 litre (4 cups) milk
25 ml (2 T) brandy or lemon juice
250 ml (1 cup) oil

TO SERVE
cinnamon or spice castor sugar
lemon slices

1. Sift the flour, baking powder, salt and castor sugar. Beat the eggs and stir the milk in gradually. Stir the milk mixture gradually into the flour mixture, first stirring to a smooth paste with just enough of the milk mixture. Stir the rest of the milk mixture in with a wooden spoon. Pour the batter through a sieve. Using a food processor makes this process easier.
2. Beat in first the brandy and then the oil in a thin stream. Make sure that the oil is completely incorporated into the pancake mixture. Leave to stand for about 1 hour at room temperature.
3. Stir well. Test for thickness: Fill a large soup ladle with batter, lift it high above the mixing bowl and let it run back into the mixing bowl in a thin stream. The mixture should be like thin cream. If the batter is too thick, stir in a little cold tap water. The batter is now ready to be used.
4. Heat a crêpe (pancake) pan or pans over moderate heat. It must not be too hot, as the batter will burn and stick before it is cooked. If your crêpe pan is correctly sealed, 1-2 ml (¼ t) oil will be enough to cook the first pancake. Drop a spoonful of batter into the pan and tilt the pan so that the batter coats the base completely. The thinner, the better. Cook the pancake for ± 60 seconds on one side, turn and cook for a further 30 seconds.
5. TO SERVE: The cooked pancakes may be left to cool completely, or kept warm over a saucepan of hot water. Spread the pancakes left to cool lightly with butter, sprinkle with the chosen sugar and fold in quarters or roll up. Place them on a microwave-safe plate and reheat them in the microwave at 100% power: 1 minute for every 4 pancakes. Serve with lemon slices.

FOLK WISDOM
In the past it was believed that the first pancake was always unsuccessful and it was the cook's to eat; the rest were for the family.

Cape pancakes

(MAKES 6 SERVINGS)

First prepare the ginger butter and the batter. Refrigerate the butter to firm while the batter is left to thicken. Remember: Making pancakes is a family effort – one cooks, one spreads the jam, one spreads the butter and the fourth folds up the pancakes. Read again (left) how to keep the pancakes hot or to reheat them afterwards.

½ quantity pancake mixture (see left)

GINGER BUTTER
250 g (250 ml / 1 cup) butter
100 g (125 ml / ½ cup) castor sugar
25 ml (2 T) finely grated lemon
*   and / or orange rind*
25 ml (2 T) ginger liqueur or Van der Hum
25 ml (2 T) brandy

OTHER INGREDIENTS
125 ml (½ cup) very smooth apricot jam
5 ml (1 t) vanilla essence
few drops almond essence
48 pancakes, cooked as recipe

1. Beat the butter until light and fluffy and stir castor sugar in gradually. Stir in half the rind. Beat in half the liqueur and half the brandy. Repeat with remaining rind, liqueur and brandy. Do not add rind, liqueur and brandy all at the same time – the mixture could separate. The sugar should have dissolved completely. Refrigerate until firm, but not hard.
2. Heat the jam until runny and beat in the essences. Spread thinly over the pancakes and spread the ginger butter on top. Fold into quarters and serve.

Brandy sauce

(MAKES 1 LITRE / 4 CUPS)

600 g (750 ml / 3 cups) sugar
750 ml (3 cups) water
15 g (15 ml / 3 t) butter
3 sticks cinnamon
1 ml (pinch) salt
125 ml (½ cup) brandy
15 ml (3 t) vanilla essence

1. Place the sugar in a saucepan, stir in the water and heat over low heat. Stir until the sugar has dissolved completely. Add the butter, cinnamon and salt and boil for 5 minutes. Remove from the heat and leave to infuse for at least 1 hour.
2. Remove the cinnamon and add the brandy and vanilla. Use with steamed Cloutie dumpling (suet pudding) and to pour over any other baked puddings.
3. AS A DESSERT SAUCE: Reduce the sugar syrup, after infusion with the cinnamon, over moderate heat until 500 ml (2 cups) remains. Dissolve 25 ml (2 T) cornflour or custard powder in a little water and stir into the sauce. Boil until the sauce clarifies, remove from the heat and stir in the brandy and vanilla. If preferred, beat 50 ml (4 T) ice-cold butter into the hot sauce, knob by knob, at the end.

Port sauce

(MAKES 250 ML / 1 CUP)

120 g (150 ml / ⅗ cup) sugar
125 ml (½ cup) water
75 g (75 ml / 6 T) butter
15 ml (3 t) cornflour, rubbed through a sieve
grated rind and juice of 2 lemons
grated rind and juice of 1 orange
150 ml (⅗ cup) port
grated nutmeg

1. Place the sugar in a saucepan and stir in the water. Heat over low heat, stirring until the sugar has dissolved. Increase the heat and boil for 15 minutes. Mix the butter and cornflour. Remove the syrup from the heat and beat in the cornflour mixture. Return the mixture to the heat and boil for 3 minutes, stirring constantly.
2. Remove from the heat and stir in the rind, juice and port. Season well with nutmeg. Heat to just under boiling point. Remove from the heat and allow to stand for 1 hour. Pour, through a sieve placed over a funnel, into a clean bottle and store in the refrigerator. Heat over low heat before use.

CAPE PANCAKES

Orange syrup sauce

(MAKES 500 ML/2 CUPS)

Many South Africans do not like alcohol in desserts. Orange syrup sauce is ideal for pouring over any baked pudding.

100 g (125 ml/½ cup) sugar
50 ml (4 T) water
finely grated rind and juice of 6 oranges to
*   make at least 500 ml (2 cups) orange juice*
50 g (50 ml/4 T) salted butter

1. Mix the sugar and water in a large saucepan and stir over very low heat until the sugar has dissolved. Add the grated rind and half the juice and heat gradually to boiling point. Reduce the heat and simmer for 15 minutes. Remove from the heat, allow to stand for 1 hour and pour through a sieve.
2. Add the remaining juice and return to moderate heat. Beat in the butter, knob by knob, and serve.

VARIATION: SPICED ORANGE SAUCE
Prepare as above, but add a clove and a small piece of stick cinnamon or cassia to the sugar syrup while it cooks.

Milk tart

(MAKES 6-8 SERVINGS)

Serve the milk tart lukewarm as a dessert, with preserves – whole or chunks.

500 g puff pastry

FILLING
500 ml (2 cups) milk
peel of 1 naartjie
1 stick cinnamon
15 ml (3 t) cornflour
45 ml (3 large T) cake flour
1 ml (pinch) salt
60 g (75 ml/6 T) sugar
4 extra-large eggs, separated
15 g (15 ml/3 t) butter
1 ml (few drops) almond essence

TO SERVE
cinnamon sugar

STEAMED PUDDING

1. IN ADVANCE: Line the rim of the tart dish with a 40 mm wide strip of puff pastry. Brush a little ice-cold water over and cover with another strip of pastry. Brush again with water. Cut out a round of puff pastry 15 mm wider than the tart dish, place in the dish and crimp the edge. Brush a little whisked egg white over the pastry in the base and refrigerate. Preheat the oven to 220 °C (450 °F).
2. Heat the milk, naartjie peel and stick of cinnamon until hot and leave to infuse for 45 minutes. Heat to boiling point. Pour through a sieve. Mix the cornflour, flour, salt, sugar and egg yolks to a paste with a little of the flavoured milk. Stir into the milk and return to the stove. Beat until the mixture is cooked and thick. Remove from the heat and spoon the butter on top. Wait until the butter has melted, then tilt the saucepan until the butter covers the custard. Whisk the egg whites and essence until stiff peaks form and fold into the custard mixture. Spoon into pastry case and bake for 10 minutes. Reduce the heat to 180 °C (350 °F) and bake for a further 15 minutes.
3. Sprinkle cinnamon sugar over the tart and serve lukewarm.

HINT: If available, heat 3-4 apricot kernels with the milk. It is an old Boland custom to beat a knife point (less than 1 ml) of turmeric into the cooked custard mixture. Sometimes, 6-8 cardamom seeds are heated with the milk.

Van der Hum tart

(MAKES 8 SERVINGS)

Lesley Faull introduced this recipe; this version is my adaptation.

BASE
30 g (30 ml/6 t) butter
30 g (40 ml/8 t) sugar
50 g (125 ml/½ cup) finely chopped
*   Brazil nuts*
40 g (125 ml/½ cup) lightly roasted coconut

FILLING
4 extra-large egg yolks
100 g (125 ml/½ cup) sugar
10 g (15 ml/3 t) gelatine
65 ml (¼ cup) water
grated rind of 1 orange
250 ml (1 cup) Crème fraîche (p. 34) or cream
75 ml (6 T) Van der Hum
250 ml (1 cup) gooseberries,
*   washed and patted dry*

TO SERVE
250 ml (1 cup) Chantilly cream (p. 182)
gooseberries in their 'capes'

1. BASE: Beat the butter and sugar until light and fluffy. Add the nuts and coconut and mix. Press into a 200 mm (8 in) diameter tart dish. Place in the refrigerator. Heat the oven to 180 °C (350 °F) and bake the crust for ± 15 minutes.
2. FILLING: Beat the egg yolks and sugar over steam until the mixture is thick and light. Meanwhile, sprinkle the gelatine over the water and leave to sponge. Clarify in the microwave at 100% power for 40 seconds, or over steam on a stove. Stir the hot gelatine mixture into the hot egg yolk mixture. Remove from heat and pour mixture through a sieve into a clean mixing bowl. Stir in orange rind. Place mixture over ice cubes and ice-water and stir until mixture is just about to set. In the meantime, beat cream and Van der Hum until the first stiff peaks form. Fold cream mixture into egg yolk mixture. Spoon gooseberries into tart base and spread evenly. Cover with Van der Hum mixture and leave in refrigerator to set.
3. TO SERVE: Spoon cream into a piping bag with a rose nozzle and pipe rosettes onto the set filling. Finish off each rosette with a gooseberry – pull each 'cape' back to make it stand erect to resemble a dried leaf. Serve a small slice of tart with an individual helping of Snow pudding (p. 164) on Strawberry coulis (p. 171).

VARIATION
Orange segments or any other chunky citrus jam cut into strips may be used for this recipe instead of gooseberries.

Corn flake tart

(MAKES 6-8 SERVINGS)

In the 1950s the Afrikaans rural communities referred to this tart as *Engelse melktert* (English milk tart or Post Toastie tart).

BASE
65 g (65 ml/ ¼ cup) butter
250 ml (1 cup) crushed Corn flakes
50 g (65 ml/ ½ cup) sugar
10 ml (2 t) ground cinnamon

FILLING
25 ml (2 T) cornflour
100 g (125 ml/ ½ cup) sugar
3 extra-large eggs, separated
5 ml (1 t) vanilla essence
500 ml (2 cups) milk
12,5 ml (1 T) butter
1 ml (pinch) salt
50 ml (4 T) castor sugar

1. BASE: Melt butter in a saucepan, remove from heat, add Corn flakes, sugar and cinnamon and mix well. Set aside 25 ml (2 T) of mixture. Spoon remaining mixture into a 200-225 mm (8-9 in) tart dish and press in firmly, using the back of a spoon.
2. FILLING: Mix the cornflour and the sugar. Beat the egg yolks and the vanilla and add to the cornflour mixture. Add a little of the milk and stir to a smooth, runny paste.
3. Heat the rest of the milk until hot and stir in the egg yolk mixture. Stirring constantly, cook the mixture to a thick, smooth 'porridge'. Remove from the heat and stir in the

butter. Whisk the egg whites and salt until stiff peaks just form. Gradually whisk in the castor sugar. Add ⅓ of the egg white mixture to the 'porridge' and fold in. Spoon the mixture into the crumb base and stack the rest of the egg white mixture, like a cloud, on top of the filling. Sprinkle the reserved crust mixture over the egg white mixture. Bake for 10 minutes in a preheated oven at 180 °C (350 °F). Cool completely and serve.

Ginger tart

(MAKES 6-8 SERVINGS)

In the long-gone past, the highlight of the Day of the Covenant on 16 December was the ginger tart. The recipe for this tart appeared in the very first issue of *Cook and Enjoy*. Over the years the recipe underwent some changes and the one below is one of the best versions of this old favourite.

BASE
1 packet (200 g) ginger snaps
125 g (125 ml/ ½ cup) butter,
    melted and foam skimmed
3 ml (½ t) ground ginger or ground cinnamon

FILLING
250 ml (1 cup) boiling water
250 ml (1 cup) golden syrup
3 ml (½ t) ground ginger
30 ml (6 t) finely chopped preserved ginger
30 ml (6 t) cornflour
30 ml (6 t) custard powder
30 ml (6 t) cold water

CHANTILLY CREAM
250 ml (1 cup) cream, stiffly
    beaten with:
12,5 ml (1 T) vanilla essence and
25 ml (2 T) castor sugar
slices preserved ginger

1. BASE: Pulse ginger snaps in a food processor or crush with a rolling pin between 2 sheets of paper or in a plastic or flour bag. Mix butter and ground ginger and stir in crumbs. Press crumbs into a lightly oiled tart dish with a diameter of 200 mm (8 in). Do not press crumbs too tightly. If you really have a taste for ginger, arrange a few pieces of preserved ginger on the tart base.
2. FILLING: Mix boiling water, syrup, ground and preserved ginger in a saucepan. Heat and boil for 1 minute.
3. In the meantime, mix cornflour and custard powder with cold water until mixture is smooth and runny. Spoon some of the boiling syrup into the custard mixture and stir through. Spoon custard mixture into the remaining syrup and stir through. Return to heat, stirring constantly until the mixture thickens and reaches boiling point. Boil for 3 minutes. Remove from heat, leave to cool slightly and spoon into prepared base. Set aside to cool completely.
4. Cover the tart lightly with cling wrap and place in the refrigerator. Allow to set completely. Spoon prepared cream into a piping pag with a star nozzle and pipe rosettes onto the filling. Finish off each rosette with a slice of preserved ginger. Serve the tart as dessert with a small helping of ginger or vanilla ice-cream.

Index

Page numbers in **bold** refer to photographs.